AF887225

Global Public Interest in International Investment Law

The strengths of international investment law – above all, a strong focus on investor interests and an effective adjudication and enforcement system – also entail its weaknesses: it runs the danger of impeding or even sanctioning the host states' legitimate regulatory interests and ignoring other fields of public international law. How does it cope with public interest concerns such as human rights, the environment, or the fight against corruption? At the heart of this book lies a fresh approach towards a general theory of such global public interest considerations in the investment realm. Delineating how and why those considerations matter, and why the current system does not accommodate them properly, Andreas Kulick fleshes out general principles and customary international law as defences the host state may raise against alleged investor rights infringements, and promotes proportionality as the appropriate balancing mechanism.

ANDREAS KULICK is currently finishing his Bar training at the Berlin Higher Regional Court (Kammergericht).

CAMBRIDGE STUDIES IN INTERNATIONAL AND COMPARATIVE LAW

Established in 1946, this series produces high quality scholarship in the fields of public and private international law and comparative law. Although these are distinct legal sub-disciplines, developments since 1946 confirm their interrelations.

Comparative law is increasingly used as a tool in the making of law at national, regional and international levels. Private international law is now often affected by international conventions, and the issues faced by classical conflicts rules are frequently dealt with by substantive harmonisation of law under international auspices. Mixed international arbitrations, especially those involving state economic activity, raise mixed questions of public and private international law, while in many fields (such as the protection of human rights and democratic standards, investment guarantees and international criminal law) international and national systems interact. National constitutional arrangements relating to 'foreign affairs', and to the implementation of international norms, are a focus of attention.

The series welcomes works of a theoretical or interdisciplinary character, and those focusing on the new approaches to international or comparative law or conflicts of law. Studies of particular institutions or problems are equally welcome, as are translations of the best work published in other languages.

General Editors James Crawford SC FBA
Whewell Professor of International Law, Faculty of Law, University of Cambridge
John S. Bell FBA
Professor of Law, Faculty of Law, University of Cambridge

A list of books in the series can be found at the end of this volume.

Global Public Interest in International Investment Law

Andreas Kulick

Dissertation at the Eberhard Karls University, Tübingen D 21

CAMBRIDGE
UNIVERSITY PRESS

CAMBRIDGE
UNIVERSITY PRESS

Shaftesbury Road, Cambridge CB2 8EA, United Kingdom

One Liberty Plaza, 20th Floor, New York, NY 10006, USA

477 Williamstown Road, Port Melbourne, VIC 3207, Australia

314–321, 3rd Floor, Plot 3, Splendor Forum, Jasola District Centre, New Delhi – 110025, India

103 Penang Road, #05–06/07, Visioncrest Commercial, Singapore 238467

Cambridge University Press is part of Cambridge University Press & Assessment, a department of the University of Cambridge.

We share the University's mission to contribute to society through the pursuit of education, learning and research at the highest international levels of excellence.

www.cambridge.org
Information on this title: www.cambridge.org/9781107021761

© Andreas Kulick 2012

This publication is in copyright. Subject to statutory exception and to the provisions of relevant collective licensing agreements, no reproduction of any part may take place without the written permission of Cambridge University Press & Assessment.

First published 2012

A catalogue record for this publication is available from the British Library

Library of Congress Cataloging-in-Publication data
Kulick, Andreas, 1982–
Global public interest in international investment law / Andreas Kulick.
p. cm.
"Dissertation at the Eberhard Karls University, Tübingen" – ECIP t.p.
ISBN 978-1-107-02176-1 (hardback)
1. Investments, Foreign – Law and legislation. 2. Investments, Foreign (International law) 3. Arbitration and award, International. I. Title.
K3830.K85 2012
346′.092 – dc23 2012007320

ISBN 978-1-107-02176-1 Hardback

Cambridge University Press & Assessment has no responsibility for the persistence or accuracy of URLs for external or third-party internet websites referred to in this publication and does not guarantee that any content on such websites is, or will remain, accurate or appropriate.

Meiner Mutter

Dissertation of the University of Tübingen
D 21

Contents

Foreword

International investment agreements (otherwise known as BITs) deal, mostly if not exclusively, with the protection of foreign investment, and are generally seen as doing so from the perspective of investor rights. As it happens, unlike human rights treaties, they are not articulated as conferring substantive individual rights. But when combined with the powerful procedural tool of investor–state arbitration, that is their effect. However, as experience has shown and as fierce opposition to the creation of a multilateral framework has demonstrated, investment disputes often engage matters of the public interest, e.g. human rights, corruption, regulation of waste or chemicals, or more generally the environment. It is an unresolved question how well investment Tribunals are taking such factors into account.

Andreas Kulick, who has studied at Freiburg, Geneva, Berlin, New York and has received a Ph.D. from the University of Tübingen, finished the thesis on which this book is based at Cambridge's Lauterpacht Centre. At the heart of his work is the (current and potential) influence of what he calls, in capitals, the Global Public Interest on international investment law and on the jurisprudence of the Tribunals. Borrowing from the Global Administrative Law movement and from Constitutionalization theory, he sees investment law as public law. Basing himself on a comparative analysis with European law and the European Convention on Human Rights, he argues that general (customary) international law and general principles of law can be employed by the host State as defences against investment claims; these should be balanced against each other according to the principle of proportionality. Of particular interest is how the defence of necessity (ILC Articles on State Responsibility, Article 25) has been used (or rejected) by the Tribunals as a means to serve the public interest.

His book seeks to draw out the pressing need for including public interest considerations in the realm of international investment law and to identify the challenges this entails. He focuses on three examples that epitomize this challenge: human rights, the environment and corruption.

Capitalised Concepts are not without their difficulties, and this is certainly true of the Global Administrative Law, which seems to posit a system of *vires* and nullity without any of the accompanying institutions or procedures of review. In the common law tradition, at least, modern administrative law was the consequence, not the cause, of such institutions and procedures. On the other hand, international law went for much of its life with few or no institutions and with rudimentary procedures, yet it managed to generate general and constraining ideas. There is no reason to assume such potentiality has disappeared. While one might prefer to induce public interest on a case-by-case basis, a more *a priori* method may serve – and certainly Andreas Kulick presents a good argument for it. This is a welcome addition to the literature on international investment law at a time when the general and the particular are actively contesting the field.

James Crawford
Lauterpacht Centre for International Law
University of Cambridge

Acknowledgments

A Ph.D. thesis is a long-term project. This one has been no exception. That it came to life and that it eventually crystallized into the book the esteemed reader now holds in his or her hands is due to inspiration and support of various kinds and from various sources. Without them there would be a much weaker or even no book at all. Both people and institutions have contributed to its successful conclusion, to whom and which I owe the utmost gratitude.

First and foremost, I wish to thank my supervisor, Professor Dr. Martin Nettesheim, who was an inspiring mentor with the rare ability to combine unambiguous support for me and my project with the amount of critique necessary to transform good but sometimes lofty ideas into a thought-through and thorough thesis. Moreover, I am indebted to Professor Dr. Wolfgang Graf Vitzthum for so timely providing the second report on my Ph.D. thesis.

I had the great privilege to find time and inspiration to write in the New World as well as in the old. Hence, I am grateful to Professors José Alvarez and Robert Howse of New York University School of Law, who introduced me to the world of international investment law during my LL.M. year at NYU, and particularly to Professor James Crawford, SC, FBA of Cambridge University, who gave me the opportunity to find a peaceful and inspiring environment at the Lauterpacht Centre for International Law in the spring of 2010 and wrote such a learned foreword to this book.

Additionally, I have to thank many more people for their valuable comments on drafts of my work, above all the three anonymous readers at Cambridge University Press.

Moreover, without financial support from several institutions the academic extravagancies I was so lucky to pursue would never have been possible. Thus, many thanks go to the Fulbright Commission and the Friedrich

Ebert Foundation for supporting my LL.M. studies at NYU, where first ideas started to ripen into the result of which I reap hereby. The German Academic Exchange Service (DAAD) sponsored my time at the Lauterpacht Centre.

Last but not least I wish to thank Cambridge University Press and above all Nienke van Schaverbeke for accompanying my book project from first proposal to final publication.

Andreas Kulick

Table of Cases

ICSID and UNCITRAL cases

NAFTA cases

ICJ and PCIJ cases

GATT and WTO Panel and Appellate Body reports

European Court of Human Rights cases

European Court of Justice and European Court of First Instance cases

Cases decided by domestic courts

Cases decided by other tribunals and courts

Table of Treaties and Other Documents

Agreement Between Canada And . . . . For The Promotion And Protection of Investments, available at ita.law.uvic.ca/documents/Canadian2004-FIPA-model-en.pdf 72
Agreement Between the Kingdom of Norway And . . . . For The Promotion and Protection of Investments, issued December 19, 2007, available at http://ita.law.uvic.ca/investmenttreaties.htm 73
Basel Convention on the Control of Transboundary Movements of Hazardous Wastes and their Disposal, done March 22, 1989, available at www.basel.int/text/documents.html 232, 240–44, 259
"Bolivian tension mounts as roadblock deadline looms," CNN, March 10, 2000, available at http://archives.cnn.com/2000/WORLD/americas/10/03/bolivia.protests.reut/index.html 294
Canadian 2004 Model Foreign Investment Protection Agreement, available at ita.law.uvic.ca/documents/Canadian2004-FIPA-model-en.pdf 72, 75
Canadian Charter of Rights and Freedoms, § 1, available at http://laws.justice.gc.ca/en/charter/ 176–77
Comments On The Model For Future Investment Agreements, English translation, issued December 19, 2007, available at http://ita.law.uvic.ca/investmenttreaties.htm 73
Convention Concerning the Protection of the World Cultural and Natural Heritage, Adopted in Paris, November 16, 1972, available at http://whc.unesco.org/en/conventiontext 212
Convention for Cooperation in the Protection and Sustainable Development of the Marine and Coastal Environment of the North-East Pacific (The Antigua Convention) 227
Convention for the Protection of Human Rights and Fundamental Freedoms, concluded November 4, 1950, entered into force September 3, 1953, available at http://conventions.coe.int/Treaty/Commun/QueVoulezVous.asp?NT=005&CL=ENG 118, 120

1 Introduction

International investment law has focused, so far, on the protection of investment and thus on investor rights. Throughout the past two decades we have been witnessing an impressive proliferation of bilateral investment treaties (BITs), which introduce an elaborate set of substantive investor protection provisions on the one hand and arbitration clauses on the other, generally referring an investor–host State arbitration to, inter alia, the International Centre for the Settlement of Investment Disputes (ICSID), which has subsequently become the crucial – though not the only – forum before which investment disputes are resolved.

BITs mainly, and in a plethora of cases exclusively, deal with investor rights. Inter alia, they grant prompt, adequate and effective compensation in case of expropriation; they guarantee fair and equitable, national and most favored nation treatment; and quite often they contain the prohibition of performance requirements and an umbrella clause. However, as past experience has shown and fierce opposition to the creation of a multilateral framework has demonstrated, investments do not take place in a vacuum and thus disputes that eventually come to the stage of ICSID or other investment arbitration fora involve a multitude of different issues, some concerning investor rights, others concerning matters of mainly public interest, e.g. human rights, corruption or the environment. While soft law instruments exist that stress certain responsibilities of corporate non-State actors on the international stage, particularly vis-à-vis the three said public interest issues,[1] their legal reach in a dispute settlement

[1] See Report of the World Summit on Sustainable Development, Johannesburg, August 26 to September 4, 2002, available at http://daccess-ods.un.org/TMP/7699301.html; Agenda 21, Chapter 1: Preamble, Para. 1.1, available at www.un.org/esa/sustdev/documents/agenda21/english/agenda21chapter1.htm; The UN Global Compact, available at

system referring to a myriad of clear-cut treaties dealing exclusively with investor rights is considerably limited.[2]

This book seeks to both flesh out the pressing need for including such aforementioned public interest considerations within the realm of international investment law, and identify the challenges they entail. I will subsequently refer to this complex as the public interest challenge. This challenge comprises, among others, the host State's need (and constitutional, or otherwise, remit) to protect third party interests or common interests. The present legal framework offers the host State only very limited options to pursue such interests. That is, because it elevates such issues to the international level and tests them against the backdrop of, as I will argue, investor rights serving as international law "trump cards" and enjoying primacy and supremacy over domestic law.

What is more, such interests – for example, the right of a worker to join a union or the preservation of flora and fauna in proximity to an industrialized area – do not merely constitute domestic concerns but frequently also expand to the international level and translate into international law rules or principles that the host State has undertaken to observe. The fact that such public interests enshrined in international legal obligations of the host State compel the latter to integrate and to protect them in its domestic law system hence means giving them effect on the domestic as well as the international level. I will refer to such harmonization, or even enmeshment, of the domestic and the international

www.unglobalcompact.org/AboutTheGC/index.html; on the drafting history of the Compact see E. Morgera, "The UN and Corporate Environmental Responsibility: Between International Regulation and Partnerships," *Eur. Com. & Int'l Env. L. Rev.*, 15 (2006), 93; Millennium Development Goals, adopted at the UN Millennium Summit in New York, September 18, 2000: see www.un.org/millenniumgoals/; The OECD Guidelines for Multinational Enterprises, Revision 2000, available at www.olis.oecd.org/olis/2000doc.nsf/LinkTo/daffe-ime-wpg(2000)9; on the OECD Guidelines, see further R. Jones, "The 1999 Review of the OECD Guidelines for Multinational Enterprises" in R. Blanpain (ed.), *Multinational Enterprises and the Social Challenges of the XXIst Century* (Kluwer Law International, 2000), p. 141 at pp. 143 f.

[2] On the – naturally – limited legal force as well as on the legal influence they may nonetheless exert see P. Muchlinski, *Multinational Enterprises and the Law*, 2nd edn. (Oxford University Press, 2007), pp. 568 ff. My book does not deal with those – admittedly potentially considerable – effects of soft law instruments on public interest issues within the realm of international investment law. The eventual solution I will promote will be – deliberately so, as I will explain throughout this book and particularly in the concluding remarks – a quite doctrinal one. However, while I thus risk excluding some possibly fruitful inspirations, the theory I will flesh out in the subsequent chapters and which leaves little room for soft law instruments to assume a relevant role, in my opinion best encapsulates the specifics of international investment law.

by regulatory action through treaties, decisions by international bodies such as the UN Security Council or other international instruments, as a "global" phenomenon. International investment law, as I will contend, on the one hand represents such cutting through and mélange of the domestic and the international, and thus on the other touches upon and is faced with public interest challenges bearing relevance on both the domestic and international levels by piercing their dichotomy. Therefore, the public interest this book is concerned with will be called the "*Global* Public Interest."

This term, for the sake of the analysis undertaken in this book, shall comprise all interests inhering a pivotal importance for the international community and bearing relevance on both the domestic and international levels. However, to clarify the purpose of the book and in order to obviate disappointment, my analysis is not so much concerned with discerning *what* Global Public Interest in international investment law actually comprises, but rather *how* to legally translate it and reconcile it with competing investor rights. The former issue requires a separate study of a rather sociological and international relations based approach. Since I am more interested in the "how" than in the "what," the structure of this book falls in two main parts: Part I fleshes out the public interest challenge and thereinafter seeks to develop a general theory as an adequate response to such challenge, including its legal translations as well as doctrinal structure and mode of reconciliation with investor rights. Part II undertakes three case studies in exemplary Global Public Interest issues – the environment, international human rights and corruption – viewing the investment arbitration case law against the backdrop of the general theory and doctrine developed in Part I.

Hence, this book focuses on theory and its potential to shape practice, which naturally means a preponderance of Part I. Therefore, several considerations underlie the point of departure of my analysis. Looking at the strongly favorable position BITs give to the investors, two main questions arise: Firstly, does this situation create an imbalance that is unacceptable given the importance of a Global Public Interest issue? And secondly, if we answer the first question in the affirmative, is there a way to argue for a doctrinal foundation to infer such Global Public Interest concerns as within the realm of international investment law?[3] Naturally, in order

[3] For the sake of clarity and in order to avoid confusion, I refer to "international investment law" as the general framework set by both procedural and substantive provisions. Differentiating between investment law (substance, i.e. BITs) and investment

to counter such alleged imbalance, the way Global Public Interest concerns will play out doctrinally is through defenses the host State may raise against investor rights infringements claimed by the investor. If one acknowledges, say, the environment as a licit issue to bring up legally, it is simply inevitable that such matter will very often be introduced as a defense against an infringement of investor rights.

To say as much, my answer to both questions will be yes. My argumentation is structured in three parts. In Chapter 2, I seek to shed light on the relationship of domestic and international law under the realm of international investment law. It will be my argument that the role of international law under the general applicable law clause of Article 42(1) second sentence ICSID, which provides a pattern for applicable law clauses in most international investment agreements, has constantly grown. International law's prominence has now arrived at a stage where Tribunals not only acknowledge its supremacy over domestic law within the realm of international investment law, but also grant the former the role as the primary source in an investment dispute. I call this development the "internationalization" of international investment law. Moreover, I opine that investment arbitration case law describes the legal order applicable in investment disputes as a specific mélange of domestic and international law that defines a clear-cut hierarchy of the two sources from which it draws, with international law at the top. I will refer to this phenomenon of interdigitation of different legal sources as the "integration" of international investment law. What my conclusion entails is that as long as Global Public Interest concerns can only be addressed on the level of domestic law, they represent no viable defense against the supreme international law investor rights with which they might collide. Thus, there appears to be a need for possible defenses the host State may raise as justification for investor rights infringement it commits in pursuit of the Global Public Interest.

Chapter 3 demonstrates that neither current doctrinal discussions regarding international legal obligations of Multinational Enterprises nor BIT practice at the present stage are able to adequately respond to the challenges my observations as to "internationalization" and "integration" of international investment law entail. Therefore, Chapter 4 delineates what

arbitration (procedure, i.e. ICSID or other arbitration rules) I find futile, given the influence procedure and substance have on each other – as I demonstrate in Chapter 4. Hence, I will only refer to "investment arbitration" in case I seek to specifically emphasize an exclusively procedural aspect.

I call the Global Public Interest theory. It argues that international investment law has an inherently public law character, which, however, in its specific nature may not be explained by either the classical model of public international law or current and evolving approaches that can only capture certain and insular aspects of it but are unable to explain their interplay and interrelation. Comparing it with similar legal systems that share the alleged public law character of international investment law, my argument is that balancing the individual with the public interest is a defining feature of every public law system, i.e. also of a Global Public Law system such as international investment law. In this Global Public Law system, so I will argue, the Global Public Interest finds its legal translation in certain general principles and customary international law norms. Chapter 5 doctrinally categorizes those legal translations as defenses the host State may raise against investor rights infringements, argues for employing proportionality analysis as the tool to balance the Global Public Interest with the interest of the investor, and proposes to introduce a procedural mechanism in order to prevent the host State from abusing Global Public Interest considerations for protectionist or other illicit purposes.

As regards the methodological approach, the emphasis in this book will be on systemic analysis. As has been foreshadowed above, I will scrutinize how international investment law functions and compare it with other legal systems sharing distinct features with the former, such as "integration" – compared with the European law system – or "internationalization" as regards the function of international law as "trump cards" – compared with the European Convention on Human Rights system. To say as much, I will categorize international investment law as what I call a "Global Public Law system." In short, such denomination seeks to capture my assessments of international investment law as (1) a public law system that is concerned with the control of the exercise of (the host State's) public authority, and as (2) a legal régime that is characterized by the enmeshment of the domestic and the international levels and creates a (to some extent) constitutional system by the phenomena I have referred to earlier as "integration" and "internationalization."

At this point I have to emphasize that among the plethora of thought-provoking pieces that have been published on international investment law in the past decade, two works in particular have inspired me to tackle the *problematique* of the present book, for it partially builds on their ideas and undertakes to push the argument several steps further or even to draw new conclusions from them or their combination. The first one is, as the ardent follower of the recent investment debate already might have suggested, Gus Van Harten's *Investment Treaty Arbitration as Public Law*.[4] His descriptive study of international investment arbitration as a public law system has not only proven tremendously instructive to my analysis but, among other major influences, actually incited me to start thinking about the (Global) Public Interest in international investment law in the first place.[5] However, as the focus on investment *arbitration* makes apparent, Van Harten's systemic analysis concentrates on the consequences of bringing international investment issues before an arbitration forum tailored after a commercial arbitration system for disputes between private entities. Thus, his assessment mainly, albeit not exclusively, pertains to procedural aspects. My analysis, however, adds a substantive dimension to the procedural assessment by drawing conclusions from the phenomena of "internationalization" and "integration" for the public law nature of international investment *law*, i.e. the combination of procedure and substance. Moreover, while Van Harten detects the public interest challenge, his response, since being related to his mainly procedural perspective, naturally is procedural or institutional – he proposes to create a permanent Investment Arbitration Appellate Court. Here, again, my approach seeks to advance the argument and to provide substantive solutions to the public interest challenge that emerges from the concoction of procedural as well as substantive elements that create the specific features of international investment law that I have categorized as Global Public Law.

Less influential, although nonetheless very helpful for expanding my argument, particularly as just described, was Stephan Schill's *Multilateralization of International Investment Law*.[6] My analysis has heavily profited from his assessment that the investment treaty system, consisting mostly of bilateral investment treaties, is no mere rag-rug of scattered and contradictory rules, but establishes a rather harmonious régime of investment protection that provides for a thrust of highly similar norms and thus arguably represents a de facto multilateral system. Building on this concept, I will push the argument as to harmonization and the existence of a general framework of international investment law to a further level by arguing for a comprehensive understanding of an investment régime

[4] G. Van Harten, *Investment Treaty Arbitration and Public Law* (Oxford University Press, 2007).

[5] Van Harten refers rather to "arbitration" instead of "law," but I prefer – as explained previously – the term "international investment law" due to the reasons given earlier.

[6] S. W. Schill, *The Multilateralization of International Investment Law* (Cambridge University Press, 2009).

which integrates Global Public Interest defenses that must be balanced against investor rights and which thus expands the general framework to a full public law system.

The response to the public interest challenge this book promotes, the Global Public Interest theory, seeks to correspond to the current state of public international law. Therefore, although I undertake to define a new category to capture the distinct features of international investment law, my theory takes account of the current antagonism of the potential public international law *Grundnorms* of sovereignty vs. humanity. Thus, the solution the Global Public Interest theory provides will attempt to accomodate both the growing value-orientation of public international law on the one hand and its State-centeredness on the other. This localization of international investment law as part of public international law but with characteristics going way beyond the confines of a classical understanding of the latter is a major concern of this book. To conclude this Introduction, some of the assertions and conclusions that will be made subsequently may appear audacious – albeit, of course, I am convinced they are accurate. However, despite its strong emphasis on theory and the fact that it is relying on contentious concepts that not everybody may share, it is my intention to build a theory that translates well into practice and is as convincing to scholars as it is easy for practioners to implement.

Part I Towards the Global Public Interest theory

2 The "internationalization" of international investment law

The ensuing chapter, together with Chapter 3, is intended to set the stage for my Global Public Interest theory to be developed subsequently in Chapter 4. A relatively narrow doctrinal issue, i.e. analyzing the relationship of international and domestic law in international investment law through the applicable law lens will, so I shall contend, uncover the avenue to the much broader question of how (global) public interest shapes international investment relations and thereby international investment law – which entails both doctrinal and theoretical aspects. For this purpose, Article 42(1) second sentence of the ICSID Convention shall be analyzed in some detail. This is not to limit the discussion and my theory to the ICSID realm and neglect that significant investment arbitration occurs before other fora as well. However, most bilateral investment treaties (BITs) embrace applicable law provisions very similar or identical to Article 42(1) second sentence ICSID. This and the fact that ICSID still is by far the most important investment arbitration forum give thrust to its model character in the entire international investment realm.

What I seek to reveal subsequently is that the more prominence international law has been assuming in international investment law – what I will call "internationalization" – and the more international and domestic law have become intertwined – what I will refer to as "integration" – the lack of public interest considerations in the by far most prominent source of international law in an investment dispute, i.e. BITs, makes apparent a challenge. This challenge – the "public interest challenge" – lies in the host States' responsibility to further the public interest on behalf of their subjects. Domestic law offers answers – some desirable, some rather undesirable – to a conflict of the individual (investor) and the public interest. Once domestic law steps into the background and international law steps into the foreground, this route is closed. What role to assume for the public interest on the international level and how to do so is the challenge tackled in Chapters 4 and 5. The purpose of this chapter is to flesh out said challenge.

A. A first glance at Article 42(1) ICSID

The Washington Convention on the International Centre for the Settlement of Investment Disputes (ICSID Convention), the main focus of my analysis in this chapter,[1] contains the following rule on the law applicable in an investment dispute:

"*Article 42*

(1) The Tribunal shall decide a dispute in accordance with such rules of law as may be agreed by the parties. In the absence of such agreement, the Tribunal shall apply the law of the Contracting State party to the dispute (including its rules on the conflict of laws) and such rules of international law as may be applicable.
(2) The Tribunal may not bring in a finding of *non liquet* on the ground of silence or obscurity of the law.
(3) The provisions of paragraphs (1) and (2) shall not prejudice the power of the Tribunal to decide a dispute *ex aequo et bono* if the parties so agree."

Article 42(1) second sentence is of particular interest in this regard. I will demonstrate in the ensuing chapter that this provision and its interpretation by ICSID Tribunals have – in a considerable part due to the proliferation of BITs – undergone a remarkable development in the past years that indicates not only a major change in the view on international investment law but serves well as a basis for building the approach aimed at by this book.

1. *Context: general principle of Article 42 ICSID is freedom of choice*

The first sentence of Article 42(1) ICSID incorporates a fundamental principle of commercial arbitration into the investor–State dispute settlement system, i.e. that the parties may agree which law has to be applied to the dispute.[2] This freedom of choice derives from the general rationale of party autonomy and gives the parties a flexible means to relate the

[1] On the reasons why that is so, see also *infra* 2 D. 1.

[2] W. L. Craig, W. W. Park and J. Paulsson, *International Chamber of Commerce Arbitration*, 3rd edn. (Oceana Publications, 2000), p. 319; T. Várady, J. J. Barceló III and A. T. von Mehren, *International Commercial Arbitration – A Transnational Perspective*, 3rd edn. (Thomson/West, 2006), p. 616.

dispute to any law or rules which they think are most suitable to resolve the dispute.[3]

Viewed from today's perspective, it may appear odd that party autonomy, which is rooted in the idea of private law coordinating the relationship of peers, underpins an investor–State dispute.[4] But at the time of the adoption of the ICSID Convention, the common view was to give a framework to investment arbitration by basically referring to the existing and well-functioning system of commercial arbitration.[5]

While the first sentence of Article 42(1) ICSID is not the subject matter of this analysis, it has to be kept in mind that the second sentence only comes into play if the parties are unwilling or unable to exercise their autonomy to determine the law applicable to the investment dispute. Thus, party autonomy overrides the subsidiary rule of Article 42(1) second sentence ICSID as regards the applicable law. Most interestingly, however, even if the parties choose the applicable law according to the first sentence, they usually emulate the clause enshrined in the second sentence.[6]

2. Possible cases in which international law may be applicable under Article 42 ICSID

Looking merely at its text, there exist five possible cases in which international law may be applicable under Article 42(1) ICSID:[7]

(1) If the parties have agreed to apply international law according to the first sentence of Article 42(1) ICSID.
(2) If the domestic law of the host State calls for the application of international law.

[3] In this respect, paragraph (1) can be read in conjunction with paragraph (3), which bestows the parties with the ability to permit an *ex aequo et bono* decision by the Tribunal; see C. Schreuer, *The ICSID Convention – A Commentary* (Cambridge University Press, 2001), Art. 42, para. 2.

[4] See G. Van Harten, *Investment Treaty Arbitration and Public Law* (Oxford University Press, 2007), pp. 130 f.; G. Van Harten and M. Loughlin, "Investment Treaty Arbitration as a Species of Global Administrative Law," *Eur. J. Int'l L.*, 17 (2006), 121 at 145 ff.

[5] A. Broches, "The Convention on the Settlement of Investment Disputes between States and Nationals of other States," *Recueil des Cours*, 136 (1972 II), 329 at 388 ff.

[6] See instead of many Treaty Between The Government Of The United States of America And The Government Of. . . . . . Concerning the Encouragement And Reciprocal Protection of Investment, US Model BIT 2004, available at www.ustr.gov/assets/Trade_Sectors/Investment/Model_BIT/asset_upload_file847_6897.pdf, Art. 30 (2) (b).

[7] See Broches, "The Convention," 392 f. It must be noted, however, that this list does not make any reference as to the scope to which international law may be applied. This question, however, is addressed in several parts of the analysis under 2 D. and E.

(3) If the domestic law – fully or in part – does not address the issue or does not provide for a solution.
(4) If the subject matter or issue is directly regulated by international law.
(5) If the domestic law or action taken under that law is inconsistent with international law.

Case (1) has been addressed above.[8] As regards case (2), domestic law may call for the application of international law either by direct reference to a specific treaty or treaty provision, or may, as some constitutions do,[9] declare some parts of international law generally as supreme over all or some parts of the domestic law. Case (3) is more difficult to discern, since in some situations domestic law may deliberately contain no rule on the issue. Further, a solution may only be found by thorough knowledge of the domestic law and its underlying principles, which may provide a challenge in an arbitral system, where the arbitrators may not be experts on the domestic law at issue. Case (4) occurs in particular if there is a treaty, e.g. a bilateral investment treaty between the investor's home State and the host State, which deals with investment issues, but may also be considered if customary international law applies in the case at hand. Finally, case (5) is critical, for the applicability of international law depends on the degree of inconsistency: does one require that international law must actually be violated or does it suffice that domestic law merely differs from international law, to name but the two extremes on the scale of "inconsistency."

3. *International law as applicable even in case of an exclusive choice of domestic law according to Article 42(1) first sentence ICSID*

Before proceeding to section B., and foreshadowing some observations to be made in section C., it must be added that ICSID Tribunals have found international law to be applicable in a further, sixth case. According to the Tribunal in *SPP* v. *Egypt*, international law may even be referred to if the parties under Article 42(1) first sentence chose domestic law to be exclusively applicable to the dispute.[10] The Tribunal reasoned that

[8] See *supra* 2 A. 1.

[9] See e.g. Art. 59(2) of the Grundgesetz, the German Federal Constitution, which declares customary international law as supreme over federal and state statutes but not over constitutional law; and Art. 31 of the Argentine Constitution, according to which international treaties trump domestic law.

[10] *Southern Pacific Properties (Middle East) Limited* v. *Arab Republic of Egypt* (ICSID Case No. ARB/84/3), Award, May 20, 1992, *ICSID Reports*, 3 (1992), 189 (hereinafter: *SPP* v. *Egypt*) at 352 ff., para. 80.

the domestic law did not provide for a solution of the issue at hand, and therefore it might have recourse to international law according to Article 42(1) second sentence ICSID, which declares international law applicable in case of such loopholes.[11]

While one must concede that case (6) strongly resembles case (3) in that domestic law does not provide for a solution, it nonetheless seems preferable to distinguish those two cases. Case (6) is primarily a choice of law situation under Article 42(1) first sentence ICSID, i.e. the flipside of case (1) – instead of international law the parties have chosen domestic law to govern the case. Case (3) is an Article 42(1) second sentence situation, i.e. domestic law is not applicable, not due to the parties' choice of law but due to a provision of the ICSID Convention itself absent a party agreement. What makes case (6) noteworthy is that although Article 42(1) is premised on the principle that primarily the parties may decide which law is to be applied to their dispute,[12] and despite their decision for domestic law, this law is nonetheless not exclusively applied but still leaves room for international law to fill loopholes.

B. Drafting history of Article 42(1) second sentence ICSID

Originally, i.e. in the Preliminary Draft of ICSID, the predecessor of Article 42(1) second sentence read as follows:

> In the absence of agreement between the parties concerning the law to be applied, and unless the parties shall have given the Tribunal the power to decide *ex aequo et bono*, the Tribunal shall decide the dispute submitted to it in accordance with such rules of law, whether national or international, as it shall determine to be applicable.[13]

Many developing countries, not surprisingly at that time,[14] denounced the draft as granting international law too prominent a role in the absence of an agreement on the applicable law and further underlined that the

[11] *Ibid.*, para. 84. [12] See *supra* 2. A. 1.

[13] Cited from A. Broches, "The Convention on the Settlement of Investment Disputes between States and Nationals of Other States: Applicable Law and Default Procedure" in P. Sanders (ed.), *International Arbitration, Liber Amicorum Martin Domke* (Martinus Nijhoff Publishers, 1967), p. 12 at p. 13.

[14] See United Nations General Assembly Res. 3171 (XXVII) of December 17, 1973, www.un.org/documents/ga/res/28/ares28.htm and United Nations General Assembly Res. 3281 (XXIX) of December 12, 1974, www.un.org/documents/ga/res/29/ares29.htm representing the then predominant view among developing countries at the United Nations General Assembly.

Tribunal should not be forced to choose either national or international law, as the word "or" suggested.[15]

Intending to address the latter concern, but expressly not in order to limit the scope of international law, the World Bank submitted a new document, the First Draft, to the Legal Committee. It replaced the last passage of the Preliminary Draft with the phrase "in accordance with such rules of national and international law as [the Tribunal] shall determine to be applicable" and added a definition of international law, which referred to Article 38 of the Statute of the International Court of Justice.[16]

Looking at the discussion in the Legal Committee regarding the First Draft, it appears at first glance that most members seem to favor a very limited role for international law. Confronted with objections by developing, particularly Latin American countries, to applying international law, even the representatives from Western nations accepted that, as Mr. Gourevitch (USA) stated, "national law would usually be applied."[17] In other words, domestic law should be the primary source. They insisted, however, that international law should be part of the applicable law, for "it would seem strange if a Tribunal which was admittedly international would be excluded from the application of international law."[18]

When the revised version[19] was submitted to a vote, Mr. Broches, the Legal Committee's chairman, explained: "international law . . . would [be brought] into play both in the case of a lacuna in domestic law as well as in the case of inconsistency between the two."[20] The Committee then adopted the draft by a majority of twenty-four to six. However, motions by delegates from Dahomey[21] and India to insert express limitations to the scope and application of international law failed.[22] Moreover, the Final Draft, as the text of ICSID, did not contain a definition of international law, as did, by contrast, the First Draft.[23]

Summarizing the brief outline of the drafting history of Article 42(1) second sentence ICSID as described above, it is fair to say that several delegates, particularly from developing countries, attempted to limit or even

[15] See Broches, "Applicable Law," pp. 14 f. [16] *Ibid.*, p. 15.

[17] Convention on the Settlement of Investment Disputes between States and Nationals of other States, Documents Concerning the Origin and Formulation of the Convention, International Centre for the Settlement of Investment Disputes, Vol. II, Pt. 2, 1968, 803.

[18] See the statement of the German representative, Mr. Bertram, *ibid.*, 801.

[19] Which became the final version of ICSID, except for the introductory phrase changed from "Failing such agreement" to "In absence of such agreement"; see Broches, "Applicable Law," p. 16.

[20] See Convention on the Settlement of Investment Disputes, *supra* n. 17, at 804.

[21] Which is now the Republic of Benin. [22] See n. 20. [23] *Ibid.*

exclude the applicability of international law to ICSID investment disputes. While the view that domestic law should "usually be applied"[24] generally prevailed, even among Western countries, motions to put express limitations on international law failed, however. Instead, developed countries insisted that international law had to play a role in deciding international investment disputes. Thus it appears that the final text of Article 42(1) second sentence deliberately leaves a lot of leeway for interpreting the role of international law, as the delegates could not find a compromise on how to exactly define its relationship to domestic law.

The statement that "international law... would [be brought] into play both in the case of a lacuna in domestic law as well as in the case of inconsistency between the two"[25] in this context materializes as representing the then view on a rather open-ended Article 42(1) second sentence ICSID. Such open-endedness does not set in stone the prevalent view at the time of the adoption of such a provision, but leaves room for a dynamic interpretation, particularly by future judicial bodies. Accordingly, the open-ended wording of Article 42(1) second sentence ICSID appears to have been used on purpose. As Aaron Broches put it in 1967:

> Article 42(1) leaves open a number of questions, particularly questions on substantive international law... Its importance lies in the fact that it *opens the way for Tribunals to pronounce themselves on these questions and thus to contribute to the further development of international law in this field.*[26]

Consequently, Article 42(1) may be read as an open provision, which intends to expand – or at least does not disfavor – the role of international law over time, as interpreted by investment Tribunals.

C. The role of BITs in international investment law

1. *BITs as a recent phenomenon*

Considering their high number, it is hard to believe – from a contemporary perspective – that BITs are a fairly recent phenomenon. While the first BIT was concluded in 1959 between the Federal Republic of Germany and Pakistan,[27] the proliferation of BITs did not occur until the late 1980s.[28] In fact, the first case under ICSID arbitration to involve a BIT was decided

[24] *Ibid.* [25] *Ibid.*

[26] See Broches, "Applicable Law," p. 15 (emphasis added).

[27] See A. Lowenfeld, *International Economic Law*, 2nd edn. (Oxford University Press, 2008), p. 554.

[28] K. Vandevelde, *United States Investment Treaties – Policy and Practice* (Kluwer, 1992), pp. 19 ff.

in 1990.[29] This was due to the fact that several capital-exporting States, particularly the United States, until then relied on their old Friendship, Commerce and Navigation Treaties (FCN)[30] to grant protection to their investors. With the growing reluctance of capital-importing countries to adhere to conventional investor protections, as evinced by several UN General Assembly Resolutions,[31] the tide shifted. All capital-exporting countries initiated a major campaign to conclude BITs with capital-importing countries, which led to a current number of BITs exceeding 2,600.[32]

2. *Codification and promotion of international law through BITs*

Despite considerable differences in wording and scope of protection, the major issues addressed in different BITs are strikingly similar: almost all contain a definition of investors and investment, a number of investor rights – admission, fair and equitable treatment, full protection and security, prompt adequate and effective compensation, national treatment, most favored nation treatment – and the general consent to binding investment arbitration, i.e. ICSID or otherwise.

Regardless of how broadly one defines the scope of customary international law in international investment law,[33] it is undeniable that a BIT creates an elaborate framework of express international law rules to govern the relationship both between the contracting parties and – by way of Article 42(1) second sentence ICSID – between the investor and the host State. However, it will emerge from the succeeding analysis of the case law that the fact of having detailed and express international law provisions on the subject matter creates a considerable dynamic for interpreting the relationship of international and domestic law under Article 42(1) ICSID.[34]

While the effect of BIT proliferation on the relationship of international and domestic law under international investment case law will be elaborated later, at the present stage it suffices to underline the similar

[29] *Asian Agricultural Products Limited* v. *Democratic Socialist Republic of Sri Lanka* (ICSID Case No. ARB/87/3), Award, June 27, 1990, *ICSID Review – FILJ*, 6 (1991), 526 (hereinafter: *AAPL* v. *Sri Lanka*).

[30] See K. Vandevelde, *United States Investment Treaties*, pp. 14 ff.

[31] See n. 14.

[32] For an updated list of BITs, see http://icsid.worldbank.org/ICSID.

[33] See the discussion in R. Dolzer and C. Schreuer, *Principles of International Investment Law* (Oxford University Press, 2008), pp. 11–17.

[34] See *infra* 2 D. 3.–5.

structure and substantive rights in almost all BITs.[35] Those similarities permit interpretations accruing from comparison between different BITs and recourse to internatonal investment case law, which may have recurrent effect on subsequent BIT interpretation.

D. The relationship of domestic law and international law

1. *Preliminary remarks*

In this part, which represents the core of Chapter 2, I will attempt to analyze the case law regarding the relationship of domestic and international law under Article 42(1) second sentence ICSID. Concerning case law, I confine myself to ICSID cases exclusively, omitting those awards decided by Tribunals under the Additional Facility rules. Under these rules, the ICSID Convention is not applicable and the relevant choice-of-law clause does not contain a provision comparable to Article 42(1) second sentence ICSID. This focus on ICSID case law is not to exclude, for the conclusions to be drawn in later parts, investment cases deriving from other fora. However, the ICSID Convention represents the only arbitration forum that expressly provides for an applicable law clause and hence is the one most prone to this issue arising and being discussed.

The analysis takes a chronological approach. I deem this the proper way to demonstrate the development that, in my opinion, has taken place regarding the interpretation of Article 42(1) second sentence ICSID. Thus I will start by describing the long-prevailing view both in case law and scholarly opinion – what I call the *Klöckner-Amco* doctrine – and how it evolved and its rationale (2). Thereinafter, my analysis will draw on recent case law to illustrate that the confidence in the *Klöckner-Amco* doctrine gradually waned (3), particularly when a Tribunal expressly chose a new approach – what I call the *Wena* doctrine (4). Finally, I opine that the Argentine crisis Tribunals, while adopting its basic reasoning, took the *Wena* doctrine one

[35] The wording and therefore the scope of the substantive rights clauses vary, however; see Dolzer and Schreuer, *Principles*, p. 22. Nonetheless, although protection may be broader under some BITs and narrower under others, they all deal with the same principles and thereby employ the same underlying rationales. See on this issue A. Lowenfeld, "Investment Agreements and International Law – The Regulation of Foreign Direct Investment," *Col. J. Transnt'l L.*, 42 (2003–04), 123 at 128; S. M. Schwebel, "The Influence of Bilateral Investment Treaties on Customary International Law," *Am. J. Int'l L.*, 98 (2004), 27; and J. E. Alvarez, "A BIT on Custom," *N.Y.U. J. Int'l L. & Pol.*, 42 (2010), 17 at 77 ff., even going so far as to argue that the law enshrined in BITs has accrued to customary international law. Moreover see Schill, *The Multilateralization of International Investment Law* (Cambridge University Press, 2009), pp. 367 ff.

step further, in that they further stressed the importance of international law under Article 42(1) second sentence ICSID.

Before entering into the study, three general considerations regarding ICSID arbitration have to be recalled. Firstly, ICSID Tribunals are established ad hoc and their interpretation of the legal issues before them, including the relationship of international and domestic law under Article 42(1) ICSID, is only binding among the parties to the particular dispute. Therefore, there is no common law type system of precedents and *stare decisis*. On the contrary, as holds true for almost all decisions of international judicial bodies, neither the findings nor the reasoning of previous ICSID Tribunals may bind the arbitrators in any way.[36] However, previous decisions of ICSID Tribunals on the same subject matter may well serve as persuasive "precedent" in that arbitrators may refer to them in order to buttress their reasoning. This leads to the second consideration, i.e. that ICSID case law plays a considerable role in interpreting the ICSID Convention. Multiple Tribunals have referred to previous decisions in order to justify their own interpretation of both BIT and ICSID provisions.[37]

Finally, there exist two kinds of ICSID decisions, which are very different in nature: the decision of a Tribunal and the decision of an Annulment Committee. The following analysis of ICSID case law draws on both. Therefore, I deem it necessary to point out the difference between the two. Whereas all ICSID arbitration starts with the establishment of a Tribunal that decides on the issues raised by the parties, an Annulment Committee only comes into play as a second phase, i.e. after the Tribunal has rendered its award and if one of the parties sees some considerable flaws in the Tribunal's decision. This annulment procedure, however, is not an appeal. According to Article 52(6) ICSID, in case of an annulment, the dispute shall, at the request of the parties, be submitted to a new Tribunal, different to the first one, whose decision has been annulled. Basis for an annulment is, among others, that the Tribunal has manifestly exceeded

[36] See *Saipem SpA* v. *People's Republic of Bangladesh* (ICSID Case No. ARB/05/7), Decision on Jurisdiction and Recommendation on Provisional Matters, March 21, 2007, para. 67, available at http://icsid.worldbank.org/ICSID/FrontServlet (hereinafter: *Saipem* v. *Bangladesh*); *AES Corporation* v. *Argentine Republic* (ICSID Case No. ARB/02/17), Decision Jurisdiction, July 13, 2005, paras. 30–32, available at www.investmentclaims.com/decisions/AES-Argentina_Jurisdiction.pdf; see also P. Sands, R. Mackenzie and Y. Shany, *Manual on International Courts and Tribunals* (Butterworths, 1999), pp. 4 ff.

[37] See P. M. Norton, "A Law of the Future or a Law of the Past? Modern Tribunals and the International Law of Expropriation," *Am. J. Int'l L.*, 85 (1991), 474 at 497 ff.

its powers (see Article 52(1)(b) ICSID). Such a case occurs particularly if the Tribunal failed to apply the correct law governing the dispute.[38]

However, since it is not an appellate division, the Annulment Committee's scope of review is very limited, for it may only annul the Tribunal's decision if the latter obviously misconstrued the applicable law. Furthermore, the Annulment Committee's task is to find whether the Tribunal has chosen a wrong interpretation of Article 42(1) ICSID, not to spell out the correct one. Therefore, any opinion expressed by the Annulment Committee regarding its view on how the relationship of international and domestic law should precisely be defined may only appear as a dictum. However, since the concept of *stare decisis* does not exist in ICSID arbitration, it is only the persuasiveness of the argument that may make a reasoning of a previous arbitral body authoritative for the arbitrators. In that respect, dicta, if well reasoned, may be as persuasive as findings.

Keeping these considerations in mind, I will now proceed to analyze both the case law and scholarly opinion on Article 42(1) second sentence ICSID.

2. *The* Klöckner-Amco *doctrine*[39]

(a) Case law under ICSID

(i) "Supplemental and corrective functions" of international law

The first case in which an ICSID arbitral body had the opportunity to elaborate its view on the relationship of domestic law and international law under Article 42(1) second sentence ICSID was the annulment decision in a dispute between Klöckner Industrie-Anlagen GmbH, a German company, and the United Republic of Cameroon.[40] The former Tribunal, which rendered the award that was scrutinized by the ad hoc Annulment Committee, had held that a particular variation of the principle of good faith as existent in French contract law had to be applied in the present

[38] *Klöckner Industrie-Anlagen GmbH and others* v. *United Republic of Cameroon and Société Camerounaise des Engrais* (ICSID Case No. ARB/81/2), Decision on Annulment, May 3, 1985 (hereinafter: *Klöckner* v. *Cameroon*, Decision on Annulment), *ICSID Reports*, 1 (1990), 90 at 109, paras. 57ff.; see also C. F. Dugan, D. Wallace, Jr., N. D. Rubins and B. Sabahi, *Investor-State Arbitration* (Oxford University Press, 2008), pp. 631 f.

[39] This subsection draws partly on A. Kulick, "The Integration of International Investment Law" in N. Lavranos *et al.* (eds.), *Hague Yearbook of International Law*, 23 (2010), 159.

[40] *Klöckner* v. *Cameroon*, Decision on Annulment.

case. According to the Tribunal, although Cameroonian law was applicable, the relevant Cameroonian law was "based on French law."[41] It found that:

> the principle according to which a person who engages in close contractual relations, based on confidence, must deal with his partner in a frank, loyal and candid manner is a basic principle of French civil law, as is indeed the case under other national codes which we know of.[42]

Thus the Tribunal inferred its reasoning from a principle of French law which it assumed to be applicable under Cameroonian law and appears to base this view on a comparative analysis of "other national codes which we know of."[43]

Remarkably, the Annulment Committee interpreted this recourse to principles "under other national codes we know of" as the Tribunal referring to "general principles of law," one source of international law according to Article 38(1)(c) of the ICJ Statute.[44] Having identified the former Tribunal's interpretation, in its view, as in fact a recourse to international law, the ad hoc Committee then went on to analyze the relationship of international law and domestic law under Article 42(1) second sentence ICSID.

As a starting point, the Committee stressed that Article 42(1) second sentence speaks of "*such principles of international law as may be applicable*"[45] in contrast to "rules of law" or "law of the Contracting State party." It thereby concluded, without further reasoning, that the ICSID Convention "gives these principles . . . a dual role, that is, *complementary* (in the case of 'lacuna' in the law of the State) or *corrective*, should the State's law not conform on all points to the principles of international law."[46] This dual role, the Annulment Committee stated, means that arbitrators have to apply a two-stage test, under which they (1) have to inquire into the domestic law before they (2) may refer to the "principles of international law."[47]

Looking at the text of Article 42(1) second sentence ICSID, it has to be noted that only the French version speaks of "principes," whereas the English and Spanish versions use the terms "rules" or "normas." The

41 *Klöckner Industrie-Anlagen GmbH* v. *United Republic of Cameroon* (ICSID Case No. ARB/81/2), Award of the Tribunal, October 21, 1983, 1983 WL 510000 (APPAWD) (hereinafter: *Klöckner* v. *Cameroon*, Award of the Tribunal), VI. B.

42 *Ibid.*

43 *Klöckner* v. *Cameroon*, Decision on Annulment, 111, para. 67.

44 *Ibid.*, 112, para. 69. 45 *Ibid.* (emphasis in the original). 46 *Ibid.* 47 *Ibid.*

Annulment Committee rendered its decision in French, so the reference to "principles" in contrast to "rules" and "law" is understandable, yet not entirely convincing as a starting point of interpretation, given the wording in the two other official versions of the ICSID Convention.

Moreover, the Committee's conclusion that the Tribunal's recourse to principles under other national legal orders constitutes a reference to international law is very dubious. In fact, one may see this recourse to other legal orders merely as a means of interpreting the domestic law. As a matter of fact, for example, the Swiss federal Tribunal, the highest court in Switzerland, has used a comparative law approach as a means of interpretation since the 1960s.[48]

International law in the sense of both Article 42(1) ICSID and Article 38 of the ICJ Statute means primarily public international law,[49] whereas the Tribunal's comparative approach, interpreted by the Annulment Committee as "international law," may well be seen as a reference to private international law. However, even if one generally regards private international law as part of "international law" in Article 42(1) ICSID or views the Tribunal's interpretation as referring to a general principle of law according to Article 38(1)(c) of the ICJ Statute, in the case at hand it may well be argued that the Tribunal applied domestic law and merely used a comparison to other national codes as a means for interpreting the domestic law. In this view, no issue regarding the relationship of international and domestic law under Article 42(1) second sentence ICSID arose in the *Klöckner* case. The Tribunal exclusively applied domestic law, which it allegedly may have interpreted by illicit means. However, that is not a proper basis for an annulment according to Article 52(1)(c) ICSID. The Annulment Committee, by contrast, appears to think that a comparative interpretation of domestic law means applying "international law" according to Article 42(1) second sentence ICSID. Such an interpretation, however, can be called, at least, unconventional.

Given all these particularities of both the facts involved and the Committee's dubious and overly succinct reasoning, one may think that subsequent Tribunals would have been cautious to adopt the Annulment Committee's interpretation of Article 42(1) second sentence ICSID. The next

48 See K. Zweigert and H. Kötz, *Introduction to Comparative Law*, 2nd edn. (Oxford University Press, 1993), pp. 48 ff.

49 See A. Zimmermann, C. Tomuschat and K. Oellers-Frahm (eds.), *The Statute of the International Court of Justice – A Commentary* (Oxford University Press, 2006), Art. 38, paras. 73 ff.; see also I. Brownlie, *Principles of Public International Law*, 7th edn. (Oxford University Press, 2008), pp. 4 f.

ICSID arbitral body dealing with the relationship of international and domestic law, however, directly followed the route chosen by *Klöckner* v. *Cameroon*.[50]

According to the ad hoc Committee in *Amco* v. *Indonesia*, again ruling on an application on annulment, "rules of international law" may only be referred to in order "to fill up lacunae in the applicable domestic law and to ensure precedence to international law norms where the rules of the applicable domestic law are in collision with such norms."[51] Therefore, according to the Annulment Committee, domestic law is in principle the law governing the dispute[52] and international law merely has a "supplemental and corrective role"[53] to play. Citing *Klöckner* v. *Cameroon* as an authority to sustain its interpretation,[54] the Committee provided two arguments to support its reasoning: "the thrust of" Article 54(1) ICSID – making the award enforceable in every Member State of ICSID – and Article 27 ICSID – precluding the investor from recourse to diplomatic protection – "make sense only under the supposition that the award involved is not violative of applicable principles and rules of international law."[55]

These arguments are, however, somewhat ambiguous, since they may merely justify the prevalence of international law over domestic law and do not explain why its function under international investment law is confined to a "supplemental" role.

Notwithstanding these considerations, the "supplemental and corrective role" of international law, which I will refer to hereinafter as the first principle of the *Klöckner-Amco* doctrine,[56] seemed to express, at least until recently, the more or less unanimous interpretation of Article 42(1)

[50] *Amco Asia Corporation and others* v. *Republic of Indonesia* (ICSID Case No. ARB/81/1), Decision on the Application for Annulment, May 16, 1986, *ICSID Reports*, 1 (1990), 509 (hereinafter: *Amco* v. *Indonesia I*).

[51] *Ibid.*, 514, para. 20. [52] *Ibid.*, para. 21. [53] *Ibid.*, para. 22. [54] *Ibid.* [55] See n. 52.

[56] This term is adopted from E. Gaillard and Y. Banifatemi, "The Meaning of 'and' in Article 42(1), Second Sentence, of the Washington Convention: The Role of International Law in the ICSID Choice of Law Process," *ICSID Review – FILJ*, 18 (2003), 375 at 393. On the scholarly analysis of the case law see also C. Schreuer, *The ICSID Convention – A Commentary* (Cambridge University Press, 2001), Art. 42, paras. 140 ff.; I. F. I. Shihata and A. R. Parra, "Applicable Substantive Law in Disputes between States and Private Foreign Parties: The Case of Arbitration under the ICSID Convention," *ICSID Review – FILJ*, 9 (1994), 183; Broches, "Applicable Law," p. 12; "The Convention," 389 ff.; B. Goldman, *Le droit applicable selon la Convention de la BIRD, du 18 mars 1965, pour règelement des différends relatifs aux investissements entre États et ressortissants d'autres États, in Investissements Étrangers et abitrage entre États et personnes privées*, La Convention BIRD du 18 mars 1965, (1969), 151.

second sentence ICSID[57] and was accepted by subsequent ICSID Tribunals over a considerable period of time.[58]

(ii) Domestic law as the primary source

Intertwined with the "supplemental and corrective function" of international law is the notion that domestic law is deemed as the primary source to determine the law applicable under Article 42(1) ICSID; I will hereinafter refer to this as the second principle of the *Klöckner-Amco* doctrine. In *Klöckner* v. *Cameroon* the Tribunal established the two-stage test outlined above that it first has to look at domestic law and only thereafter may apply international law.[59] Additionally, it held that the arbitrators are not entitled to base their decision solely on international law.[60]

Subsequent Tribunals recognizing "the law of the contracting State party... as paramount within its own territory"[61] stated that "the law of the host State is, in principle, the law to be applied in resolving the dispute"[62] or did not apply international law at all.[63] The notion of domestic law as the primary source therefore can be detected as a second principle that was prevailing among Tribunals regarding the relationship of international and domestic law according to Article 42(1) second sentence ICSID.

(iii) Conclusion

The prevalent view on the relationship of international law and domestic law until the 1990s, the *Klöckner-Amco* doctrine, consists of three corresponding principles: (1) international law plays a "supplemental and corrective function" vis-à-vis domestic law, (2) domestic law is the primary source for the law applicable to resolve an investor–State dispute and therefore (3) the Tribunal in the first instance has to apply the domestic

57 See Gaillard and Banifatemi, "The Meaning of 'and'"; Broches, "The Convention," 389 ff; ICSID Convention, Analysis of Documents Concerning the Origin and the Formulation of the Convention, vol. II/1, 804 (Washington, DC, 1970).

58 *Liberian Eastern Timber Corporation (LETCO)* v. *The Government of the Republic of Liberia*, Recovery of Damages for Breach of a Concession Agreement, March 31, 1986, *ILM*, 26 (1987), 647 at 658; *SPP* v. *Egypt*, 352 ff., para. 84.

59 See *supra* 2 D. 2. (a).

60 *Klöckner* v. *Cameroon*, Decision on Annulment, para. 69.

61 *LETCO* v. *Liberia*, 658.

62 *Amco* v. *Indonesia I*, 514, para. 21.

63 *Société Ouest Africaine des Bétons Industriels* v. *Senegal* (ICSID Case No. ARB/82/1), Award, February 25, 1988, *ICSID Review – FILJ*, 4 (1989), 125, at 159, para. 5.02 (hereinafter: *SOABI* v. *Senegal*).

law of the host State and only thereafter may have recourse to international law.

(b) Approaches in scholarly writing

This part will briefly outline approaches undertaken in scholarly writing towards the interpretation of Article 42(1) second sentence ICSID. To start with, I will portray scholarly writing that led to or supported the *Klöckner-Amco* doctrine (see (i) below). Thereinafter, subsection (ii) describes the critiques of the *Klöckner-Amco* doctrine. Further, an alternative approach introduced by an eminent scholar will be given short consideration (see (iii) below).

(i) Scholarly writing promoting the Klöckner-Amco *doctrine*

The *Klöckner-Amco* doctrine did not come out of the blue. As a matter of fact, it seems to reflect a common understanding of how the role of international law was supposed to be defined under Article 42(1) ICSID, a view which prevailed among scholars and practitioners until recently.[64] For example, Aaron Broches, in his 1972 Hague Academy course on the ICSID Convention, stated:

> My submission as to the relationship between the law of the host State and international law in the second sentence of 42(1) is as follows. The Tribunal will first look at the law of the host State and that law will in the first instance be applied to the merits of the dispute. Then this result will be tested against international law.[65]

This opinion basically foreshadows the third *Klöckner-Amco* principle.[66] Broches' underlying rationale is rooted in the view that it is a "fact that the investment which has given rise to the dispute is made within a national jurisdiction and in the absence of a stipulation to the contrary... should in the first instance be examined in the light of the law of that jurisdiction,"[67] which corresponds with the second *Klöckner-Amco* principle.[68]

Remarkable, however, regarding the first *Klöckner-Amco* principle,[69] i.e. that international law has a mere "supplemental and corrective function"

[64] See C. Schreuer, *The ICSID Convention – A Commentary* (Cambridge University Press, 2001), Art. 42, paras. 140 ff; I. F. I. Shihata and A. R. Parra, "Applicable Substantive Law in Disputes between States and Private Foreign Parties: The Case of Arbitration under the ICSID Convention," *ICSID Review – FILJ*, 9 (1994), 183; B. Goldman, *Le droit applicable selon la Convention de la BIRD*, 151.

[65] See Broches, "The Convention," 392. [66] See *supra* 2 D. 2. (a) (iii).

[67] Broches, "The Convention," 390. [68] See n. 66. [69] *Ibid.*

under Article 42(1) ICSID, is the passage that directly follows the one cited above:

> That process [i.e. that domestic law has to be applied first and then the result must be tested against international law] will not involve the confirmation or denial of the validity of the host State's law, but may result in not applying it where that law, or action taken under that law, violates international law. In that sense... international law is hierarchically superior to national law under Article 42(1).[70]

The passage provokes three observations: First, as regards the "corrective function," Broches sees international law as trumping domestic law when the latter "violates" the former. Whether, in his view, "violation" differs from "inconsistency" or "conflict" cannot be deduced from this passage. Second, he opines that international law is "hierarchically superior" to domestic law, but holds that this does not mean the latter's nullity, but merely its inapplicability. Third, Broches does not mention here – or in any other part of his piece – the "supplemental function" of international law.[71] From the fact that he regards domestic law as the primary source one cannot automatically conclude that in his opinion international law may be applied to fill up lacunae in domestic law. The lack of any reference to this kind of function seems to suggest that Broches sees the role of international law as even more limited than the *Klöckner-Amco* doctrine, for the "supplemental" function of international law does not appear on his list of situations in which he regards international law as applicable under Article 42(1) ICSID.[72] This would mean that international law could only be applied to correct domestic law – or if domestic law makes international law applicable – but in the case of lacunae in the domestic law could not add any rule or principle to resolve the dispute.

(ii) Critique of the Klöckner-Amco *doctrine*

In contrast to the consensus throughout the early years of ICSID, the *Klöckner-Amco* doctrine has been subject to fierce criticism in recent years.[73]

70 Broches, "The Convention," 390.

71 Although the *Amco I* annulment decision cites him as a reference; *Amco* v. *Indonesia I*, 49, para. 22.

72 See Broches, "The Convention," 392 f.

73 See Gaillard and Banifatemi, "The Meaning of 'and'", 393; W. M. Reisman, "The Regime for Lacunae in the ICSID Choice of Law Provision and the Question of its Threshold", *ICSID Review – FILJ*, 15 (2000), 362; P. Weil, "The State, the Foreign Investor and International Law: The No Longer Stormy Relationship of a Ménage à Trois," *ICSID Review – FILJ*, 15 (2000), 401.

In particular, the basic assumption of the doctrine, i.e. that domestic law contains lacunae that may be filled up by international law, is severely disputed.[74] Given that every legal order is constructed as comprehensive, i.e. claims to address every issue arising, the argument runs, the assumption that domestic law may contain lacunae is simply erroneous.

Under a comprehensive legal order, all legal questions must generally be resolved by resort to rules existent within the order. For example, a US judge confronted with a legal question cannot hold *non liquet* but must decide the issue at hand. If there is no statute and no case law that provide for, e.g., a remedy, the natural conclusion is that there is in fact no remedy and not that there is a loophole in the law. As a matter of fact, in a highly developed domestic legal system, one may well argue, there do not exist any lacunae at all, for the system provides the instruments – general principles, rules of interpretation, case law methodology – to find a solution for every legal issue that may possibly arise.[75]

Therefore, to stay with the example of remedies, if the domestic statutory law does not contain remedies regarding a particular issue, those remedies can either be derived by resort to the aforementioned legal instruments or are not granted because the lawmaker deliberately decided not to do so. In any event, the domestic legal system does not necessarily have to contain loopholes, if it does not expressly provide for a rule regarding a particular issue.

While it may occur that domestic law in fact contains lacunae, under a developed legal system such cases are very rare. Additionally, while enforcement and adjudication may be less reliable, most developing countries' legal system is highly sophisticated – as a matter of fact, many of them adopted Western legal theory and tradition.

Therefore, the scope for international law in its "supplemental function" is very narrow, for lacunae very rarely exist in domestic legal systems. Consequently, if one takes the *Klöckner-Amco* doctrine's premise seriously, i.e. domestic law is the primary source of the applicable law under Article 42(1) second sentence ICSID, in an ICSID dispute international law would hardly ever be applied to supplement domestic law. Moreover, any ICSID arbitration would require the arbitrators to be experts in the domestic law of the host State, for without thorough knowledge of the domestic legal system and all its specific instruments – general principles,

[74] See Reisman, "The Regime for Lacunae," 371 ff.; Gaillard and Banifatemi, "The Meaning of 'and'," 394 ff.

[75] See Reisman, "The Regime for Lacunae," 371.

case law methodology and interpretative tools – they would never be able to discern whether there is a lacuna or whether the law provides for a solution.

Thus the aforementioned considerations seriously question the viability of a mere "supplemental function" of international law under Article 42(1) second sentence ICSID, if not to say the viability of domestic law as the primary source of international investment law after all.

(iii) Reisman: Corrective function only when collision with fundamental norms of international law

Calling into question the notion of lacunae in domestic law and therefore the "supplemental function" of international law according to the *Klöckner-Amco* doctrine, Professor Reisman also introduces a new concept to define the corrective function of international law under Article 42(1) second sentence ICSID.

Under his concept, international law may only have a corrective function in case of "collision" with domestic law.[76] In contrast to "inconsistency," according to Professor Reisman, "collision" means that international law, in order to prevail, must be violated by application of the domestic rule, which, in his view, is only possible if there is a peremptory norm of international law; in other words, in case of *ius cogens*.[77]

This view, however, fundamentally limits the scope of international law and almost completely excludes BITs from such international law that may have a "corrective function" – unless BITs incorporate a rule of *ius cogens*, which would only very rarely be the case. Rather, it is dubious whether any international law rule will be applicable under this standard, given the restrictive criteria and the very limited number of accepted *ius cogens* rules.[78]

Moreover, Professor Reisman's interpretation departs essentially from the text of Article 42(1) second sentence ICSID. If "international law" had to be read as "international *ius cogens*," it would not make sense to refer to "such rules of international law as *may* be applicable," since *ius cogens* is always applicable. Further, as Gaillard and Banifatemi point out in their response to Reisman, under such an interpretation, Article 42(1) ICSID would be redundant, for it would merely repeat the obvious, i.e. that peremptory norms have to be observed.[79]

[76] *Ibid.*, 375. [77] *Ibid.*, 375 ff. [78] See Brownlie, *Principles*, 510 ff.
[79] See Gaillard and Banifatemi, "The Meaning of 'and'," 401.

3. *The dissolution of the* Klöckner-Amco *doctrine*

(a) First doubts: the *Amco* resubmitted case award

On May 30, 1990 a newly established Tribunal issued the award in the resubmitted case of *Amco* v. *Indonesia*.[80] Confronted with the same facts as the Annulment Committee, one might suggest the outcome of the interpretation of Article 42 ICSID would be to endorse the *Klöckner-Amco* doctrine. The Tribunal in the resubmitted case, however, held that:

> applicable domestic laws . . . must be checked against international laws . . . Thus international law is *fully* applicable and to classify its role as 'only' supplemental and corrective seems a distinction without a difference.[81]

It is noteworthy that the Tribunal speaks of "international *laws*," whereas *Klöckner* speaks of "principles." This seems to suggest two things: Firstly, the Tribunal regards international law rather as a comprehensive body of rules than as a conglomerate of diffuse principles. The term "laws," as used by the Tribunal for describing both the domestic and the international realm, suggests a more concrete and systematic body of rules than the term "principles" – particularly in the context of the *Klöckner-Amco* doctrine, which reserves only a supplemental and corrective, i.e. secondary role, to international law.

This observation, secondly, lets one further suggest that the Tribunal sees international and domestic law on an equal footing. Referring to "domestic laws" and "international laws" respectively, the Tribunal appears to regard both orders more or less as equal, refraining from giving absolute preference to domestic law.

However, while one may well see such observations as simple logomachy, it has to be admitted that the Tribunal regards international law as "fully applicable," although it does not explain what it means by this exactly. Nonetheless, without providing much reasoning, the Tribunal casts some doubts on the viability of the *Klöckner-Amco* doctrine. The Tribunal was not ready to completely depart from the beaten path, however, since it follows the two-stage analysis of the *Klöckner-Amco* doctrine, i.e. to first look at domestic law and only as a second step take international law into consideration.[82]

[80] *Amco Asia Corporation and others* v. *Republic of Indonesia* (ICSID Case No. ARB/81/1), Resubmitted Case, Award, May 30, *ICSID Reports*, 1 (1990), 569 (hereinafter: *Amco* v. *Indonesia II*) (emphasis added).

[81] *Ibid.*, 579, para. 40. [82] *Ibid.*

(b) The advent of BITs

As alluded to in A., the advent of BITs in the ICSID arena changed the substantive law of international investment to a quite considerable extent. Defining the investor–host State relationship in an international law instrument, a BIT sets out the investor's rights in an express, clear and detailed manner. In contrast to the somewhat ambiguous rules of customary international law, whose scope and even existence can be fairly disputed, a BIT is a more or less comprehensive body of rules, comparable to – or sometimes even more elaborate than – domestic law on investment.

Under these circumstances, it does not surprise that in *AAPL* v. *Sri Lanka*,[83] the first BIT case under ICSID, the Tribunal considered the BIT as the primary source regarding the applicable law and contended that other "international or domestic legal relevant rules" were merely a "supplementary source."[84] Looking at these findings against the backdrop of the *Klöckner-Amco* doctrine, however, the fundamental change in the view on the role of international law becomes apparent.

(c) The growing role of international law

In the first years following *AAPL* and *Amco II*, the *Klöckner-Amco* doctrine was not confronted with a fundamental challenge. The case law on Article 42(1) ICSID was somewhat diffuse. However, subsequent Tribunals incrementally seemed to give more credit to the growing importance of international law in ICSID disputes.

As has been mentioned above,[85] in *SPP* v. *Egypt* the Tribunal decided to apply relevant principles and rules of international law, even though the parties made an exclusive choice of domestic law according to Article 42(1) first sentence ICSID.[86] The Tribunal reasoned that the domestic law did not provide for a solution of the issue at hand and therefore it might have recourse to international law according to Article 42(1) second sentence ICSID, which, according to the Tribunal, declared international law applicable in case of such loopholes.[87]

Furthermore, in *Tradex Hellas* v. *Albania* the Tribunal referred to international law as a means of interpretation. Although it had found earlier in the award that it only had jurisdiction under the Albanian 1993 Law on

[83] *Asian Agricultural Products Limited* v. *Democratic Socialist Republic of Sri Lanka* (ICSID Case No. ARB/87/3), Award, June 27, 1990, *ICSID Review – FILJ*, 5 (1990), 526 (hereinafter: *AAPL* v. *Sri Lanka*).

[84] *Ibid.*, 549. [85] *Supra* 2 A. 3. [86] *SPP* v. *Egypt*, 352 ff., para. 80. [87] *Ibid.*, para. 84.

Investment and therefore only this domestic law represented the applicable law in the dispute at hand, it used international law as an interpretative instrument, since the 1993 Law on Investment was adopted to transform Albanian BIT obligations into domestic law.[88]

While this case may seem somewhat similar to the *Klöckner* dispute, for "international law" is used to interpret domestic law, *Tradex Hellas* differs from *Klöckner* in that in *Tradex Hellas* the relevant law was modeled after the BIT and thus arguably informed by international law, whereas in *Klöckner* the Tribunal arbitrarily referred to a comparative interpretation.

Finally, the award in *Santa Elena* v. *Costa Rica* deserves some attention:[89] In discussing the applicable law according to Article 42(1) second sentence ICSID, the Tribunal started its analysis by restating a part of the first *Klöckner-Amco* principle, i.e. that international law prevails over domestic law in case of "inconsistency." However, the Tribunal did not cite the other part of the first *Klöckner-Amco* principle, i.e. the supplemental function of international law, but only tested the domestic Costa Rican law against international law. It appears that the Tribunal implicitly abandoned the notion that domestic law is the primary source and opted for the primacy of international law instead.

Holding that "to the extent that there may be any inconsistencies between the two bodies of law, the rules of public international law must prevail,"[90] the Tribunal reasoned that otherwise the international protection of property would be denied. In its view, this would run counter to a main purpose of the ICSID Convention, which is to create a procedural framework for promoting the protection of property as guaranteed under international law. Therefore, the Tribunal came to the conclusion that "in the end, international law is controlling."[91]

The *Santa Elena* award differs considerably, therefore, from the *Klöckner-Amco* doctrine. On the one hand it only stresses the corrective function of international law, and on the other does not regard domestic law as the primary source of law to govern the investment dispute, but by contrast regards the protection of international law rights as the very

[88] *Tradex Hellas SA* v. *Republic of Albania* (ICSID Case No. ARB/94/2), Award, April 29, 1999, *ICSID Review – FILJ*, 14 (1999) (hereinafter: *Tradex Hellas* v. *Albania*), 197 at 216, para. 69. See also *Cable Television of Nevis, Ltd. and Cable Television of Nevis Holdings, Ltd. v. Federation of St. Kitts and Nevis* (ICSID Case No. ARB/95/2), Award, December 16, 1996, *ICSID Review – FILJ*, 12 (1997), 330 (hereinafter: *Cable Television of Nevis* v. *Nevis*) at 385, para. 6.25., where the Tribunal also referred to international law as a means of interpretation.

[89] *Compañia del Desarrollo de Santa Elena SA* v. *Republic of Costa Rica* (ICSID Case No. ARB/96/1), Final Award, February 17, 2000, *ICSID Review – FILJ*, 15 (2000), 169 (hereinafter: *Santa Elena* v. *Costa Rica*).

[90] *Ibid.*, 191, para. 64.

[91] *Ibid.*, para. 65.

purpose of ICSID and therefore opts for the primacy of international law. Thereby it implicitly challenges two *Klöckner-Amco* principles, i.e. (1) international law plays a "supplemental . . . function" vis-à-vis domestic law, and (2) domestic law is the primary source for the law applicable to resolve an investor–State dispute.[92]

However, *Santa Elena* cannot be deemed as representing a complete departure from the *Klöckner-Amco* doctrine. While it emphasizes the "controlling" role of international law, the notion that international law trumps domestic law in case of "inconsistency" is hardly a new concept, since *Klöckner-Amco* already accepted the "corrective function" of international law. Consequently, despite the aforementioned reservations, the *Santa Elena* award can still be seen as roughly in line with the *Klöckner-Amco* doctrine, for it is rooted in the same initial reasoning and does not offer an entirely new concept.

4. *A new doctrine:* Wena

As we have seen in the previous paragraphs, the Tribunals that dealt with the relationship of domestic and international law under Article 42(1) second sentence ICSID throughout the 1990s used the *Klöckner-Amco* doctrine as a starting point or at least as a point of reference for their analysis. Most of the said Tribunals, however, granted international law a more prominent role than the original *Klöckner-Amco* doctrine suggested. To name but two, *AAPL* regarded the BIT as the primary source of the law applicable and gave domestic law merely a "supplemental" role instead. Moreover, the *Santa Elena* Tribunal referred to the purpose of the ICSID Convention in order to buttress its opinion that international law was "controlling."

Therefore, it became apparent that, whilst they still used it as a point of departure, the confidence of ICSID Tribunals in the accuracy of the *Klöckner-Amco* doctrine eroded during the 1990s. Despite some serious doubts, no effort was undertaken to substitute the doctrine with a fundamentally new concept. This pattern changed in 2002 with the *Wena* decision.

(a) The *Wena* decision[93]

As *Klöckner* and *Amco I*, *Wena Hotels Ltd.* v. *Arab Republic of Egypt*[94] was a decision on annulment, rendered by an ad hoc Committee under Article 52

[92] See *supra* 2 B. 1. (c).
[93] This subsection draws on A. Kulick, "The Integration."
[94] *Wena Hotels Ltd.* v. *Arab Republic of Egypt*, Decision on Annulment, February 28, 2002, *ILM*, 41 (2002), 933 (hereinafter: *Wena* v. *Egypt*).

ICSID. The question submitted to the Annulment Committee was whether the Tribunal exceeded its power by not referring to Egyptian law as the primary source and conferring the UK–Egypt BIT, the Agreement for the Promotion and Protection of Investments ("IPPA"), a prominent role.[95]

The Annulment Committee's decision reads in relevant part:

> 38. This discussion brings into light the various views expressed as to the role of international law in the context of Article 42(1).... In Klöckner I the ad hoc Committee introduced the concept of international law as complementary to the applicable law in case of lacunae and as corrective in case that the applicable domestic law would not conform on all points to the principles of international law...
>
> 39. Some of these views have in common the fact that they are aimed at restricting the role of international law and highlighting that of the law of the host State. Conversely, the view that calls for a broad application of international law aims at restricting the role of law of the host State. There seems not to be a single answer as to which of these approaches is the correct one. *The circumstances of each case may justify one or another solution*.... Further, the use of the word 'may' in the second sentence of [Article 42(1) ICSID] indicates that *the Convention does not draw a sharp line for the distinction of the respective scope of international and domestic law and, correspondingly, that this has the effect to confer on the Tribunal a certain margin and power of interpretation*.
>
> 40. What is clear is that the sense and meaning of the negotiations leading to the second sentence of Article 42(1) *allowed for both legal orders to have a role*. The law of the host State can indeed be applied in conjunction with international law if this is justified. *So too international law can be applied by itself if the appropriate rule is found in this other ambit*.[96]

Looking at the Annulment Committee's reasoning, it expressly declined from accepting the "supplemental and corrective functions" of international law, as suggested by Egypt, the Applicant. By contrast, it held that the word "may" in Article 42(1) second sentence ICSID indicates that there is no clear distinction between the respective scope of international and domestic law.[97]

Moreover, as can be derived from the drafting history of Article 42(1) ICSID, "both legal orders have a role to play."[98] Therefore, according to the Committee, it was erroneous to make the application of international law dependent on the application of a domestic law rule. In the Tribunal's opinion, nothing in the wording of Article 42(1) ICSID justified giving

[95] *Ibid.*, 939, para. 21.
[96] *Ibid.*, 940 f., paras. 37–40 (emphasis added).
[97] *Ibid.*, 941, para. 39.
[98] *Ibid.*, para. 40.

international law merely a supplemental role to play, i.e. that it may only be applicable if domestic law contained a loophole. In contrast, the *Wena* Committee held that international law can be applied "by itself,"[99] that is international law, just as domestic law, is deemed to be a comprehensive legal order, which independently can serve as a source of the law applicable to the dispute.

Given the assumption, as stated above, that, from the outset, no clear line can be drawn between the realm of international law and the realm of domestic law, the *Wena* Committee found that a Tribunal has a considerable margin of discretion in how much room it gives the one or the other. How broadly or how narrowly international law will be applied cannot be answered in a general way, but "the circumstances of each case may justify one or another solution."[100]

Consequently, according to the Tribunal, the role of international law is not initially limited to a merely secondary role, i.e. "supplemental and corrective," but has to be decided using a case-by-case approach. In other words, there is no precast pattern as to the role of either domestic law or international law before the Tribunal enters into the analysis of the "circumstances of each case." Before it looks at the circumstances of the case, all bets are off. Therefore, in the case under discussion, the Annulment Committee concluded that international law was to have the upper hand, since Egyptian law granted treaty rules primacy over domestic laws.

In conclusio, the findings in the *Wena* decision can be summarized as follows: (1) from the outset, international law is fully and independently applicable to the dispute and stands on an equal footing with domestic law; (2) which of the two prevails depends on the particular circumstances in each case; (3) a Tribunal, ruling on the relationship of international law and domestic law under Article 42(1) second sentence ICSID preserves a considerable margin of discretion in determining and interpreting those circumstances.[101]

(b) The first years after *Wena*: some ambiguities

Subsequent ICSID Tribunals did not immediately adopt the pragmatic approach[102] towards the applicable law taken by the *Wena* Committee.

99 *Ibid.* 100 *Ibid.*, 941, para. 39.

101 *Ibid.* It has to be noted that the Annulment Committee makes it clear that it conveys the Tribunal this discretion and does not limit it to the competence of an Annulment Committee.

102 See Gaillard and Banifatemi, "The Meaning of 'and'," 393.

As a matter of fact, the three decisions issued from 2002 to 2005 dealing with Article 42(1) second sentence ICSID did not mention *Wena*. The first case, *Middle East Cement* v. *Egypt*,[103] avoided the question of how to define the relationship of international and domestic law since Article 11 of the Egypt–Greece BIT contained a choice of law clause in the sense of Article 42(1) first sentence ICSID. It is noteworthy, however, that the Tribunal takes "recourse to rules of general international law to supplement those of the BIT," despite the fact that general international law was not mentioned in the choice of law clause which provided exclusively for the application of the BIT and domestic law if more favorable.[104]

In the following case, *Vivendi I*,[105] an annulment decision, the ad hoc Committee did not consider *Wena*, although Article 42(1) second sentence ICSID was applicable. In defining the relationship of international and domestic law, the Tribunal held a rather dualistic view. Asserting that the lawfulness of an act under domestic law does not affect the lawfulness of the same act under international law, the Tribunal cited the ICJ in the *ELSI* case: "Compliance with municipal law and compliance with the provisions of a treaty are different questions."[106] Thus, the Annulment Committee maintained that domestic law might not override or even affect international law.

Consequently, the Annulment Committee came to the conclusion that domestic law could not represent the primary source of the law applicable and therefore the international law rule at hand was controlling the dispute. However, since this was not a question submitted to the Committee, it did not expressly rule on the reverse question, i.e. whether and to what extent international law may trump domestic law.[107]

In the *Autopista* v. *Venezuela* award, the third case, the Tribunal expressly mentioned *Wena*, but decided to endorse the *Klöckner-Amco* doctrine.[108] Referring to the "corrective" function of international law according to

[103] *Middle East Cement Shipping and Handling Co. SA* v. *Arab Republic of Egypt* (ICSID Case No. ARB/99/6), Award of the Tribunal, April 12, 2002, *ICSID Review – FILJ*, 17 (2002), 602 (hereinafter: *Middle East Cement* v. *Egypt*).

[104] *Ibid.*, 622, para. 87.

[105] *Compañía de Aguas del Aconquija SA and Vivendi Universal (Formerly Compagnie Générale des Eaux)* v. *The Argentine Republic*, Decision on Annulment, 3 July 2002, *ILM*, 41 (2002), 1135 (hereinafter: *Vivendi I*).

[106] *Ibid.*, 1154, paras. 95, 97.

[107] Which was not necessary in the present dispute, since the mere question arose, whether domestic law may affect the BIT provisions; see *ibid.*, paras. 90 ff.

[108] *Autopista Concesionada de Venezuela, C.A.* v. *Bolivarian Republic of Venezuela* (ICSID Case No. ARB/00/5), Award of the Tribunal, September 23, 2003 (hereinafter: *Autopista* v. *Venezuela*), 31, para. 102, available at http://icsid.worldbank.org/ICSID/FrontServlet.

that doctrine, i.e. that in case of "conflict" international law prevails, the Tribunal differentiated between "inconsistency" with and "violation" of international law. In a two-stage analysis, it has to be determined, according to the Tribunal, (1) whether there exist inconsistencies between domestic and international law, and (2) whether such inconsistencies amount to a violation of international law. Only in the latter case, the Tribunal contended, international law would prevail.[109] While, on first glance, this finding seems to be a major setback to the *Wena* doctrine, a more thorough analysis reveals *Wena*'s influence even on this case.

The Tribunal started its interpretation of Article 42 ICSID with the notion that "the role of international law in ICSID practice is not entirely clear."[110] Then it cited *Wena* and went on:

> Whatever the extent of the role that international law plays under Article 42(1) (second sentence), this Tribunal believes that there is no reason *in this case*... to go beyond the corrective and supplemental functions of international law.[111]

Consequently, the Tribunal at least endorsed the last two findings of the *Wena* decision, that is, the case-by-case approach and the Tribunal's margin of discretion to choose the respective role of international law suitable in the case at hand.

Exercising its "certain margin and power of interpretation," the Tribunal expressly pointed out "that there is no reason in this case, *considering especially that it is a contract and not a treaty arbitration*, to go beyond the corrective and supplemental functions of international law."[112] Therefore, the Tribunal's rationale for granting international law only the limited role as under the *Klöckner-Amco* doctrine appears to be due to the fact that there was no BIT in place between the investor's home State and the host country. Thus, the lack of a comprehensive set of concrete and explicit rules as enshrined in a BIT seemed to have severely influenced the Tribunal's interpretation,[113] which in fact provides for the narrowest role for international law in the past two decades.

(c) Confirmation and interpretation of the *Wena* doctrine

Whereas the Tribunals established directly after *Wena* were somewhat ambiguous regarding their approach towards the new doctrine – or in some part rejected it, e.g. *Autopista* – in recent years a considerable number

[109] *Ibid.*, 32, paras. 103 f. [110] *Ibid.*, 31, para. 102.
[111] *Ibid.*, 31 f., para. 102 (emphasis added). [112] *Ibid*, 32, para. 102 (emphasis added).
[113] *Ibid.*, 32, para. 102.

of ICSID Tribunals have expressly endorsed it.[114] Although, as will be demonstrated below,[115] some of them went beyond *Wena*, all the decisions use its ruling as a basis, or at least as a starting point for their own reasoning on the applicable law. In particular, the phrases "both sources have a role to play" and "international law can be applied by itself" (or very similar ones) find their way into all of the decisions.[116] So, the Tribunals all strongly emphasize the first notion of the *Wena* doctrine, i.e. international law is fully and independently applicable to the dispute and stands – at least – on an equal footing with domestic law. As regards the two other notions, as I will show subsequently, the Tribunals expand the role of international law beyond the *Wena* decision.[117]

5. *The Argentine crisis Tribunals and beyond*[118]

As becomes obvious when reviewing the case law cited in section D. 4. (c), firstly, all the Tribunals generally endorsed *Wena*; secondly, all dealt with disputes arising out of the Argentine crisis; and thirdly, all disputes were BIT arbitrations.[119] While the details of this crisis are not relevant in this context, it nonetheless is worth noting that all the cases centered around the question whether Argentina was able to raise the state of necessity,

114 *CMS Gas Transmission Company* v. *Argentine Republic* (ICSID Case No. ARB/01/8), Award, May 12, 2005 (hereinafter: *CMS* v. *Argentina*), 34, paras. 116 ff., available at http://icsid.worldbank.org/ICSID/FrontServlet; *Azurix Corp.* v. *Argentine Republic* (ICSID Case No. ARB/01/12), Award, July 14, 2006 (hereinafter: *Azurix* v. *Argentina*), 20, para. 66, available at http://icsid.worldbank.org/ICSID/FrontServlet; *LG&E Energy Corp., LG&E Capital Corp. and LG&E International Inc.* v. *Argentine Republic* (ICSID Case No. ARB/02/1), Decision on Liability, October 3, 2006, *ICSID Review – FILJ*, 20 (2005), 203 at 227 (hereinafter: *LG&E* v. *Argentina*), para. 96; *Siemens AG* v. *Argentine Republic*, Award, February 6, 2007 (ICSID Case No. ARB/02/8), 2007 WL 1215068 (APPAWD) (hereinafter: *Siemens* v. *Argentina*), para. 77; *Enron Corporation & Ponderosa Assets* v. *Argentine Republic*, Award, May 22, 2007 (hereinafter: *Enron* v. *Argentina*) (ICSID Case No. ARB/01/3), 2007 WL 5366471 (APPAWD), para. 207; *Sempra Energy International* v. *Argentine Republic* (ICSID Case No. ARB/02/16), Award of the Tribunal, September 28, 2007 (hereinafter: *Sempra* v. *Argentina*), 68 f., para. 236, available at http://icsid.worldbank.org/ICSID/FrontServlet.

115 See *infra*, 2 D. 5.

116 *CMS* v. *Argentina*, para. 116; *Azurix* v. *Argentina*, para. 66; *LG&E* v. *Argentina*, para. 96; *Siemens* v. *Argentina*, para. 77; *Enron* v. *Argentina*, para. 207; *Sempra* v. *Argentina*, para. 236.

117 On the three notions of the *Wena* doctrine, see *supra* 2 D. 4. (a).

118 This subsection draws on A. Kulick, "The Integration."

119 On the Argentine crisis and its repercussions in the ICSID realm, see W. Burke-White and A. von Staden, "Investment Protection in Extraordinary Times: The Interpretation and Application of Non-Precluded Measures Provisions in Bilateral Investment Treaties," *Va. J. Int'l L.*, 48 (2007–08), 307 at 337 ff.; A. Szodruch, "Necessity and Beyond – the Legal Aftermath of the Argentine Financial Crisis before the German Federal Constitutional Court," *Ger. Yb. Int'l L.*, 50 (2007), 523 ff.; H. Samra, "Five Years Later – the CMS Award placed in the Context of the Argentine Financial Crisis and the ICSID Arbitration Boom," *U. Mia. InterAm. L. Rev.*, 38 (2007), 667 ff.

both under the BIT and under customary international law, in order to justify its otherwise more or less obvious violations of the respective BIT provisions.

Three findings of the Argentine crisis Tribunals go beyond the notions of the *Wena* decisions and will be elaborated subsequently: international and domestic law are mutually complementary comprehensive legal orders (a), international law is ultimately supreme over domestic law (b) and there is no dichotomy between international and domestic law; i.e. both, being complementary, can arguably be regarded as forming an integrated legal order (c).

(a) International and domestic law as comprehensive legal orders

As mentioned earlier, the *Wena* decision for the first time explicitly regarded international law not merely as secondary source pertaining to the law applicable under Article 42(1) second sentence ICSID,[120] but as a comprehensive legal order, fully applicable to the dispute, without the need to rely on domestic law as the "primary source." This notion was expressly espoused by the *LG&E*, *Siemens* and *Enron* Tribunals, but underpinned the reasoning of the other decisions as well.[121] To quote the *LG&E* Tribunal:

> 95. The intention in the language of the original draft [of Article 42(1) second sentence ICSID] was not to establish an order of preference, but rather to establish the possibility of alternatives. Initially, scholarly authorities and some ICSID Tribunals admitted that the conjunction 'and' means 'and in the case of lacunae, or should the law of the Contracting State be inconsistent with international law.' [footnote omitted] *However, any limitation to the role of international law under these terms would imply accepting that international law may be subordinate to domestic law and would obviate the fact that there are a growing number of arbitrations initiated on the basis of bilateral or multilateral investment treaties.*
>
> 96. *It is the Tribunal's opinion that 'and' means 'and'*, so that the rules of international law, especially those included in the ICSID Convention and in the Bilateral Treaty as well as those of domestic law are to be applied.[122]

On the other hand, as the cited passage demonstrates, domestic law does not completely disappear from the stage of Article 42(1) second sentence ICSID under the Tribunal's concept. The notion of the *Wena* decision that "both legal orders have a role to play" is reiterated and advanced by the

[120] See *supra* 2 D. 4. (a).
[121] *LG&E* v. *Argentina*, paras. 88, 96; *Siemens* v. *Argentina*, para. 77; *Enron* v. *Argentina*, para. 207; see also *CMS* v. *Argentina*, para. 116.
[122] *LG&E* v. *Argentina*, paras. 95 f. (emphasis added).

Enron Tribunal stating that both international and domestic law "have a complementary role to perform."[123] It is noteworthy in this regard that, different from the first *Klöckner-Amco* principle,[124] international law is not complementary to domestic law, but both are mutually complementary. The *Enron* Tribunal, therefore, deems to read *Wena* as opining for a combination of both international and domestic law as the law applicable in investment disputes.

(b) International law as ultimately supreme

The aforesaid is not a completely new finding compared to the *Wena* doctrine, although it takes its initial notion one step further. The *LG&E* Tribunal did not leave it in the obscure whether the "circumstances of the case,"[125] in the words of *Wena*, might also possibly allow for a subordinate role of international law but instead rejected such subordinate function of international law categorically.[126]

Thus, the next concept that is common to most of the Argentine crisis Tribunals at first glance is not entirely innovative either: that international law prevails over domestic law. In fact, outlined in this generality, it seems to add nothing new to the *Klöckner-Amco* doctrine, which acknowledges the prevalence of international law, if domestic law is in conflict with it. New, however, is the argumentation provided and constantly repeated by the Tribunals and the extent to which international law is regarded as supreme over domestic law.

The Argentine crisis Tribunals employ two lines of argumentation to stress the primacy of international law within the realm of international investment law. The first is a conflict of law argument, particularly endorsed by the *CMS* Tribunal. While it held, referring to *Wena*, that "the law of the host State can be applied in conjunction with international law" and thus argued that the law applicable in the case at hand consists of an amalgamation of domestic and international law rules, the *CMS* Tribunal stressed the primacy of international (treaty) law:

> 120. Article 31 of the [Argentine] Constitution mandates that the Constitution, the laws enacted under it and treaties are the 'supreme law of the Nation.' Indeed, the Argentine courts have a long-standing record of respect for treaties and have duly recognized their hierarchical standing above the law.[127]

123 *Enron* v. *Argentina*, para. 207.
124 See *supra* 2 D. 2. (a) (iii).
125 See *Wena* v. *Egypt*, 941, para. 39.
126 *LG&E* v. *Argentina*, para. 95.
127 *CMS* v. *Argentina*, para. 120.

While the *CMS* Tribunal did not find any specific collision between a treaty rule and a domestic law rule and therefore did not have to state expressly the prevalence of a specific rule of international law over domestic law, it left no doubt that it regarded international law as supreme. However, such an argument, relying on the conflict of law rule under the domestic constitution, cannot generally be used to prove the primacy of international law, for it is the domestic law itself, not an interpretation of the ICSID Convention, that leads to the conclusion that international law prevails.

In contrast, the second argument employed by the Argentine crisis Tribunals and first laid out in *LG&E* is much more instructive, for the Tribunal undertook a comprehensive effort to interpret Article 42(1) second sentence ICSID and similar BIT provisions.[128]

To introduce its further analysis, the Tribunal provided an argument for the above-mentioned *Wena* notion that international law is a comprehensive legal body, applicable independently from domestic law. According to the Tribunal the wording of Article 42 ("as may be applicable") was not intended to condition the application of international law. It rather "should be understood as making reference, within international law, to the competent rules to govern the dispute at issue," as evinced by the French version of ICSID, "that refers to the rules of international law 'en la matière.'"[129]

While underlining the "hierarchical relation" of international towards domestic law under the Argentine Constitution, the Tribunal further observed:

> [I]nternational treaties move away from the principle according to which foreign investment is subject to the law and jurisdiction of the host State and seek international solution of conflicts.[130]

Then it proceeded to state:

> International law *overrides* domestic law when there is a contradiction since a State cannot justify non-compliance of its international obligations by asserting the provisions of its domestic law.[131]

Thereby, the *LG&E* Tribunal refers to a customary rule of international treaty law[132] that is enshrined in Article 27 of the Vienna Convention on the Law of Treaties:

128 *LG&E* v. *Argentina*, paras. 80 ff. 129 *Ibid.*, para. 88.
130 *Ibid.*, para. 93. 131 *Ibid.*, para. 94 (emphasis added).
132 A. Aust, *Modern Treaty Law and Practice*, 2nd edn. (Cambridge University Press, 2007), p. 138: see also Lord McNair, *The Law of Treaties* (Clarendon Press, 1986), pp. 458 ff.

Article 27

Internal law and observance of treaties

A party may not invoke the provisions of its internal law as justification for its failure to perform a treaty. This rule is without prejudice to article 46.[133]

Relying on Article 27 VCLT is remarkable because of several reasons, three of which I want to discuss here that do not seem very surprising at first glance.[134] First, a rule of the law of treaties between States is applied in an investor–State relation. One may well argue that this is not very remarkable at all, since the BIT is a treaty and the investor is entitled to invoke its guarantees on its own behalf because the BIT permits this. Therefore, it is nothing but consequent to apply Article 27 VCLT.

While this may be true and dictated by logic, nonetheless it demonstrates how powerful an instrument Article 42(1) second sentence ICSID Convention in conjunction with a BIT really is. It permits investors to rely on international (treaty) law as the supreme law to govern their dispute with the host State. Since a BIT can be very detailed regarding investor protections, saying that international law is fully applicable, supreme over domestic law and not confined to a mere "supplemental and corrective function" as understood by the *Klöckner-Amco* doctrine basically means that an ICSID Member entering into a BIT cedes much more sovereignty than it may be aware of. It is practically unable to adopt any law that is inconsistent with a BIT provision, since any foreign investor can successfully file an investment claim for monetary damages. If international law is fully applicable and ultimately supreme in investment arbitration, a private entity can claim and – by way of Article 54 ICSID – enforce international law against a State to a very large extent. This might impede or even prevent the host State from revising its regulatory framework, since such changes are very likely to clash with provisions enshrined in BITs – irrespective of whether such revision might be necessary or even required due to international obligations the host State must abide by.

The second thing remarkable about employing the Article 27 argument in ICSID arbitration is that it clarifies that an investment dispute is unambiguously an international dispute. The primary source of law for international disputes naturally is international law – if the parties do not agree otherwise, which is not the case under Article 42(1) second

133 Vienna Convention on the Law of Treaties, done at Vienna on May 23, 1969. Entered into force on January 27, 1980. United Nations, Treaty Series, vol. 1155, p. 331.

134 For the other reasons see *infra* 4. D. 2. (a) and (b).

sentence ICSID and most BITs containing a choice of law clause. While under the *Klöckner-Amco* doctrine the prevalent view was that the primary source of law was domestic law – merely supplemented and corrected by international law – and thus might have cast some doubts on how international an international investment arbitration actually is, under the aforementioned reasoning it is beyond question that the dispute is an international one with international law as the primary source of the law applicable.

Eventually, the third aspect that is remarkable is the notion that according to Article 27 VCLT international law can in fact *override* domestic law. It is a truism that international law prevails on the international plane. However, this is due to the notion that a State may not justify violations of international law by way of asserting its own domestic law. This is exactly what Article 27 Vienna Convention states. Under this paradigm, domestic law simply has no role to play in the international arena. The Argentine crisis Tribunals' holding, however, that international law overrides domestic law, exhibits a pattern fundamentally different from the aforementioned: It presupposes that international and domestic law are both fully applicable and intertwined in the way described at (a), for one legal order can only override another if they are both applicable – otherwise the question would not even arise. While one might regard these findings by the Argentine crisis Tribunals dubious from a classical public international law perspective, they foreshadow that many aspects of international investment law can hardly be explained by means of conventional models.

Where domestic law does not contradict international law, the *LG&E* Tribunal, however, did not hold that supremacy of international law means that it excludes the applicability of domestic law entirely.[135] According to the Tribunal, in such a case, the treaty is more open to a "wider juridical context," which may include "rules . . . of international law character or of domestic law nature";[136] which one to choose depends on the circumstances of the case.[137] Thereby, the *LG&E* Tribunal referred to the *Wena* notion that a case-by-case approach decides which rules of domestic and international law are to be applied in the case at hand. However, to determine the applicable law the Tribunal looked first at the BIT, second at general international law and only in third place at domestic law.[138] This

135 *LG&E* v. *Argentina*, *supra* n. 114, paras. 95 ff.

136 *Ibid*., para. 97. The Tribunal cites from *AAPL* v. *Sri Lanka*, 549.

137 *Ibid*., paras. 97 f. 138 *Ibid*., para. 99.

turns the order suggested by the *Klöckner-Amco* doctrine upside-down[139] and demonstrates once more how prominent a role the *LG&E* Tribunal conferred on international law.

The awards following *LG&E*, furthermore, confirmed the differentiation between contradiction and non-contradiction of international and domestic law. The *Siemens*, *Enron* and *Sempra* Tribunals all regarded international law as supreme in case of "conflict" or "inconsistency."[140] Moreover, they relied on Article 27 VCLT and stressed the "prominent role" of international law to make their case that international law is the primary and supreme source of international law.[141] Such prominent role of international law has since been engrained in the general conscience of the investment community and bears relevance even in cases where the BIT focuses on domestic law as the main or even exclusive legal source. For example, in *Bernardus Henricus Funnekotter and Others* v. *Republic of Zimbabwe* the parties agreed that despite Article 9(3) of the Dutch–Zimbabwean BIT declaring "the applicable law is domestic law... generally international law should prevail over domestic law."[142] Similarly, the *Chevron* Partial Award on the Merits[143] stressed the primacy of international law as did the Tribunals in *ATA* v. *Jordan*[144] and *Suez, Vivendi and AWG* v. *Argentina*.[145]

To conclude, Article 27 VCLT was the main argument for the Argentine crisis Tribunals to decide the relationship of international and domestic law under Article 42(1) second sentence ICSID. Subsequent Tribunals have expressly or implicitly endorsed such interpretation.[146] Three

139 See *supra* 2 D. 2. (a) (iii).

140 *Siemens* v. *Argentina*, para. 79; *Enron* v. *Argentina*, para. 207; *Sempra* v. *Argentina*, para. 237.

141 *Enron* v. *Argentina*, paras. 207 f.; *Sempra* v. *Argentina*, paras. 236 f.

142 *Bernardus Henricus Funnekotter and Others* v. *Republic of Zimbabwe*, Award, April 22, 2009 (ICSID Case No. ARB/05/6), para. 73.

143 *Chevron Corporation (USA) and Texaco Corporation (USA)* v. *Republic of Ecuador*, Partial Awards on the Merits, March 30, 2010, UNCITRAL, para. 159.

144 *ATA Construction, Industrial and Trading Company* v. *The Hashemite Kingdom of Jordan*, Award, May 18, 2010 (ICSID Case No. ARB/08/2), paras. 121 ff. However, the cited passage may also be understood as a mere reiteration of the customary rule enshrined in Art. 27 VCLT.

145 *Suez, Sociedad General de Aguas de Barcelona SA, and Vivendi Universal SA, and AWG Group* v. *The Argentine Republic*, Decision on Liability, July 30, 2010 (ICSID Case No. ARB/03/19), para. 63.

146 Note, however, *Iaonnis Kardassopoulos and Ron Fuchs* v. *Republic of Georgia*, Award, March 3, 2010 (ICSID Case No. ARB/05/18 and 07/15), para. 222, which seems to somewhat backtrack to the *Wena* standard.

observations can be derived from relying on this argument: First, international law is deemed to be ultimately supreme over domestic law. Second, placing the power to invoke supreme and detailed international law protections in the hands of an investor forcefully – albeit not illicitly – shatters the host State's sovereignty. Third, in the Tribunals' view, an international investment dispute is undoubtedly an international dispute, the primary legal source of which naturally is international law.

E. The changing face of international investment law

A summary of the aforesaid reveals six preliminary observations regarding the relationship of international law and domestic law under Article 42(1) second sentence ICSID (see 1.). Taking these observations into account, this chapter concludes by stating that according to the analysis of the case law Tribunals grant international law a "prominent role"[147] under the realm of international investment law: It is fully applicable and supreme over domestic law (2.). Moreover, I argue that international investment law evolves as an integrated legal order (3.).

1. *Six preliminary observations*

To summarize the aforesaid, six preliminary observations can be derived from the above analysis:

- **Observation 1:** BITs are similar legal instruments, which form a comprehensive framework establishing – at least in part – the law of international investment.[148]
- **Observation 2:** Under the realm of international investment law, international and domestic law are both comprehensive and complementary legal orders.[149]
- **Observation 3:** Under the realm of international investment law, international law is supreme.[150]
- **Observation 4:** Under Article 42(1) second sentence ICSID, international law is the primary source for the applicable law.[151]
- **Observation 5:** The main reason for observations 2 to 4 is the proliferation of BITs in recent years.
- **Observation 6:** However, even absent a BIT, recent ICSID case law indicates the growing role of international law.[152]

147 *CMS* v. *Argentina*, para. 119; *Enron* v. *Argentina*, para. 207; *Sempra* v. *Argentina*, para. 236.
148 See *supra* 2 A. 149 See *supra* 2 D. 5. (a). 150 See *supra* 2 D. 5. (b).
151 See *supra* 2 D. 5. (b). 152 See *supra* 2 D. 3. (c).

2. *"Prominent role": The "internationalization" of international investment law*

In the previous parts of this analysis we have seen investment jurisprudence, especially the Argentine crisis Tribunals, developing towards the notion that international law is regarded as comprehensive and supreme over domestic law.[153] Many Tribunals, as has been mentioned before, underline the "prominent role" of international law under international investment law.[154] But not all of this is entirely new. Even the *Klöckner-Amco* doctrine recognized that international law may trump domestic law under certain circumstances, i.e. in case of "inconsistencies" between the two orders.[155] As the *LETCO* Tribunal put it, "the law of the contracting state . . . is . . . subjected to control by international law."[156]

Reviewing the case law on Article 42(1) ICSID and similar BIT provisions, however, we have observed the constantly growing role of international law under the realm of international investment law. As early as 1990, twelve years before the *Wena* decision, the *Amco II* Tribunal spoke of both domestic and "international *laws*"[157] that are to govern the dispute, arguably foreshadowing the notion of a comprehensive legal order similar and equal to domestic law.

The advent of BITs in international investment law furthered the development towards a more "prominent role" of international law. Now, international law did not merely consist of a somewhat obscure and disputable set of principles and customary law rules, but the arbitrators were provided with an explicit legal document which often was more comprehensive and elaborate than domestic investment law.

Not surprisingly, therefore, the *AAPL* Tribunal – the first to decide a case governed by a BIT – regarded the treaty as "*lex specialis*" and both "international [i.e. other than those of the BIT] and domestic legal relevant rules" as a merely "supplemental source."[158] By contrast the *Autopista* Tribunal, as late as 2003 (i.e. after the *Wena* decision) applied, more or less, the *Klöckner-Amco* doctrine to a case in which no BIT existed.[159]

It may not surprise that a BIT broadens the scope of international investor protections, since that is exactly what a BIT is intended to do. However, the combination of the extended scope, primacy and hierarchical

[153] See *supra* 2 D. 5. (b) and 2 D. 5. (c).
[154] See *Enron* v. *Argentina*, paras. 207 f.; *Sempra* v. *Argentina*, paras. 236 f.
[155] See *supra* 2 D. 2. (a).
[156] *LETCO* v. *Liberia*, 658.
[157] *Amco II*, para. 40 (emphasis added).
[158] *AAPL* v. *Sri Lanka*, para. 24.
[159] See *Autopista* v. *Venezuela*, para. 102.

superiority of international law transforms BITs together with investment arbitration into a very powerful instrument for investors, who can fully enjoy the international guarantees and do not have to worry about conflicting domestic restrictions. Since most BITs exclusively contain investor rights and no, or few, investor obligations, such a system is very preferable to investors.

Moreover, the notion, first introduced by the *LG&E* Tribunal, that the BIT in fact *overrides* domestic law under Article 42(1) second sentence ICSID because of Article 27 VCLT, provides a strong argumentative foundation for the supremacy of international (treaty) law as well as a paradigm change in the perception of the relationship of domestic and international law in international investment law as such. Furthermore, my argument is, inter alia, that the recent proliferation of BITs played and still plays an important role in the Tribunals' change of view on the relationship of international and domestic law under Article 42(1) second sentence ICSID.

But even apart from the thriving force of BITs, Tribunals recognized the growing role of international law in investment disputes. In three cases described above, the Tribunals stressed the importance and expanded the applicability of international law although a BIT did not exist or was not applicable. As mentioned earlier, in *SPP* v. *Egypt*, the Tribunal deemed international law applicable to some extent even in case of a choice of domestic law according to the first sentence of Article 42(1) ICSID.[160] The *Tradex Hellas* award held that the exclusively applicable domestic 1993 Law on Investments had to be interpreted in accordance with international law. Moreover, in *Santa Elena* v. *Costa Rica* the Tribunal's rationale pertained to the purpose of ICSID to protect foreign property by international law, which would be frustrated if international law did not prevail.[161]

Thus, the analyzed case law reveals that investment Tribunals and ad hoc Committees exhibit a constantly growing tendency towards giving more room to international law within the realm of international investment law. Again, this "prominent role" is to a considerable extent due to the proliferation of BITs containing a whole bouquet of detailed international rules to adhere to. In fact, as the *Autopista* award suggests, in absence of a BIT Tribunals are less enthusiastic to hold the primacy and unlimited applicability of international law in investment disputes. However, even absent a BIT the trend seems to tend towards giving more room to international law, as the *SPP*, *Tradex Hellas* and *Santa Elena* awards evince.

160 *SPP* v. *Egypt*, para. 80.

161 Cf. *supra* 2 D. 3. (c).

Thus, considering the aforementioned, I call the development I have described in most of this chapter the "internationalization" of international investment law. In fact, international investment law has undergone a considerable transformation from the notion of the *Klöckner-Amco* doctrine, which regarded domestic law as the dominant source, to the broad role international law enjoys according to the Argentine crisis Tribunals. International law is now deemed the primary and supreme source of international investment law. By describing such development as "internationalization," I seek to underline both the process and the actual fact that international investment law now puts international law in the center of its focus.

3. *The "integration" of international investment law*[162]

As the above analysis has demonstrated, there is a constant, if not always gradual, development in investment law jurisprudence towards a more expansive and important role of international law. If one combines the six preliminary observations as stated above, it is arguable that international investment law – at least in case Article 42(1) second sentence applies or there is a BIT between the host government and the investor's home State providing for the applicability of both domestic and international law – creates a unique mélange of international and domestic law. That mélange cannot be characterized as either the one or the other. In fact, it fiercely challenges any dichotomy between international and domestic law. As has been outlined above, the *Enron* Tribunal endorsed the *Wena* doctrine by rejecting a dichotomy between domestic and international law and granting both legal orders a "complementary role."[163] Further, we have observed that Article 27 VCLT was read as indicating that international law overrides domestic law and was applied in an investor–State context. Considering both notions together, it becomes obvious that under the Argentine crisis Tribunals' interpretation of Article 42(1) ICSID no sharp line can be drawn between international and domestic law. If one combines both notions with the first part of the *Wena* doctrine, i.e. both legal orders are comprehensive and equally and independently applicable, their relationship may be best described as an integrated legal order.

Since investment Tribunals abandoned the *Klöckner-Amco* doctrine in BIT disputes, international investment law is no longer primarily governed

162 This subsection draws on A. Kulick, "The Integration."
163 Cf. *supra* 2 D. 4. (a).

by domestic law, with a few international law principles interspersed. It is, however, also not exclusively international law, for domestic law still often will be applied to the dispute. It shows, instead, all the features of an integrated legal order. This is my seventh observation regarding the analysis of the ICSID case law.

I understand legal integration as the combination of different legal orders which creates a harmonious system of legal rules that define the hierarchy of those orders within the integrated system without nullifying, but rather making inapplicable, the colliding hierarchically lower rules. As European law, for example,[164] creates an integrated legal order by combining Community law and the domestic law of the Member States to form a harmonious set of rules, international investment law is integrated, in that it creates an amalgamation of domestic and international law in which both are applicable, but international law prevails in case of conflict.[165] Moreover, the interpretation of Article 42(1) ICSID as employed by the Argentine crisis Tribunals merely leads to the inapplicability of the hierarchically lower rules.

Article 42(1) ICSID calls upon both domestic and international law to serve as a legal basis to decide disputes in the integrated order of international investment law. Thus, international law and domestic law complement one another and thereby form such integrated legal order.

Finally, in order to define the relationship of international and domestic law, the investment Tribunals interpreting Article 42(1) second sentence ICSID abrogated the dichotomy between the two: The Tribunals used Article 27 VCLT as an argument to underlay the supremacy of international law within the context of the legal régime of international investment law.

Having said this, I am aware of the questions following from such a view. Regarding international investment law as integrated may seem bold, given the fact that the contents of what is actually integrated may vary both from domestic law to domestic law and from BIT to BIT. Different from European law, international investment law, however, integrates by creating a system of adjudication and the relationship of domestic and international law without defining a single thrust of substantive legal rules.[166]

164 This comparison is not coincidental. As a matter of fact comparing international investment law to European law will prove very instructive in the later course of this analysis; see *infra* 4. B. 2. and 3.

165 See also Broches, "The Convention," 390.

166 See further on this issue *infra* 4. B. 2.

Moreover, can an ad hoc adjudicatory system, in which no appeals chamber exists and therefore no Tribunal is bound by the ruling and findings of any other Tribunal, really be "harmonious"? While an ad hoc system admittedly bears the risk of fragmentation, it is a fact that investment Tribunals constantly refer to former decisions and, as evinced by the Argentine crisis Tribunals regarding the *Wena* premises,[167] may even follow the same path.

To conclude this chapter, I argue that international investment law is gradually developing into an integrated and harmonious system, since more and more Tribunals see their task as the *Saipem* award did, i.e. a "duty to seek to contribute to the harmonious development of investment law."[168]

4. *Outlook: The public interest challenge*

Having found that international investment law is characterized by the equal application of domestic and international law with both orders being intertwined (what I call "integration") and at the same time the primacy and supremacy of international over domestic law (what I call "internationalization"), a challenge becomes apparent: As long as international investment law had been hinging mostly on domestic law as the main legal source – i.e. during the pre-BIT era – issues of public interest such as the protection of the environment[169] could be addressed and resolved more or less effectively on the domestic law level. The investor could mostly rely only on rights deriving from the domestic realm, which were subject to the regulatory authority of the host State and thus could be altered – within certain confines, of course – according to the public interest needed. Naturally, this authority of modification was not infinite and found its limits in customary international law guarantees such as the denial of justice.[170] Nonetheless, international law's reach was very limited given its confines in both substance and applicability in the investment realm.

[167] Cf. *supra* 2 D. 4.

[168] *Saipem* v. *Bangladesh*, 20, para. 67. See also O. K. Fauchald, "The Legal Reasoning of ICSID Tribunals – An Empirical Analysis," *Eur. J. Int'l L.*, 19 (2008), 301, who argues "that there is a tendency among ICSID Tribunals to contribute to the homogeneous development of the methodology of international law."

[169] See *infra* 6.

[170] See J. Paulsson, *Denial of Justice in International Law* (Cambridge University Press, 2005), p. 82; H. W. Spiegel, "Origin and Development of Denial of Justice, "*Am. J. Int'l L.*, 32 (1938), 63.

With international law's prominence as delineated above, the picture looks dramatically different: Once we accept this notion of supremacy of international law within the integrated system of the law applicable in an investment dispute, and once we acknowledge that such applicable international law mostly consists of the law enshrined in BITs, we face a simple fact: BITs deal mainly and often exclusively with investor rights. Naturally so, one might say. Indeed, as I hinted at earlier, the creation and proliferation of BITs can be explained as a counter-reaction to the challenges by developing countries in the 1960s and 1970s to traditional patterns of investment protections, mostly in the forum of the UN General Assembly.[171] Thus, it is less than unsurprising that BITs focus on investor rights. However, this simple fact has tremendous consequences in combination with my conclusions above. To put it polemically: If international law is supreme in international investment law and the substantive international law consists mostly of BITs that almost exclusively deal with investor rights only, then, under international investment law, investor rights (and thus investor interests) are supreme.

If investor rights are supreme because they have the status of applicable international law in an investment dispute, however, any public interest the host State might legitimately pursue and enforce by way of its domestic law will be superseded in case it conflicts with an investor right, i.e. international law. Thus, any public interest measure undertaken by the host State that conflicts with the – often very broad – BIT provisions guaranteeing investor rights, will be trumped in an investment dispute. In other words, if the host State applies the public interest measure in conflict with a BIT provision, the investor has a claim under the realm of international investment law – irrespective of the urgency and the importance of applying the said measure. I shall call this *problematique* the public interest challenge: Public interest issues that could be addressed and resolved on the domestic law level as long as domestic law was the main source of international investment law, under the current state of "internationalization" and "integration" may not be adequately represented by a merely domestic legal pedigree. Even more so, if the public interest measure is based on domestic legislation that itself roots in an international treaty, the picture remains the same. The treaty, while international law, binds only the States parties to it. Investors, being non-State actors and thus unable to sign up to international treaty provisions, are not bound by them and thus, arguably, any such convention does not

[171] See *supra* 2 A. 1.

share part of the "applicable" international law as understood in Article 42(1) second sentence ICSID and most BITs' applicable law provisions.[172]

5. *Consequences of the above findings: Three hypotheticals*

Keeping these considerations in mind, and before I elaborate in the following chapter on attempts in theory and BIT practice to resolve the public interest challenge, let us consider three hypotheticals in order to further illustrate the *problematique* as outlined above. Those hypotheticals derive from three exemplary areas that constitute, in my opinion, the focal points of public interest issues arising in investment arbitration: the environment, human rights, and corruption. These three areas also play a central part in the second half of this book, where I analyze current international investment case law dealing with these three public interest issues. The solution of the hypotheticals according to my approach, which I will develop in the subsequent chapters,[173] will demonstrate both the difference and the advantage of what I will later refer to as the Global Public Interest theory[174] vis-à-vis the current state of international investment law as well as other approaches trying to include public interest considerations. Now, consider the following three hypotheticals:

(a) Environment

An investor from developed country A builds a chemical plant in developing host country B. The plant uses and produces chemicals neither the toxic nature of which is fully established, nor can it be excluded definitively. Prior to the investment and during the first years of the

[172] It should be acknowledged that naturally the relationship of international and domestic law is a matter more complex than just the question vis-à-vis the applicable law. Issues of nationality as well as "in accordance with the law of the host State" clauses, both of particular relevance regarding jurisdiction, are for the most part governed by domestic law. However, I deem it sufficient to focus on the present question, for what I have called "the public interest challenge" is fueled primarily by the primacy of international law over domestic law in case of conflict. Admittedly, domestic law may shape interpretations of international law standards such as legitimate expectations as part of fair and equitable treatment. But fair and equitable treatment or expropriation or any other BIT clauses are nonetheless international law standards that prevail over conflicting domestic law. Although domestic law and international law in this context are somewhat like jellyfish, for they interact and the one partly relies on the other to define its scope while it also may trump it, I argue that my description of their relation as a mélange, i.e. their and thus international investment law's "integration" reconcile this paradox, which will be further elaborated at 4. B. 2. and C. 2.

[173] *Ibid.* [174] See *infra* 4. C. 5.

plant's operation, B has had very lax environmental legislation, which was basically the reason why the investor chose to build its plant there. A couple of years after the plant has been completed and running, B signs on to the Stockholm Convention on Persistent Organic Pollutants[175] and implements its obligations under the Convention by adopting domestic legislation. The provisions of the Stockholm Convention are based on the precautionary principle, which basically requires the parties to undertake steps to prevent environmental harm even in case of scientific uncertainty regarding the harmfulness of the substance[176] (see Preamble, para. 8, and Article 1). Article 3 obliges the parties to prohibit and/or restrict the use and production of certain chemicals listed in Annexes A and B.

Consider now that the investor's plant uses and produces chemicals listed in Annex A, and without using and producing those chemicals the plant in its present form cannot be run profitably. Thus, the legislation implementing the Stockholm Convention forces the investor either to make an additional very considerable investment, which might even jeopardize the profitability of the whole project, or abandon the investment overall. Moreover, consider that the legislation additionally introduces considerable fines for the further use or production of those prohibited chemicals and that the investor, despite such legislation, chooses to continue to run the plant without making adjustments necessary to fulfill its obligations under domestic law. Country B imposes a fine of $20 million on the investor for such blatant violation of its legislation and shuts down the plant. The investor, however, refuses to pay the fine and insists on being able to run the plant. It initiates an ICSID arbitration proceeding and claims, inter alia, that introducing the restrictive legislation on a chemical the toxicity of which cannot be proven definitively combined with the prohibition of its use and production, the fine and the shutdown of the plant amount to expropriation, which requires prompt, adequate and effective compensation if B insists on enforcing the legislation.

While the legal position of the investor is very weak regarding domestic law, its chances to succeed on the expropriation claim based on the BIT between country A and country B are considerably high: The investor cannot make any further use of the plant if it has to fulfill all that domestic legislation asks of it, and due to the high fine and the shutdown

[175] Stockholm Convention on Persistent Organic Pollutants, done at Stockholm, May 22, 2001 (hereinafter: Stockholm Convention); see http://chm.pops.int/Convention/tabid/54/language/en-US/Default.aspx#convtext.

[176] On the precautionary principle see *infra* 6. A. 3.

of the plant may even be likely to face bankruptcy. And the Stockholm Convention does not bind the investor, but merely the States parties. International law supersedes domestic law, so the strong legal position of B under domestic law does not provide any help; the investor is very likely to recover compensation.

However, is this a preferable outcome? B has done nothing but fulfilled its international obligations. The investor has no legitimate expectation that legislation remains unchanged. Moreover, it has deliberately chosen to violate the new legislation implementing B's international law obligations under the Stockholm Convention into domestic law. Under such circumstances, it is hard to appreciate why the investor should be fully compensated, particularly regarding the fine. Taking the above conclusions into account, however, such result seems inevitable. Therefore, if we accept those conclusions, the only satisfactory solution for the dilemma described in the hypotheticals appears to find a way to argue for legal defenses of the host State that accommodate such challenges.

(b) Human rights

Investor I, incorporated in country C, had been granted a license to exploit gold in the largest mine site in country D. Over the course of several years and with tacit approval by the government of D, I had been forcing the local population to work in its mines with either very low or no payment at all. Regularly, security forces employed by I intruded into the nearby villages and coerced villagers to mount a truck, driving them to poor shelters where they were held for several weeks or even months with poor nutrition, when they were not working in the mines. Both I and the government of D were aware that such practice was quite common among mining companies in D.

Then, the government of D changed. The new president was elected mostly upon the promise to "eradicate the atrocious and abhorrent practice in our mines, to end the enslavement of our local population and to hold accountable those responsible for these horrible crimes." Subsequently, the government prosecuted the managing personnel of I as well as former senior government officials for aiding and abetting them. Moreover, it introduced legislation withdrawing the mining license of any company, foreign or domestic, having been engaged in forced labor without any compensation "in order to punish those responsible and to deter once and for all any future encroachments in this regard."

After extensive deliberations, given the tremendous profits it had been making out of the gold mine in the past and that it was expecting to make in the future, not least due to cheap labor, the board of I decided to bring a claim to the ICSID forum, despite being aware of the very negative publicity this might entail. It asserted, inter alia, that D had taken its property without any kind of compensation, violating the expropriation clause of the BIT between C and D.

Here, the infringement of this clause is rather obvious – without the license, I cannot exploit the mine and thus loses tremendous future profits as well as effectively its investment in the mining facilities which now have become useless. However, the pivotal question at hand is whether, and if answered in the affirmative, what influence should the fact that the investor had been engaged in forced labor have? Note that the prohibition of forced labor arguably is a *ius cogens* norm![177] Hence, should the investor bear the consequences of such *ius cogens* violations in the investment arbitration context? And what consequences should accrue from the fact that the former government tacitly approved of such practice being more or less common among mining companies in D before the new government entered office?

(c) Corruption

As for the third and last hypothetical, consider the following constellation: Large resources of crude oil have been recently discovered in country E. Given the measured amount of the resources, many major oil companies have pivotal interest in gaining the licence for exploitation, for profits promise to be tremendous. Foreign investor I, being headquartered in country F, seeks to build an oil drilling facility, refinery and pipeline on the site where the oil was discovered and across country E. During the negotiations with the government, however, officials indicate to the representatives of I that while its bid is generally considered the most promising, what eventually will make the difference is which of the bidders is willing to pay the highest amount of "personal donation" to the minister of economy of E, who is supervising the tender. After long deliberations and recourse to their board, I's representatives, since they are convinced that they will lose the bid otherwise – an option they are not willing to accept – agree to pay the amount of US$1 million in cash to the minister of economy. Subsequently, I wins the tender, is granted the license and constructs the drilling facilities, the refinery and the pipeline for the overall

[177] Only see A. Ramasastry, "Corporate Complicity: From Nuremberg to Rangoon – An Examination of Forced Labor Cases and their Impact on the Liability of Multinational Corporations," *Berkeley J. Int'l L.*, 20 (2002), 91 at 98 with further references.

costs of US$1 billion. After all of the facilities and the pipeline have been finished and they have been running successfully for about five months – i.e. three years after I was awarded the tender – the President of E introduces a nationwide "raid against corruption." Central to this campaign is to "cut and punish the supply side," which, so his spokesman stresses, is in line with the policy adopted in several international instruments targeted at corruption, which focus on sanctioning foreign bribers rather than the receiver of the bribe. Consequently, according to a presidential decree, any foreign investment being "tainted with corruption" falls to the government. Managing personnel are replaced with government officials and compensation will not be granted, "in order to shun malefactors to lure our officials into graft in the future."

Being directly affected by the presidential decree, I is outraged, particularly given that it was the minister of economy – who could even keep his post in the cabinet – that asked for the bribe. On the basis of the BIT between E and F, its home State, I introduces an ICSID arbitration claiming violation of, inter alia, the treaty's fair and equitable treatment clause (FET).[178] On first glance, I will win very easily on the merits:[179] The measures undertaken by the government thwart any kind of legitimate expectations the investor could hold vis-à-vis the protection of its investment. However, can I really claim in good faith the full value of its investment although it was entirely aware that the way in which it was granted entry to invest in E was obviously illegal? Is an investor's claim for full compensation for an investment that it was only able to make due to illegal conduct affected by the principle *nemo audiatur suam turpitudinem allegans*, i.e. that nobody may assert his or her own illegal conduct as ground for a claim?

[178] Leaving aside issues regarding expropriation.

[179] However, as will be considered *in extenso* in Chapter 8, several challenges lie in arguing for the Tribunal's jurisdiction.

3 Public interest and international economic law – current approaches

Scholars and drafters of BITs are starting to recognize and acknowledge the public interest challenge that I have described at the end of the preceding chapter. The main reason for this is that the need of conforming public interest considerations with the investment régime touches upon the longstanding struggle of public international law with the advent of non-State and in particular corporate actors on the international arena. Viewing the public interest challenge of international investment law in the context of this much broader debate, I will explore scholarly approaches towards international legal obligations of corporate actors and thereinafter evaluate how much they present for resolving the issue before us (A.).[1] The second part of this chapter will be dedicated to a brief analysis of current BIT practice dealing with the public interest challenge (B.).[2]

A. Scholarly approaches towards international legal obligations of MNEs

Multinational enterprises (MNEs) mostly – albeit not exclusively[3] – represent the group of investors in investor–State arbitration. One possible

[1] Approaches towards investor obligations or responsibility in specific areas, particularly in the field of human rights, will be addressed in conjunction with the case law studies in later parts of this book; see, in particular, *infra* 7. A.

[2] I am not at all oblivious to the fact that the investment debate has made further attempts to address issues of public interest beyond the question of an international legal personality of non-State actors. 7. A. seeks to take account of the debate vis-à-vis human rights. Further, see the excellent recent volume edited by Stephan W. Schill, *International Investment Law and Comparative Public Law* (Oxford University Press, 2010), particularly Schill's piece on umbrella clauses, "Umbrella Clauses as Public Law Concepts in Comparative Perspective," p. 317 at pp. 336 ff.

[3] See, for example, *Ioannis Kardassopoulos* v. *Georgia* (ICSID Case No. ARB/05/18, pending arbitration. Date Registered: October 3, 2005. Constituted: February 27, 2006.

scenario to tackle the public interest challenge is to promote international legal obligations of MNEs and thus investors. Since there exist a plethora of approaches arguing for international legal obligations of MNEs, this section is split into two subsections. The first discusses a rather pragmatic take on the subject that led to the formulation of a set of guidelines on the issue of international MNEs obligations (1.), while the second scrutinizes broader theoretical concepts that seek to approach the issue by analyzing MNEs' ability to gain or to have international legal personality (2.).

1. *A scholarly attempt to shape the practice: The Norms on the Responsibilities of Transnational Corporations and Other Business Enterprises with Regard to Human Rights*

Soft law instruments such as the UN Global Compact or the OECD Guidelines for Multinational Enterprises, while lacking a mandatory nature, at least demonstrate a growing trend in international law that acknowledges the increasing impact and importance of MNEs in fields such as human rights or the environment.[4] However, in the international law debate centering around international responsibility of MNEs there exist proponents of a much more far-reaching role for MNEs in the international arena who in fact argue for international legal obligations of business enterprises. Since it has at least the potential to be considerably instructive to the question before us, I will therefore allocate some space to highlighting and evaluating their approach. While this aspect of the debate on international responsibility of MNEs emerged in and focuses mainly on the field of international human rights, I deem it of interest to take a brief look at such approaches, for if it proves viable or at least reasonable, a similar approach may be taken vis-à-vis any other field of potential MNE – and thus investor – obligations.

The most ambitious and audacious debate that may be of interest in this regard centers around the Norms on the Responsibilities of Transnational Corporations and Other Business Enterprises with Regard to Human Rights ("the Norms").[5] Following a draft by David Weissbrodt, the

Reconstituted: January 16, 2008; hereinafter: *Kardassopoulos* v. *Georgia*), in which the investor is a natural person.

4 For a list of and references on such soft law instruments, including the two mentioned, see *supra* p. 1, n. 1.

5 Norms on the Responsibilities of Transnational Corporations and Other Business Enterprises with Regard to Human Rights, adopted August 13, 2003, UN Doc. E/CN.4/Sub.2/2003/12.

Sub-Committee on the Promotion and Protection of Human Rights of the United Nations Economic and Social Council (ECOSOC) approved the Norms on August 13, 2003 and subsequently submitted them to the then-UN Human Rights Commission[6] which requested the appointment of a Special Representative to the Secretary-General (SRSG) to "identify and clarify" the matters involved.[7]

According to their proponents, the most prominent among them being David Weissbrodt himself, the Norms differ from other instruments that set out a code of conduct, such as the above-mentioned OECD Guidelines on Multinational Enterprises,[8] in at least two regards that are of interest here: (1) They are intended not to be voluntary but rather to lay out binding rules for all kind of businesses; (2) they do not assert that their normative content is aspirational but claim to restate the current state of law instead.[9] These claims are based on two doctrinal grounds, both seeking to build on positive law foundations, while the first is purely positivist and the second assumes an underlying functionalist justification. Firstly, it is asserted that the rules enshrined in the Norms reflect the current state of treaty and customary international law applicable vis-à-vis businesses. Secondly, the voices favoring this approach hearken back to the 1948 Universal Declaration of Human Rights, which proclaims that:

> every individual and every organ of society . . . shall strive by teaching and education to promote respect for these rights and freedoms and by progressive measures, national and international, to secure their universal and effective recognition and observance.[10]

[6] Now: UN Human Rights Council.

[7] See J. G. Ruggie, "Current Developments – Business and Human Rights: The Evolving International Agenda," *Am. J. Int'l L.*, 101 (2007), 819 at 821 f.; K. Nowrot, "Die UN- Norms on the Responsibilities of Transnational Corporations and Other Business Enterprises with Regard to Human Rights – Gelungener Beitrag zur transnationalen Rechtsverwirklichung oder das Ende des Global Compact?," *Beiträge zum Transnationalen Wirtschaftsrecht*, 21 (2003), 1 at 6 ff.

[8] See *supra* 1.

[9] See D. Weissbrodt and M. Kruger, "Current Developments – Norms on the Responsibilities of Transnational Corporations and Other Business Enterprises with Regard to Human Rights," *Am. J. Int'l L.*, 97 (2003), 901 at 912 ff.; D. Weissbrodt and M. Kruger, "Human Rights Responsibilities of Businesses as Non-State Actors" in P. Alston (ed.), *Non-State Actors and Human Rights* (Oxford University Press, 2005), p. 315 at pp. 328 ff.; D. Weissbrodt, "Stefan A. Riesenfeld Symposium 2008, March 14, 2008, Berkeley, California – Keynote Address: International Standard-Setting on the Human Rights Responsibilities of Businesses," *Berkeley J. Int'l L.*, 26 (2008), 373 at 380 ff.

[10] Universal Declaration of Human Rights, GA Res. 217 (III), UN Doc. A/810, at 71 (1948).

Since worldwide operating business conglomerates such as MNEs have a considerable influence on the global stage that often surpasses that of at least some States and thus have great power to affect the realization of rights, such scholars opine that "with . . . power comes . . . responsibility."[11] To put it differently, MNEs have and can exert a strong impact on a wide range of rights, and this must be reflected by their responsibility to protect those rights and to be held accountable for violations of them.

This is, as I said, an ambitious and audacious claim. However, some questions remain. If the Norms are a restatement of the law already in place, what is their contribution beyond being a mere anthology of human right norms applicable vis-à-vis businesses? One might well say that such a "comprehensive collection of international standards and implementation mechanisms"[12] is a very valuable contribution in itself. Such assertion is generally true; however, its proponents do not seem to believe themselves. If the Norms reflect the current state of the law, why "[can] no one realistically expect business human rights standards to become the subject of treaty obligations immediately"?[13] Even more so, why is there any need beyond a mere anthological interest to frame a treaty in the first place, if the Norms already reflect existing treaty law and custom? Moreover, while they are very reluctant to admit it, it is inevitable for the proponents of the Norms to have to accept that the latter have no status other than "soft law."[14] Soft law status, however, by definition thwarts any assertion of mandatory nature. It is symptomatic in this respect that they shy away from calling them binding, but rather note the Norms' "non-voluntary" nature.[15]

However, the most important criticism of this approach lies in its lack of theoretical legal foundation. "The concept of corporate spheres of influence, though useful as an analytical tool, seems to have no legal pedigree."[16] Therefore, as Philip Alston put it so powerfully, the dilemma entails that:

> [i]f the only difference is that governments have a comprehensive set of obligations, while those of corporations are limited to their 'spheres of influence,' . . . how are the latter [obligations] to be delineated? Does Shell's sphere of influence in the Niger Delta not cover everything ranging from the right to

[11] Weissbrodt and Kruger, "Current Developments," 921.
[12] Weissbrodt, "International Standard-Setting," 390.
[13] Weissbrodt and Kruger, "Current Developments," 914. [14] *Ibid.*, 915.
[15] *Ibid.*, 913. [16] Ruggie, "Business and Human Rights," 825.

health, through the right to free speech, to rights to physical integrity and due process?[17]

The real problem of the approach underlying the Norms, being confronted with those questions, is not that those questions arise but that they lack any sound theoretical foundation to answer them. Particularly, such approach at least has to address the question of international legal personality of non-State actors, which automatically arises if MNEs are contended to have international legal *obligations*. Considering the aforementioned, the approach taken regarding the Norms does not prove satisfying for the question before us. In the ensuing part, I will therefore seek to address rather theoretical approaches towards the topic of international legal obligations of (corporate) non-State actors, that strive to derive answers from analyzing the broader question of the latter's ability to have international legal personality.

2. Scholarly approaches towards an international legal personality of MNEs

One major impediment in arguing for a wide range of public interest considerations being introduced to the realm of international investment law, at least if legally translated as investors' obligations, so it is argued, is that investors, being non-State actors, are not regarded as subjects of public international law – at least not according to the classical view.[18] Subjects of international law share a commonality: they have international legal personality, one feature of which is that they are bound by international law. This ability to be bearers of international law obligations, it is asserted,[19] is a characteristic of international legal personality. Thus, we have to take a brief look at different views that endorse or reject international legal personality of non-State actors. Since no author directly argues for an international personality of investors as such, I will again focus on the debate whether MNEs[20] are or can be subjects of international law.

[17] P. Alston, "The 'Not-a-Cat' Syndrome: Can the International Human Rights Regime Accommodate Non-State Actors?" in *Non-State Actors and Human Rights*, p. 3 at pp. 13 f.

[18] See Brownlie, *Principles of Public International Law*, 7th edn. (Oxford University Press, 2008), p. 66.

[19] N. Jägers, "The Legal Status of Multinational Corporations Under International Law" in M. K. Addo (ed.), *Human Rights Standards and the Responsibility of Transnational Corporations* (Kluwer Law International, 1999), p. 259 at p. 261.

[20] On different approaches to defining the term "Multinational Enterprises" see C. Baez, M. Dearing, M. Delatour and C. Dixon, "Multinational Enterprises and Human Rights," *Miami Int'l & Comp. L. Rev.*, 8 (1999–2000), 183 at 187 ff.

(a) Strict positivist view: only States as subjects of international law

According to the classical positivist theory, dominant for most of the past 300 years, the sole actor and mediator of international law is the State. It thus confines the legal system created by international law to the governance of the relations between States.[21] International law rules and principles are derived exclusively from studying the behavior of States. They alone create the law that governs their relations and therefore are the only addressees of international law.[22] Consequently, under positivism, only States are subjects of international law, i.e. have international legal personality.

There are what Malanczuk calls three "indicia"[23] of international legal personality, defined by three cumulative capacities: (1) The capacity to bring claims accruing from the violation of international law. (2) The capacity to enter into relations with other subjects of international law and thus to create international law by concluding valid international agreements or creating customary international law. (3) And the capacity to enjoy privileges and immunities from national jurisdiction.[24]

The positivist school explains developments such as the advent of international organizations on the international arena and their ability to conclude treaties and to interact with States as well as the phenomenon of human rights by pointing at treaties, concluded among States, that are the prerequisite for enabling non-State entities to act and interact on the international level. According to this logic, non-State actors can act internationally, because States in their sovereign capacity granted them the ability to do so. International organizations come into existence and may even create international law rules only because the contracting States decided to enshrine such capacity into the constituting treaty. Individuals can claim human rights violations because and only to the extent the States parties to the human rights treaty permit them. Non-State actors, thus, can at best be said to have a "derived" legal personality – in contrast

[21] M. Northmann, "Non-State Actors in International Law" in B. Arts, M. Northmann and B. Reinalda (eds.), *Non-State Actors in International Relations* (Ashgate, 2001), p. 59 at p. 60; S. Joseph, "An Overview of the Human Rights Accountability of Multinational Enterprises" in M. T. Kamminga and S. Zia-Zarifi (eds.), *Liability of Multinational Corporations under International Law* (Kluwer Law International, 2000), p. 75.

[22] H. Kelsen, *Introduction to the Problem of Legal Theory* (Oxford: Clarendon Press, 1996), p. 107.

[23] P. Malanczuk, *Akehurst's Modern Introduction to International Law* (Routledge, 1997), p. 91.

[24] See Northmann, "Non-State Actors," 64.

to States' "original" personality that results from their capacity to create international law and fully participate in the international realm, which is inherent in themselves and not merely granted by another entity.

Reiterating the three "indicia" outlined above, the positivist school asserts that while MNEs might in some circumstances well be able to claim international law violations before an international Tribunal they obviously lack the two other capacities, for they may not create international law and they are definitely not immune from national jurisdiction. Thus, according to positivism MNEs are not subjects of international law and thus may only be granted rights and have duties imposed on them if States, as the sole subjects of international law, decide to do so.

(b) Different approaches endorsing an international legal personality of MNEs

Approaches arguing for an international legal personality of MNEs have been largely emerging from a human rights perspective.[25] While they try to develop their rationales through the human rights lens, most of the theories and underlying ideas are applicable or at least transferable to other international law contexts. There are basically three distinguishable, albeit interlinked, takes challenging the classical positivist paradigm.

The first and most prominent one seeks to define international legal personality from a functionalist perspective. As early as 1949, the International Court of Justice (ICJ) in its famous *Reparations for Injuries* case broke with the strict positivist view that only States can be subjects of international law: "The subjects of law in any legal system are not necessarily identical in their nature or in the extent of their rights, and the nature depends on the needs of the community."[26] Though employed not vis-à-vis MNEs but as argument for a partial international legal personality of an international organization, this statement encapsulates the functionalist rationale: If the international system necessitates it, in most cases on the notions of efficiency and justice, functionalism invites actors other than the State to become subjects of international law.[27]

[25] See L.-C. Chen, *An Introduction to Contemporary International Law*, 2nd edn. (Yale University Press, 2000), p. 79; Jägers, "Legal Status," 265; Northmann, "Non-State Actors," 61 f.; S. F. Puvimanasinghe, *Foreign Investment, Human Rights and the Environment* (Martinus Nijhoff Publishers, 2007), p. 64; S. R. Ratner, "Corporations and Human Rights: A Theory of Legal Responsibility," *Yale L.J.*, 111 (2001–02), 443 at 462 f.

[26] *Reparations for Injuries Suffered in the Service of the United Nations*, *ICJ Reports*, (1949), 174.

[27] Northmann, "Non-State Actors," 62.

Therefore, the functionalist approach abandons the notion, held under strict positivism, that international legal personality is an indivisible or binary concept, i.e. one is either a subject of international law or not. The idea that international legal personality depends on the function which the actor performs automatically entails that international legal personality is not binary but gradual. This means that international legal personality thus is limited to the function which an entity is assigned to in the international community. The same entity can have international legal personality in one respect and lack it in another.[28]

As regards MNEs, the functionalist theory attributes them international legal personality with respect to their ability to bring claims against host States before an investment arbitration Tribunal.[29] Moreover, due to their economic and political influence and thus their vast potential to violate human rights or destroy the environment on a global scale,[30] some authors argue for international legal duties of MNEs in the respective areas of law.[31]

This is where the functionalist theory is intertwined with another approach endorsing an international legal personality of MNEs, i.e. a policy oriented approach. Lung-Chu Chen argues in his treatise that the classical "state-centered international law is being transformed into an international law of homocentricity."[32] While the old positivist approach was born and endorsed at a time in which sovereign monarchs decided the destinies of their peoples and realpolitik was the defining rationale of the day and thus naturally focused on the State as the principal actor, he contends that we are now moving towards a new international system that puts the human being and human dignity in the center of its consideration. Thus, international legal personality of non-State actors has to be presumed in any case and to the extent it serves the promotion of the dignity, livelihood and environment of the human being.[33] Following this

[28] See C. Leben, "The Changing Structure of International Law Revisited by Way of Introduction," *Eur. J. Int'l L.*. 8 (1997), 399 at 404; W. Friedmann, *The Changing Structure of International Law* (Columbia University Press, 1964), p. 375.

[29] Leben points at the parallels between the functionalist and the positivist paradigm as developed by Kelsen; see C. Leben, "Hans Kelsen and the Advancement of International Law," *EJIL*, 9 (1998), 287 at 304.

[30] Jägers, "Legal Status," 260; S. Subedi, "Multinational Corporations and Human Rights" in A. Arts and P. Mihyo (eds.), *Responding to the Human Rights Deficit* (Kluwer Law International, 2003), p. 171 at p. 172.

[31] Jägers, "Legal Status," 265. [32] Chen, *An Introduction*, p. 79.

[33] Northmann, "Non-State Actors," at 62 underlines that despite several similarities, what distinguishes functionalism from the policy-oriented approach is that while the former

rationale, MNEs are subjects of international law and thus are attributed international duties if their actions impede or infringe upon the human being's dignity, livelihood or environment.[34]

Finally, the third approach that may serve as a basis to argue for an international legal personality of MNEs is legal pluralism. Legal pluralism emphatically endorses the complexity that positivism seeks to avoid by accepting the international community as a complex, multipolar and multilayered society. States, the legal pluralist asserts, are in fact only one of several relevant factors in international law-making. In a globalized world the exclusive focus on territory is no longer relevant and thus "territory-based entities [such as States] exist alongside entities which do not derive the basis of their existence from territory and territorially-defined populations."[35] Consequently, albeit it fails to develop a comprehensive practicable theory, legal pluralism permits to expand international legal personality to such actors as MNEs.

(c) Conclusion

In assessing how useful the above-mentioned theories prove for the questions before us, one may well start by contesting positivism as futile to explain the contemporary international system. Indeed, international personality is a legal fiction, a model, which exists and is viable only to the extent it serves to explain reality.[36] The subject/object dichotomy and its definition alongside the three "indicia"[37] are subject to circular reasoning, for they shape their rationale according to a State-centered model: They basically say that States are the only subjects of international law because subjects of international law need to have the characteristics of States.

Rejecting this premise of positivism, however, in the end means questioning the pattern of international legal personality and subjects of international law as a whole. In fact, using those terms inevitably lures one into the trap of a binary understanding of the capacity to participate in the realm of international law. As current developments in international law demonstrate, every actor forms part of the international system to the extent it is able to participate. Therefore, as Rosalyn Higgins put it, it is quite futile to speak of "subjects" and "objects" of international law,

shares with positivism a value-free notion of international law, the latter is utterly based on values, for it seeks to ascertain that international law serves human dignity.

34 See Chen, *An Introduction*, pp. 79 ff. See also pp. 411 ff.

35 See Northmann, "Non-State Actors," 62.

36 See Jägers, "Legal Status," 262.

37 See *supra* 3 A. 2. (a).

since "there are . . . only *participants*. Individuals are participants, along with states, international organizations . . . multinational corporations, and indeed private non-governmental groups."[38]

With the subject/object model toppling, however, the entire concept that seeks to derive international duties of MNEs from their existent or non-existent international legal personality is inevitably called into question. Despite such obstacles as how to actually define MNEs or the fact that not all investors are MNEs, such an approach proves futile because it is also utterly circular. Not only is it based on a premise that it passionately rejects – the State-centered subject/object dichotomy of the positivist paradigm – its viability to serve as a theoretical basis for international investor obligations is limited to the argument that MNEs have international duties because they possess international legal personality. However, as was demonstrated above, if one abandons the subject/object dichotomy, the only way to argue for such feature of international legal personality of MNEs is by way of showing that they are actually attributed international duties. Therefore, seeking to argue for international investor obligations through the pattern of international legal personality one feels like the protagonist of Franz Kafka's *The Castle*: One marches a long distance but does not come any closer to one's goal.

Considering the aforementioned, therefore, the preferable approach to argue for international obligations of investors appears to be to develop a general concept that escapes the subject/object dichotomy trap.

B. Public interest considerations in recent BIT practice

Before turning to the elaboration of my own approach that I call the Global Public Interest theory, which among others seeks to avoid the aforementioned subject/object dichotomy trap, it is in order to briefly describe approaches that incorporate public interest considerations into recent (Model) BITs and demonstrate why they are not sufficient given the above-mentioned challenges, particularly the supremacy of international law in international investment law.

1. *Prelude: The principle of good faith and Article XX GATT*

In Chapter 11 of his book on NAFTA, Todd Weiler argues for exceptions to investor rights that the host State would be entitled to raise by suggesting

[38] R. Higgins, *Problems and Procedures – International Law and How We Use It* (Clarendon Press, 1994), p. 50 (emphasis in the original).

drawing on Article XX of the GATT.[39,40] This approach, that I will elaborate on in this brief introductory section, was inspiration to certain provisions in Model BITs, which I will analyze further below. Hence, it makes sense to get to know – and critique – Weiler's considerations which are to be kept in mind when delving into scrutinizing current BIT practice. However, before explaining and discussing Todd Weiler's proposal, I deem it necessary to make some brief introductory remarks on Article XX GATT, on which he relies as the basis for (indirect) investor obligations.

(a) Introductory remarks on Article XX GATT

GATT represents the very core of the law on world trade. Enacted in 1947 and incorporated in the WTO legal framework in 1995, it lays out the major rules on the international trade in goods. As part of the WTO agreements, GATT is a multilateral international law treaty to which States become party as soon as they accede to membership of the WTO.[41] GATT, as all WTO agreements, creates rights and obligations only vis-à-vis States. Non-State actors, although currently by far the most important actors in the international exchange of goods, are neither subject to rights nor obligations under the WTO agreements and consequently cannot become a party to a WTO dispute.[42]

Within the systematic framework of the GATT, Article XX assumes the role of a general exemptions clause which serves as the major means of justification for violations of provisions guaranteeing free trade, such as (most importantly, albeit not exclusively) national treatment.[43] Irrespective of the kind of violation, if the conditions of Article XX are met the measure undertaken is not considered contrary to the GATT.

According to the WTO Appellate Body in *US-Gasoline*, Article XX consists of two separate parts which inform the meaning of the provision: Whereas

[39] General Agreement on Tariffs and Trade; see www.wto.org/english/docs_e/legal_e/gatt47_01_e.htm.

[40] T. Weiler, "Prohibition Against Discrimination in NAFTA Chapter 11" in T. Weiler (ed.), *NAFTA Investment Law and Arbitration* (Transnational Publishers, 2004), p. 27 at pp. 37 ff.

[41] See Article XII:1 of the Marrakesh Agreement Establishing the World Trade Organization; see www.wto.org/english/docs_e/legal_e/04-wto_e.htm.

[42] However, it must be noted that since the WTO Appellate Body decision in the *EC-Asbestos* case, *amicus curiae* briefs are accepted in WTO disputes, which became a means of indirect, albeit very active participation of non-State actors; see European Communities – Measures Affecting Asbestos and Asbestos-Containing Products, Report of the Appellate Body, WT/DS135/AB/R, March 12, 2001 (01–1157), AB-2000–11.

[43] See M. Trebilcock and R. Howse, *The Regulation of International Trade*, 3rd edn. (Routledge, 2005), p. 35.

it first has to be established whether the measure undertaken meets the requirements of the specific exceptions enshrined in Article XX (a) to (j), its application secondly must also not lead to an arbitrary or unjustifiable discrimination or a disguised restriction on international trade, according to the chapeau of Article XX GATT. Only if a measure passes both steps can it be considered a licit exception to the other GATT provisions.

(b) Transferability to international investment law?

Todd Weiler seeks to harness Article XX GATT in order to argue for, among others, (indirect) international investor obligations under the realm of international investment law.[44] The doctrinal starting point of his approach is the WTO Appellate Body's assertion in *US-Shrimp/Turtles*[45] that Article XX GATT is a manifestation of the principle of good faith, which, in turn, is applicable in international law as a general principle of law.[46] Being a general principle of law, his argument runs, the principle of good faith is thus generally applicable under the realm of international investment law. Since Article XX GATT is a manifestation of that principle, according to Weiler, one may refer to its specific exceptions as justification for a violation of an investor right.[47]

Such reasoning is defective, however, both on the basis of doctrine and on the basis of logic. Doctrinally it is defective, since the WTO Appellate Body in *US-Shrimp/Turtles* merely referred to the chapeau as incorporating the principle of good faith.[48] Given the dichotomy between the chapeau and the specific provisions of Article XX (a) to (j) as established in *US-Gasoline*,[49] it is very dubious to treat them interchangeably and thus resort to, for example, measures relating to the conservation of exhaustible

[44] T. Weiler asserts his argument in the context of NAFTA and limited to the exceptions to violations of national treatment; "Prohibition Against Discrimination," p. 37. However, the challenges under NAFTA and ICSID are similar, particularly regarding the supremacy of international law; see NAFTA Art. 1131(1); The North American Free Trade Agreement (see www.international.gc.ca/trade-agreements-accords-commerciaux/agr-acc/nafta-alena/texte/chap11.aspx?lang=en#article_1131). Moreover, it is not entirely clear whether Weiler seeks to limit his argument to national treatment; see Weiler, "Prohibition Against Discrimination," p. 37.

[45] United States – Import Prohibition of Certain Shrimp and Shrimp Products, WT/DS58/AB/R, October 12, 1998, AB-1998–4 (hereinafter: *US-Shrimp/Turtles*), para. 158.

[46] See Art. 38(1) of the ICJ Statute, which outlines the licit sources of international law.

[47] T. Weiler, "Prohibition Against Discrimination," p. 38.

[48] See *US-Shrimp/Turtles*, para. 158.

[49] United States – Standards for Reformulated and Conventional Gasoline, AB-1996–1, Report of the Appellate Body, WT/DS2/AB/R, April 22, 1996 (hereinafter: *US-Gasoline*).

natural resources – Article XX (g) – as an expression of the principle of good faith.

Moreover, the reasoning is equally defective in logic. It seeks to draw a conclusion from the specific in order to inform the principle. However, the ways in which specific aspects of a principle are tailored does not automatically echo back to the general principle. The standard of treatment vis-à-vis one specific case of a broader category is not necessarily equally applicable regarding another specific case. What Weiler actually seems to say is that since apples and oranges are both fruits, what we do with apples can be applied in the same way regarding oranges. Anybody who has ever tried to bite into an orange without peeling its skin is quite skeptical about such reasoning.

Not to mention the general reservation one should have when transferring specific provisions from one legal régime to another without taking account of the general context they are situated in, the above-mentioned approach neither convinces as a matter of argument nor as a matter of practicability.

2. *Public interest considerations in BITs*[50]

Until very recently, the protection of issues other than investment and trade was more or less non-existent in BITs. However, recent BIT practice, evinced in a series of Model and Draft Model BITs issued throughout the past decade, shows some sympathy to non-investment issues being enshrined in investment treaty provisions. The current Model US BIT 2004, for example, acknowledges the potential environmental implications of FDI in its Article 12, headed "Investment and Environment":[51]

"Article 12: Investment and Environment

1. The Parties recognize that it is inappropriate to encourage investment by weakening or reducing the protections afforded in domestic environmental laws. Accordingly, each Party shall strive to ensure that it does not waive or otherwise derogate from, or offer to waive or otherwise derogate from, such laws in a manner that weakens or

[50] This section does not discuss non-precluded measures clauses pertaining to "essential security interests" of the host State, which constituted a main issue in the case law on the Argentine crisis and which hence are dealt with in the section relating to the state of necessity; see *infra* 4. C. 1. (b).

[51] Treaty Between The Government of The United States of America and the Government of...... Concerning the Encouragement and Reciprocal Protection of Investments, US Model BIT 2004, available at www.ustr.gov/assets/Trade_Sectors/Investment/Model_BIT/asset_upload_file847_6897.pdf.

reduces the protections afforded in those laws as an encouragement for the establishment, acquisition, expansion, or retention of an investment in its territory. If a Party considers that the other Party has offered such an encouragement, it may request consultations with the other Party and the two Parties shall consult with a view to avoiding any such encouragement.

2. Nothing in this Treaty shall be construed to prevent a Party from adopting, maintaining, or enforcing any measure otherwise consistent with this Treaty that it considers appropriate to ensure that investment activity in its territory is undertaken in a manner sensitive to environmental concerns.

But the leap such insertion of the environment as a matter of investment law suggests appears to be more ostensible than real. While the first sentence of Article 12(1) of Model US BIT 2004 "recognize[s] that it is inappropriate to encourage investment by weakening or reducing the protections afforded in domestic environmental laws," Article 12(1) in its entirety only lays obligations on States. They "shall strive to ensure" [sic] that, in order to provide incentives to investors, they do not fall below the threshold of environmental protection guaranteed by their domestic law. Apart from the awkward phrasing it is remarkable – and apparently deliberate – that this international law treaty harks back to domestic standards of environmental protection and thus seeks to avoid signing up to international standards. The level of protection depends on domestic legislation – which can set a very high or a very low threshold. Moreover, international environmental law principles seem thus to be excluded, for environmental protection is treated as a matter of domestic law. This, again, means that according to the aforementioned analysis[52] in case of conflict with international law, particularly treaty rights of investors, the latter prevails over domestic environmental law under Article 12(1).

Article 12(2) on first glance appears to make up for the shortcomings of Article 12(1). According to this provision, the host State is entitled to "adopt . . . maintain . . . or enforce . . . any measure . . . that it considers appropriate to ensure that investment activity in its territory is undertaken in a manner sensitive to environmental concerns." However, the measure undertaken must be "otherwise consistent with this Treaty." In other words, "inconsistencies" with investor rights enshrined in the BIT lead to the inapplicability of Article 12(2).[53] Given the broadness of this

[52] See *supra* 2, particularly D. 5. and E. 2.

[53] A similar formulation is to be found in the Norwegian Draft Model BIT of December 2007. Art. 12 makes a proviso to the right to regulate in that it covers only measures

term, Article 12(2) thus does not contribute much to international environmental protections. Moreover, as its wording seems to indicate, the measures, i.e. possible obligations, Article 12(2) discusses are of domestic rather than international law character – thus leading back to the same challenges as under Article 12(1). Additionally, it remains fairly murky what "sensitive to environmental concerns" actually means. Considering the weak wording and the qualification regarding inconsistencies with treaty rights, paragraph 2 appears to be as unsatisfying as paragraph 1. To conclude, while the progress of actually mentioning concerns other than economic ones should be acknowledged, Article 12 of the US Model BIT 2004 falls short in failing to add more than a nebulous provision that can easily be marginalized.

The same holds true regarding Article 13 of the US Model BIT 2004, stating that investment should not lead to a downgrading of domestic labor protection standards. Apart from the fact that it lacks a provision similar to Article 12(2) and thus is even less open for regulatory measures in this specific public interest area, Article 13 basically emulates its environmental counterpart – in language as well as in murkiness and insignificance.

Slightly more relevant, however, is Article 14 of the said BIT, which constitutes an opt-out clause for measures not in conformity with BIT Articles 3, 4, 8 and 9[54] adopted or maintained by certain government bodies or regarding certain sectors or in the field of public procurement. It refers to schedules listed in Annexes I to III to the treaty indicating the exempted government bodies or industries. Depending on the number of sectors, etc. listed in these schedules, limitations to investment protection stemming from this opt-out clause can be considerable. However, as this assessment indicates, Article 14 is more concerned with reducing the scope of investment protection vis-à-vis certain sectors or government measures than with actually warranting regulatory scope in the public

"otherwise consistent with this Agreement" and thus with investor protections. As its relative in Art. 12 US Model BIT of 2004, "it is not an exemption of the obligation to observe [investor] rights. Rather it is a reaffirmation that legitimate regulation in the named fields is not *per se* to be the basis of a claim." P. Muchlinski, "Trends in Internatonal Investment Agreements – Balancing Investor Rights and the Right to Regulate. The Issue of National Security" in K. P. Sauvant (ed.), *Yearbook on International Investment Law & Policy 2008–2009* (Oxford University Press, 2009), p. 35 at p. 45.

54 Dealing with National Treatment (Art. 3); Most-Favored-Nations Treatment (Art. 4); Performance Requirements (Art. 8); and the Nationality of Senior Management and Boards of Directors (Art. 9).

interest. By exempting from certain investor protections for certain sectors, etc. as indicated in annexed schedules, it resembles somehow several provisions of the WTO realm, in particular GATS or TRIPS. In this regard it should be noted that Article 14(4) refers to exceptions in the TRIPS Agreement.

Such parallelism to or inspiration from international trade law is not entirely unfamiliar to other Model BITs. Of particular interest in this aspect is the Canada Model BIT 2004.[55] Remarkably so, it – by result – embraces Todd Weiler's approach[56] and provides for a general exceptions clause resembling GATT Article XX:

"Article 10

General Exceptions

1. Subject to the requirement that such measures are not applied in a manner that would constitute arbitrary or unjustifiable discrimination between investments or between investors, or a disguised restriction on international trade or investment, nothing in this Agreement shall be construed to prevent a Party from adopting or enforcing measures necessary:
   (a) to protect human, animal or plant life or health;
   (b) to ensure compliance with laws and regulations that are not inconsistent with the provisions of this Agreement; or
   (c) for the conservation of living or non-living exhaustible natural resources.
2. Nothing in this Agreement shall be construed to prevent a Party from adopting or maintaining reasonable measures for prudential reasons, such as:
   (a) the protection of investors, depositors, financial market participants, policy-holders, policy-claimants, or persons to whom a fiduciary duty is owed by a financial institution;
   (b) the maintenance of the safety, soundness, integrity or financial responsibility of financial institutions; and
   (c) ensuring the integrity and stability of a Party's financial system."

Indeed, while it refrains from introducing the entire list of specific exceptions enlisted in GATT Article XX (a) to (j), the first paragraph is almost identical in wording with the latter's chapeau and provisions (b), (d) and (g). While Article 10(1) (a) and (c) mean a broad introduction to the

[55] See Agreement Between Canada And . . . . . . For The Promotion And Protection of Investments, ita.law.uvic.ca/documents/Canadian2004-FIPA-model-en.pdf.

[56] See *supra* 3 B. 1.

international investment law stage of specific environmental measures as defenses against investor rights infringements, it remains to be seen whether a Tribunal discussing Article 10 will apply on this stage the well-established WTO jurisprudence on GATT Article XX[57] indiscriminately and in an unmodified manner. Moreover, it must be recalled that Canada – at least at the time of writing – is not a party to the Washington Convention, although preparations are in progress for it to join the ICSID club.[58] Apart from this general exceptions clause, Article 9 of the Canadian Model BIT contains a provision emulating almost word-by-word Article 14 US Model BIT as described above. The same holds true for Article 11 being very similar – particularly regarding the loftiness of its wording – to Article 12(1) and 13 US Model BIT. Hence, the Canadian BIT, while slightly more responsive to the public interest challenges than the US Model BIT, either contains clauses equally ineffective to those of its US counterpart or – pertaining to the general exceptions provision – inserts a language associated with trade law into the investment régime, which is at least a very dubious undertaking.

A much broader and bolder approach towards public interest considerations being enshrined in treaty language constitutes the 2007 Norwegian Draft Model BIT.[59] This document delineates a comprehensive attempt to insert the entire bouquet of public interest concerns into the investment realm: The preamble refers to topics ranging from public health and safety, the environment, labor rights, democracy, the rule of law, and human rights, to the prevention of corruption or even the principles enshrined in the United Nations Charter.[60] In its Commentary on the Draft Model BIT, issued jointly with the Draft, the Norwegian government lays out its main incentives and considerations in underlying its BIT edifice with all the aforementioned issues:

If Norway concludes investment agreements, it will be possible for us to lead the *development from one-sided agreements* that only safeguard the interests of the investor *to comprehensive agreements* that safeguard the regulative needs of both

57 See *infra* 5 B. 1. (a) and Trebilcock and Howse, *The Regulation of International Trade*, pp. 514 ff. See also the ruling of the *Continental Casualty* Tribunal in the Argentine crisis cases involving the state of necessity, *infra* 4. C. 1. (b).

58 See http://tradelawyersblog.com/blog/archive/2008/june/article/canada-has-not-ratified-icsid-convention-yet.

59 Agreement Between the Kingdom of Norway And . . . . . . For The Promotion and Protection of Investments, issued December 19, 2007, available at http://ita.law.uvic.ca/investmenttreaties.htm.

60 See *ibid.*, Preamble, paras. 3, 7, 8, 11.

developed and developing countries, *making investors accountable while ensuring them predictability and protection*. Future investment agreements should address the *totality of international legal agreements* by referring to agreements of *relevance to the regulatory authority* of the states as regards, for example, sovereignty over resources and environmental regulations.[61]

However, the Norwegian Draft Model BIT does not let it suffice merely to mention the said considerations in the preamble, but actually specifies them in a number of substantive provisions tailored to address the needs and objectives as set out in the above-cited passage. Article 11 stresses that parties should not lower their threshold of protection regarding environmental or health standards in order to lure investors. Apart from warranting a certain level of protection in the said areas, this provision is particularly intended to prevent a race to the bottom among capital importing countries' regulatory framework. Moreover, "[t]he purpose of the provision is to ensure that a state does not receive rewards in the form of increased investments for omitting to make socially beneficial regulations."[62] As these two last objectives demonstrate, Norway appears not to be simply concerned with the public interest in the individual host States but seems to assume the existence and possibility of enhancing a rather communal understanding and observation of the public interest by seeking to somewhat educate the host State in a certain way. In that context, the treaty explicitly bestows parties with the "right to regulate" (Article 12) in order to ensure investments are made in a manner sound with the environment, health etc. However, as per Article 12(2) US Model BIT 2004, this right to regulate is made subject to the reservation that the measure undertaken must be "otherwise consistent with the agreement," which limits its scope dramatically. Nevertheless, as the Commentary states:

[t]he provision signals that the parties have national regulatory needs associated with health, environment and safety that are legitimate and must be respected...From a legal point of view, the main significance of the provision is as an additional interpretive factor for the scope of the protection provisions of the agreement.[63]

Much more bite, however, is shown in the exceptions clauses enshrined in Section 5 of the Norway Draft Model BIT. In Article 24 the draft treaty

[61] Comments On The Model For Future Investment Agreements, English translation, issued December 19, 2007, available at http://ita.law.uvic.ca/investmenttreaties.htm, p. 10 (emphasis added).
[62] *Ibid.*, p. 27. [63] *Ibid.*, p. 28.

follows the Canadian 2004 Model BIT in providing a general exceptions clause tailored according to WTO provisions, i.e. Article XIV GATS,[64] as the Commentary informs us.[65] Again, the question remains – and the Commentary, for whatever reason, does not even mention it – whether or not a Tribunal applying the provision is supposed to follow the interpretative *acquis* of the WTO jurisprudence. Apart from the general exceptions clause, Articles 25 to 28 introduce exceptions for specific areas such as prudential regulation, tax measures or legislation targeted at promoting linguistic and cultural diversity. As the wordings indicate ("nothing . . . shall be construed as"; "this agreement shall not apply"), the Norway Draft Model BIT understands "exceptions" doctrinally not as excuses but rather as exemptions from the general scope of application of investor rights.[66]

Eventually, the draft treaty obliges the parties "to encourage investors to conduct their investment activities in compliance with the OECD Guidelines for Multinational Enterprises and to participate in the United Nations Global Compact."[67] The main purpose of this provision is to streamline developing countries and emerging economies that are not members of the OECD along the lines of corporate social responsibility objectives.[68]

Given how broad and – as a consequence – how dubious and murky many of the aforementioned provisions are, it was not to the utmost surprise that the Norwegian government, in 2009, abandonded the Draft Model BIT in the form as outlined above.[69] Hence, the aforementioned exhibits quite impressively two things: Firstly, important economic powers recognize the growing need for public interest considerations in the investment régime given a certain degree of imbalance towards investment protections and a legitimate interest of the host State to preserve the power to regulate for certain purposes. This may be mostly due to several major economies, in particular the USA, turning from merely large exporters of capital into both capital exporting and capital importing economies and thus themselves experiencing the leashes of BITs lacking

64 Which is, in fact, very similar to Article XX GATT.

65 See n. 61, p. 45.

66 On the differentiation between "excuses," which merely serve as a defense against an infringement of a right, and exemptions or "exculpations," which exclude the wrongfulness of the conduct, see V. Lowe, "Precluding Wrongfulness or Responsibility: A Plea for Excuses," *Eur. J. Int'l L.*, 10 (1999), 405 at 409.

67 Art. 32.

68 Norway Draft Model BIT Commentary, p. 48.

69 See D. Vis-Dunbar, "Norway Shelves its Draft Model Bilateral Investment Treaty," *investmenttreatynews*, June 8, 2009, available at www.investmenttreatynews.org/cms/news/archive/2009/06/08/.

any leeway for public interest considerations. The second observation to be made, however, is that drafters of BITs are still struggling to find the right answers to the challenges that are to be addressed and resolved. Either the Model BITs are rather ineffective in this regard and thus are inadequate to address the needs, or they find improper solutions by referring to the WTO realm or inserting broad exceptions for specific fields that may be easily exploited. Hence, the question evolves, whether the issue of public interest considerations may be adequately resolved by BIT drafting. While I do not intend to fully answer it at this stage, I do not conceal that the approach I will promote in the next chapter will take a different path.

4 The Global Public Interest theory

A. Setting the stage: International investment law as Global Public Law

As the development that I described above as "internationalization" of international investment law reveals,[1] in the past investment Tribunals regarded themselves as somewhat odd brothers of international commercial arbitration Tribunals.[2] Supported by the fact that until the 1990s (a) most arbitrators had a commercial arbitration background, and (b) public international law did not play a dominant role under the investment realm due to the lack of a coherent body of rules on the international level, investment arbitration was regarded and treated rather as a private law system. While the consequences of this view still can unfold powerfully in sporadic cases,[3] I will delineate my understanding of international investment law as a public law system. Such delineation pertains both to procedural and substantive aspects – procedural in that I will flesh out investment arbitration's character as a system of global administrative adjudication (1.) and substantive in that I will identify the function of (international) investor rights as trump cards[4] that enable the individual to seek for sanctions for the abuse of public authority through an independent third party (1. (b) (i) and 2.). Finally, section 3 will explain how, in my view, these two different concepts may be combined and reconciled

[1] See *supra* 2 E. 2.

[2] See G. Cordero Moss, "Commercial Arbitration and Investment Arbitration: Fertile Soil for False Friends?" in C. Binder *et al.* (eds.), *International Investment Law for the 21st Century – Essays in Honour of Christoph Schreuer* (Oxford University Press, 2009), p. 782 at pp. 791 ff.

[3] See, for example, the *World Duty Free* case, *infra* 8 C. 2. (b).

[4] See *infra* 4 A. 2. (c).

and moreover I will delineate a model that adequately captures all the identified features of international investment law.

1. *The Global Administrative Law face of international investment law*

Moving towards developing a new approach, in this part of the analysis I will briefly describe the emerging concept of Global Administrative Law. As will be shown, this movement, despite some reservations that I will identify, may serve as a means to explain certain particularities of international investment law and proves very instructive for constructing my theory in the later parts of this chapter.

(a) Global Administrative Law as a concept[5]

The Global Administrative Law movement is a fairly recent concept[6] though some aspects of it have already been foreshadowed in earlier writings.[7] It departs from the premise that in a considerable amount of cases no sharp line can be drawn any more between the international and the domestic levels. Rather, one can observe the phenomenon that international and domestic legal mechanisms are strongly intertwined. The implementation of the so-called smart sanctions[8] régime of the UN Security Council on the domestic and regional, i.e. European,[9] levels or the control by the bodies of the WTO dispute settlement system of domestic policies allegedly affecting international trade[10] are but two of a myriad of different examples.

Taking this "enmeshment" of the international and the domestic levels into account, the Global Administrative Law concept further proceeds with the observation that currently several instruments of global

[5] This subsection draws partly on A. Kulick, "The Integration of International Investment Law" in N. Lavranos *et al.* (eds.), *Hague Yearbook of International Law*, 23 (2010), p. 159.

[6] See B. Kingsbury, N. Krisch and R. B. Stewart, "The Emergence of Global Administrative Law," *Law & Contemporary Problems*, 68 (2005), 15, 31 ff., 39 f.; "Symposium: Global Governance and Global Administrative Law in the International Legal Order," *EJIL*, 17 (2006), 1–278.

[7] See, e.g. H. H. Koh, "Transnational Legal Process" in G. Simpson, *The Nature of International Law* (Ashgate, 2001), p. 311 at p. 314.

[8] See United Nations Security Council Res. 1373 (2001), adopted by the Security Council at its 4,385th meeting, September 28, 2001, at http://daccess-ods.un.org/TMP/3086396.html.

[9] See Joined Cases C-402/05 and C-415/05 P: *Yassin Abdullah Kadi* v. *Council of the European Union & Al Barakaat International Foundation* v. *Council of the European Union*, 2008 WL 4056300, [2008] 3 CMLR 41, Celex No. 605J0402, ECJ, September 3, 2008. On the debate related to the whole complex of smart sanctions see M. Nettesheim, "UN Sanctions Against Individuals – a Challenge to the Architecture of European Union Governance," *CML Rev.*, 44 (2007), 567.

[10] See *US-Shrimp/Turtles*.

governance are existent which do not fit into the conventional pattern of public international law as a system of coordination between sovereign and equal actors. Rather, the mechanisms of regulation resemble typical administrative law functions: "the setting and application of rules by bodies that are not legislative or primarily adjudicative in character."[11]

Global Administrative Law is concerned with the accountability of regulatory bodies the decisions of which have impacts of a global instead of a merely domestic nature.[12] It can occur in a plethora of different forms. Thus, Kingsbury/Krisch/Stewart identify five different types of globalized administrative regulation as distinguishable categories, which in practice, however, may often overlap or combine several features: (1) administration by international organizations, i.e. intergovernmental organizations established by treaties set rules that are directed towards individuals – the "smart sanctions" régime of the UN Security Council being the most prominent example; (2) administration based on collective action by transnational networks, i.e. the cooperation of national regulators in the absence of a binding formal decision-making structure such as the Basle Committee;[13] (3) administration by domestic regulatory bodies that decide on issues of global concern, e.g. the measures undertaken by the US authorities targeted at the protection of sea turtles, which triggered off a trade dispute in the WTO realm;[14] (4) administration by hybrid intergovernmental–private arrangements, that is bodies combining private and governmental actors such as the Codex Alimentarius Commission, which adopts standards on food safety by involving both State and non-State representatives in the decision-making process; (5) administration by private institutions that perform regulatory functions, such as the International Standardization Organization (ISO), which is a private body that seeks to harmonize product and process rules on a global level.[15]

[11] N. Krisch and B. Kingsbury, "Symposium: Global Governance and Global Administrative Law in the International Legal Order – Introduction: Global Governance and Global Administrative Law in the International Legal Order," *Eur. J. Int'l L.*, 17 (2006), 1, 3.

[12] B. Kingsbury, N. Krisch, R. B. Stewart and J. B. Wiener, "Foreword: Global Governance as Administration – National and Transnational Approaches to Global Administrative Law," *Law & Contemp. Probs.*, 68 (2004–05), 1 at 5.

[13] For an overview on the Basle Committee on Banking Supervision see www.bis.org/bcbs/index.htm.

[14] See *US-Strimp/Turtles*.

[15] Kingsbury/Krisch/Stewart, "Emergence of Global Administrative Law," 20 ff.

Looking preliminarily at international investment law,[16] arguably it may be described as a category (3) type of Global Administrative Law.[17] Here, the administrative character of global governance involved is characteristically different from the four other categories: The primary regulatory function is performed by the host State in, at least at first glance, a merely domestic realm. Whereas in category (1) cases an International Organization body sets rules that affect the individual, here the relationship of the host government and the investor appears to be an internal one at first glance. What transforms this relationship into a global one, however, is the possibility for an investor to let an international Tribunal review the legality of the host State's conduct on the basis of an international law instrument, i.e. a BIT. The raison d'être of administrative law is to control public authority. Therefore, Global Administrative Law, in this more advanced form, allegedly may explain global mechanisms of adjudication against the exercise of public authority, which provide enforceable public law remedies, such as under international investment law.[18]

Consequently, Global Administrative Law describes the phenomenon that there exists a body of global governance regulation and review which is hard to describe using the classical dichotomy of the international and domestic levels. It may on the one hand comprise the rule-making of international "executive" bodies, which affect domestic decision-making, e.g. UN Security Council Resolutions on so-called "smart" or "targeted" sanctions.[19] On the other hand it may involve the review of domestic regulation by an international Tribunal, such as WTO Panel and Appellate Body decisions.[20]

Global Administrative Law is an open rather than a closed concept. It still leaves a myriad of questions in the obscure[21] and is an object of criticism.[22] However, it undeniably describes a thriving trend in global

[16] A more detailed examination follows below; see *infra*, 4 A. 1. (b) (ii) and 3.

[17] Kingsbury/Krisch/Stewart, "Emergence of Global Administrative Law," 36.

[18] G. Van Harten and M. Loughlin, "Investment Treaty Arbitration as a Species of Global Administrative Law," *EJIL*, 17 (2006), 121 at 149; Kingsbury/Krisch/Stewart, "Emergence of Global Administrative Law," 39 f.

[19] See UN SC Res. 1373.

[20] See *US-Shrimp/Turtles*, which held a US regulation on the protection of sea turtles as inconsistent with GATT Article III:4.

[21] These cannot be addressed here. See, however, on these issues: Krisch/Kingsbury, "Global Governance and Global Administrative Law," 10 ff.; Kingsbury/Krisch/Stewart, "Emergence of Global Administrative Law," 61.

[22] See C. Harlow, "Global Administrative Law: *The Quest for Principles and Values*," *EJIL*, 17 (2006), 187.

governance – that the dichotomy between the international and domestic levels is dissolving and that regulatory and review régimes are emerging that are best analogized to administrative law.

(b) International investment law as Global Administrative Law?

Given the features that shape the enmeshment of international and domestic law as described above, it becomes apparent that international investment law shares some main features with Global Administrative Law. Following the argumentation as outlined by Van Harten and Loughlin,[23] I will describe four pivotal characteristics of international investment arbitration and outline the differences to international commercial arbitration which illustrate the Global Administrative Law character of international investment arbitration. However, such assessment of international investment law has limits. Therefore, despite striking common features, I will argue that the Global Administrative Law movement, albeit proving very instructive, cannot entirely capture the special character of international investment law.

(i) Four characteristics of international investment arbitration

International investment arbitration, i.e. the adjudication of investment disputes before an international Tribunal, in its present form has four distinctive features that bear relevance in the context at hand. Firstly, it permits individual claims of private entities against States before an international Tribunal.[24] Article 27 ICSID excludes the investor's recourse to diplomatic protection, which shows the aim of ICSID to make arbitration directly available to investors as the only dispute settlement instrument. The fact that most BITs derogate from the obligation to exhaust local remedies[25] plays into the hands of this principle. Regarding the host State, by its general consent to the arbitration of all future investment disputes, it accepts it will be subject to claims by private entities in an international forum. It thereby critically limits its sovereignty and acknowledges the authority of a Tribunal to adjudicate disputes which otherwise would have been decided within its realm.

[23] G. Van Harten and M. Loughlin, "Investment Treaty Arbitration as a Species of Global Administrative Law," *EJIL*, 17 (2006), 121; G. Van Harten, *Investment Treaty Arbitration and Public Law* (Oxford University Press, 2007).

[24] See Van Harten and Loughlin, "Investment Treaty Arbitration," 127 ff.; Van Harten, *Investment Treaty Arbitration and Public Law*, pp. 96 ff.

[25] See, e.g., the US Model BIT, *supra* 3 B. 2.

The second characteristic of international investment arbitration further promotes the State's waiver to its immunity, i.e. its sovereignty: the direct enforceability of the arbitration awards.[26] Whereas under general public international law the principle of State immunity prevents domestic courts from enforcing a claim against a State,[27] Article 54 ICSID allows for enforcement of ICSID awards before the courts of *any* ICSID Member State. Consequently, not merely must the courts of the host State and the courts of the investor's home State enforce an award, but the investor may seek enforcement before the courts of any of the 156 Member States of the ICSID Convention.

Thirdly, international investment arbitration provides for damages as remedy for a breach of an obligation by the host State.[28] Those damages are intended to encounter a deterrent effect and therefore serve as a sanction, i.e. a public law remedy, vis-à-vis the host State. In contrast to other systems, which provide for damages claims by individuals outside the domestic level, damages in international investment arbitration are neither limited by certain substantive qualifications, as under the *Francovich* doctrine of the ECJ,[29] nor by the notion that monetary damages sometimes are inadequate to compensate non-monetary violations of human rights, as applied by regional human rights courts.[30] In investment arbitration, however, damages are granted when the investor's rights have been violated, and those violations in most cases directly entail an economic loss which can be measured in monetary terms.

Finally, by the various means to establish subsidiaries in different countries, BITs facilitate forum shopping by the investor and consequently expand the reach of investment arbitration as a means of international adjudicative review.[31]

(ii) Conclusion

As has been demonstrated above, administrative review means the review of the exercise of public authority vis-à-vis a private entity, which entails

[26] See Van Harten and Loughlin, "Investment Treaty Arbitration," 133 ff.

[27] See M. N. Shaw, *International Law*, 6th edn. (Cambridge University Press, 2008), pp. 697 ff.

[28] See Van Harten and Loughlin, "Investment Treaty Arbitration," 131 ff.; Van Harten, *Investment Treaty Arbitration and Public Law*, pp. 101 ff.

[29] See ECJ, Case C-479/93, *Francovich* v. *Italy* [1995] ECR I-3843; K. P. E. Lasok, *Law & Institutions of the European Union*, 7th edn. (Butterworths, 2001), pp. 148 f.

[30] See M. W. Janis, R. S. Kay and A. W. Bradley, *European Human Rights Law*, 3rd edn. (Oxford University Press, 2008), pp. 98 ff.

[31] See Van Harten and Loughlin, "Investment Treaty Arbitration," 137 ff.

enforceable public law remedies against the State.[32] Considering, moreover, that international investment law provides for the protection of investors' rights against violative domestic regulation by the host State, it becomes apparent that international investment law currently may be the best example of Global Administrative Law.

Firstly, international investment arbitration holds several distinctive features of administrative review: (1) The investor can directly initiate a claim against the host State's actions; see Article 27 ICSID which exempts from the local remedies rule. (2) Those actions accrue directly from the exercise of the State's public authority.[33] (3) In case a violation is found, the reviewing body awards a remedy, i.e. compensation for damages suffered. (4) The awarded remedies are enforceable within the realm of the legal régime see Article 54 ICSID.

Secondly, the body of substantive rules which governs an international investment dispute consists of an enmeshment of international and domestic law rules and principles that are interwoven and employ no clear dichotomy. Instead of being two separate orders, international and domestic law are both in general comprehensively applicable and complementary within the realm of international investment law. Moreover, within this realm, international law trumps domestic law in case of conflict. Consequently, international investment law is composed of both domestic and international rules on investment, which are intertwined and form a harmonious legal régime to govern the investor–host State relationship. Without prejudice to a thorough analysis at B. 2., this feature mirrors the integration of European and domestic law of the Member States. Nowhere does it become as apparent as in the case of administrative law.

Thirdly, and again foreshadowing somewhat a subsequent assessment at 3., the combination of the two previous observations reveals that international investment law displays all the characteristics of public law: "it is not based on a reciprocal relationship of juridical equals, but engages a regulatory relationship of the State and an individual."[34] No other international adjudicatory system creates a review and remedy mechanism which is that close in its features to domestic administrative adjudication.

[32] See *supra* 4 A. 1. (b) (i).

[33] It must be noted, however, that in international investment arbitration any exercise of public authority can be subject to arbitral review, be it executive, legislative or judicial; see Van Harten and Loughlin, "Investment Treaty Arbitration," 146.

[34] Van Harten and Loughlin, *ibid.*, 149.

It controls the exercise of public authority and provides for universally enforceable public law remedies.

International investment disputes are not fought between States. Instead, international investment arbitration enables the investor to bring an international claim directly against the host State. Furthermore, international investment law provides a hierarchical set of legal rules, derived from both the international and the domestic levels, the violation of which makes the host State subject to enforceable remedies for its exercise of public authority.

The aforesaid provides impressive argumentation for understanding international investment law as an example par excellence of Global Administrative Law. However, although nothing in the previous assessment may misrepresent the defining features of international investment law, it is also true that it leaves out some characteristics of both international investment law and arbitration on the one hand and (global) administrative law on the other which prove either quite hard to reconcile or simply cannot be explained when looking through the lens of Global Administrative Law. To begin with, measures adopted by the host State on the domestic level that affect the investor's international rights very often are – viewed from an internal perspective – taken by the legislature rather than by the executive. Tax legislation, general regulatory régimes in the energy sector or simply expropriation by a formal law are only three examples in this regard. Moreover, even a domestic court decision depriving the investor of guarantees enshrined in BITs may be the basis of an investment claim. Hence, depicting State conduct originating from all three branches of government as "administrative" is in fact inaccurate. Indeed, categorizing international investment law as administration by domestic regulatory bodies that decide on issues of global concern,[35] as was asserted earlier, required making some considerable modifications to what Kingsbury/Krisch/Stewart regard as ideal type (3) Global Administrative Law.[36] While it is true that the adjudicatory control of the exercise of public authority is a typical feature of review by administrative courts, it is equally true that such control is not an exclusive feature of administrative adjudication either. In fact, since *Marbury* v. *Madison*[37] it has become conventional wisdom that at least in democracies based on the modern

[35] See ideal type Global Administrative Law category (3) as described at 4 A. 1. (a) *supra*.

[36] Kingsbury/Krisch/Stewart, "Emergence of Global Administrative Law," 32.

[37] *William Marbury* v. *James Madison*, 5 US (1 Cranch) 137 (1803), decided February 24, 1803 (hereinafter: *Marbury* v. *Madison*).

rule of law acts of the legislature also may be subject to judicial (constitutional) review, not to mention decisions by (lower) courts.

The latter observation alludes to another aspect that a mere Global Administrative Law assessment of international investment law neglects. The enmeshment of the domestic and the international that investment law displays results in investor rights, being international law, trumping domestic law and thus entitling the investor, similar to the individual in a domestic constitutional order, to raise those "trumps" against the State exercising its public authority. This issue will be addressed and assessed below.

2. *Constitutional elements in international investment law*

In the preceding section I described international investment law as a system of administrative adjudication on a global scale exhibiting a regulatory and thus vertical relationship of the State and the investor. However, as I have already foreshadowed before, there is more to it. While I do not intend to reverse it, the following section extends the said statement. I will unveil the constitutional features of international investment law. I will argue that the hierarchical system it creates among domestic and international law and the role it assigns to investor rights as trump cards that enable the investor to pierce the sovereignty shield a host State attempts to raise are typical patterns of a constitutional structure. After a brief overview of the Constitutionalism debate in current public international law theory (a), I will move to a description of a special offshoot of this debate (b) and then eventually demonstrate that international investment law displays constitutional features, but may also not be entirely captured by the Constitutionalization debate (c). Both (b) and (c) will prove important support in building what I will later call the Global Public Interest theory.[38]

(a) Constitutionalization in public international law theory

Observed with Argus eyes, if not with fierce skepticism, by prominent proponents of realist[39] and neo-realist[40] perspectives on international relations theory, Constitutionalism as a public international law theory

[38] See *infra* 4 C. 4.–6.

[39] Only see one of the most prominent examples, H. J. Morgenthau, *Politics Among Nations: The Struggle for Power and Peace* (McGraw-Hill, 1948 (repr. 1993)).

[40] See K. Waltz, *Theory of International Politics* (McGraw-Hill, 1979), which constitutes the most influential work of neo-realism to date.

model, though burgeoning much earlier,[41] has been blossoming after the end of the Cold War as a predominantly,[42] albeit not exclusively,[43] German initiative. If I understand the international order as anarchy rather than displaying a more or less coherent body of rules, cue ball to the mechanics of international politics, I regard any attempt to bring order into that chaos and inflict normative elements by attributing constitutional features to an international legal framework a futile, if not naïve, undertaking.[44]

What the realist/neo-realist school of thought hence would call naïveté is the boldness of Constitutionalism to infer a normative element from the framework that constructs what it calls the "international community" and thus "constitutes" public international law.[45] Two main threads of Constitutionalism can be unraveled: One emphasizes and demands close parallels to the understanding of "constitution" in the domestic realm. Thus, those proponents ask for an institutional framework emulating a separation of power system with organs that have legislative, executive and judicial features.[46] Naturally so, to them the UN Charter is the

[41] Major projects had been launched in the pre-World War II era; see H. Kelsen, *Reine Rechtslehre* (1934), pp. 115–119; G. Scelle, *Pacte des Nations et sa Liaison avec le Traité de Paix* (Sirey, 1919), pp. 101–107; A. Verdross, *Die Verfassung der Völkerrechtsgemeinschaft* (J. Springer, 1926). Even at that time, however, German and Austrian scholars were a dominant voice in this regard. See on the historical dimension and development of the debate B. Fassbender, "Grund und Grenzen der konstitutionellen Idee im Völkerrecht" in O. Depenheuer *et al.* (eds.), *Staat im Wort: Festschrift für Josef Isensee* (C. F. Müller Verlag, 2007), p. 73.

[42] H. Mosler, "The International Society as a Legal Community," *Recueil des Cours*, 140 (1974), 1; B. Simma, "From Bilateralism to Community Interest in International Law," *Recueil des Cours*, 250 (1994), 217; C. Tomuschat, "Obligations Arising from States Without or Against their Will," *Recueil des Cours*, 241 (1993), 195; "International Law: Ensuring the Survival of Mankind on the Eve of a New Century," *Recueil des Cours*, 281 (1999), 1, particularly 72–90. See also J. Habermas, "Hat die Konstitutionaliseriung des Völkerrechts noch eine Chance?" in J. Habermas (ed.), *Der gespaltene Westen – Kleine Politische Schriften X* (Suhrkamp, 2004), p. 113 on the development and future of the debate.

[43] See e.g. P.-M. Dupuy, "The Constitutional Dimension of the Charter of the United Nations Revisited" in *Max Planck Y.B. United Nations L.*, 1 (1997), 1; T. M. Franck, "Is the UN Charter a Constitution?" in J. A. Frowein *et al.* (eds.), *Verhandeln für den Frieden – Negotiating for Peace*, Liber Amicorum *Tono Eitel* (Springer, 2003), p. 95; E. de Wet, "The Prohibition of Torture as an International Norm of Jus Cogens and its Implications for National and Customary Law," *Eur. J. Int'l L.*, 15 (2004), 97.

[44] Cf. Waltz, *Theory of International Politics*, pp. 102 ff.

[45] See A. von Bogdandy, "Constitutionalism in International Law: Comment on a Proposal from Germany," *Harv. Int'l L. J.*, 47 (2006), 223 at 225 ff.

[46] See on these elements M. Nettesheim, "Von der Verhandlungsdiplomatie zur internationalen Verfassungsordnung – Zur Entwicklung der Ordnungsformen des

example par excellence for a "constitution of the international community."[47] It creates organs that at least somewhat resemble the three branches of government on the domestic level – Legislature (General Assembly), Executive (Security Council) and the Judiciary (International Court of Justice) – and defines their competencies and spheres of influence.[48] However, such emphasis on institutional features should not be confounded with what the New Haven School[49] calls "constitutive process" and describes as "authoritative power exercised to provide an institutional framework for decision and to allocate indispensable functions."[50] Looking at law from a "policy perspective," the New Haven School thereby promotes the view that the "changing features of 'world constitutional law' are to be understood by perceiving the intimacy of interplay between law and the entire social process of the world community."[51] Hence, as alluded to before, the normative understanding of the international community for the New Haven School unfolds in a comparatively loose process[52] rather than being framed in a "constitution"-like structure as Constitutionalism theory propagates.

While the institutional emphasis of this first thread of Constitutionalist thinking runs the risk of concealing its normative core from the inexperienced observer, the second thread allows an easier discernment of the concept of value-orientation. It rather puts the hierarchy of norms in international law in its focus and intertwines this phenomenon, particularly the emergence of peremptory norms, with a non-voluntaristic notion.[53] In this understanding, the old *Lotus* principle, i.e.

internationalen Wirtschaftsrechts" in C. D. Claassen *et al.* (eds.), *"In einem vereinten Europa dem Frieden der Welt zu dienen . . . "* Liber amicorum *Thomas Oppermann* (Duncker & Humblot, 2001), p. 381 at p. 391, though it needs mentioning that Nettesheim's list exceeds mere institutional elements.

47 P.-M. Dupuy, "Constitutional Dimension," 2; B. Fassbender, "Grund und Grenzen," pp. 573 ff.; B. Simma, "From Bilateralism," 256 ff.

48 See e.g. Article 12 UN Charter on the relationship of the General Assembly and the Security Council on matters of international peace and security.

49 On the New Haven School see W. M. Reisman, "The View from the New Haven School of International Law," *Am. Soc'y Int'l L. Proc.*, 86 (1992), 118.

50 M. S. McDougal *et al.*, "The World Constitutive Process of Authoritative Decision" in M. S. McDougal and M. Reisman (eds.), *International Law Essays: A Supplement to International Law in Contemporary Perspective* (Foundation Press, 1981), p. 191 at p. 192.

51 *Ibid.*, at p. 195.

52 Only see R. Higgins, *Themes and Theories – Selected Essays, Speeches, and Writings in International Law*, Vol. I (Oxford University Press, 2009), pp. 19 ff.

53 On this issue see in particular C. Tomuschat, "Obligations for States," 195.

[t]he rules of law binding upon States . . . emanate from their own free will as expressed in conventions or by usages generally accepted as expressing principles of law,[54]

has lost much of its validity. The concept of *ius cogens* norms and – as their usual, albeit not necessary corollary[55] – obligations *erga omnes* are considered the most prominent examples for such development. Similar in their hierarchical meaning, though not identical in a doctrinal understanding,[56] are universal conflict of norms rules such as Article 103 UN Charter.[57] While they do not invalidate conflicting norms but rather render the latter inapplicable while and to the extent that there exist inconsistencies with the hierarchically higher norms, it is the hierarchical system they create and their universal applicability that they share with *ius cogens* norms. Both *ius cogens* norms and universal conflict of norms rules "constitute" the public international law system in that they define the hierarchy of norms and the system's normative outer limits in a way very similar to a domestic constitution.[58] Moreover, remaining in this domestic analogy, comparable to civil liberties or fundamental rights, which are a core component of the domestic constitutional realm, the core body of human rights serves as a "trump" on the international level that the individual may raise against the regulatory or prosecutorial power of the State as a matter of international law.[59]

The underlying rationale that both threads have in common is what Constitutionalism theory scholars call "community interest."[60] What is meant by this term in the present context is the understanding of public

[54] *The Case of the SS "Lotus," France* v. *Turkey*, September 7, 1927, PCIJ, Series A, No. 9, 18.

[55] That is, no *ius cogens* norm is perceivable without inferring obligations *erga omnes*; however, obligations *erga omnes* do not exclusively emerge from *ius cogens* norms. See further on this Shaw, *International Law*, pp. 124 f. and M. Ragazzi, *The Concept of International Obligations Erga Omnes* (Oxford University Press, 1997); A. Hoogh, "The Relationship between Jus Cogens, Obligations Erga Omnes and International Crimes: Peremptory Norms in Perspective," *Austrian Journal of Public International Law*, 42 (1991), 183.

[56] Simma, "From Bilateralism," 287.

[57] Since virtually all States are members of the United Nations, it is fair to claim that its provisions and thus also Article 103 are universally applicable.

[58] See L. Hannikainen, *Peremptory Norms (Jus Cogens) in International Law – Historical Development, Criteria, Present Status* (Finnish Lawyers Publishing Company, 1988), pp. 67 ff. For an early assessment see M. Virally, "Réflexions sur le 'jus cogens'," *Annuaire Français de Droit International*, 12 (1966), 5.

[59] See M.-B. Dembour, *Who Believes in Human Rights?: Reflections on the European Convention* (Cambridge University Press, 2006), pp. 73 ff.

[60] The term is adopted from Simma, "From Bilateralism," 233. Cf. on similar terminology Mosler, "International Society," 10; Tomuschat, "Obligations for States," 211.

international law as a system inhering normative features. Those features provide both its frame and its foundation. *Ius cogens* norms are the prime example for such notion: Their peremptory character is rooted "in the communality of the interests of the entire international society."[61] Consequently, beyond the variety of aspects such as institutional features, hierarchical structure or "trump" card, it is the value-orientation that is the core characteristic of Constitutionalism theory.

(b) Incremental development from a State-centric to a value-based system of public international law

Considering the aforementioned, it was Christian Tomuschat in his General Course at The Hague Academy of International Law in 1999 who further advanced the Constitutionalist notion by stating that some rules of public international law fulfill a constitutional function both on the domestic and the international levels:

> We take it that international law is not an objective in and for itself and that, instead, it has a general function to fulfill, namely to safeguard international peace, security and justice in relations between States, and human rights as well as the rule of law domestically inside States for the benefit of human beings, who, in substance, are the ultimate addressees of international law.[62]

Thus, "[t]he essence of the constitutional argument is that the core principles of international law address and limit all forms of political power."[63] What Tomuschat contends is that replacing the *Lotus* principle by a Constitutionalist perspective means a shift in the tide – from a State-centric to a value-oriented system of public international law. It is not that States are the "ultimate addressees of international law,"[64] as they used to be under the classical Vattelian concept prevalent in public international law for most of the past three-and-a-half centuries.[65] Instead, the focus is on the human being. Examples in ICJ case law are myriad, in which the World Court referred to "elementary considerations of humanity,"[66] "the

[61] Simma, "From Bilateralism," 288. On the differentiation between "international society" and "international community" see also K. Wellens, "General Observations" in T. Komori and K. Wellens (eds.), *Public Interest Rules of International Law – Towards Effective Implementation* (Ashgate, 2009), p. 15 at p. 16.

[62] Tomuschat, "Survival of Mankind," 23.

[63] Von Bogdandy, "Constitutionalism," 226.

[64] Tomuschat, "Survival of Mankind," 23.

[65] See E. de Vattel, *Le droit des gens ou principes de la loi naturelle appliqués à la conduite et aux affaires des nations et des souverains*, 1758 and D. Armstrong, T. Farrell and H. Lambert, *International Law and International Relations* (Cambridge University Press, 2007), pp. 53 ff.

[66] ICJ, *The Corfu Channel Case*, Merits, Judgment of April 9, 1949, *ICJ Reports*, (1949), 4 at 22.

principles and rules concerning the basic rights of the human person"[67] or "fundamental principles" of human rights and humanitarian law.[68] Therefore, pertaining to the concept of *ius cogens*, Martti Koskenniemi stressed that:

[s]ome norms seem so basic, so important, that it is more than slightly artificial to argue that States are legally bound to comply with them simply because there exists an agreement between them to that effect, rather than because, in the words of the International Court of Justice... non compliance would 'shock the conscience of mankind' and be contrary to 'elementary considerations of humanity.'

...

[I]t is really our certainty that genocide or torture is illegal that allows us to understand State behavior and to accept or reject its legal message, not State behavior itself that allows us to understand that these practices are prohibited by law. It seems to me that if we are uncertain of the latter fact, then there is really little in this world we can feel confident about.[69]

The emphasis on humanity spotlights the human being. It is the benchmark in the solar system of public international law. The *Grundnorm* of public international law, so to speak,[70] is shifting from sovereign equality to humanity. However, as Tomuschat acknowledges, while such description of public international law captures some ongoing processes of fundamental paradigm change, we are not quite there yet.[71] The State still plays the most prominent role in public international law.[72] It is its chief actor, the main international law-maker – through treaties and custom[73] – and forms the membership in those international organizations that have

[67] *Case Concerning the Barcelona Traction, Light and Power Company, Limited (Belgium* v. *Spain)*, Second Phase, Judgment of February 5, 1970, *ICJ Reports*, 3 (1970), 32, para. 34.

[68] *Case Concerning United States Diplomatic and Consular Staff in Teheran (United States of America* v. *Iran)*, Judgment of May 24, 1980, *ICJ Reports*, (1980), 3 at 42; *Military and Paramilitary Activities in and against Nicaragua (Nicaragua* v. *United States of America)*, Merits, *ICJ Reports*, (1986), 14 (hereinafter: *Nicaragua Case*) at 125, para. 242.

[69] M. Koskenniemi, "The Pull of the Mainstream," *Mich. L. Rev.*, 88 (1990), 1946 at 1946 f. and 1952.

[70] Cf. on the term as understood by Kelsen generally see U. Bindreiter, *Why Grundnorm? – A Treatise on the Implications of Kelsen's Doctrine* (Kluwer Law International, 2002); M. Haase, *Grundnorm – Gemeinwille – Geist* (Mohr Siebeck, 2002), pp. 40 ff.

[71] For a more skeptical analysis see U. Haltern, "Tomuschats Traum: Zur Bedeutung von Souveränität im Völkerrecht," in P.-M. Dupuy *et al.* (eds.), *Völkerrecht als Wertordnung – Common Values in International Law: Festschrift für Christian Tomuschat* (N.P. Engel Verlag, 2006), p. 867.

[72] Tomuschat, "Survival of Mankind," 161.

[73] Although this is debatable to some extent; see *infra* 4 C. 6. (a).

a status similar to States in public international law.[74] Moreover, the force inherent in the principle of sovereign equality should not be underestimated. Gross and large-scale violations of human rights and the laws of war occur in many countries around the globe on an almost day-to-day basis. In fact, if we were to number the States whose governments engage in such violations or on the territories of which such violations are committed, the list would be frighteningly long.

Nonetheless, public international law is no longer governed exclusively by the rationales of realpolitik, and while the ruthless and cunning State is still a familiar companion in international relations, none of its perpetrations – or, in fact, the perpetrations of individuals[75] – remain unobserved and uncommented on by the international community. And in increasing numbers they do not go unsanctioned or even unpunished. So, in a nutshell, values prop up the public international law system despite the prominence enjoyed by the State, its chief actor.

(c) Constitutional features of international investment law

Lacking a mentionable institutional setting, ICSID – which is more of a forum than an organization – or other arbitration fora such as UNCITRAL and hence international investment law definitely have no constitutional features as understood by the first thread[76] of the Constitutionalism debate. However, its constitutional features are to be found in the second thread. By the "interdigitation" of domestic and international law that Article 42 ICSID and the vast majority of BITs provide for and by giving supremacy to international law, international investment law, as I have argued above,[77] creates a system of normative hierarchy. With international law – and thus particularly investor rights enshrined in BITs – at the top of the hierarchical order, international investment law hands a trump card[78] to the investor: The latter can assume that it

[74] In fact, many public international law scholars would actually argue that they derive their status exclusively from the membership of States.

[75] For the evolution of international criminal law and the mushrooming of ad hoc and permanent international criminal Tribunals, see H. Olásolo, *The Criminal Responsibility of Senior Political and Military Leaders as Principals to International Crimes* (Hart Publishing, 2009), pp. 2 ff.; G. Werle, *Principles of International Criminal Law*, 2nd edn. (T. M. C. Asser Press, 2009), pp. 7 ff.

[76] See *supra* 4 A. 2. (a). [77] See *supra* 2 E. 2.

[78] It must be noted that, although this terminology is inspired by Dworkin, I do not fully embrace his model. For Dworkin, a right "trumps" if it in itself supersedes "some background justification for political decisions that states a goal for the community as a whole." Hence, a balancing with conflicting interests precedes the actual evaluation

has a strong position as regards the protection of its interest as cast in individual rights provisions in BITs.[79] Thus, its rights may be described as prima facie positions[80] in its favor.

Such prima facie character does not mean that, eventually, its claim turns out to be illusory.[81] It simply means that the investor is preliminarily placed in a position to assume – and thus the Tribunal likewise has to assume – that its claim succeeds, if no other position is asserted that supersedes the investor right.

Providing such prima facie positions by compelling the State to justify any infringement of those rights is a typical feature of a constitutional

as a "trump." A right in the Dworkinian sense only is a "trump" – and, in fact, only is a right – if it prevails over "some background justifications." Therefore, by his understanding, once there is a right, it prevails – otherwise it would not be called a "right." By contrast, I understand "trump" – and hence "right" – as a prima facie position that provides a preliminary position. It provides an assumption that it eventually prevails, if a balancing with conflicting interests is unable to prove the latter's supremacy. So, while for me, "trump" or "trump card" means winning the battle, for Dworkin it means winning the war. See on Dworkin's theory of rights R. Dworkin, *Taking Rights Seriously* (Harvard University Press, 1977) and R. Dworkin, "Rights as Trumps" in J. Waldron (ed.), *Theories of Rights*, 6th impr. (Oxford University Press, 1995), p. 153. I deem it preferable to regard "rights" as prima facie positions and leave the balancing to a level separate from the content of the "right," for Dworkin's categorization neglects that conflicts very often occur not between individual rights and "goal[s] for the community as a whole," but between different individual rights. To say that a "right" only exists if it "trumps" the conflicting interest is rather illogical if the conflicting interest is itself a right. My right to privacy exists even if another person's right to freedom of speech that conflicts with my said right eventually prevails when I balance both against each other. Both rights exist, it is merely that our legal order regards one of the two as more valuable given the particular circumstances of the specific conflict.

79 See also on this issue P. Behrens, "Towards the Constitutionalization of International Investment Protection," *Archiv des Völkerrechts*, 45 (2007), 153; D. Schneiderman, *Constitutionalizing Economic Globalization – Investment Rules and Democracy's Promise* (Cambridge University Press, 2008), pp. 37 f.

80 See R. Alexy, *Theorie der Grundrechte*, 1st edn. (Suhrkamp, 1986), pp. 87 ff. The term "*prima facie* positions" originally derives from W. D. Ross, *The Right and the Good*, ed. P. Stratton-Lake (Oxford University Press, 2002), pp. 21 ff. As a side note and for clarification purposes, I stress that here, again, I differ from Dworkin's terminology. I think that rights have a double nature, for they can display features of both rules and principles; see Alexy, *ibid.*, pp. 122 ff.; on Dworkin's terminology see Dworkin, *Taking Rights Seriously*, pp. 24–26. Moreover, I contend – differently to Dworkin, who appears to purport that rules have an all-or-nothing character (see Dworkin, *ibid.*, pp. 24, 26) – that rules can have a prima facie character: If one rule conflicts with another, such conflict may only be reconciled by granting one of them prevalence as far and as long as the conflict persists, without invalidating the rule as such. See on this issue Alexy, *ibid.*, pp. 88 f.

81 See Ross, *The Right and the Good*, p. 21.

order.[82] The hierarchy of norms that international investment law exhibits neither nullifies conflicting norms of lower rank – which maintain their validity, but are merely rendered inapplicable for the time and to the extent of the conflict – nor anticipates the actual outcome of the legal analysis. What it does, however, is give supremacy to international law and thereby to investor rights in particular.

Moreover, as I have mentioned earlier[83] and as Stephan Schill recognizes in his recent book, the public law dimension of international investment law, i.e. the control of the exercise of public authority by sanctions for violation of individual rights, exhibits constitutional features:

> Like constitutions, [BITs] restrict State action and, as part of an international public order, create and safeguard the interests of an international community in the function of the global economic system. Investment treaties comprise constitutional traits by establishing legal principles that serve as a yardstick for the conduct of States vis-à-vis foreign investors.[84]

Such function of international investment law – to curb State action – has an additional dimension. States no longer have the final say in how they treat investors – or at least cannot attain the possibility of entering into political bargains with the investor's home State, as is the case in diplomatic protection. By agreeing to submit an investment dispute to an international Tribunal they transfer considerable power to an independent third party.[85] Such power of review of State action – whether executive, judicial or legislative – incites comparison of the arbitral Tribunal in this regard to domestic constitutional or supreme courts that are bestowed with the power to finally decide whether the respective State action is reconcilable with the pillars of the legal system they are operating in.[86] Investment Tribunals hence assume a role to some extent comparable with the third branch of government in a domestic constitution.[87]

[82] See Alexy, *Theory der Grundrechte*, pp. 87 ff. [83] See *supra* 4 A. before 1., and 2.

[84] S. W. Schill, *The Multilateralization of International Investment Law* (Cambridge University Press, 2009), p. 373.

[85] *Ibid.*, p. 374.

[86] Consider, e.g., the role of the German Federal Constitutional Court under the German *Grundgesetz* or of the US Supreme Court under the Constitution of the United States.

[87] Some commentators rightly purport that this is not an exhaustive description of a Tribunal's role in an investment dispute. As Schill, in *Multilateralization*, p. 374 stresses, "[t]he function of investment Tribunals is not restricted to applying pre-existing principles to the facts of a case, but rather involves developing more precise rules that govern international investment relations. Standards like fair and equitable treatment

As has been foreshadowed, however, in the discussion about a State-centric vs. a value-based system of public international law, despite an undeniable gradual development towards the latter and investor rights bestowing the investor with trump cards against the host State's exercise of public authority, I acknowledge that Constitutionalization has clearly discernible limits, both as a general theory and in its viability to characterize international investment law. In the first regard reservations derive from the impossibility of transposing models and terminology originating in a domestic legal and political context to the international plane. Neither are domestic constitutional systems identical – in fact, even among Western liberal democracies, they differ considerably and so do the understandings of constitutional values – nor does the international level even come close to displaying institutions and organs as stable and powerful as exist on the domestic level. Regarding Constitutionalization's suitability to describe international investment law it is obvious that ICSID or any other arbitral framework that allows introduction of investment disputes displays institutional features only faintly comparable to either a domestic constitutional architecture or the structure of the United Nations. Moreover, the enmeshment of the domestic and the international that is so prominent in investment law being based on the integrated mélange of domestic and international law evaporating the dichotomy between the domestic and the international levels is a feature the Constitutionalization debate is not concerned with. Given such limitations, the question arises whether there exists or may be developed a model more adequate to capture the defining features of international investment law.

3. *International investment law as Global Public Law*

I have thus identified the viable claims as well as the well-founded skepticism vis-à-vis characterizing international investment law as either Global Administrative Law or according to Constitutionalization theories. As much as investment law and arbitration create a system of adjudicatory control of the exercise of public authority and provide the investor with trump cards superseding the domestic law realm, yet it is equally hard

or indirect expropriation serve as "general clauses" that effectively transfer substantial rule-making powers to arbitral bodies that are established on a case-by-case basis and that lack genuine democratic legitimacy to develop restrictions for public acts of States under international law . . . Above all, unlike in the domestic context, there is no legislator for international investment law that could easily counteract mis-developments of the arbitral jurisprudence." See also V. Been and J. C. Beauvais, "The Global Fifth Amendment," *N.Y.U. L. Rev.*, 78 (2003), 30.

to contest that the government action contained by international investment law is not merely administrative in character and that the Constitutionalization debate still has many aspects that are more wishful thinking than actual assessments of the current state of public international law.

Hence, we find ourselves forced to acknowledge that international investment law cannot be entirely captured by either of the models outlined. Its distinct features necessitate putting it into a different category. In this regard, let me add a third model, already foreshadowed,[88] which will prove very instructive for developing what I will call the Global Public Interest theory. In his astute study of the investment arbitration system Gus Van Harten describes it as a public law system captured in a private law procedural frame.[89] To him, public law is characterized by the control of the exercise of public authority by sovereign entities. Investment law's distinct public law features, so he opines, lie firstly in it providing an adjudicatory framework for reviewing the host State's exercise of public authority vis-à-vis the investor and secondly in the general consent to investment arbitration the host State signs up to when concluding BITs. The former feature has been elaborated extensively in the section on Global Administrative Law.[90] Regarding general consent, Van Harten stresses that this BIT clause has an extraordinary meaning for the nature of investment law and arbitration, since submitting all disputes arising out of foreign investments to international arbitration is a unique expression of a host State's sovereignty. It means a severe limitation of sovereignty by bestowing an international Tribunal with the capacity to rule bindingly on the relationship of the host State and its foreign investors and thus on large parts of the host State's regulatory framework. However, such limitation simultaneously means exercising sovereignty, for giving up such broad competencies requires possessing them in the first place:

> Only the state can consent generally to arbitration because only the state has the authority to regulate individuals in its territory and to authorize the compulsory adjudication of disputes between the state and individuals who are subject to its regulatory authority. In this respect, the general consent transforms international arbitration from a form of reciprocally consensual adjudication into a governing arrangement.[91]

88 See *supra* 4 A. 1.

89 Van Harten, *Investment Treaty Arbitration and Public Law*, pp. 45 ff.

90 See *supra* 4 A. 1.

91 Van Harten, *Investment Treaty Arbitration and Public Law*, p. 64.

Taking Van Harten's assessment – which I think is an accurate one – as a basis, I want to add another aspect. Public law, dealing with the control of the exercise of public authority, usually has two dimensions. Firstly, it is concerned with the everyday relationship of the State and individuals (or other private actors, such as companies) exercised by individual measures on the basis of simple statutes, regulations, etc., subject to judicial review by the ordinary, low-level courts. This may be called the administrative dimension. And secondly, it deals with fundamental rights, civil liberties, etc. the individual may raise as trumps against State conduct – be it executive, legislative or judicial – too intrusive on the sphere of liberty, privacy or dignity, etc. guaranteed for in the founding document of a *polis*. We may call this the constitutional dimension of public law. As my above analysis exhibits, international investment law displays both dimensions. This is not to deny my earlier assessment that neither the Global Administrative Law movement nor Constitutionalization theory may fully explain the special features of international investment law. Instead, I argue that understanding it as a public law system allows combining aspects of both pedigrees.

Again, describing international investment law as a public law system that has both (Global) administrative and constitutional features is not a contradiction. Both administrative law and constitutional law are public law in that they grant the individual rights against the State in a regulatory relationship. In the domestic realm constitutional law often sets the frame that administrative law then fills and shapes through administrative procedures or adjudication. While the individual right thus usually has a constitutional pedigree such as the Bill of Rights or the fundamental rights section in the German *Grundgesetz*, it is the task of administrative law to provide the actual mechanisms, both via administrative procedure and adjudication, in order to sanction the violation of the individual right and to restore the *status quo ante*.

I acknowledge that my description of international investment law as public law, though sharing some major aspects, differs from Van Harten's. In particular, he focuses on the procedural features of investment *arbitration*, characterizing it as an adjudicatory framework serving the control of public authority. As will be developed in the subsequent sections, while I share such assessment, my concept of understanding investment *law* as public law is more substantive. It departs from the same premise, i.e. that at the core of the international investment system lies the idea of taming government action. However, it proceeds further[92] and compares the investment realm to basic features and principles of administrative and constitutional law, such as individual rights as supreme trump cards or public law's major task to strike a balance between the individual and the public interest.[93]

Moreover, promoting Constitutionalist features of international investment law means to some extent accepting the increasing value-orientation of public international law exerting influence on the investment régime. For the sake of avoiding confusion with Van Harten's concept, I hence denominate international investment law a system of Global Public Law. Thereby, I take notice that it (1) provides an adjudicatory framework for the control of the exercise of public authority; (2) dissolves the dichotomy of the domestic and international levels by declaring a mélange of both domestic and international law the applicable law and by bestowing an international Tribunal with the power of review over measures a host State takes vis-à-vis foreign investors within its otherwise sovereign realm; and (3) hands trump cards to the investor, derived from an international legal source, i.e. a BIT, that it may raise against the host State's exercise of its public authority and thus pierce the sovereignty veil a State may usually cloak itself in according to the conventional concept of public international law. Hence, international investment law is a Public Law system because it involves the adjudicatory control of the exercise of public authority, providing non-State entities with rights that pierce the sovereignty shield of the host State. And it is Global because it makes this Public Law system applicable on a global scale and epitomizes the enmeshment of the domestic and the international.

Before proceeding to a comparative analysis of international investment law and the European law and ECHR systems – my next step in building the Global Public Interest theory – let me address some criticism towards characterizing international investment law as (Global) Public Law as advanced by Moshe Hirsch. He contends that international investment law exhibits private law rather than public law features.[94] He asserts basically two arguments to corroborate his statement: (1) The investment

[92] In fact, international investment law is the perfect example for the intricate nature of substance and procedure and how the fact that they are intertwined may be made fruitful. See in particular *infra* 5 G. 2.

[93] See on this *infra* 4 C. 4.

[94] M. Hirsch, "Investment Tribunals and Human Rights: Divergent Paths" in P.-M. Dupuy, F. Francioni and E.-U. Petersmann (eds.), *Human Rights in International Investment Law and Arbitration* (Oxford University Press, 2009), p. 97 at pp. 107 ff.

contract; (2) investment arbitration's reliance on most of the *acquis* of international commercial arbitration.

To start with the first argument, it is true enough that in many investment disputes the investor concludes an investment contract with the host government laying down the basic framework and terms of the rights and obligations the investor enjoys regarding its investment in the host State. Usually, those contracts are of a private law nature comparable with a private law contract between private entities or between a domestic economic actor and the government acting *de iure gestionis*. Hence, so Hirsch implies, investment disputes being based partially or in some instances even exclusively on the investment contracts do not substantially differ from ordinary contract law claims under domestic law, for they are rooted in a reciprocal relationship.[95]

However, Hirsch neglects the fact that nowadays the rôle of investment contracts is considerably reduced. While instances in which there exists an investment contract but no BIT are very scarce, the reverse situation occurs frequently. Moreover, if both investment contract and BIT exist – given my above assessment that international law trumps domestic law in case of conflict[96] – the Tribunal will apply the former only to those issues that are not addressed in the BIT.

Furthermore, Hirsch conflates the factors determining the public or private law character of a legal system. Assume Hirsch's equation in a purely domestic system: The government concludes a private law contract with a domestic private entity. Undisputably, the contract itself is of a private law nature and if either side defaults on its obligations, the dispute arising is equally of a private law character. However, what if the State does not act as a private entity but in its capacity as a public entity bestowed with public authority, i.e. seizing the other side's assets, arresting its employees or adopting legislation effectively eradicating the rights enshrined in the contract? This is no coordinative relationship of legal peers. The relationship is clearly vertical rather than horizontal, for the State apparently does not act in its private capacity but employs instruments of *puissance publique*. Such disputes, whether predominantly administrative or constitutional in character, involve individual rights the private entity can raise against the exercise of public authority by the government and are thus undoubtedly of a public law character. This situation, and only this, parallels an investment dispute.

[95] *Ibid.*, pp. 108 f. [96] See *supra* 2 E. 2.

Hirsch is right, however, in depicting the investment arbitration system as heavily borrowing from international commercial arbitration.[97] Ad hoc Tribunals, an *inter partes* system and monetary damages and compensation as the pivotal remedy are but three of several more traits investment and commercial arbitration have in common.[98] While this may to some extent explain investment Tribunals' myopia vis-à-vis what Hirsch calls "public policy issues"[99] in the past, it cannot change the substantive law character of investment law being inherently public rather than private, as has been elaborated in detail above. Not to forget, in spite of all the said parallels with commercial arbitration, (procedural) investment arbitration is intertwined with and hence unthinkable without (substantive) investment law. Therefore procedural mechanisms such as the enforcement of arbitral awards (in particular), while also existing under the clearly private law realm of international commercial arbitration, attain a completely different character, for combined with the public law features of substantive investment law they turn into public law sanctions against illicit exercise of public authority.

B. Comparative insights

The ensuing section puts together both familiar and unfamiliar companions. While comparison of systemic features of international investment law with international human rights frameworks such as the European Convention on Human Rights (ECHR) has been undertaken before,[100] fleshing out striking similarities between the investment régime and the European legal order is much less common. The choice of these two systems is not random, of course. The Global Public Law character as described at 4. A. 3. above will both be mirrored and informed by the ECHR and European law systems paralleling many features of what I have denominated the constitutional and administrative dimensions of international investment law.

1. *Recall the seven observations on international investment law*

Before turning to comparisons with other legal systems, I recall the seven observations of Chapter 2:[101]

[97] Hirsch, "Investment Tribunals and Human Rights," 110 ff.; see also Moss, "Commercial Arbitration and Investment Arbitration," pp. 791 ff.

[98] *Ibid.*, pp. 112 f. [99] *Ibid.*, p. 112. [100] See the references *infra* 4 B. 3.

[101] See *supra* 2 E. 1. and 2.

- **Observation 1:** BITs are similar legal instruments, which form a comprehensive framework establishing – at least in part – the law of international investment.
- **Observation 2:** Under the realm of international investment law, international and domestic law are both comprehensive and complementary legal orders.
- **Observation 3:** Under the realm of international investment law, international law is supreme.
- **Observation 4:** Under Article 42(1) second sentence ICSID, international law is the primary source for the applicable law.
- **Observation 5:** The main reason for observations 2 to 4 is the proliferation of BITs in recent years.
- **Observation 6:** However, even absent a BIT, recent ICSID case law indicates the growing role of international law.
- **Observation 7:** International investment law is on the verge of becoming an integrated legal order.

Highlighting two of these observations, the supremacy, i.e. the "internationalization" of international law and the "integration" of domestic and international law under the realm of international investment law, I add an eighth observation that follows from the above analysis viewing international investment law through the lens of Global Administrative Law[102] and describing it as a public law system.[103] Different from the coordinative system of classical public international law, international investment law creates a system of judicial control of the exercise of public authority by the host State. The relationship of the host State and the investor that such system entails is vertical and regulatory rather than horizontal and coordinative. In fact, it resembles to a large extent the typical pattern of administrative adjudication. Considering these observations, particularly the very last one, I shall proceed to make profitable insights gained from analysing characteristics of another integrated system that shares features with administrative law, i.e. the European legal order. It is through a comparison with European law and viewed against the backdrop of general public international law that we will see international investment law in a new light (2.), which shall serve as a basis for the theory that I will lay out further below. Similarly, the constitutional features to be found in international investment law inspire a comparison with the European Convention on Human Rights system that provides equal support for constructing my theory (3.).

[102] See *supra* 4 A. 1. [103] See *supra* 4 A. 3.

2. *The European law system*

(a) Characteristic features of the European law system

Keeping the considerations of international investment law as Global Public Law in mind, I will advance with the development of my approach by drawing on a comparison with the European law system. This necessitates, as a first step, describing the characteristic features of the latter (a) before actually comparing them to those of international investment law – often viewed against the backdrop of general public international law (b).

(i) Supremacy and direct effect

Considering which characteristic features define the system of European law, the two doctrines of supremacy and direct effect are surely among the first to mention. Their full importance and thriving force becomes apparent only if one acknowledges them as intertwined and interrelated, for it is their combination that distinguishes European law from public international law and provides the main contribution to the European Exceptionalism I will refer to at (ii).

Both doctrines lack an express foundation in the text of the Treaty on the Functioning of the European Union (TFEU) and were developed in the early 1960s by a rather dynamic teleological interpretation by the European Court of Justice.[104] To start with the doctrine of supremacy, this notion, even at the time, did not seem very innovative, for just as Union law trumps domestic law in case of conflict, so does international law in general – as it is stated, e.g. for the law of treaties, in Article 27 VCLT. Conflicting domestic law is not annulled but merely rendered inapplicable so far and so long as it collides with Union law. However, in order to understand what makes the ECJ's holding in *Costa/ENEL*[105] – the first decision, dating from 1964, on the supremacy of Union (then Community) law – quite revolutionary, we have to consider two other characteristics of European law.

First of all, in contrast to public international law, which in most cases relies on the dichotomy vis-à-vis domestic law, Union law and domestic law amalgamate and are thus both equally applicable to a dispute. This phenomenon, which Rudolf Streinz refers to as "interdigitation"

[104] J. H. H. Weiler, "The Transformation of Europe," *Yale L.J.*, 100 (1990–91), 2403 at 2413.

[105] European Court of Justice, Case 6/64, *Flaminio Costa* v. *ENEL* [1964] ECR 585 (hereinafter: *Costa/ENEL*), 593.

("*Verzahnung*"),[106] can be observed both on the substantive and the procedural side and is most obvious in administrative law, where Union law relies on the established procedures of domestic law but complements and sometimes corrects it. What creates this "interdigitation" of Union and domestic law is the second doctrine, i.e. direct effect, which at the same time is the second characteristic of European law and makes the notion of supremacy so extraordinary.

According to the ECJ in its famous judgment *Van Gend & Loos* of 1963, the doctrine of direct effect means that all Union law norms, both primary and secondary, which are clear, precise and self-sufficient (not requiring further legislative measures by the authorities of the Union or the Member States)[107] are directly applicable within the domestic legal orders of the Member States of the Union.[108] It creates enforceable legal obligations between the Member States and individuals as well as among individuals themselves. Moreover, due to their direct effect, Union norms may be invoked before domestic or Union courts as well as before any other branch of government, both on the domestic and the Union level.[109] While this concept is not entirely new as such, particularly not to constitutional orders endorsing monism, such as the United States,[110] what makes it remarkable is that direct applicability is made the general rule in contrast to the exception of self-executing norms.[111]

Groundbreaking vis-à-vis the classical public international law conception are two aspects of the doctrine of direct effect. Firstly, direct effect allows for piercing the veil of sovereignty in that it takes away the State's ability to determine the method and extent to which international law may produce effects for individuals within the internal legal order.[112]

106 R. Streinz, *Europarecht*, 5th edn. (C. F. Müller Verlagsgesellschaft, 2001), pp. 69 f.

107 J. H. H. Weiler, "Transformation," 2413.

108 European Court of Justice, Case 26/62, *NV Algemene Transporten Expeditie Onderneming van Gend en Loos* v. *Nederlandse Aministratie der Belastingen* [1963] ECR 1 (hereinafter: *Van Gend & Loos*), 12 f.

109 T. Oppermann, *Europarecht*, 2nd edn. (C. H. Beck Verlag, 1999), p. 234; P. Craig and G. De Búrca, *EU Law – Text, Cases, and Materials*, 4th edn. (Oxford University Press, 2008), pp. 178 ff.; T. C. Hartley, *The Foundations of European Community Law*, 6th edn. (Oxford University Press, 2007), p. 192.

110 See Article VI(2) of the US Constitution.

111 See J. H. H. Weiler, "Transformation," 2418; on the issue of self-executing treaty provisions under US law see *Asakura* v. *City of Seattle*, US Supreme Court, 265 US 332 (1924) and *United States* v. *Postal*, US Court of Appeals, 589 F.2d 862 (5th Cir. 1979).

112 See J. H. H. Weiler, *ibid.*, 2413.

Secondly, under the classical doctrine of public international law, States are the only actors and thus an individual cannot itself invoke an international obligation directly against the State. It has to rely on diplomatic protection, i.e. on its home State to take up the matter against the host State in an inter-State claim. Direct effect means that as a general rule non-State actors can bring direct claims against States on the basis of rights bestowed upon them.

Considering both doctrines, supremacy and direct effect, together, both their thriving force as well as their revolutionary character become apparent: It is not innovative that Union law trumps domestic law. It is equally unspectacular that a Union law rule may be directly applicable in the domestic legal order. However, what is extraordinarily innovative and spectacular is that as a general rule, non-State actors engage in a direct legal relationship with States on the basis of Union law, which they may invoke vis-à-vis any act of public authority and which generally trumps any conflicting domestic law. As Joseph Weiler put it:

> [t]he combination of the two doctrines means that Community [now Union] norms that produce direct effects are not merely the Law of the Land but the 'Higher Law' of the Land.[113]

Having outlined these two fundamental doctrines of European legal integration, I will now proceed to describe how they, in combination with other factors, create the autonomous legal order that is characteristic of the notion of European Exceptionalism, which I will elaborate below.

(ii) European Exceptionalism: An autonomous legal order

The ECJ, in order to argue for the above-mentioned doctrines of supremacy and direct effect, more or less *en passant* outlined its view of the European legal order that differs considerably from the classical concept of public international law. In *Costa/ENEL*, the highest court of the European legal system observed that:

> [b]y contrast with the ordinary international treaties, the EEC Treaty [the predecessor of the TFEU] has created its *own legal system* which, on the entry into force of the Treaty, became an integral part of the legal systems of the Member States and which their courts are bound to apply.[114]

[113] *Ibid.*, 2415. [114] *Costa/ENEL*, 593 (emphasis added).

Moreover, in the famous words of *Van Gend & Loos*:

The objective of the EEC Treaty, which is to establish a Common Market, the functioning of which is of direct concern to interested parties in the Community, implies that this Treaty is *more than an agreement which merely creates mutual obligations between the contracting states* . . .

The conclusion to be drawn from this is that the Community constitutes a *new legal order of international law* for the benefit of which the states have limited their sovereign rights, albeit within limited fields, and the subjects of which comprise not only Member States but also their nationals.[115]

This "new legal order of international law," European Exceptionalism, is characterized by the supremacy of Union law, the direct applicability of Union legal norms, the direct and vertical legal relationship of the individual and the State, the "interdigitation" of Union and domestic law and the autonomy from the realm of public international law.[116] While some critics[117] contest this notion of European Exceptionalism – and indeed the ECJ's reasoning in *Van Gend & Loos* and *Costa/ENEL* is not necessarily imperative from a viewpoint of legal logic – the persistent case law confirming it and the acceptance by both the Member States and the Union have long ago transformed European law into an autonomous legal order.[118]

Different from classical public international law, European law rejects the dichotomy of the international and the domestic levels. It is an enmeshment of Union law, either primary or secondary, and domestic law, forging both legal orders into one new amalgamation that consists of a hierarchical order of norms and a vertical, administrative law type

[115] *Van Gend & Loos*, 12 (emphasis added).

[116] P. Pescatore, *Le Droit de l'Intégration* (A. W. Sijthoff, 1972), p. 37; É. Cerexhe, *Le Droit Européen* (Bruylant/Nauwelaerts, 1989), pp. 275 f.; J. H. H. Weiler, "Transformation," 2418 f.; Streinz, *Europarecht*, pp. 73 f.; P. S. R. F. Mathijsen, *A Guide to European Union Law*, 9th edn. (Sweet & Maxwell, 2007), p. 40.

[117] See T. Schilling, "The Autonomy of the Community Legal Order: An Analysis of Possible Foundations," *Harv. Int'l L.J.*, 37 (1996), 389; also see D. Wyatt, "New Legal Order, or Old?," *Eur. L. Rev.*, 7 (1982), 147.

[118] See J. H. H. Weiler and U. Haltern, "The Autonomy of the Community Legal Order – Through the Looking Glass," *Harv. Int'l L.J.*, 37 (1996), 411 at 420. See on the debate N. Walker, "Sovereignty and Differentiated Integration in the European Union" in Z. Bankowski and A. Scott (eds.), *The European Union and its Order* (Blackwell Publishers, 2000), p. 31 at p. 37; D. Grimm, "Does Europe Need a Constitution?," *Eur. L. J.*, 1 (1995), 282; J. Habermas, "Remarks on Dieter Grimm's 'Does Europe Need a Constitution?'," *Eur. L. J.*, 1 (1995), 303; J. H. H. Weiler, "Does Europe Need a Constitution? – Demos, Telos and the German Maastricht Decision," *Eur. L. J.*, 1 (1995), 219.

relationship of the State and the individual that is defined by mutual obligations. This special relationship of the individual and the State plays a considerable role in the following analysis.

(iii) Relationship of the State and non-State actors

European law, once one accepts its Exceptionalism, creates a myriad of different and complex relationships among the actors involved in its application. Leaving the relationship of the European institutions and the Member States or between the individual and the European institutions aside, I will focus, for the sake of our present analysis, on how the State–individual relationship plays out under the European law system.

As I stated before, as a consequence of the "interdigitation" of Union and domestic law, Union law avails itself of the respective domestic administrative law and procedures to unfold its full effectiveness vis-à-vis the individual.[119] Running on the tracks laid by domestic law, European law accepts the vertical relationship of the individual and the State that the internal administrative law, being public law, creates.

In contrast to the horizontal relationship among actors in private law or classical public international law,[120] public law describes a direct but vertical relationship of the State and non-State actors. This means that on the one hand the State is accepted as sovereign, acting according to the public interest of its constituency, i.e. the people, and by the authority of which non-State actors have to abide. On the other hand, the State has to accept non-State actors as subjects of law and thus as bearers of rights and obligations, which may be rooted both in Union law and domestic law – so long as the latter does not conflict with the former.[121]

Infringing the rights of non-State actors may only be justified by an obligation that reflects the public interest of the State's constituency. If the State lacks such justification by a non-State actor's obligation that can be traced back to a public interest, public law provides the latter with a remedy against the State – most commonly a claim before a court. Under the European law system, the non-State actor can claim violations of both Union and domestic law before domestic courts.[122] If the dispute involves an unresolved question of Union law, the court can or, if there is no possibility of an appeal against its decision, even has to submit the question to

[119] See *supra* 4 B. 2. (a) (i).

[120] See for public international law A. Cassese, *International Law*, 2nd edn. (Oxford University Press, 2005), pp. 48 ff.

[121] See on that issue Streinz, *Europarecht*, pp. 201 ff.

[122] J. H. H. Weiler, "Transformation," 2414; Oppermann, *Europarecht*, p. 234.

the ECJ.[123] Not very surprisingly, much of the aforementioned is reminiscent of the features of Global Administrative Law. And indeed, European law appears to be a very advanced version of Global Administrative Law that combines many aspects of the five types of Global Administrative Law identified above.[124]

(iv) Creation of Union legal norms

To conclude my brief study of the characteristics of the European law system, we have to take a quick glance at the different kinds of Union legal norms and how they are created. A common distinction runs between primary and secondary Union law. However, as has been noted before, the doctrine of direct effect makes all Union legal norms directly applicable to all actors within the European law system so long as they are clear, precise and self-sufficient.[125]

Primary Union law consists of the treaty itself, the general principles that can be derived from its interpretation and customary Union law – the latter being considerably rare.[126] As for the first and most important of the three sources of primary Union law, treaty rules are created and amended by a consensus of the Member States – a process not very unlike the rules of general public international law. However, primary treaty law shares with secondary Union law the characteristic that both sources rely on positively enshrined rules that seek to regulate a certain issue, mostly – albeit not exclusively in the case of secondary Union law[127] – in a general and abstract manner similar to a domestic law. Thus, a second type of distinction may be introduced, i.e. between written and unwritten Union law.

Written secondary Union law is created by Union organs established by written primary Union law. It may take four different forms: (1) Regulations, i.e. abstract and general norms that are addressed directly at individuals in the Member States and thus share the closest resemblance with domestic laws;[128] (2) Directives, i.e. abstract and general norms that are addressed at the Member States but not directly at individuals, for they provide guidance but leave the Member States with some flexibility as to how they want to translate that guidance into their domestic legal systems;[129] (3) Decisions by the Council or the Commission, i.e.

[123] See Art. 267 TFEU. [124] See *supra* 4 A. 1. [125] See *supra* 4 B. 2. (a) (i).
[126] See Oppermann, *Europarecht*, pp. 182 ff.; Mathijsen, *Guide*, pp. 48 ff.
[127] E.g. decisions issued by the Commission; See Oppermann, *ibid.*, p. 214.
[128] See Art. 288(2) TFEU. [129] See Art. 288(3) TFEU.

concrete and individual decisions that are directed at a specific person regarding a specific issue;[130] (4) Recommendations by the Council or the Commission, i.e. statements that are not of a mandatory character.[131] Of particular interest here are the first-mentioned Regulations, for they, being de facto European laws,[132] may provide for direct obligations of individuals.

Regarding unwritten Union law, which is mostly primary Union law, leaving the almost common law type jurisprudence of the ECJ aside,[133] there exist basically two kinds of sources: (1) Customary Union law; and (2) General principles of law. Customary Union law, which evolves by the same rules as customary international law,[134] is considerably rare and mostly concerns institutional issues, such as the possibility for Member States to be represented in the Council by officials below the ministerial level.[135] However, at least according to some authors,[136] customary Union law contains a few rules directly concerning individuals, most notably the direct effect of Directives if certain conditions are met.[137]

Much more prominent is the second category of unwritten primary Union law. The general principles of law have been playing a pivotal role in ECJ case law for about forty years. Such principles comprise, among others, proportionality, legitimate expectations, non-discrimination, transparency and, most importantly, fundamental rights. Being identified by the ECJ, they are dogmatically located in primary Union law, although the Court often does not bother to make such reference. For the sake of the analysis before us, it suffices if I limit myself to a brief description of the general principle of fundamental rights.

The introduction and acceptance of fundamental rights within the realm of European law was a complex and gradual process that has developed an impressive dynamic over the course of time.[138] Starting with

130 See Art. 288(4) TFEU. 131 See Art. 288(5) TFEU. 132 See Case 8/55 [1955/56], 227.

133 On this issue see Craig and De Búrca, *EU Law*, pp. 96 ff. and H. Rasmussen, *On Law and Policy in the European Court of Justice* (Martinus Nijhoff Publishers, 1986), p. 62.

134 On the creation of customary international law see Brownlie, *Principles of Public International Law*, 7th edn. (Oxford University Press, 2008), p. 6; ICJ, *North Sea Continental Shelf Cases, ICJ Reports*, (1969), 43.

135 See Oppermann, *Europarecht*, p. 185. 136 *Ibid.*

137 This, however, is controversial, for one may well argue that such notion is due rather to a common law type case law of the ECJ than to customary Union law. See on this issue and on the conditions for a Directive exerting direct effect U. Haltern, *Europarecht – Dogmatik im Kontext* (Mohr Siebeck, 2005), pp. 187 ff.

138 See J. Kühling, "Fundamental Rights" in A. von Bogdandy and J. Bast (eds.), *Principles of European Constitutional Law* (Hart Publishing, 2006), p. 501.

utter reluctance[139] but inspired by a not always friendly dialog[140] with the German Federal Constitutional Court, the ECJ accepted and established fundamental rights as a pivotal principle of Union law,[141] a principle which has become one of the defining characteristics of the European law system.[142]

The ECJ roots fundamental rights both in the constitutional traditions of the Member States and international human rights treaties (the European Convention on Human Rights in particular) to which the Member States are parties.[143] Fundamental rights may serve their classical function as ground for a claim against an action by either the Community organs or the Member States.[144] Moreover, as the ECJ has found in recent cases, fundamental rights may serve as a justification for infringing fundamental freedoms or fundamental rights. Thus, the ECJ held in *Schmidberger* that the thirty-hour blockade of a tunnel caused by the inaction of Austrian authorities in clearing the area of protesters, which was acknowledged as an infringement of the fundamental freedom of the movement of goods,[145] was justified due to the protesters' fundamental rights to freedom of speech and freedom of assembly which the Austrian State had to respect.[146] In fact, the ECJ granted Austria a "wide margin of discretion"[147] regarding the level of protection of fundamental freedoms against private conduct that itself constitutes the exercise of a fundamental right. What makes the judgment so remarkable is that the Court acknowledged the State's delicate position, for it had to deal with two

139 See European Court of Justice, Case 11/70, *Internationale Handelsgesellschaft* v. *Einfuhr- und Vorratsstelle Getreide* [1970] ECR 1125; Case 25/70, *Einfuhr- und Vorratsstelle* v. *Köster* [1970] ECR 1161.

140 German Federal Constitutional Court, *Solange-I-Beschluss*, May 29, 1974, BVerfGE 37, 271; German Federal Constitutional Court, *Solange-II-Beschluss*, October 22, 1986, BVerfGE 73, 339.

141 See European Court of Justice, Case 44/79, *Hauer* v. *Rheinland-Pfalz* [1979] ECR 3727 (hereinafter: *Hauer* v. *Rheinland-Pfalz*) and subsequent case law.

142 See Kühling, "Fundamental Rights," 503.

143 See *Hauer* v. *Rheinland-Pfalz*, 3727.

144 It has to be noted, however, that the principle that fundamental rights can directly be made subject of a claim is not equally deeply entrenched in the constitutional tradition of the Member States of the European Union; see, e.g., on France, L. Favoreu, P. Gaïa, R. Ghevontian, J.-L. Mestre, O. Pfersmann, A. Roux and G. Scoffoni, *Droit constitutionnel*, 9th edn. (Dalloz, 2006), pp. 806 ff.

145 See Art. 34 TFEU.

146 European Court of Justice, Case C-112/00, *Schmidberger* v. *Austria* [2003] ECR I-5659 (hereinafter: *Schmidberger* v. *Austria*).

147 *Ibid.*, para. 90.

conflicting obligations[148] – the protection of fundamental freedoms on the one hand and the protection of fundamental rights on the other – and thus provided Austria with the opportunity of invoking fundamental rights as a justification for an infringement of the freedom of movement of goods,[149] the very pillar of the economic freedoms guaranteed under the TFEU.

(v) Conclusion

Looking at the defining features of European law, I have identified a number of important characteristics. The doctrines of supremacy and direct effect of Union law break with the classical concept of public international law and make it possible for non-State actors to interact in a vertical administrative law type relationship with the State on the basis of both domestic and Union law. The "interdigitation" of the two legal orders, in respect of both substantive and procedural law, combined with the doctrines of supremacy and direct effect, have transformed the European law system into a "new legal order," separate and autonomous from public international law. Within this order, legal norms are created by the Union organs and the Member States respectively, or are – in the form of customary Union law or general principles of Union law – identified by the ECJ. In particular, the general principle of fundamental rights has had a pivotal impact on the European law system and has developed a dynamic that has acknowledged those rights not only as protections against State interference but also as justification for State action infringing upon fundamental freedoms that seeks to protect the fundamental rights of other individuals.

(b) International investment law system vs. the European law system: Five comparators

Considering the foregoing analysis of characteristic features of the European law system I will now turn to a comparative approach that seeks to use the juxtaposition of European law vis-à-vis international investment

[148] G. Gonzales, "EC Fundamental Freedoms v. Human Rights in the Case C-112/00 Eugen Schmidberger v. Austria [2003] ECR I-5659," *Legal Issues of Economic Integration*, 31 (2004), 219 at 220 f., 223.

[149] See also European Court of Justice, Case C-36/02, *Omega* v. *Germany* [2004] ECR I-9609, where the ECJ accepted the protection of human dignity as a justification for the German authorities prohibiting a company from operating a game called "laserdrome" that simulates the killing of human beings by shooting them with lasers.

law as a vehicle to a better understanding of the latter.[150] While doing this, I will often view the two systems against the backdrop of general public international law. Discussing both the similarities and differences of European vs. international investment law, I will also address the potential critiques of my approach that may arise considering the differences of the two systems.

In order to analyze potential similarities between the European and the international investment law systems viewed against the backdrop of public international law, I will employ five comparators: (i) the hierarchy of norms; (ii) the participation of non-State actors in the respective systems; (iii) the relationship of the State and non-State actors; (iv) the types of legal norms, including their creation, that play a role in the respective systems; and (v) the institutional and treaty setting in the respective systems.

(i) The hierarchy of norms

Starting with the first comparator, the hierarchy of norms, it may surprise that on first glance there exist striking similarities between all three systems. Just as Union law trumps domestic law in case of conflict so does international law, both in the international investment law system and under general public international law. While the supremacy of Union law is rooted in the case law of the ECJ, proclaiming a "new legal order," it is a general principle of international law as enshrined in Article 27 VCLT that a State may not invoke its domestic law as justification for a violation of international law.[151] The *LG&E* Tribunal, followed by subsequent Tribunals, endorsed this principle as the foundation of its finding that international law is hierarchically superior to domestic law within the realm of international investment law.[152]

So, preliminarily, and one might say naturally, international investment law seems to be closer to general public international law than to European law, since it appears to rely on a classical public international law rationale – Article 27 VCLT – instead of expressly invoking a "new legal order" as a reason for supremacy. Yet, this is only the first impression. The rationale behind the supremacy of international law under general public international law is simply that domestic law does not play a role at all. General public international law treats domestic law as a different universe, a realm that is segregated from international law and thus is

[150] This subsection draws on A. Kulick, "The Integration of International Investment Law" in N. Lavranos *et al.* (eds.), *Hague Yearbook of International Law*, 23 (2010), 171 ff.

[151] See *supra* 2 D. 5. [152] See *supra* 2 D. 5. (b).

not supposed to interfere with it.[153] International investment law, on the other hand, consists of a mélange, an amalgamation of domestic and international law. Both are equally applicable to an investment dispute.[154] This phenomenon, to which I refer as integration of legal orders,[155] resembles much more the "interdigitation" of Union and domestic law under European law than the segregation endorsed by general public international law. Supremacy in both international investment law and European law serves a hierarchical cause to resolve conflicts in an integrated system of law that is nurtured from two different, albeit equally applicable, legal sources.

(ii) The participation of non-State actors

Moreover, and here I come to the second comparator, as under European law, the doctrine of supremacy must be analyzed in conjunction with the way non-State actors participate in the respective systems. According to classical public international law, the only subjects and thus the only actors of international law are States. Therefore, originally, the protection of investments was a matter of the law of aliens and subject to diplomatic protection in a State–State relationship. If an investor wanted to allege a violation of its rights, it had to appeal to its home State to take up the issue on its behalf with the host State. A legal relationship on the international law level existed merely between the investor's home State and its host State; the investor itself was not directly involved in the dispute at all.[156]

In sharp contrast to this, the ICSID Convention and most dispute settlement clauses enshrined in BITs introduce the possibility of investors directly engaging in a dispute with the host State – in fact the ICSID Convention expressly excludes diplomatic protection by the home State as a legal option.[157] As I have demonstrated above, in combination with the vast investor rights enshrined in BITs, viewed together with the notion of integration and hierarchical order among domestic and international

153 I am aware that what I am presenting here is a dualistic view that is not necessarily commonly shared among all scholars. However, even proponents of monism concede that the way the international system is currently structured, State practice at least mostly regards domestic law as irrelevant under the realm of international law. See on the dualism/monism debate and its relevance for the actual practice G. Fitzmaurice, "General Course on Public International Law," *Recueil des Cours*, 92 (1957) II, 68.

154 See *Wena* and the Argentine crisis Tribunals, *supra* 2 D. 4. (a) and 5. (a).

155 See *supra* 2 E. 3.

156 See R. D. Bishop, J. Crawford and W. M. Reisman, *Foreign Investment Disputes* (Kluwer Law International, 2005), p. 3; Shaw, *International Law*, p. 818.

157 See Art. 27 ICSID.

law, such direct interaction between the investor and the host State creates a thriving force that moves international investment law much closer towards a system comparable with the European legal order.

While European law, through the doctrine of direct effect, allows individuals to invoke hierarchically superior Union law together with domestic law vis-à-vis a State in an administrative law type claim before a judicial body, international investment law does virtually the same by permitting investors to initiate a public law type claim before a Tribunal directly against the host State on the basis of both domestic law and international law – the latter being hierarchically superior to the former. Referring to my analysis at (i), the combination of the supremacy of international law with the way investors may participate in international investment law breaks with the classical dualistic dichotomy of the international and the domestic levels, for international law overrides the domestic law that is not regarded as part of a segregated universe but is an integral part of the law applicable.

I am perfectly aware that until this point I carefully avoided mentioning a detail that may easily be employed to challenge this parallel between the European and the international investment law systems: While European law issues can be and are mostly adjudicated before domestic courts, international investment law claims come exclusively before an international Tribunal. Whereas a dispute arising under international investment law is a genuinely international one, as I have acknowledged earlier,[158] a European law dispute is first and foremost a domestic one. This is because direct effect means that Union law becomes the law of the land of the Member States.[159] By contrast, the respective BIT does not enjoy a similar privilege by virtue of the ICSID Convention or the applicable law clauses of such BIT. International law may be supreme, but it does not become the law of the land of the host State – both orders are applied equally to the dispute on the international, not the domestic level. How the host State actually treats the investor through its courts remains untouched within its sovereign realm – it merely has to respond to violations of investors' rights on the international plane.

Be that as it may, this observation cannot change the fact that under both systems, an individual can bring a public law type claim against the exercise of public authority on the basis of a mélange of two equally applicable legal orders that stand in a hierarchical relationship to each other. Moreover, also under European law, the dispute always can – and, if

[158] See *supra* 2 D. 5. (b). [159] See J. H. H. Weiler, "Transformation," 2415.

there is no possibility of an appeal, even has to – be made subject to control by the ECJ by virtue of Article 267 TFEU. Thus, European law also provides for judicial review mechanisms regarding the hierarchically superior of the two applicable legal orders.

It may be true that within the realm of international investment law international law does not become the law of the land of the host State. However, for the present analysis this fact is simply irrelevant. For deciding a dispute, the "law of the land" means no more and no less than the law applicable before the respective judicial body, the *lex fori*. Thus while for Union law becoming the law of the land means becoming the *lex fori* before the domestic courts, Article 42(1) ICSID or similar clauses in BITs define both international and domestic law as the *lex fori* before the investment Tribunals. The only difference exists in perspective: While it is a peculiarity that before a domestic judicial body Union law is applicable to the dispute, it is also a peculiarity that before an international judicial body domestic law is applicable. Moreover, what we are looking at is how the relationship of the State and the individual may influence their rights and obligations vis-à-vis each other under the two systems of European law and international investment law. What is relevant for such an analysis is not the level *on which* but the way *in which* this relationship plays out.

(iii) The relationship of the State and non-State actors

Much has already been said in the foregoing about the relationship of the actors involved, so I can confine myself to a few brief additional comments. Under the classical doctrine of public international law, the relationship of the actors is horizontal and coordinative. Since statehood is a prerequisite for membership in the exclusive club of subjects of public international law, non-State actors play no direct role in the relationship among the legal actors.[160]

By contrast, in both European and international investment law, non-State actors directly interact with the State. They are enabled to introduce direct claims against the exercise of public authority by the State, thus their relationship vis-à-vis the State is of a vertical and regulatory character. Within the realm of international investment law I have described such administrative law type relationship through the lens of Global

[160] Of course, this statement in its entirety and absoluteness only captures the classical view on public international law before 1945 and has been confronted with several challenges and modifications since the end of the Second World War. See on all this Brownlie, *Principles*, pp. 58 ff.

Administrative Law.[161] Investors can seek judicial control of the exercise of public authority that threatens or violates their rights and are provided – given their claim was successful – with a universally enforceable remedy against the host State. Such relationship of the investor and the State resembles much more that of an individual and the State under domestic administrative law than the coordinative and horizontal system of general public international law. Moreover, it is very similar to the European law system, where Union law is integrated in domestic administrative law and procedures. Here as well, the exercise of public authority is subject to judicial control on the basis of a hierarchical system of two integrated legal orders. To sum up, international investment law is considerably distinct from general public international law as regards the relationship of the State and non-State actors. It is, indeed, in that respect much closer to European or even domestic administrative law,[162] for it describes the vertical and regulatory control of public authority by a judicial body.

(iv) The types of legal norms, including their creation, which play a role in the respective systems

As a fourth comparator, I will examine the different types of legal norms that play a role in the respective systems. This will also include a brief look at how those norms are created.

In all three systems – international investment law, European law and general public international law – agreements among States constitute an important pillar of the respective system of norms that are applicable in the respective realm. European Member States alone conclude and amend the EC Treaty, and Member States of ICSID alone may conclude and amend the ICSID Convention; the same is true for BITs or for any treaty in the general public international sphere. In this regard, even the European system endorses the club-like exclusivity that reserves the ability to conclude treaties to States only.

As regards the role of domestic law, the picture looks different. Domestic branches of government, subject to domestic procedures, create domestic law. As Article 27 VCLT and the general principle underlying it make abundantly clear, domestic law is irrelevant within the realm of international law. It ought not to be considered at all. By contrast, under the European legal order, domestic law is the applicable law so long as it does not collide with Union law. A similar pattern is true for international investment law: Article 42(1) ICSID declares both international and

[161] See *supra* 4 A. 1.

[162] With the reservations as outlined at 4 A. 1. (b) (ii).

domestic law applicable and according to the case law discussed above, both are equally applicable to an investment dispute, while the former trumps the latter in case of conflict.

A third category of legal norms is customary law. It is known in all three systems, although it is important to note some differences. Firstly, the customary law in the European legal order is, first and foremost, customary Union law, i.e. created by and applicable to only the Member States of the European Union within the autonomous legal order of European law. Secondly, while customary international law plays an important role in a coordinative system that lacks a comprehensive legal framework such as general public international law, customary Union law as well as customary international law within the realm of international investment law are much less prominent due to a considerable number of positive provisions, both domestic and international/European, that are specifically tailored to govern the respective dispute.

Finally, all three systems draw on general principles of law – again, the European legal order is only concerned with general principles of law within its autonomous system. General principles of European law are extracted from the spirit of the TFEU by way of the ECJ's jurisprudence.[163] General principles of law, relevant both in international investment law[164] and general public international law, constitute one of the sources of public international law as referred to in Article 38(1) of the ICJ Statute, which is generally regarded as an authoritative list of the sources of public international law.[165] Each international Tribunal may identify such principles – however, considering its role in the public international law system, the ICJ has the most authoritative voice in this respect.

So, while all three systems grant a similar role to international agreements and to general principles of law, which both may provide an important source of law for the respective systems, international investment law differs from general public international law as concerns the role of domestic law, which is much closer to the role domestic law plays in the European legal order. As regards customary law, though its role is

[163] See *supra* 4 B. 2. (a) (iv).

[164] Only see Dolzer and Schreuer, *Principles of International Investment Law* (Oxford University Press, 2008), pp. 265 ff.

[165] See M. Koskenniemi (ed.), *Sources of International Law* (Ashgate, 2000), Introduction, p. xi. For a critique of the common understanding of general principles of public international law see M. Koskenniemi, "General Principles: Reflections on Constructivist Thinking in International Law" in M. Koskenniemi (ed.), *Sources of International Law* (Ashgate, 2000), p. 359.

somewhat reduced in international investment law as a matter of fact due to the plethora of express BIT provisions, it is yet accessible as a potential source.

(v) The institutional and treaty setting in the respective systems

Turning to the last comparator, the institutional and treaty setting, this might constitute the occasion on which one might become skeptical as to whether a comparative approach vis-à-vis the European law system proves fruitful overall. True, the institutional setting the European system provides as well as its treaty framework are inherently different from both international investment law and public international law.[166] This comparator, the skeptic might well argue, is the utter proof that international investment law is much closer to general public international law and that, in fact, a differentiation between the two is futile, i.e. that international investment law, despite some peculiarities, is public international law.

Where ICSID is a loose accumulation of States, linked only by a very limited treaty that establishes merely a Secretariat that is not provided with any considerable authority,[167] the European system creates a close economic and political union with a myriad of different organs that are given broad competences, including law-making.[168] While the TEU and TFEU are multi-topic multilateral agreements, the international investment law system consists of bilateral treaties on one singular topic, i.e. investment – the multilateral ICSID Convention is not comparable to the TFEU or TEU in that respect given that it contains no substantive provisions and deals merely with jurisdictional and procedural matters.

Moreover, and even more importantly, the special institutional and treaty framework of the European legal order seems to be a fundamental rationale that led the ECJ to endorse and advance European Exceptionalism, beginning with *Van Gend & Loos* and *Costa/ENEL*. The notion of the "new legal order" leading to direct effect and supremacy of Union law basically rests on the specific setting of the TFEU/TEU and the institutions they create:

166 See on the specifics of the European institutional order and its distinct Constitutional traits D. Thym, "'United in Diversity' – The Integration of Enhanced Cooperation into the European Constitutional Order," *German L. J.*, 6 (2005), 1731 at 1742 ff.

167 See Dugan, Wallace, Rubins and Sabahi, *Investor-State Arbitration*, pp. 50 f.

168 See R. H. Lauwaars, "Institutional Structure" in P. J. G. Kapeteyn, A. M. McDonnell, K. J. M. Mortelmans and C. W. A. Timmermans, *The Law of the European Union and the European Communities*, 4th (rev.) edn. (Kluwer Law International, 2008), pp. 175 ff.; K. P. E. Lasok, *Law & Institutions of the European Union*, 7th edn. (Butterworths, 2001), pp. 207 ff.

> By creating a Community of unlimited duration, having its own institutions, its own personality, its own legal capacity and capacity of representation on the international plane and, more particularly, real powers stemming from a limitation of sovereignty or a transfer of powers from the States to the Community, the Member States have limited their sovereign rights, albeit within limited fields, and have thus created a body of law which binds both their nationals and themselves.[169]

> The objective of the EEC Treaty, which is to establish a Common Market, the functioning of which is of direct concern to interested parties in the Community, implies that this Treaty is more than an agreement which merely creates mutual obligations between the contracting states.[170]

So, given these considerations, is it appropriate to draw parallels between European law and international investment law that go beyond mere odd, coincidental resemblance? I concede that international investment law lacks either a considerable institutional or a multilateral treaty framework. However, if we look at the issues separately, it is surprising, to start with the treaty setting, that although the MAI project failed spectacularly in 1998,[171] it is an undisputable fact that most BITs are strikingly similar.[172] They contain a large number of investor rights (national treatment and most favored nation clauses, provisions on fair and equitable treatment, prompt, adequate and effective compensation and performance requirements as well as an umbrella clause),[173] a dispute settlement clause and no (or almost no) defenses for the host State. Thus, though there might still exist differences that have to be acknowledged, it seems fair to say and reflects actual practice[174] that Tribunals refer to former decisions by different Tribunals on different BITs as if they dealt with the same legal framework. This is, I contend, simply because BITs are in fact basically the same.[175]

As regards the lack of institutional setting in international investment law that allegedly drove the rationale behind *Van Gend & Loos* and *Costa/ENEL*, two arguments stand against the notion that such differences shun from drawing a comparison. Firstly, the mere fact that the rationale relies on different pillars does not automatically mean that the result

[169] *Costa/ENEL*, 593. [170] *Van Gend & Loos*, 12.

[171] See Trebilcock and Howse, *Regulation of International Trade*, p. 458.

[172] See *supra* 2 A. 2.; Lowenfeld, "Investment Agreements"; Schill, *Multilateralization*, pp. 362 ff.

[173] See Dolzer and Schreuer, *Principles*, p. 164.

[174] See P. M. Norton, "A Law of the Future or a Law of the Past? Modern Tribunals and the International Law of Expropriation," *AJIL*, 85 (1991), 474 at 497 ff.

[175] See also Stephan Schill's argument that the investment régime is de facto turning into a multilateral system: Schill, *Multilateralization*, pp. 365 ff.

cannot be very similar nonetheless. While the investment system lacks institutions comparable to those of the Union, this does not change the fact that both orders share all the similarities I pointed at under the first four comparators. The only consequence entailing the different institutional setting is that conclusions from such comparative approach must be drawn with care and sensibility vis-à-vis the underlying rationales. Secondly, the ECJ, in *Van Gend & Loos*, *Costa/ENEL* and many subsequent decisions, relies on a teleological argument, i.e. the promotion of effectiveness of the EC Treaty provisions, the so-called "*effet utile*."[176] Such reasoning, however, is not unknown to investment case law, either. In *Santa Elena* the Tribunal argued, as I described above, that the purpose of the ICSID Convention, i.e. to serve the protection of property, requires the supremacy of international law over domestic law.[177] Just as the establishment of a Common Market is employed as a rationale in *Van Gend & Loos*, the *Santa Elena* award emphasizes the protection of property as the underlying *telos*.

Hence, it becomes apparent that the institutional setting is of rather minor importance when comparing international investment law with the European legal order. Indeed, firstly systems may share major communalities albeit their origins differ; and secondly the institutional framework is of little relevance if it is the functioning and interaction of the applicable law itself that is the main focus of the comparative analysis. Consequently, the differences as outlined in this last subsection do not compromise the comparative thrust this section has invigorated.

3. *The European Convention on Human Rights system*

The second system I turn to for comparative insights is the European Convention on Human Rights (ECHR).[178] Comparison between investor rights and human rights is not at all far-fetched given their past common roots in the law on the treatment of aliens and their current common feature as individual rights positions of non-State actors against a State on the public international law plane.[179] In fact, many investment Tribunals cite

176 Kapeteyn, McDonnell, Mortelmans and Timmermans, *Law of the European Union*, p. 77.

177 See *Santa Elena*, para. 44.

178 Convention for the Protection of Human Rights and Fundamental Freedoms, concluded November 4, 1950, entered into force September 3, 1953, available at http://conventions.coe.int/Treaty/Commun/QueVoulezVous.asp?NT=005&CL=ENG.

179 See on this issue J. E. Alvarez, "Critical Theory and the North American Free Trade Agreement's Chapter Eleven," *U. Miami Inter-Am. L. Rev.*, 28 (1996–97), 303 at 308 ff., who stresses the similarities and calls "the NAFTA investment chapter . . . a human rights

ECtHR jurisprudence, particularly regarding issues of expropriation.[180] As Thomas Wälde pointed out in his separate opinion in *International Thunderbird Gaming Corp.* v. *United Mexican States*, the ECtHR exhibits "[t]he judicial practice most comparable to treaty-based investor-state arbitration."[181] Given such considerations, a comparative study of several features of the ECHR system and international investment law promises to grant some instructive insights into the nature and functioning of the latter that may be made use of in the analysis afterwards. Similarly to section 2. above, I will employ five comparators ((a) to (e)) in order to flesh out distinct characteristics international investment law shares with the ECHR system and where it even goes beyond it. However, presupposing general familiarity with the overall concept and structure of human rights, I forbear from giving an introduction here as I did in the preceding section comparing international investment law with the European law system.

(a) Institutional and treaty setting

I will start this comparative analysis with the last comparator I used vis-à-vis the European law system and international investment law, which is, as in the former case, the most divisive. The most common ground – although even here there are considerable differences – is to be found in the importance the treaties ascribe to the judicial body as compared to the role of the other institutions established by the Convention: Both under the ICSID Convention and the ECHR, the main role is to be played by the Tribunal or the ECtHR. Different to, say, the UN Charter where the ICJ as the judicial organ of the United Nations plays one role in the concert of several primary organs,[182] under both the ICSID Convention and the ECHR

treaty for a special-interest group." See also P.-M. Dupuy, "Unification Rather than Fragmentation of International Law? The Case of International Investment Law and Human Rights Law" in P.-M. Dupuy, F. Francioni and E.-U. Petersmann (eds.), *Human Rights in International Investment Law and Arbitration* (Oxford University Press, 2009), p. 45 at p. 46 citing the UNCITRAL arbitration *Biloune* v. *Ghana* in which the Ghanaian authorities had arrested a Syrian investor, held him without charge and eventually deported him from Ghana to Togo (*Biloune and Marine Drive Complex Ltd* v. *Ghana Investments Centre and the Government of Ghana*, UNCITRAL, Award on Jurisdiction and Liability, October 27, 1989, *ILR*, 184).

180 See J. D. Fry, "International Human Rights Law in Investment Arbitration: Evidence of International Law's Unity," *Duke J. Int'l & Comp. L.*, 18 (2007), 77 at 83 ff.

181 *Int'l Thunderbird Gaming Corp.* v. *United Mexican States* (*US* v. *Mex.*), 2006 WL 247692, para. 141 (NAFTA Ch. 11 Arb. Trib. 2006) (separate opinion of Thomas W. Wälde).

182 See J. Crawford and T. Grant, "International Court of Justice" in T. G. Weiss and S. Daws (eds.), *The Oxford Handbook on the United Nations* (Oxford University Press, 2007), p. 193 at pp. 202 ff.

the other treaty bodies are allocated a mere auxiliary and supporting role vis-à-vis the chief purpose of the respective treaty, that being the adjudication of individual rights against a State. However, it must not be forgotten that whereas under ICSID the role of the Secretariat and the Administrative Council is a very limited one, i.e. basically administrative, the Council of Europe, the Committee of Ministers (even after the entry into force of Protocol No. 11[183]) and the Secretary General each hold a much more prominent position under the ECHR, including, among others, considerable supervisory functions as to the Member States' implementation of the provisions of the Convention[184] or the Court's judgments.[185,186]

Already displaying certain differences, this is basically where similarities end between the ICSID Convention and the ECHR regarding the institutional and treaty setting. The ECHR is a multilateral treaty enshrining both procedural and substantive matters with a limited, i.e. regional, scope of membership, creating a permanent judicial body. By contrast, the ICSID Convention, open for universal membership, only sets a procedural framework without delineating substantive provisions – which in the vast majority of instances are enshrined in bilateral treaties to be concluded separately between each and every Member State – providing only for ad hoc Tribunals to be set up for every dispute. In other words, multilateralism for a regional avant-garde and a permanent body on the one hand, and a mixed multilateral/bilateral framework that is challenged to comfort a plethora of different attitudes towards the stated purpose of the Convention and the discontinuity and thus potential incoherence of the adjudication system on the other. It does not need much analysis to conclude that those said differences are considerable. However, the fact that they exist does not necessarily mean that they are relevant for the analysis at hand and prohibit drawing conclusions from a comparison of

[183] Which marked a complete revision of the ECHR's supervisory system, abolishing the Committee of Ministers' competence to hear individual cases and creating a permanent Court taking the place of the European Commission of Human Rights and the old Court; see Protocol No. 11 to the Convention for the Protection of Human Rights and Fundamental Freedoms, restructuring the control machinery established thereby, Strasbourg, May 11, 1994, entered into force November 1, 1998, available at http://conventions.coe.int/treaty/EN/Treaties/html/155.htm.

[184] Art. 52 ECHR. [185] Art. 46(2) ECHR.

[186] On these supervisory functions see L. Zwaak, "Chapter 1 – General Survey of the European Convention" in P. van Dijk, F. van Hoof, A. van Rijn and L. Zwaak (eds.), *Theory and Practice of the European Convention on Human Rights*, 4th edn. (Intersentia, 2006), p. 1 at pp. 44 ff.; L. Zwaak, "Chapter 3 – Supervisory Task of the Committee of Ministers" in P. van Dijk *et al.*, *ibid.*, p. 291; J. Schokkenbroek, "Chapter 4 – The Supervisory Function of the Secretary General of the Council of Europe" in P. van Dijk *et al.*, *ibid.*, p. 323.

the two systems that may inform our view on international investment law.[187]

(b) Hierarchy of norms

As for the second comparator, vis-à-vis the hierarchy of norms in the respective systems, at first glance the differences appear to dominate here as well. Whereas international investment law, as I described in Chapter 2, sets up an integrated system, a mélange of domestic and international law equally applicable but granting the latter supremacy in case of conflict, in the ECHR realm in the strict sense no such issue arises.[188] Admittedly, the ECtHR has to consider domestic law as well. However, domestic law is not the *lex fori*, i.e. it is not applicable as such with the individuals being entitled to claim its violation independently from a violation of the ECHR. The Court may only consider domestic law as a possible justification of a Convention right infringement according to the limitations clauses enshrined in several provisions of the ECHR.[189] Put differently, while international investment law – in absence of any alternative agreement (see Article 42(1) first sentence ICSID) – permits investor claims exclusively on the basis of a violation of domestic law, even if such violation does not result in a violation of a BIT provision, under the ECHR system domestic law only plays a role by way of detour through the limitations clause of the Convention, i.e. if it fulfills the requirements of the clause. Hence, the judge scrutinizing domestic law as to its capacity to meet the conditions as delineated in the limitations clause does not apply domestic law as such; rather, he or she applies the provisions of the Convention, finding whether domestic law corroborates the assertion of the State made vis-à-vis the limitation of the right allegedly violated.

Thus, the classical public international law pattern[190] of a dichotomy of domestic and international law applies in the ECHR context: On the international plane, in the separate realm of public international law, international law is "supreme" over domestic law in that it trumps the latter in case the State seeks to assert its domestic law as a justification for infringing an international law norm. Again, this differs from a case

[187] Particularly considering the multilateralization argument promoted by Schill, *Multilateralization*, pp. 365 ff.

[188] See *supra* 2 E. 2.

[189] See R. Bernhardt, "The Convention and Domestic Law" in R. St. J. Macdonald, F. Matscher and H. Petzold (eds.), *The European System for the Protection of Human Rights* (Martinus Nijhoff Publishers, 1993), p. 25 at pp. 30 ff.

[190] See *supra* 4 B. 2. (b) (i).

in which the State contends that the domestic law under scrutiny does not violate the Convention, for it meets the conditions of the limitations clause of the right allegedly violated. Such latter assertion is licit because international law, i.e. the limitations clauses enshrined in the Convention, allows for it, and not because domestic law – without an international law pedigree ordering recourse to it – is per se a valid justification. As the customary rule enshrined in Article 27 VCLT underlines,[191] a State may not seek justification of an international law violation by asserting domestic law. Consequently under the ECHR system, international law (i.e. the Convention provisions) is not hierarchically superior to domestic law in the strict sense, for no hierarchy actually exists: Domestic law, by itself, is not applicable, only in the sense as explained above, which is, again, by way of the Convention.

However, while in theory this appears to be a considerable difference, we should recall that a main argument of the Argentine Tribunals to corroborate the absolute supremacy of international over domestic law in international investment law was exactly the reference to Article 27 VCLT. While, admittedly, and as I have pointed out in the relevant section above,[192] the recourse to this provision was peculiar, if not ill advised from a doctrinal viewpoint, it nonetheless demonstrates the interconnectedness of the issues. Moreover, from a finalistic rather than a doctrinal vantage point, the result is very similar in both systems: Under international investment law as well as under the ECHR system, international law trumps domestic law in case of conflict.[193]

(c) Constitutional traits

The last-mentioned characteristic of the two systems is a fundamental aspect of the third comparator I employ here vis-à-vis international investment law and the ECHR realm. As has been elaborated earlier,[194] the effect of individual rights as "trump cards" guaranteeing a minimum standard of protection against State conduct displays constitutional traits of either of the two systems.[195] Both the ECHR and BITs lay out a core of fundamental rights on the international plane setting a floor of minimum

191 See *supra* 2 D. 5. 192 See *supra* 2 E. 2.

193 In the case of the ECHR, again, justification through domestic law fulfilling the requirements of the limitations clause does not mean justification by domestic law per se, but through a provision inherent in the Convention itself, referring to domestic law.

194 Albeit only regarding international investment law; see *supra* 4 A. 2.

195 On this issue see E.-U. Petersmann, "Constitutional Theories of International Economic Adjudication and Investor-State Arbitration" in P.-M. Dupuy, F. Francioni and E.-U. Petersmann (eds.), *Human Rights in International Investment Law and Arbitration* (Oxford

treatment of individuals in their relationship to the State. As regards this last-mentioned relationship of the individual to the State and thus – viewed procedurally – between the two parties to a dispute, both systems assume a regulatory rather than a coordinative relationship. Different to the classical public international law paradigm of coordinative relationship among legal peers, both in international investment law and under the ECHR system, a non-State actor is confronted with a sovereign State and is bestowed with the right to refer the dispute to an international judicial body that is called upon to adjudicate the exercise of public authority vis-à-vis internationalized individual rights. Moreover, both the ECtHR and ICSID Tribunals are competent to deliver final decisions on this issue: There is no appeal possible, neither on the international nor on the domestic level, against a (Grand Chamber) decision of the ECtHR, nor is there an appeal mechanism[196] nor judicial oversight by domestic courts within the investment realm.[197]

Another aspect of human rights/investor rights being trump cards vis-à-vis the domestic law provisions and thus adding to their constitutional trait is their transformatory and harmonizing effect on the domestic law of the (host) State. A State that wants to honor its commitments in the ECHR and in its BITs – due to political, normative or simply pragmatic reasons (given the high amount of many ICSID awards) – will inevitably bring its laws into conformity with the rules enshrined in the "constitutional" treaty, for any failure to do so will result in high costs – political, ethical or financial – it makes no sense to pay if it is the State's intention to remain party to such treaty. Admittedly, viewed separately, this aspect is not very spectacular, for any treaty has such effect if it provides for effective sanctions. However, the particularly high costs of coming short of the treaty provisions – mostly ethical and political in the case of the ECHR and mostly financial in the case of ICSID/BITs – in conjunction with the aforementioned make a strong case for the similar constitutional

University Press, 2009), p. 137; E.-U. Petersmann, "Introduction and Summary: 'Administration of Justice' in International Law and Adjudication?" in P.-M. Dupuy *et al.* (eds.), *ibid.*, p. 3 at pp. 27 ff.; L. Wildhaber, "A Constitutional Future for the European Court of Human Rights," *Hum. Rts. L. J.*, 23 (2002), 161.

196 The annulment procedure, Art. 52 ICSID, is not to be confused with an appeal mechanism, which is a substantially different instrument of review; see *supra* 2 C. 1.

197 Which is typically the case in international commercial arbitration, where domestic courts retain limited competency to review an award. For a collection of materials on the issue see J.-F. Poudret and S. Besson, *Comparative Law of International Arbitration*, 2nd edn. (Sweet & Maxwell, 2007), pp. 478 ff.; H. Smit and V. Pechota, *International Commercial Arbitration and the Courts*, 4th edn. (Juris Publishing, 2004), A1.

character of international investment law and the ECHR system. While the degree of the harmonizing effect may be higher in the case of the ECHR system due to the ECtHR being a permanent body and the ECHR being a multilateral treaty, the functional characteristics of such effect as a constitutionalizing device are no different in international investment law.

(d) Degree of "internationalization"

Linked to the constitutional aspects (see section (e) below), the fourth comparator pertains to the degree of "internationalization" of the respective systems. By "internationalized" I mean in this context the level to which the adjudicatory mechanisms – the core of both ICSID and the ECHR – are detached from domestic law and decision-making processes. While both clearly establish an international adjudicatory system, the first impression might well be that the degree of "internationalization" is higher in the ECHR realm, for in contrast to international investment law it does not grant domestic law the role as the *lex fori* but allows its applicability merely by way of international law.[198] However, this is quite a limited perspective and neglects another aspect relevant in this regard: Different to the ECHR system, where a claimant needs to go through the domestic court system before he or she is allowed to knock at the doors of the ECtHR,[199] international investment law does not require exhaustion of local remedies[200] but usually permits submission of the dispute directly at the international level.[201]

Such more far-reaching detachment from the domestic sphere of the international investment vis-à-vis the ECHR realm inheres two aspects, both having an effect on the constitutional traits of the respective systems linked to the domestic constitutional architecture. If an investor under ICSID does not have to refer the dispute to the domestic courts but may directly present its claim to an international Tribunal, the effect is twofold: Firstly, it means more autonomy of the international Tribunal and thus a high level of protection guaranteed in the first place, independent from the sphere of influence of the host State. Secondly, it means that such possibility of direct referral to an international Tribunal that

[198] See *supra* 4 B. 3. (b). [199] See Art. 35(1) ECHR. [200] See Art. 26 ICSID.

[201] See U. Kriebaum, "Is the European Court of Human Rights an Alternative to Investor-State Arbitration?" in P.-M. Dupuy *et al.* (eds.), *supra* n. 195, p. 219 at pp. 228 ff.; C. Tomuschat, "The European Court of Human Rights and Investment Protection" in C. Binder *et al.* (eds.), *International Investment Law for the 21st Century – Essays in Honour of Christoph Schreuer* (Oxford University Press, 2009), p. 636 at pp. 641 f.

is competent to award high amounts of compensation places a lot of pressure on the domestic executive and particularly the legislature to bring administrative practice and legislation into conformity with the obligations signed onto in BITs.

By contrast, within the ECHR system that does not allow for the applicability of domestic law per se but requires the exhaustion of local remedies, the pressure is not only on the domestic executive and on the legislature, but on all instances of the third branch of government as well. Although formally it is no appeal to domestic (even Supreme or Constitutional) court decisions, in fact this is exactly what is the perception both of the public and increasingly of domestic judges.[202] Strasbourg is often regarded as the last instance to be addressed when domestic courts fail to grant the claimant what it seeks.[203] The term "instance" demonstrates the current practice and public perception that the ECtHR attains the final word in protection of fundamental individual rights cases after a long march through the courts, i.e. it replaces the Supreme Court/ Constitutional Court/Court of Cassation, etc. in this regard. Moreover, the fact that every Member State has transformed the Convention into domestic law and thus that every individual may generally request compliance with the Convention before the domestic courts, supports the aforesaid.

Consequently, the requirement to exhaust local remedies in combination with a strong Court and a high level of compliance with its judgments entails a higher embedment in a constitutional system shaped by the rights enshrined in the ECHR and by their interpretation by the Court. As I have explained above, international investment law compensates such lack of "constitutional judicial review" by integrating domestic and international law and defining a clear-cut hierarchy in this mélange.[204]

(e) Participation of non-State actors

Eventually and very briefly, I turn to the fifith and final comparator, the participation of non-State actors in the respective adjudicatory systems.

[202] Although the *Görgülü* case exhibits the limits of that perception, see European Court of Human Rights, *Görgülü* v. *Germany*, App. No. 74969/01, Final Judgment of May 26, 2004 and M. Hartwig, "Much Ado About Human Rights: The Federal Constitutional Court Confronts the European Court of Human Rights," *German Law Journal*, 5 (May 1, 2005), available at www.germanlawjournal.com/index.php?pageID=11&artID=601.

[203] The recent decisions against Germany overruling judgments of the Federal Constitutional Court bear good witness in this regard. Only see European Court of Human Rights, *M.* v. *Germany* (App. No. 19359/04), Judgment of December 17, 2009 on the (unjustified) retroactive extension of a prisoner's preventive detention.

[204] See *supra* 4 B. 2. (b) (ii), (iii).

Both the ECHR and ICSID grant non-State actors access to international Tribunals in order to submit the exercise of public authority by the (host) State to judicial review on the international plane. Different to the European law system, the ECHR system and international investment law in their core are international review mechanisms.[205] Direct effect and thus the possibility for an individual to claim violations of an international treaty directly on the basis of that treaty before a domestic court is absent in both the ECHR and the ICSID systems.

However, the way in which non-State actors participate in the adjudication of the rights enshrined in the respective document is not so different at all in the three systems mentioned. While under the ECHR – different to the European law system – the treaty itself does not become the law of the land by way of direct effect,[206] the Convention provisions have been transformed into domestic law. Whereas the exact status of the Convention in the constitutional architecture of the Member States differs, for it is for each Member State to decide individually how to integrate the ECHR provisions into its domestic legal framework, in each and every Member State the Convention – i.e. its content – has become the law of the land. This fact contributes to the harmonization of domestic law I have referred to earlier as a constitutional trait of the ECHR system.[207] Any individual may claim violation of the transformed ECHR provisions within the domestic system of a Member State while traversing the instances in order to exhaust local remedies. Before the Court he or she can claim rights violations on the basis of the Convention itself – but with the very same content as the transformed provisions relied on before domestic courts. Hence, the classical public international law face the ECHR appears to display – the dichotomy of the domestic and the international; an international treaty merely applicable on the international stage – at second glance mostly vanishes and exhibits features not that different in effect from the European legal system, at least vis-à-vis the particpation of non-State actors.

The same holds true for international investment law. Having already elaborated its similarities with the European legal system in this regard, I contend its similarity with the ECHR system as well. While its integration of domestic and international law displays a resemblance with the European law system, its exclusively international adjudicatory system and its indirect harmonizing effect by putting pressure on the executive and legislature to conform administrative practice and legislation to the

[205] See *supra* 4 B. 2. (b) (ii). [206] *Ibid.* [207] See *supra* 4 B. 2. (b) (iii).

BIT provisions, are features it shares with the ECHR system. Therefore, to conclude, since the ECHR system's lack of legal integration on the one hand is somewhat compensated on the other by creating a permanent judicial body and by a multilateral treaty thus fostering the harmonizing and hence constitutionalizing effect on the domestic law of the Member States, in my view the similarities of international investment law and the ECHR system – also viewed against the backdrop of the European legal system and public international law – are considerable.

C. The Global Public Interest theory

After such systemic analysis at A. and instructive comparative insights into characteristic features of European law, the ECHR and international investment law respectively at B., now the stage is set for building what I will later refer to as the Global Public Interest theory. The essence of these two preceding sections will both inspire and corroborate my approach. Before making profit from the lessons learned, however, I shall delve into a thorough analysis of two areas exemplifying how investment Tribunals currently handle public interest issues within the realm of international investment law.

1. Two examples of public interest considerations in international investment case law

Although investment Tribunals' reasoning currently comes short of presenting a coherent theoretical foundation, public interest considerations permeate a considerable number of ICSID and other investment awards. Two of these considerations, encapsulated in the general principle of international public policy (a) and the customary international law rule of the state of necessity (b), will serve to exemplify that investment Tribunals incrementally tend to consider public interest issues as possible defenses against investor rights infringements.

(a) International public policy: *Inceysa* and *Fraport*

The first example from international investment case law that supports such logic, i.e. *in concreto* to apply general international law principles that play out as de facto defenses against investor rights infringements,[208]

[208] Of course, the awards made no explicit reference at all to such considerations.

represent the recent *Inceysa*[209] and *Fraport*[210] awards. To start with *Inceysa*, the dispute involved a service contract for installation, management and operation of mechanical inspection stations for vehicles between the Ministry of the Environment and Natural Resources of the Republic of El Salvador and Inceysa Vallisoletana, SL, a Spanish company.[211] While Inceysa asserted that El Salvador de facto terminated the contract in an unjustifiable manner, leading to an indirect expropriation, the host government countered that Inceysa, during the procurement procedure, had illicitly influenced the outcome of the tender by a multitude of fraudulent acts, among them making false financial statements, submitting forged documents and misrepresenting its actual level of experience in the field of vehicle inspections.[212] Thus, El Salvador challenged the Tribunal's jurisdiction on the ground of Article 25 ICSID and Articles I and XI of the Spain–El Salvador BIT, contending that its scope of consent to ICSID arbitration was limited to investments made in accordance with its laws. In its view, Inceysa's investment, subject to fraudulent behavior, was not supposed to qualify in this respect. The definition of "investment" in Article I of the Spain–El Salvador BIT comprises only such investments made in accordance with the law of the host State. Article XI of the same BIT submits any dispute arising within the realm of the BIT, i.e. subject to the definition of Article I, to ICSID arbitration, among others.[213] Article 25 ICSID reads in pertinent part:

> (1) The jurisdiction of the Centre shall extend to any legal dispute arising directly out of an investment, between a Contracting State (or any constituent subdivision or agency of a Contracting State designated to the Centre by that State) and a national of another Contracting State, which the parties to the dispute consent in writing to submit to the Centre. When the parties have given their consent, no party may withdraw its consent unilaterally.

Interpreting Article 25 ICSID in conjunction with Articles I and XI of the BIT, the Tribunal harked back to several general principles of law in order to take account of Inceysa's fraudulent behavior. Basing its reasoning mainly on the principle of good faith and on the principle that nobody should benefit from fraud – *Nemo Auditur Propriam Turpitudinem*

[209] *Inceysa Vallisoletana, SL* v. *Republic of El Salvador* (ICSID Case No. ARB/03/26), Award, August 2, 2006 (hereinafter: *Inceysa* v. *El Salvador*).

[210] *Fraport AG Frankfurt Airport Services Worldwide* v. *Republic of the Philippines* (ICSID Case No. ARB/03/25), Award, August 16, 2007 (hereinafter: *Fraport* v. *Philippines*).

[211] For a detailed description of facts and issues involved in the *Inceysa* award see *infra* 8 C. 2. (c).

[212] *Inceysa* v. *El Salvador*, paras. 37, 53.

[213] *Ibid*., paras. 133, 163.

Allegans – the Tribunal argued that Inceysa could not expect the BIT to include such investments undertaken by fraud and therefore the Tribunal had no jurisdiction over the matter.[214] In other words, the *Inceysa* award acknowledged that an investor's rights depend to some extent on the legality of its own conduct.[215] To put it another way, by excluding investments acquired by fraudulent conduct, the award indirectly creates the obligation for an investor not to engage in fraud when making the investment. Arguably, the *Inceysa* Tribunal thus recognized general principles of law as a vehicle to make an investor accountable for conduct not tolerated under general public international law.

Moreover, in the *Fraport* case, dealing with an issue similar to the one in *Inceysa*, the Tribunal acknowledged the existence of investor obligations and introduced the notion of an element of reciprocity as enshrined in BITs. In the words of the Tribunal:

> [a]s for policy, BITs oblige governments to conduct their relations with foreign investors in a transparent fashion. *Some reciprocal if not identical obligations* lie on the foreign investor. *One of those* is the obligation to make the investment in accordance with the host State's law.[216]

While the *Fraport* Tribunal came short of discussing the principle of good faith as an international law principle, the passage quoted above marks the first case in which an ICSID Tribunal expressly referred to investor obligations emerging from the legal framework provided by international investment law, i.e. the combination of ICSID and the respective BIT. Remarkably, it describes such investor obligations as "*reciprocal if not identical*" to the obligations of the host State, which seems to consider a notion of equivalence, at least in their normative content. Whereas the Tribunal expressly referred to issues of transparency, it left it somewhat in the obscure whether it regarded the reciprocal or identical investor obligations as limited to that field or open to issues other than transparency concerns. The phrase "*one of those*," however, hints at the latter consideration.

[214] *Ibid.*, paras. 230 ff.

[215] Arguably, the same notion can be extracted from the majority opinion in *Fraport* v. *Philippines*; see particularly paras. 334 ff. However, though dealing with a very similar issue, the majority's reasoning in *Fraport* relied exclusively on domestic law and thus considered the principle of good faith on the domestic level instead of employing it as a means of interpretation vis-à-vis the ICSID and BIT provisions relating to jurisdiction. Cremades' dissenting opinion in *Fraport* criticizes such shortcoming. See also *infra* 8 C. 2. (d).

[216] *Fraport* v. *Philippines*, para. 402 (emphasis added).

In both *Inceysa* and *Fraport*, the Tribunals eventually hinged on general principles of law pertaining to or dealing with what they referred to as "international public policy," in order to thwart otherwise licit rights infringements claimed by the investors.[217] *Inceysa* even explicitly relied on "international public policy" that it regarded and treated as an independent principle of international law.[218] Admittedly, as will be elaborated *in extenso* in the chapter dealing with the case study on corruption and other irregularities,[219] doctrinally the Tribunals did not place this debate at the merits stage following a thorough analysis and thorough assessment of investor rights infringements but rather declined jurisdiction in the first place.[220] In spite of such differing doctrinal location, the rulings in *Fraport* and *Inceysa* are nevertheless remarkable for stressing investors' responsibility and accountability inhering a "reciprocal" nature vis-à-vis the obligations the host State owes to investors within the investment realm.

(b) The state of necessity: the Argentine crisis awards

As a second example of public interest considerations gaining ground in international investment arbitration, the case law revolving around the 2001/02 Argentine financial crisis – which has already played a prominent role in the dramaturgy of this book[221] – is a very interesting object of study. Much has been written about both the crisis itself and the ICSID Tribunals' decisions that seem to have left scholars and practitioners alike helpless and restless given their differing, if not contradictory, findings and reasonings appearing to thwart any glimmer of hope for consistency in ICSID jurisprudence.[222] After a brief summary of the crisis

217 *Ibid.*, para. 364. 218 *Inceysa* v. *El Salvador*, para. 245. 219 See *infra* 8 D.

220 *Inceysa* v. *El Salvador*, para. 278; *Fraport* v. *Philippines*, para. 413.

221 See *supra* 2 D. 5.

222 The following is only a small selection of the tremendous amount of literature this crisis has produced: J. E. Alvarez and K. Khamsi, "The Argentine Crisis and Foreign Investors – A Glimpse into the Heart of the Investment Regime" in K. P. Sauvant (ed.), *Yearbook on International Investment Law & Policy 2008–2009* (Oxford University Press, 2009), p. 379; A. Bjorklund, "Economic Security Defenses in International Investment Law" in K. P. Sauvant (ed.), *ibid.*, p. 479; W. Burke-White, "The Argentine Financial Crisis: State Liabilty under BITs and the Legitimacy of the ICSID System," *Asian J. WTO & Int'l Health L and Pol'y*, 3 (2008), 199; W. Burke-White and A. von Staden, "Private Litigation in a Public Law Sphere: The Standard of Review in Investor-State Arbitration," *University of Pennsylvania Law School, Public Law and Legal Theory Research Paper Series, Research Paper* No. #09–23; C. Leben, "L'état de necessité dans le droit international de l'investissment," *Gazette du palais – cahier de l'arbitrage* (2005), 32; G. Mayeda, "International Investment Agreements Between Developed and Developing Countries: Dancing with the Devil?

and the background facts of the decisions (i), I will juxtapose the eight decisions[223] – seven awards and one annulment decision – having been issued on the matter at the time of writing and will reveal where they differ as well as where there are surprising similarities to be found (ii) which may show the path to some interesting conclusions (iii).

(i) Summary of the crisis and the background facts

The events leading to the crisis as well as the facts underlying the disputes were as follows:[224] Initiated by its 1989 State Reform Law, Argentina privatized several utilities as a move to overcome a previous economic crisis in the late 1980s. Among those were Argentina's gas transportation and distribution as well as electricity services monopolies. The Gas Law and Electricity Law of 1992 established the legal framework for this privatization, creating the industry regulators Ente Nacional Regulador del Gas (ENARGAS) and Ente Nacional Regulador de Electricidad (ENRE) respectively. All claimants but one[225] acquired shares in the privatized entities.

Regarding the relevant regulatory framework, the 1991 Convertibility Law provided for the convertibility of the Argentine currency (the peso),

Case Comment on the Vivendi, Sempra and Enron Awards," *JSDLP*, 4 (2008), 189; A. Reinisch, "Necessity in International Investment Arbitration – An Unnecessary Split of Opinions in Recent ICSID Cases? – Comments on CMS v. Argentina and LG&E v. Argentina," *J. World Invtm't & Trade*, 8 (2007), 191; S. W. Schill, "International Investment Law and the Host State's Power to Handle Economic Crises – Comment on the ICSID Decision in LG&E v. Argentina," *J. Int'l Arb.*, 24 (2007), 265; M. Waibel, "Two Worlds of Necessity in ICSID Arbitration: CMS and LG&E," *Leiden J. Int'l L.*, 20 (2007), 637.

223 I will not include *Metalpar SA and Buen Aire SA* v. *The Argentine Republic* (ICSID Case No. ARB/03/5), Award, June 6, 2006 (hereinafter: *Metalpar* v. *Argentina*) in my discussion of the case law on necessity. Although Argentina also raised the necessity defense in this dispute, different to all the other decisions I will analyze subsequently, the Tribunal did not find that the measures undertaken by Argentina in reaction to the crisis negatively affected the claimants' investments and thus did not regard it necessary to discuss the viability of the necessity defense in this case; *Metalpar* v. *Argentina*, paras. 211, 233.

224 For an overview of the facts and the unfolding of the crisis, also consult *BG Group PLC* v. *Argentine Republic*, UNCITRAL, Final Award, December 24, 2007 (hereinafter: *BG* v. *Argentina*), paras. 16–82; *CMS* v. *Argentina*, paras. 53–67; *CMS* v. *Argentina*, Annulment, paras. 30–40; *Continental Casualty Company* v. *Argentine Republic* (ICSID Case No. ARB/03/9), Award, September 5, 2008 (hereinafter: *Continental Casualty* v. *Argentina*), paras. 100–159; *Enron* v. *Argentina*, paras. 61–79; *LG&E* v. *Argentina*, Liability, paras. 34–71; *National Grid PLC* v. *Argentine Republic*, UNCITRAL, Award, November 3, 2008 (hereinafter: *NG* v. *Argentina*), paras. 51–60; *Sempra* v. *Argentina*, paras. 82–92; and Alvarez/Khamsi, "The Argentine Crisis," 388–390.

225 Except for Continental Casualty, which had made an investment in the workers' compensation insurance services industry. In this regard, the pesification measure described subsequently in this section had a tremendously negative influence on its investment portfolio; see *Continental Casualty* v. *Argentina*, paras. 16 ff.

which was at that time pegged to the US dollar. The industry regulators, ENARGAS and ENRE, were to set transportation and distribution tariffs under the Gas Law and Electricity Law respectively, which were to remain at "fair and reasonable" levels, however ensuring a "reasonable rate of return."[226] Moreover, investors benefited from a number of so-called "stabilization" guarantees, including preset tariffs over a five-year period, calculation of the tariffs in dollars with a guarantee to convert them to pesos at a fixed rate, semi-annual tariff review based on the US Producer Price Index (PPI) and no rescission of the license without the licensees' consent.[227]

In the wake of the economic crisis, due to deflation in Argentina and inflation in the USA, the original PPI adjustments would have resulted in significantly higher rates for consumers. Hence, the Argentine government negotiated a postponement of the PPI adjustment for a six-month period in January 2000, and a two-year postponement in July that same year. In November 2001, ENARGAS announced that no further adjustments to tariffs would be made.[228]

Argentina's crisis worsened significantly in late 2001. Poverty and unemployment soared, with half the population living below the poverty line and unemployment at 25 percent, which spurred serious social unrest. By the end of 2001, Argentina was experiencing difficulties repaying its foreign debt. Due to Argentines fearing default on their bank deposits and thus making massive withdrawals from their accounts, in December 2001 the government restricted bank withdrawals and prohibited international currency transfers. This measure became known as the "Corralito."[229]

In late December 2001, President de la Rúa had to resign due to violent public upheavals and Argentina experienced a succession of four further presidencies within a two-weeks period. In January 2002, Argentina passed its "Emergency Law," abolishing the currency board pegging the peso to the dollar, which hence resulted in rapid and severe devaluation of the peso. Furthermore, the Law terminated the right of companies in the utilities sector to calculate their tariffs in dollars and according to the US PPI, and redenominated tariffs in pesos at a rate of 1:1 to the dollar.[230]

226 *CMS* v. *Argentina*, paras. 132 f., 179. In the following, since the factual framework was the same in all cases, I will only cite *CMS* for references in case law on the facts.

227 *Ibid.*, paras. 136 ff.

228 *Ibid.*, paras. 62 f.

229 Decree No. 1570/01, December 1, 2001. See Alvarez and Khamsi, "The Argentine Crisis," 389.

230 *CMS* v. *Argentina*, paras. 65 f.

In March 2002, the government ordered ENARGAS and ENRE respectively to discontinue all tariff reviews and to refrain from adjusting tariffs in any respect. On May 25, 2003, an election having been held on April 26, Néstor Kirchner took office as President of Argentina. Since then, Argentina's economy has weathered the crisis and has grown steadily. At the time of the decisions in the disputes underlying the ensuing analysis, the claimants' licenses[231] had not been successfully renegotiated and attempts to increase natural gas tariffs had been thwarted.[232]

(ii) Necessity or not? The Tribunals' differing decisions

It is no secret that the Argentine crisis Tribunals, though almost identical in their evaluation of investor rights infringements,[233] were severely divided pertaining to the issue of necessity as a licit defense under the particular circumstances underlying the cases. Although the factual matrixes and the Tribunals' eventual rulings differed slightly in some respects, it is nonetheless fair to distinguish two opposing factions: The majority of decisions rejected Argentina's necessity defense,[234] based on reasoning diverging only to a marginal extent – which offers some interesting insights, nonetheless.[235] By contrast, the Tribunals in *LG&E* and *Continental Casualty* endorsed Argentina's allegations regarding the state of necessity – here, however, the Tribunals' underlying considerations differ considerably. The following is a selection of those issues relevant for understanding how investment Tribunals deal with such references to the Global Public Interest and is pivotal to my conclusions on the matter under (iii).

To start with, a very important issue to decide was the relationship of the customary international law rule on the state of necessity as expressed in Article 25 of the ILC Articles on State Responsibility[236] and the emergency clause in Article XI of the US–Argentina BIT,[237] applicable in most cases

[231] Naturally, this does not apply to Continental Casualty, as I have noted earlier.

[232] See Alvarez and Khamsi, "The Argentine Crisis," 390.

[233] See Alvarez and Khamsi, "The Argentine Crisis," 393; Reinisch, "Necessity in International Investment Arbitration," 194; Schill, "Comment on the ICSID Decision in LG&E," 284; Waibel, "Two Worlds of Necessity in ICSID Arbitration," 639.

[234] *BG*, *CMS* Award, *Enron*, *National Grid*, *Sempra*.

[235] See this subsection below and (iii).

[236] The International Law Commission's Articles on Responsibility of States for Internationally Wrongful Acts, *Yearbook of the International Law Commission*, 2001, vol. II (Pt II), Annex to General Assembly Resolution 56/83 of December 12, 2001, corrected by document A/56/49(Vol. I)/Corr.4, available at http://untreaty.un.org/ilc/texts/9_6.htm.

[237] Treaty Between the United States of America and the Argentine Republic Concerning the Reciprocal Encouragement and Protection of the Investment, signed November 14,

except for *BG* and *National Grid*.[238] Both provisions dealing with issues of emergency and the right to self-preservation, the question arose whether – in the case one regards Article 25 ILC and Article XI of the US–Argentina BIT as generally applicable to an economic crisis such as the 2001/02 Argentine collapse[239] – there is a certain order in which the Tribunal must consider them and whether the treaty provision excludes the application of the customary rule by way of the *lex specialis* principle.[240]

The *CMS*, *Enron* and *Sempra* Tribunals focused on Article 25 ILC and only referred to Article XI of the BIT in a subsidiary and cursory manner, equating the requirements set out in both norms. As the ad hoc Committee in the *CMS* Annulment decision rightly noted, such order of consideration seriously conflates the doctrinal structure of the customary rule and the treaty provision: It is not only that Article 25 ILC delineates numerous thresholds, whereas Article XI of the US–Argentina BIT merely states that the measures undertaken must be "necessary" to address the "essential security interest". Even more importantly:

> Article XI is a threshold requirement: if it applies, the substantive obligations under the Treaty do not apply. By contrast, Article 25 is an excuse which is only relevant once it has been decided that there has otherwise been a breach of those substantive obligations.[241]

In other words, whereas the consequence ensuing from Article XI is that no breach of investor rights has occurred in the first place, Article 25, in a second step, may justify infringements of the BIT having been found beforehand. Hence, both provisions must be distinguished carefully and Article XI of the BIT, given its doctrinal structure as a threshold

1991, entered into force October 20, 1994, available at www.unctad.org/sections/dite/iia/docs/bits/argentina_us.pdf. Article XI reads as follows:

> "This Treaty shall not preclude the application by either Party of measures necessary for the maintenance of public order, the fulfillment of its obligations with respect to the maintenance and restoration of international peace and security, or the protection of its own essential security interests."

238 These two disputes were founded on the UK–Argentina BIT, which does not contain a clause comparable to Article XI BIT; see *BG* v. *Argentina*, para. 381; *National Grid* v. *Argentina*, para. 253.

239 This, however, is debatable regarding both Article 25 ILC and Article XI of the US–Argentina BIT. As to the appropriateness of the customary rule in case of economic crises see (iii) below. On such discussion pertaining to the treaty provision see, e.g., Reinisch, "Necessity in International Investment Arbitration," 209, stating that the BIT passage "essential security interests," on which the Tribunals based the applicability of Article XI, "primarily relate[s] to military and strategic considerations."

240 See *CMS* Annulment, paras. 101 ff. and 128 ff.

241 *Ibid*., para. 129.

requirement, must be considered before Article 25, which merely provides a defense against a measure breaching the BIT.

Contrasting with the rulings in *CMS*, *Enron* and *Sempra*, the Tribunals in the *LG&E* and *Continental Casualty* disputes put the emphasis of their analysis on Article XI and referred to Article 25 ILC either as a merely auxiliary provision supporting the interpretation of the BIT rule (*LG&E*)[242] or in fact not at all (*Continental Casualty*).[243] While, in general, *LG&E* and *Continental Casualty* alike were more cognizant vis-à-vis the doctrinal structures of Articles XI of the BIT and 25 ILC repectively than *CMS*, *Enron* and *Sempra* and thus consequently started their analysis with the former, their findings on the interpretation of this treaty clause diverge to a notable extent – whereas in the final outcome, however, they arrive more or less at the same result.[244] Viewed against the backdrop of the standard set out in the *CMS* Decision on Annulment, *LG&E* is the less consistent of the two, falling short of strictly distinguishing between Article XI and Article 25 and considering the latter as a support of its conclusions on the former.[245] Additional to its cursory overall consideration of Article XI, lacking a thorough step-by-step analysis of the individual requirements of the provision,[246] the Tribunal mingled customary law requirements with those of the treaty rule and eventually stated that Article 25 ILC "alone does not establish Argentina's defense," but read in conjunction with Article XI, Argentina succeeds with its plea on necessity.[247]

In this regard at least, *Continental Casualty* was much more consistent, focusing on Article XI of the BIT and therefore refraining from a discussion of the customary rule at all after having found that the measures taken by Argentina met the requirements of the treaty provision.[248] Rather unsettling, however, was the Tribunal's interpretation of "necessary" in Article XI. In its view, such wording has no relevant connection to the state of necessity under customary international law, but originates in the FCN treaties of the USA, which in its view the US–Argentina BIT was modeled after, and the Tribunal thus concluded that "necessary" must rather be interpreted along the lines of Article XX of the GATT [sic!], given that this provision allegedly finds its roots in the very same US FCN treaties.[249] While such reasoning is already audacious to say the least, given the fact that the USA adopted BITs instead of FCNs specifically

242 *LG&E* v. *Argentina*, Liability, paras. 245, 258.
243 *Continental Casualty* v. *Argentina*, para. 192.
244 *LG&E* v. *Argentina*, Liability, para. 259; *Continental Casualty* v. *Argentina*, paras. 236, 304.
245 *LG&E* v. *Argentina*, Liability, para. 245. 246 *Ibid.*, paras. 230–242.
247 *Ibid.*, para. 258. 248 *Continental Casualty* v. *Argentina*, para. 192. 249 *Ibid.*

because the latter were inadequate to address the needs of investment protection,[250] tearing a provision of the WTO legal framework out of the complex architecture of the GATT and inserting it into an investor–State relationship appears completely inadequate. Not only that the GATT – as in fact the entirety of WTO provisions – consists exclusively of inter-State provisions, obliging and entitling States. Referring to the WTO case law on Article XX GATT is out of place, since the WTO Appellate Body's interpretation of "necessary" in Article XX (c) etc. GATT relies on the distinct relationship of the specific provisions in Article XX (a) to (j) GATT and the chapeau of Article XX GATT providing that a measure may not lead to an "arbitrary or unjustifiable discrimination or a disguised restriction on international trade."[251] Article XI of the US–Argentina BIT naturally does not take account of such elaborate architecture and hence cannot be interpreted by way of reference to Article XX GATT.

Besides the relationship of Article XI BIT and Article 25 ILC, other highly controversial issues among the Tribunals pertain to the actual application and interpretation of the customary international law rule on the state of necessity in the context of the measures undertaken by Argentina to weather the 2001/02 economic crisis. For a better overview, note the wording of Article 25 ILC, which I have already referred to earlier:

"Necessity

1. Necessity may not be invoked by a State as a ground for precluding the wrongfulness of an act not in conformity with an international obligation of that State unless the act:
   (a) Is the only way for the State to safeguard an essential interest against a grave and imminent peril; and
   (b) Does not seriously impair an essential interest of the State or States towards which the obligation exists, or of the international community as a whole.
2. In any case, necessity may not be invoked by a State as a ground for precluding wrongfulness if:
   (a) The international obligation in question excludes the possibility of invoking necessity; or
   (b) The State has contributed to the situation of necessity."[252]

[250] See *supra* 2 C. 1.

[251] See in particular the respective passages in *Korea-Beef* and *US-Gambling* the *Continental Casualty* Tribunal cites in paras. 193, 195. See also WTO Appellate Body Report, *Korea – Measures Affecting Imports of Fresh, Chilled and Frozen Beef*, WT/DS161/AB/R, December 11, 2000, paras. 164 ff.

[252] The International Law Commission's Articles on Responsibility of States (see n. 236); hereinafter: ILC Articles on State Responsibility.

The first topic in this regard concerns the interpretation of the "essential interest" that must be at stake in order to invoke the necessity defense. Interestingly so, *CMS* and *Enron* use the gravity of the crisis as the decisive benchmark for determining whether Argentina's interest at stake qualified as "essential."[253] James Crawford notes the link between "essential interest" and the "grave and imminent peril" from which it is to be safeguarded.[254] Hence, both requirements are intertwined and interrelated and consequently hard to separate. Considering the gravity of the circumstances during the crisis, both the *CMS* and *Enron* Tribunals acknowledged that they were severe. However, arguing that they were not severe enough, since economists were not unanimous in evaluating whether the crisis amounted to "catastrophic proportions"[255] and because the Argentine constitutional framework did not entirely collapse,[256] the Tribunals rejected the notion that the events qualified as pertaining to an "essential interest." Such reasoning appears to be defective if not to say absurd. As *Continental Casualty* underlined regarding the similar requirement in Article XI of the US–Argentina BIT, in order to qualify as pertaining to an "essential interest," the crisis does not have to have degenerated to an irreversible level, for "[t]here is no point in having such protection [i.e. the state of necessity] if there is nothing left to protect."[257] In fact, it appears completely absurd for the *Sempra* Tribunal to argue in this regard that the crisis was not severe enough because Argentina witnessed five presidencies within little more than a week without the constitutional framework entirely collapsing.[258] Moreover, as is the case in almost every academic discipline, economics scholars will always differ in their evaluation of the severity of crises. If just the mere fact that there is more than one view on the matter suffices to foreclose recourse to the necessity defense, such requirement becomes meaningless for it is simply impossible to fulfill. The fact that the *CMS* and *Enron* Tribunals alike dedicated only one paragraph to assessing the gravity of the crisis[259] is additional support that their findings on the matter are simply untenable. Therefore, the *LG&E* Tribunal affirming the "essential interest"[260] requirement

[253] *CMS* v. *Argentina*, paras. 319–322; *Enron* v. *Argentina*, paras. 305 f.

[254] J. Crawford, *The International Law Commission's Articles on State Responsibility – Introduction, Text and Commentaries* (Cambridge University Press, 2002), p. 183, Art. 25, para. 15.

[255] *CMS* v. *Argentina*, para. 320; see also *Enron* v. *Argentina*, para. 305.

[256] *Enron* v. *Argentina*, para. 306.

[257] *Continental Casualty* v. *Argentina*, para. 180.

[258] *Sempra* v. *Argentina*, para. 332.

[259] *CMS* v. *Argentina*, para. 320; *Enron* v. *Argentina*, para. 306.

[260] While interpreting "essential security interest" in Article XI of the US–Argentina BIT, which, however, does not differ in this regard from the requirement in Article 25 ILC.

after recapitulating in great detail the cataclysmic events triggering and ensuing from the crisis[261] seems the much more adequate position.

Similar reasoning, at least as to *CMS*, *Enron* and *Sempra*, applies to the requirement enshrined in Article 25(1)(a) that the measures undertaken constituted the "only way" to address the "grave and imminent peril": Here again, the *CMS* Tribunals would not accept that Argentina met this requirement simply because economists differed on the assessment of whether there were measures possible to overcome the crisis other than those adopted by the Argentine government.[262] Even more briefly, the *Enron* and *Sempra* Tribunals stated in almost identical wording that "there are always many approaches to address and correct those critical events."[263,264] As Michael Waibel has pointed out, "[a]s such divergence of views lies in the nature of economic policy, the *CMS* test is essentially meaningless."[265] However, whereas the approach taken by *CMS*, *Enron* and *Sempra* hence deforms the "only way" requirement in Article 25(1)(a) ILC to an absurd threshold impossible to pass, the *LG&E* Tribunal tackled the issue as a question to be answered in the abstract: The Tribunal merely considered if there was an alternative to an economic recovery package in general, which it answered in the negative.[266] While I am rather sympathetic to giving more deference to the host State in choosing the appropriate measure to respond to the crisis and thus tend more towards the *LG&E* than the *CMS*, *Enron* and *Sempra* approach, I nevertheless deem *LG&E* to be too lenient in this regard. Simply referring to Argentina adopting any kind of recovery package renders the "only way" requirement as absurd as requiring that all economists agree that the measures adopted by the host States were the only ones possible to overcome the crisis. Otherwise, any kind of reaction would qualify, which makes this requirement similarly meaningless. Hence, despite some judicial restraint necessary here, the Tribunal should at least determine in such an instance whether the measures adopted were appropriate and reasonably connected to the crisis

261 *LG&E* v. *Argentina*, Liability, paras. 231–237.

262 *CMS* v. *Argentina*, paras. 323 f.

263 *Enron* v. *Argentina*, para. 308; *Sempra* v. *Argentina*, para. 350: "there are always many approaches to addressing and resolving such critical events."

264 Furthermore, it must be noted that the Tribunals declining Argentina's recourse to the necessity defense also applied very similar reasoning in responding to whether Argentina had itself contributed to the situation of necessity: see Art. 25(2)(b) ILC; *CMS* v. *Argentina*, para. 329; *National Grid* v. *Argentina*, para. 260 stating that Argentina failed to fulfill this requirement since endogenous factors to the crisis were not entirely absent.

265 Waibel, "Two Worlds of Necessity in ICSID Arbitration," 646.

266 *LG&E* v. *Argentina*, Liability, para. 257.

and whether they constituted the least restrictive measures reasonably available.[267]

Finally, as a last issue mentionable at this point, the *CMS* Tribunal referred to Article 27 ILC in order to corroborate its findings on the state of necessity, arguing that due to this provision, Argentina would be obligated to pay compensation even if it succeeded with asserting the necessity defense.[268] Article 27 ILC provides:

"*Consequences of invoking a circumstance precluding wrongfulness*
The invocation of a circumstance precluding wrongfulness in accordance with this chapter is without prejudice to:

(a) Compliance with the obligation in question, if and to the extent that the circumstance precluding wrongfulness no longer exists;
(b) The question of compensation for any material loss caused by the act in question."[269]

While Article 27 ILC will be dealt with extensively at (iii), at the present stage it remains to note that the *CMS* Tribunal making reference to Article 27 after having rejected Article 25 ILC is quite dubious, for, as held in the *CMS* Decision on Annulment, if Article 25 does not apply, Article 27 is not applicable either.[270] The *LG&E* Tribunal, by contrast, "opines that [Article 27] does not specifically refer to the compensation for one or all the losses incurred by an investor as a result of the measures adopted by a State during a state of necessity."[271] However, by considering Article 27 ILC, *LG&E* is as inconsequential as *CMS*, since finding that the threshold requirement of Article XI BIT is applicable – as did the *LG&E* Tribunal – excludes permissible recourse to the consequential rule of Article 25 ILC

267 Similarly Reinisch, "Necessity in International Investment Arbitration," 201, who seeks to introduce a proportionality test to Article 25(1)(a) ILC. While he does not further elaborate on his proposal, I, however, would be skeptical about inserting a proportionality *stricto sensu* into Article 25(1)(a) ILC, which in my view would overload this requirement. Equally skeptical, albeit presumably due to different considerations, A. Newcombe and L. Paradell, *Law and Practice of Investment Tribunals – Standards of Treatment* (Kluwer Law International, 2009), p. 520. On proportionality *stricto sensu* see *infra* 5 D. 3.

268 See *CMS* v. *Argentina*, para. 390: "The Tribunal is satisfied that Article 27 establishes the appropriate rule of international law on the issue."

269 Art. 27 ILC Articles on State Responsibility.

270 *CMS* v. *Argentina*, Annulment, para. 150. Also see Crawford, *The ILC's Articles on State Responsibility*, p. 189, Art. 27, para. 1.

271 *LG&E* v. *Argentina*, para. 260.

which is merely an "excuse"[272] and hence does not apply if already there is no breach of an investor right.[273]

(iii) Conclusion

After such detailed analysis of the findings in the Argentine crisis cases, let me move some steps back and regard the entire necessity issue from a more distant viewpoint. When doing so, beyond all the nitty-gritties of the individual requirements of Article 25 ILC and Article XI of the US–Argentina BIT and their mutual relationship, what comes to mind is whether the customary law rule on the state of necessity is actually applicable vis-à-vis an investor. Investors, being non-State entities, are quite different to the right-holders and duty-bearers originally intended by the ILC Articles on State Responsibility. By declaring that "[e]very internationally wrongful act of a State entails the international responsibility of that State," the very first ILC Article on State Responsibility makes it fairly obvious that the rules enshrined in these Articles are focusing primarily on States.[274] While in most instances of investment disputes this fact is of minor importance, for the customary law on State responsibility is applied – implicitly or explicitly – against the State to the advantage of the investor, the question does not appear to be answered so easily if the host State actually invokes the ILC Articles to justify an investor right infringement, i.e. if the law on State responsibility is applied against the investor to the advantage of the host State. However, Article 25 ILC, as with all provisions in Part One Chapter V of the ILC Articles, if successfully raised by the host State in an investment dispute, entails exactly such effect: "precluding the wrongfulness of conduct that would otherwise not be in conformity with the international obligations of the State concerned."[275] Hence, the question arises as to the applicability and doctrinal foundation of the customary rule on the state of necessity in investment disputes.[276]

272 *CMS* v. *Argentina*, Annulment, para. 129. 273 *Ibid.*, para. 146.

274 See Crawford, *The ILC's Articles on State Responsibility*, p. 80, Art. 1, para. 7: "The articles deal only with the responsibility of States."; V. Pechota, "The Limits of International Responsibility in the Protection of Foreign Investments" in M. Ragazzi (ed.), *International Responsibility Today – Essays in Memory of Oscar Schachter* (Martinus Nijhoff Publishers, 2005), p. 171 at pp. 176 f.

275 Crawford, *The ILC's Articles on State Responsibility*, p. 160, Ch. V, para. 1.

276 There exist other grounds on which to doubt the applicability of the customary state of necessity in the Argentine crisis. Some scholars remind of its roots in the practice on the use of force and the right to self-defense and regard the inconsistent judgments of the Argentine crisis Tribunals as evidence for the inappropriateness of such defense in economic crises, although they admit that the case law of international arbitration Tribunals does not generally exclude extreme financial distress as a ground for

Most Tribunals in the Argentine crisis cases were quite oblivious of this issue. The *CMS* Tribunal merely stated that Article 25 ILC "adequately reflect[s] the state of customary international law on the question of necessity"[277] and did simply assume its applicability vis-à-vis the investor. Similarly, according to *Enron* and *Sempra*, the customary law rule as enshrined in the ILC Articles on State Responsibility represented the "state of customary law on the matter."[278] By contrast, in the *BG* award we find the following dictum:

> Article 25 may relate exclusively to international obligations between sovereign States. From this perspective, Article 25 would be of little assistance to Argentina as it would not disentitle BG, a private investor, from the right to compensation under the UK–Argentina BIT.[279]

Eventually, the Tribunal did not deem it necessary to rule on this particular matter, for it found that in any event Argentina had not met the conditions set out in Article 25 ILC.[280] Nonetheless, what might have induced the *BG* Tribunal to raise the issue of applicability of the customary rule on the state of necessity was the fact that – different to the cases arbitrated under the US–Argentina BIT – the UK–Argentina BIT did not contain a provision similar to Article XI of the former BIT.[281] Thus lacking a treaty-based necessity clause, the applicability of which to an investor–state dispute was out of question, the Tribunal seemed to have been more vigilant vis-à-vis the viability of a necessity claim against an investor under customary international law.

To some, this dictum, as in fact the entire issue of questioning the applicability of Article 25 ILC in an investor–State arbitration, might appear rather odd. Indeed, if one regards an investment dispute simply as the continuation or mirror of the inter-State relationship of alien protection, the ground for application of any kind of international law rule, be it treaty-based or customary, originates in the relationship of the investor's home State and its host State. In such an understanding of investor rights as merely derivative, any kind of entitlements the investor is vested with

necessity; see Russian Indemnities case (*Russia* v. *Turkey*), PCA, Award of the Arbitral Tribunal, November 11, 1912, *UNRIAA*, vol. XI, 421 at 443: "[L]'obligation pour un Etat d'exécuter les traits peut réfléchir 'si l'existence meme de l'Etat vient être en danger, si l'observation du devoir international est . . . self destructive.". Moreover, see Waibel, "Two Worlds of Necessity in ICSID Arbitration," 648 promoting a lack of payment capacity defense instead; see also Reinisch, "Necessity in International Investment Arbitration," 197 ff.

277 *CMS* v. *Argentina*, para. 315.

278 *Enron* v. *Argentina*, para. 303; *Sempra* v. *Argentina*, para. 344.

279 *BG* v. *Argentina*, para. 408.

280 *Ibid*, paras. 410–412.

281 *Ibid.*, para. 381.

would be strictly accessory and thus bound to the scope of the rights – and their limits – the investor's home State enjoys.

Such view on investor rights as only derivative was entertained by Mexico in two disputes arising under NAFTA's Chapter XI.[282] In the face of a trade dispute between Mexico and the United States over sweeteners used in soft drink beverages, three US companies, having invested in the Mexican artificial sweetener industry, challenged legislation introducing a 20 percent tax on the transfer and importation of soft drink beverages containing sweeteners other than cane sugar adopted by the Mexican government as a countermeasure in response to alleged breaches of WTO provisions by the USA.[283] While one of the Tribunals considered it generally viable for the host State to have recourse to the countermeasures defense under customary international law as enshrined in Articles 22 and 49 *et seq.* ILC, but found that in the case at hand Mexico did not meet the conditions set out in the Articles,[284] both a concurring opinion in this case and the Tribunal in *CPI* v. *Mexico* denied the applicability of the countermeasures defense in an investor–State dispute.[285] The latter stressed that the very purpose of NAFTA Chapter XI is "to remove such claims from the inter-State plane and to ensure that investors could assert rights directly against a host State."[286] As judge Stephen Schwebel points out in a passage cited by arbitrator Arthur Rovine in the said concurring opinion,

> those procedures embrace the direct right of the company to invoke international law in defense of its interests. Certainly it is hard to maintain the contrary. How odd it would be if States were to conclude treaties such as the ICSID Convention or the Algiers Declaration providing for the Iran–United States Claims Tribunal, and were to conclude contracts with aliens providing for exclusive arbitration of disputes arising thereunder, and at the same time were to be deemed to have debarred the alien claimants and companies which are central to these processes from direct reliance upon international law to sustain their claims.[287]

282 *Archer Daniels Midland Company and Tate & Lyle Ingredients Americas, Inc.* v. *United Mexican States* (ICSID Case No. ARB (AF)/04/5 (NAFTA)), Award, November 21, 2007 (hereinafter: *ADM* v. *Mexico*); *Corn Products International, Inc.* v. *United Mexican States* (ICSID Case No. ARB (AF)/04/1 (NAFTA)), Decision on Responsibility, January 15, 2008 (hereinafter: *CPI* v. *Mexico*).

283 *ADM* v. *Mexico*, para. 110; *CPI* v. *Mexico*, para. 62.

284 *ADM* v. *Mexico*, paras. 120 f., 123, 151–160.

285 *ADM* v. *Mexico*, Concurring Opinion of Arthur W. Rovine; *CPI* v. *Mexico*, para. 161.

286 *CPI* v. *Mexico*, para. 161.

287 S. M. Schwebel, *Justice in International Law* (Cambridge University Press, 1994), p. 211; see also *ADM* v. *Mexico*, Concurring Opinion, para. 24.

Since thus "the NAFTA confers upon investors substantive rights separate and distinct from those of the State of which they are nationals,"[288] countermeasures are not applicable vis-à-vis an investor, for they must be directed against the State that has committed the internationally wrongful act, which simply is not possible in an investor–host State relationship.[289]

This much more preferable position as to investor rights as separate and distinct rights of the investor rather than derivative and thus merely accessory reflections of the home State's relationship with the host State[290] appears also to have inspired the *National Grid* Tribunal in one of the Argentine crisis cases. Different to those cases based on the US–Argentina BIT, in the two cases involving the UK–Argentina BIT – *BG* and *National Grid* – the issue arose whether Argentina was precluded from having recourse to the customary state of necessity defense due to the United Kingdom allegedly being a persistent objector to such rule. Interestingly so, here it was the investor – in both *BG* and *National Grid* – raising such argument and hence suggesting that the scope of its rights was tied to the scope of its home State's rights vis-à-vis the host State of the investment.[291] The *National Grid* Tribunal rejected such inter-State perspective, however clouded its findings in murky language, by merely stressing that Article 25 ILC was applicable irrespective of the bilateral relationship of Argentina and the UK, as long as those countries had not expressly agreed otherwise in the BIT.[292] In this regard, it would have been preferable if the Tribunal had chosen language as unequivocal as did the *CPI* award discussed above by reminding that the investor's rights are separate and distinct from the relationship of the host and the home State, which is evinced best in the fact that the investor is entitled to bring its claim against the host State even if its home State disapproves of introducing an investment dispute.[293]

If therefore, in my view, it is untenable to disregard "that controversies between foreign investors and host States are insulated from political and diplomatic relations between states,"[294] the bilateral relationship of

288 *CPI* v. *Mexico*, para. 167.

289 *Ibid.*, paras. 163 f. Similarly, albeit not completely renunciating countermeasures in international investment law, M. Paparinskis, "Investment Arbitration and the Law of Countermeasures," *Brit. Yb. Int'l L.*, 79 (2008), 264 at 351 ff.

290 Agreeing with this position Z. Douglas, *The International Law of Investment Claims* (Cambridge University Press, 2009), pp. 32 ff.

291 *BG* v. *Argentina*, para. 400; *NG* v. *Argentina*, para. 256.

292 *NG* v. *Argentina*, para. 256.

293 See *CPI* v. *Mexico*, para. 173.

294 *CPI* v. *Mexico*, Concurring Opinion of Andreas F. Lowenfeld, para. 1.

the investor's host and its home State cannot provide a doctrinal basis for the applicability of Article 25 ILC. Furthermore, the Argentine crisis Tribunals' reasoning vis-à-vis the requirements of Article 25 ILC as well as Article 27 ILC seem to further challenge necessity as a licit defense in the investment context. As noted at (ii) above, the *CMS*, *Enron* and *Sempra* Tribunals set a threshold so high, in order to determine the severity of the crisis and whether the measures adopted by the Argentina government were the "only way," that it was virtually impossible to pass it. Moreover, taking seriously the rulings in these awards, in order to be entitled to raise the necessity defense a host State faced with a situation of economic emergency would be forced to let the crisis escalate and to stand by with its hands tied until the crisis reached an irreversible level of deterioration, where, in the words of *Continental Casualty*, there was "nothing left to protect."[295] In such scenario, there would be no point in raising the necessity defense any more. Further, *CMS* referring to Article 27 ILC saying that even if Article 25 ILC applies, the host State is not exempted from its obligation to pay compensation,[296] calls into question the whole point of accepting the state of necessity as a licit defense in investor–State arbitration: Different to inter-State disputes, where States care much about their reputation and thus precluding the wrongfulness of the conduct in itself is a valuable prospect, investor-State claims are all about money. If hence a host State successfully raising the necessity defense paid the same amount of compensation as a host State not being entitled to do so, there simply would not be much point in permitting recourse to Article 25 ILC after all. Given all these findings by those Argentine crisis Tribunals rejecting Argentina's necessity claim, the Tribunals setting absurdly high thresholds and asserting that the monetary consequence of a successful necessity defense would be no different to that of an unsuccessful one, incites the impression that these Tribunals actually did not deem Article 25 ILC applicable in an investment dispute.

This suggestion, which I consider fairly adequate, is as sobering as it is astonishing. Why would investment Tribunals make so much fuss about discussing Article 25 ILC, if they actually doubt its applicability? In my opinion, this approach, which almost all Tribunals – with the exception of *LG&E* and *Continental Casualty* – chose vis-à-vis the customary state of necessity, is a strong indicator of the Tribunals' perception that not allowing at least for the theoretical possibility of raising such defense would have been unacceptable. Why unacceptable? A State in extreme financial

[295] *Continental Casualty* v. *Argentina*, para. 180. [296] *CMS* v. *Argentina*, para. 390.

distress that has no choice but to take immediate action and adopt measures that affect investors as much as any other economic actors should not and – as a simple factual matter – cannot be treated the same as a State under normal economic conditions. As *force majeure* and different to, for example, countermeasures,[297] necessity is a defense that does not root in the reciprocal relationship of two States. The source of a situation triggering such defenses originates in outside circumstances that cannot be attributed to another State or group of States but are, such as nature (*force majeure*) or the economy (necessity), due to events not completely in the hands of international actors or concern the sheer existence and survival of the State, where there is no choice but to act.

Moreover, it must be noted that the *CMS* Tribunal was not entirely correct in stating that Article 27 ILC did not debar Argentina from its obligation to pay compensation from its investor rights infringements.[298] While it is true that the customary state of necessity inheres the notion that affected third parties should not automatically suffer financially from a State invoking that defense,[299] this does not mean that the investor under Article 27 ILC is entitled to the same amount of compensation as if the requirements of Article 25 ILC had not been fulfilled. In fact, Article 27(b) states that invoking Articles 20 to 25 is without prejudice to "the question of compensation for any *material loss* caused by the act in question."[300] As James Crawford explains in his Commentary on the ILC Articles on State Responsibility:

> Although article 27(b) uses the term 'compensation,' it is not concerned with compensation within the framework of reparation for wrongful conduct, which is the subject of article 34. Rather it is concerned with the question whether a State relying on a circumstance precluding wrongfulness should nonetheless be expected to make good any material loss suffered by any State directly affected. The reference to 'material loss' is narrower than the concept of damage elsewhere in the articles: article 27 concerns only the adjustment of losses that may occur when a party relies on a circumstance covered by Chapter V.[301]

[297] See *CPI* v. *Mexico*, para. 161. [298] *CMS* v. *Argentina*, para. 390.

[299] Crawford, *The ILC's Articles on State Responsibility*, p. 190, Art. 27, para. 5, citing the ICJ in the *Gabcíkovo-Nagymaros* case, noting that "Hungary expressly acknowledged that, in any event, such a state of necessity would not exempt it from its duty to compensate its partner" (*ICJ Reports*, (1997), 7 at 39, para. 48).

[300] Emphasis added.

[301] Crawford, *The ILC's Articles on State Responsibility*, para. 4. See also S. Ripinsky and K. Williams, *Damages in International Investment Law* (British Institute of International and Comparative Law, 2008), p. 343.

Hence, the investor must be fully compensated for its losses, but may not claim lost profits: it is entitled only to *damnum emergens*, not to *lucrum cessans*. This is the consequence of Article 27 ILC and adequately reflects the situation of both the investor righteously claiming BIT rights infringements and the host State righteously claiming necessity under Article 25.

All these conclusions considered, the state of necessity under customary international law is a further expression of the public interest. While all Argentine crisis Tribunals adopted dubious reasonings – either reducing the necessity claim to absurdity (*CMS*, *Enron*, *Sempra* and to a lesser degree *BG* and *National Grid*) or prying the door wide open for abuse by the host State (*LG&E*) or untenably interpreting the term "necessary" by reference to Article XX GATT and WTO case law (*Continental Casualty*) – they all acknowledge the general need for vesting the host State with a necessity claim in case of extreme financial distress. If understood as outlined above, the customary international law rule on the state of necessity provides a licit defense of the host State. The latter's right to self-preservation in the interests of both the community it constitutes, i.e. its people, and the international community exemplifies, therefore, the public interest consideration inherent in the concept of the necessity defense that thus is present also in international investment law.

2. *Lessons learned from the comparative insights*

Recalling the various similarities between international investment law on the one hand and European law and the European Convention on Human Rights régime on the other,[302] in the subsequent section I will briefly condense the lessons learned from those comparative insights and thus seek to make profit from them in constructing my theory.

I have contended that international investment law arguably has transformed into a legal régime integrating domestic and international law and defining a clear hierarchical system.[303] Moreover, international investment law creates a relationship of the investor and the host State that differs considerably from the classical concept of public international law and which can be described – by looking through the lens of what I call Global Public Law – as a vertical and regulatory public law type control of the exercise of public authority.[304] In this respect, apart from many others, it is very similar to the European legal order.[305]

[302] See *supra* 4 B. 2., 3. [303] See *supra* 2 E. 2.
[304] See *supra* 4 A. 3. [305] See *supra* 4 B. 2. (b).

Drawing on this public law character of the two systems, as the European experience demonstrates, general principles of law, existing in both orders, may serve as a basis for introducing limitations of investors' rights that may serve as justifications for infringements of those rights: In *Schmidberger* the ECJ allowed Austria to rely on the general principle of fundamental rights as a defense for an infringement of economic freedoms in a vertical regulatory administrative law type exercise of public authority very similar to a typical investor–State relationship.[306] Just as the blocking of the tunnel infringed Schmidberger's fundamental freedom of the movement of goods as guaranteed by Article 34 TFEU, any expropriation without compensation, lack of fair and equitable treatment, etc. of an investor may infringe an investor right enshrined in a BIT. Given the numerous similarities between the two systems as described earlier, there exists thorough argumentation to allow a host State in an investment dispute endorsing the same rationale as in *Schmidberger*: Both fundamental freedoms and investor rights constitute legal expressions of private entities' economic interests and public interest challenges such as in *Schmidberger* arise in both contexts. Considering all the parallels we have identified between the EU law system and the investment régime, it does not seem far-fetched to draw on those parallels in the issue at hand. General principles of law exist and are applied quite often in international investment law. Indeed, such principles are adopted in an almost unmodified fashion from general public international law.[307] Thus, it is nothing but a matter of logic and coherence to apply general principles that serve as a limitation to the investor's rights and thus may constitute a justification for the State's conduct infringing on the said right. The same rationale applies regarding customary law.[308]

To play devil's advocate, one may well reply to such considerations that *Schmidberger* was a special case, for the Austrian State was faced with the dilemma to choose between two conflicting interests: the fundamental freedom of Schmidberger on the one hand, and the fundamental rights of the protesters on the other. Either way, it would have infringed an individual interest. But if the host State invokes a general principle of law or a rule of customary international law as justification for an infringement of an investor right, the situation is different.

[306] See *supra* 4 B. 2. (b) (iv).

[307] See, e.g., the Argentine crisis cases regarding the state of necessity, *supra* 4 C. 1. (b) and 2 B. 5. (b).

[308] Particularly if one endorses Oppermann's view that fundamental rights are customary Union law rather than general principles; see Oppermann, *Europarecht*, p. 280.

However, such reasoning is misguided. Most domestic legislation regulating the conduct of investors seeks to serve – at least among others – the interest of other individuals, either as such or as part of a group or as part of society. While domestic law loses its relevance when international law trumps it in case of conflict, the rationale behind invoking general principles or customary international law as justification for infringing investor rights is the same as under domestic law: Protecting either the interest of one individual or of a collective of individual human beings – both of which pertain to the public interest.[309] Whether such interest clashes directly with the interest of the investor or is translated into a legal provision serving such interest seems a minor and negligible difference.

With *Schmidberger* demonstrating how European law – sharing all the aforementioned features with international investment law – may well inspire public interest defenses within the investment régime, the parallels between investment law and the ECHR system equally need to be considered, particularly given the human rights reference in this said case. International investment law shares with both the European law system and the ECHR system the public law character in that all three deal with the control of the exercise of public authority. However, beyond this, international investment law and the ECHR system have in common that they exert such control by handing trump cards to non-State actors that can pursue their rights, originating in an international law source, before an international Tribunal. Furthermore, within the investment realm – and different to the ECHR system – investors do not even need to exhaust local remedies but may directly introduce a claim before an international Tribunal.[310] Recognizing that international investment law hence exhibits a legal system very similar to the ECHR system with regard to what I have called constitutional traits, we can again observe that the latter, as the European law system, provides for entry points of public interest considerations as defenses the State infringing an individual right may raise for justifying its conduct. As I have fleshed out in some detail above, the European Convention on Human Rights in many places permits infringement of its provisions, if the measure undertaken was "necessary in a democratic society," i.e. if it was proportional.[311] As a matter of fact, even where the Convention does not expressly mention such justification clause, the ECtHR has ruled that it applies as a matter of general principle.[312] Hence, here again we observe an example of a public

[309] See, for a more elaborate analysis of this notion, *infra* 4 C. 5. (a).
[310] See Art. 26 ICSID. [311] See *supra* 4 B. 3. [312] *Ibid.*

law system sharing many defining features with international investment law allowing for defenses against individual rights infringements by way of general principles or customary law.

3. *The State as the agent of public interest*

Recapitulating the conclusions drawn from the Constitutionalization debate, while values focusing on humanity and thus the human being are permeating all aspects of public international law, it is still State-centered in that the State remains its chief actor.[313] However, although "the state remains the most important *actor* on the international plane . . . it assumes a *role* . . . in a *play* written and directed by the international community."[314] As Christian Tomuschat asserted in his General Course at The Hague Academy in 1999, public international law "has become a multi-faceted body of law that permeates all fields of life, wherever governments act for promoting a public purpose."[315] Such public purpose, in a value-oriented system that focuses on the human being, cannot mean what the State considers best for its own interests as a sovereign. It can only mean what is best for the totality of human beings constituting the most important stakeholder of the international community. In the words of Professor Tomuschat:

> States are no more than instruments whose inherent function it is to serve the interests of their citizens as legally expressed in human rights.[316]

Hence, the State's role in such system of public international law is the one of an intermediary or agent for the interests of human beings. Since public international law still grants the State the position of the chief actor of international law, the latter is the motor that spurs the mechanics revolving around the human being as the benchmark. To paraphrase the imagery employed above, while it is the international community that writes and directs the *play*, it needs – at least at the current state

[313] See *supra* 4 A. 2. (b).

[314] A. von Bogdandy, "The Telos of International Law – Christian Tomuschat's General Course and the Evolution of the Universalist Tradition" in P.-M. Dupuy *et al.* (eds.), *Völkerrecht als Wertordnung*, p. 703 at p. 707 (emphasis in the original).

[315] Tomuschat, "Survival of Mankind," 70 f.

[316] *Ibid.* See, with similar understanding, albeit with some limitations as regards the current state of the law, C. Tomuschat, "Möglichkeiten und Grenzen der Globalisierung" in J. Schwarze (ed.), *Globalisierung und Entstaatlichung des Rechts – Ergebnisse der 31. Tagung der Gesellschaft für Rechtsvergleichung vom 20. Bis 22. September 2007 in Halle, Vol. 1: Beiträge zum Öffentlichen Recht, Europarecht, Arbeits- und Sozialrecht und Strafrecht* (Mohr Siebeck, 2008), p. 21 at pp. 31 ff.

of public international law – the State as its *protagonist* to convey the message.

Another consideration adds to this: Nowadays, the vast majority of States are democracies. The fact that many of them often do not live up to what they provide for in their constitutions is of no relevance here. It cannot alter the existence of the general perception that government by the people *for* the people is the ultimate end of a State and the justification for its monopolization of force and its exercise of power over its citizens.[317] Such view is mirrored in Article 25 of the International Covenant on Civil and Political Rights which states that every citizen has the right to take part in the conduct of public affairs, either directly or indirectly through freely elected representatives.[318] Due to its 165 parties, the Covenant can fairly serve as expression of an almost universal opinion among States.

If the very purpose of the State thus is to promote the interest of its citizens, determined both by its internal constitutional goals and by an external, international rule, the fact that the State is situated in a value-based public international law system focusing on the human being means that, on the international plane also, the State must serve as the agent of the interest of the human being. *In conclusio*, if the rationale of public international law is humanity but the State is still the most important actor in international relations, it assumes the role of an agent that must use its capacity to act in the interest of human beings.

[317] See J. Crawford, "Democracy and the Body of International Law" in G. H. Fox and B. R. Roth (eds.), *Democratic Governance and International Law* (Cambridge University Press, 2000), p. 91 at pp. 92 f.

[318] Art. 25 of the ICCPR reads as follows:

> "*Article 25*
>
> Every citizen shall have the right and the opportunity, without any of the distinctions mentioned in article 2 and without unreasonable restrictions:
>
> (a) To take part in the conduct of public affairs, directly or through freely chosen representatives;
> (b) To vote and to be elected at genuine periodic elections which shall be by universal and equal suffrage and shall be held by secret ballot, guaranteeing the free expression of the will of the electors;
> (c) To have access, on general terms of equality, to public service in his country."

International Covenant on Civil and Political Rights, adopted and opened for signature, ratification and accession by General Assembly Resolution 2200A, (XXI) of December 16, 1966, entry into force March 23, 1976, in accordance with Art. 49, available at http://www2.ohchr.org/english/law/ccpr.htm.

4. Lessons learned from international investment law as Global Public Law

(a) Equilibrium between the individual and the public interest

Harking back to my observations that international investment law displays features of an administrative adjudication system, as mirrored in the European law system, and exhibits Constitutionalist traits, as paralleled in the ECHR system, I want to reiterate that both these observations lead to the conclusion that international investment law can be described as a Global Public Law system.[319] It deals with the exercise and control of public authority vis-à-vis the individual, integrates domestic and international law and provides the investor with trump cards to pierce the sovereignty shield of the host State. If we thus embrace the notion that international investment law inheres a Global Public Law character, it must be considered that balancing the individual with the public or with other individual interests is a general feature of every exercise of public authority and thus of public law.[320] The raison d'être of each State is to serve its constituencies, be its political system democratic, communist or of any other kind. Thus, it is inherent in every public law relationship of the State and the individual (or any other private entity) that the individual's rights must be weighed against the interests that are of importance to the respective constituencies: in other words, the public interest.[321] As I have argued earlier, since there exists a widespread consensus nowadays that democracy is the most appropriate form of governance, as evinced in Article 25 ICCPR,[322] the relevant constituency is the people, i.e. the (collective of) individual human beings.

Public interest in a system displaying constitutional and hence value-based features, however, does not necessarily mean the primacy of what appears best for the collective or the majority. In fact, it also means the protection of minority rights and particularly of individual liberties against intrusion by others, whether those others are the State, the democratic majority or other individuals. Consequently, public interest has two dimensions, both of them equally valuable and applicable as a balance against the conflicting interest. Firstly, it has a *collective* dimension, i.e. measures that are to the benefit of society as a whole, as decided through

319 4 A. 3.

320 R. Seerden, "Comparative Remarks" in R. Seerden, *Administrative Law of the European Union, its Member States and the United States – A Comparative Analysis* (Intersentia, 2007), p. 401 at p. 406.

321 *Ibid.* 322 See *supra* 4 C. 4.

democratic, that is majoritarian decision-making, such as the construction of an airport. Secondly, it has an *individual* dimension, i.e. measures undertaken to protect the interest of a fraction of society or even of only one of its members, such as their or its physical integrity. Both the individual and the collective can be on either side of the balance, which leads to four possible combinations: (1) collective-collective; (2) individual-individual; (3) collective-individual; and (4) individual-collective. Staying with our aforementioned examples, combination (1) would be building an airport vs. establishing a nature sanctuary on the same area. Those conflicts are usually the easiest to resolve in a democratic decision-making process, for it is eventually the majority that decides such conflict by direct vote or through elected representatives. Combination (2) cannot be resolved by majoritarian vote. An example for the pair individual-individual would be my interest to sleep well at night and not to be confronted with an unbearable amount of noise vs. an airline's interest to pursue its business objective by operating flights in high frequency and during any time of the day and night. The collective-individual conflict (3) would, in our example, constitute the general economic benefit of building and operating an airport vs. my interest of physical integrity (cf. (2)). Combination (4) is the reverse situation of (3), i.e. the collective seeks protection against intrusion by the individual – possible but rather rare in highly developed regulatory States. Of course, those four combinations are ideal types that may overlap, most likely in combinations (2) and (3) – the individual interest of the airline goes hand in hand with the collective interest of enhancing the economy. Considering the mechanics of a free market economy, the more leverage the individual, here the airline, has, the more likely it is to affect the collective interest as well.

Those are the typical considerations regarding public interest on the domestic level. However, what constitutes the public interest if we leave the domestic realm? What is the public interest relevance in international investment law?

(b) Why the public interest is global

To address this question, we have to realize that due to the applicability of domestic law in international investment law, each dispute, besides the investment claim being fought on the international plane, has a domestic and moreover most frequently a (domestic) constitutional dimension. The public interest issues on the domestic level usually revolve around the combinations (2) and (3) that I have described at (a). The investor's individual interest either conflicts with the collective interest as pursued by the host State's government or it conflicts with another individual or minority interest that the host State takes up on behalf of the individual or minority.

However, the primary and hierarchically superior source in an investment dispute is international law.[323] Furthermore, it is one of ICSID's core innovations to unhinge the investor–host State dispute from the domestic realm and lift it to the international level. The enmeshment of the domestic and international that I have described through the lens of Global Administrative Law and the embedment in a global Constitutional setting, in other words the specific Global Public Law character, are defining features of international investment law. Thus, being informed by the rules and general principles of public international law as well as pertinent aspects of the concepts of Global Administrative Law and Constitutionalism, such public interest relevant in international investment law can be nothing else but an international or, to be more precise in terminology, a global one. If we describe international investment law as an example of global governance,[324] such governance necessarily entails the resolution of conflicting interests, individual and collective; and a relevant public interest in a global governance scheme that plays out on the international level, as an international investment dispute does,[325] can only be a global one. By saying global I do not contend that the public interest always has to originate in the international arena. Thus, an environmental issue enshrined in domestic legislation, to name but one example, may perfectly qualify as such a global public interest. Instead, what makes the interest a global one is that it has legal relevance both on the domestic and the international stage. The word "global" in contrast to "international" is supposed to illustrate the "interdigitation," i.e. the integration of the domestic and the international,[326] that is so characteristic of international investment law: A regulatory régime that resembles domestic public law constellations but is arbitrated before an international Tribunal on the basis of a mélange of both domestic and international law, while the latter provides the investor with trump cards to pierce the sovereignty shield of the host State. In such a Global Public Law type setting, as the comparative insights[327] and my further analysis at (a) above have revealed, the individual interest always finds its counterweight in the public interest. Considering the ongoing development of normative features imbuing public international law, which spotlights

[323] See *supra* 2 E. 2. [324] See *supra* 4 A. 1. [325] See *supra* 2 D. 5. (b).
[326] See *supra* 2 E. 3. [327] *Supra* 4 B.

the human being as the center of the system, it is the *Global* Public Interest – enshrining both the collective and the individual interests of third parties – that becomes the ultimate rationale in international investment law.

Hence, putting together all the puzzle pieces analyzed before, the picture that emerges becomes what I call the Global Public Interest theory: In a globalized legal setting that displays constitutional and thus normative features, inspired by and embedded in public international law that focuses on the human being but still conveys the role of principle actor to the State, it must be the latter that assumes the role of agent for the individual and collective interests that unfold relevance on both the domestic and the international stages. A core consideration of the Global Public Interest theory therefore is to provide the host State with legal instruments with which to pursue the Global Public Interest in international investment law.

5. The legal translation of Global Public Interest

Consequently, the question of how to translate such conclusions into workable legal categories remains. The following section will undertake the effort of responding to this challenge. By displaying the current characteristics of how customary international law (a) and general principles of law (b) emerge from the conduct and perceptions of and within the international community viewing them against the backdrop of the Global Public Interest, it will become apparent that the answer is to be found in these sources of general public international law.

(a) The emergence of customary international law

Despite some fierce attacks on its viability as a source of public international law,[328] customary international law maintains a major role in the public international law realm. According to Article 38(1) lit. b of the Statute of the International Court of Justice, identifying it – together with treaty law – as one of the two primary sources of public international law, "international custom" is defined as "evidence of general practice accepted as law." Hence, this most widespread definition identifies two

[328] See F. D. Fidler, "Challenging the Classical Concept of Custom: Perspectives on the Future of Customary International Law," *Ger. Yb. Int'l L.*, 37 (1996), 216; J. L. Goldsmith and E. A. Posner, "Understanding the Resemblance between Modern and Traditional Customary International Law," *Virg. J. Int'l L.*, 40 (1999/2000), 640. See also the critique in S. Estreicher, "Rethinking the Binding Effect of Customary International Law," *Virg. J. Int'l L.*, 44 (2003/04), 5.

elements of custom: Firstly, a "general practice" by the relevant international actor and, secondly, the acceptance of this practice as obligatory, the so-called *opinio iuris*.[329]

However, this is where consensus basically ends. In the traditional doctrine both elements, practice and *opinio iuris*, are constitutive of the emergence of a customary rule:[330]

> Not only must the acts concerned amount to a settled practice, but they must also be such, or be carried out in such a way, as to be evidence of a belief that this practice is rendered obligatory by the existence of a rule of law requiring it.[331]

While thus the traditional view requires both practice and *opinio iuris* cumulatively in order to constitute custom, the International Court of Justice recognized in the *North Sea Continental Shelf Cases*, from which I cited the preceding passage, that the way in which the one or the other element is composed may vary from case to case:

> Although the passage of only a short period of time is not necessarily, or of itself, a bar to the formation of a new rule of customary international law on the basis of what was originally a purely conventional rule, an indispensable requirement would be that within the period in question, short though it might be, State practice, including that of States whose interests are specifically affected, should have been both extensive and virtually uniform in the sense of the provision invoked.[332]

This quote offers three insights into the ICJ's view on the emergence of a customary rule: Firstly, practice as a constitutive element of customary international law itself consists of three elements – duration, consistency, and generality of the practice. Secondly, those three elements of practice are mutually reverse sliding scales, i.e. each one can be realized to a different or even minor degree, if the sum of the three jointly reaches a certain degree of practice. So, to illustrate it by numbers, if we assume the three sliding scales ranged from 0 (very low) to 10 (very high) and the combined sum had to be, say, 21 in order to qualify as custom, if duration

[329] See Art. 38, Statute of the International Court of Justice, available at www.icj-cij.org/documents/index.php?p1=4&p2=2&p3=0. According to Art. 92 of the UN Charter, the Statute forms an integral part of the Charter.

[330] Only see *W. Heintschel* v. *Heinegg*, in K. Ipsen, *Völkerrecht*, 5th edn. (C. H. Beck, 2004), p. 213; Brownlie, *Principles*, p. 6; R. Bernhardt, "Customary International Law" in R. Bernhardt (ed.), *The Encyclopedia of Public International Law*, Vol. I (North Holland, 1992), p. 899.

[331] ICJ, *North Sea Continental Shelf Cases*, *ICJ Reports*, 3 (1969), 44.

[332] *Ibid.*, at 43.

is only at 1, consistency and generality of the practice both have to be at 10 to compensate for the short period of time.

These sliding scales as regards the three elements of practice, in this view, however, do not alter the conventional structure of customary international law: It still requires the two monoliths of practice on the one hand and *opinio iuris* on the other. Different to such traditional view, some authors deny the need for or at least the autonomy of *opinio iuris*.[333] One *critique* of the *opinio iuris* requirement reproaches it with circular reasoning. Indeed, it has some troubles in responding to the paradox that a sense of a legal obligation is difficult to imagine without the existence of the legal obligation itself. If *opinio iuris* is a constitutive element of customary international law together with practice, it must, as its precondition, exist before the legal obligation comes into being itself.[334]

However, such argument is actually not very convincing for it falls into its own trap and thus may be twisted against itself – it presupposes that practice is a constitutive requirement of customary international law; however, if I question the traditional paradigm of the two elements structure, it becomes rather difficult to explain why I do not question the practice requirement. Without practice as a requirement, though, there is no paradox – if a sense of legal obligation suffices to create the legal obligation, the latter exists, when the former is proven. Hence, the former must not exist before the latter and consequently there is no contradiction. Therefore, this said critique of *opinio iuris* is circular itself and thus prone to its own criticism.

As another critique of the *opinio iuris* requirement, Goldsmith and Posner[335] argue that States do not comply with customary rules because of a sense of a legal obligation, but simply because it is in their – political – interest to do so. As with treaty law, they do not conclude treaties or accede to them out of a sense of legal obligation regarding the rules enshrined in the treaty – indeed, if that were so, there would not be much need to conclude the treaty after all – but because it is their political decision to bind themselves. What Goldsmith/Posner thus do is to reject any normative element in the creation of customary international law. This is

333 See M. Akehurst, "Custom as a Source of International Law," *Brit. Yb. Int'l L.*, 44 (1976), 1 at 32, particularly referring to the great positivists of the twentieth century, Kelsen and Guggenheim; see *ibid.*, 32, n. 5 and 33, n. 2. However, as Akehurst recalls, both of them altered their view later; see *ibid.*, 34. In our age, Goldsmith and Posner are the most prominent proponents of such view, however with different reasoning; see J. L. Goldsmith and E. A. Posner, "A Theory of Customary International Law," *U. Chic. L. R.*, 66 (1999), 1113.

334 See Akehurst, *ibid.*, 34. See also, with similar reasoning, Goldsmith and Posner, *ibid.*

335 See Goldsmith and Posner, "Theory," 1113.

well in line with the New Haven School, however, not the line of thought I follow in this book.[336] While there are other arguments to underline the importance of *opinio iuris*,[337] I think there is sufficient evidence for normative considerations in the creation of customary international law rules, which is to be found in the case law of international Tribunals.

Following the above-cited *North Sea Continental Shelf Cases*, which already strongly affirmed the *opinio iuris* element, the *Nicaragua* case hints at the growing importance of *opinio iuris* as an expression of a normative consideration. In this case, the ICJ had to rule on the customary international law status of the prohibition of the use of force and the principle of non-intervention due to alleged responsibility of the United States for acts committed by armed opposition groups in Nicaragua supported and funded by the US government.[338] The Court starts by pointing at the reduced relevance of a consistent practice vis-à-vis the prohibition of the use of force:

It is not to be expected that in the practice of States the application of the rules in question should have been perfect, in the sense that States should have refrained, with complete consistency, from the use of force or from intervention in each other's internal affairs. The Court does not consider that, for a rule to be established as customary, the corresponding practice must be in absolutely rigorous conformity with the rule. In order to deduce the existence of customary rules, the Court deems it sufficient that the conduct of States should, in general, be consistent with such rules, and that instances of State conduct inconsistent with

[336] *Supra* 4 A. 2. For references on the New Haven School see 4 A. 2. (a).

[337] E.g. since practice alone may neither explain why States nonetheless feel obligated to follow a certain rule, even if it might not be in their utmost political interest, nor how a legal norm may be distinguished from mere considerations of morality or courtesy, see Akehurst, "Custom," 33 and the ICJ in the *North Sea Continental Shelf Cases*, 45:

> "The essential point . . . is that even if these instances of action . . . were much more numerous than they in fact are, they would not, even in the aggregate, suffice in themselves to constitute the *opinio juris*; for in order to achieve this result, two conditions must be fulfilled. Not only must the acts concerned amount to a settled practice, but they must also be such, or be carried out in such a way, as to be evidence of a belief that this practice is rendered obligatory by the existence of a rule of law requiring it. The need for such a belief, i.e. the existence of a subjective element, is implicit in the very notion of the *opinio juris sive necessitatis*. The States concerned must therefore feel that they are conforming to what amounts to a legal obligation. The frequency, or even habitual character of the acts is not in itself enough. There are many international acts, e.g., in the field of ceremonial and protocol, which are performed almost invariably, but which are motivated only by considerations of courtesy, convenience or tradition, and not by any sense of legal obligation."

[338] *Nicaragua Case*, 21. See also J. P. Müller and L. Wildhaber, *Praxis des Völkerrechts*, 3rd edn. (Stämpfli Verlag AG Bern, 2001), p. 24.

a given rule should generally have been treated as breaches of that rule, not as indications of the recognition of a new rule. If a State acts in a way *prima facie* incompatible with a recognized rule, but defends its conduct by appealing to exceptions or justifications contained within the rule itself, then whether or not the State's conduct is in fact justifiable on that basis, the significance of that attitude is to confirm rather than to weaken the rule.[339]

Therefore, the World Court decided to put its focus on the *opinio iuris*:

The Court has however to be satisfied that there exists in customary international law an *opinio juris* as to the binding character of such abstention. This *opinio juris* may, though with all due caution, be deduced from, *inter alia*, the attitude of the Parties and the attitude of States towards certain General Assembly resolutions, and particularly resolution 2625 (XXV) entitled 'Declaration on Principles of International Law concerning Friendly Relations and Co-operation among States in accordance with the Charter of the United Nations.' The effect of consent to the text of such resolutions cannot be understood as merely that of a 'reiteration or elucidation' of the treaty commitment undertaken in the Charter. On the contrary, it may be understood as an acceptance of the validity of the rule or set of rules declared by the resolution by themselves. The principle of non-use of force, for example, may thus be regarded as a principle of customary international law, not as such conditioned by provisions relating to collective security, or to the facilities or armed contingents to be provided under Article 43 of the Charter. It would therefore seem apparent that the attitude referred to expresses an *opinio juris* respecting such rule (or set of rules), to be thenceforth treated separately from the provisions, especially those of an institutional kind, to which it is subject on the treaty-law plane of the Charter.[340]

Given its importance in the international community and its prominence in the Charter of the United Nations – which undoubtedly has normative foundations[341] – the prohibition of the use of force assumes a customary

[339] *Nicaragua Case*, 98.
[340] *Ibid.*, 100.
[341] Only compare the Preamble of the Charter:

"WE THE PEOPLES OF THE UNITED NATIONS DETERMINED

- to save succeeding generations from the scourge of war, which twice in our lifetime has brought untold sorrow to mankind, and
- to reaffirm faith in fundamental human rights, in the dignity and worth of the human person, in the equal rights of men and women and of nations large and small, and
- to establish conditions under which justice and respect for the obligations arising from treaties and other sources of international law can be maintained, and
- to promote social progress and better standards of life in larger freedom,

international law status, so the ICJ argued, even if the practice is not consistent. Though the Court comes short of expressly mentioning it, it is the embedment in normativity – as shaped, here, by the UN Charter – that makes the prohibition of the use of force a rule of custom, even if States are constantly disregarding it. Similar rationale is to be found in the *Tadic* case, where the ICTY[342] – as Professor Tomuschat pointed out[343] – came to the conclusion that customary rules had emerged allowing penalization for the commission of breaches of humanitarian law rules in internal armed conflict, albeit there was no such State practice on the international plane at that time.[344]

What further derives from such case law is that the prevalent view on customary international law doctrine deems to develop towards a "preponderance"[345] of *opinio iuris*.[346] This is most obvious regarding *ius cogens*. In a passage I have cited earlier,[347] Martti Koskenniemi asserts the following:

> Some norms seem so basic, so important, that it is more than slightly artificial to argue that States are legally bound to comply with them simply because there exists an agreement between them to that effect, rather than because, in the words of the International Court of Justice . . . non compliance would 'shock the conscience of mankind' and be contrary to 'elementary considerations of humanity.'
>
> . . .
>
> [I]t is really our certainty that genocide or torture is illegal that allows us to understand State behavior and to accept or reject its legal message, not State

AND FOR THESE ENDS

- to practice tolerance and live together in peace with one another as good neighbours, and
- to unite our strength to maintain international peace and security, and
- to ensure, by the acceptance of principles and the institution of methods, that armed force shall not be used, save in the common interest, and
- to employ international machinery for the promotion of the economic and social advancement of all peoples,

HAVE RESOLVED TO COMBINE OUR EFFORTS TO ACCOMPLISH THESE AIMS."

See www.un.org/en/documents/charter/preamble.shtml.

342 International Criminal Tribunal for the Former Yugoslavia.

343 Tomuschat, "Survival of Mankind," 326.

344 See *Prosecutor* v. *Dusko Tadic*, Judgment of October 2, 1995, *ILM*, 35 (1996), 35, at 70 f, paras. 128–137.

345 Tomuschat, "Survival of Mankind," 325.

346 See also Müller/Wildhaber, *Praxis des Völkerrechts*, p. 27.

347 See *supra* 4 A. 2. (b).

behavior itself that allows us to understand that these practices are prohibited by law. It seems to me that if we are uncertain of the latter fact, then there is really little in this world we can feel confident about.[348]

Indeed, it would make no sense to accept the concept of peremptory norms, which underlie the normative consideration that any breach of them is illegal because they express pivotal values of the international community, but yet at the same time require for State practice as a second constitutive element.[349]

There is, moreover, a tendency in contemporary international legal thinking to reject practice as a necessary requirement of customary international law altogether, albeit with differing reasoning and theoretical pedigree.[350] Andrew Guzman, for example, contends that State behavior may be explained by rational choice. Hence, according to his model, States are driven by preserving their reputation in international relations and thus hold much to compliance. While this then means that an affected State's own view on whether a particular norm is binding or not cannot be relevant – and thus that its own view cannot be relevant for determining the *opinio iuris* – it is all about reputation and hence perception by other States, i.e. *opinio iuris*, as to how customary international law comes into being:

If states as a group believe there is a legal obligation, this is enough to generate reputational (and perhaps direct) sanctions. The question of practice is not directly relevant to the issue.[351]

Practice, so Guzman argues, may have a considerable role as an indicator or proof of the *opinio iuris*. However, it is not a constitutive element of customary international law, merely a subsidiary means to give evidence to the sense of a legal obligation.[352] Moreover, he asserts that since his model is based on rational choice and thus purely on State interest, any reference to moral or normative grounds of the *opinio iuris* is flawed and misconstrues the nature of customary international law.[353]

348 M. Koskenniemi, "The Pull of the Mainstream," 1952.

349 However, note that Koskenniemi argues that *ius cogens* is thus not part of customary international law but a distinct category; see *ibid.*

350 A. T. Guzman, "Saving Customary International Law," *Mich. J. Int'l L.*, 27 (2005), 115 at 148 ff.; A. T. Guzman and T. L. Meyer, "Customary International Law in the 21st Century" in R. A. Miller and R. M. Bratspies (eds.), *Progress in International Law* (NV, 2008), 197 at 206 ff.; L. Hannikainen, "The Collective Factor as a Promoter of Customary International Law," *Baltic Yb. Int'l L.*, 6 (2006), 125 at 138.

351 Guzman, *ibid.*, 153. 352 *Ibid.* 353 *Ibid.*, 156.

Regarding the subsidiary role of practice, it appears to me that asserting that State practice is still a constitutive element of customary international law, but more emphasis must be put on the *opinio iuris*, or alleging that practice is no requirement for customary international law but is the most important evidence for the *opinio iuris*, is a distinction without a difference. Even Guzman, after purportedly having thwarted the relevance of practice, still assumes quite a prominent role for it to play eventually, for it is undeniable that in the vast majority of instances *opinio iuris* reveals itself in the examination of State practice, however we define such practice.[354] And the opposing view, conversely, is ready to accept the emergence of international criminal law as rules of customary international law without any sufficient State practice, neither on the domestic nor international levels, more or less simply on the basis of the perception that this is – or must – constitute a legally binding rule.

Furthermore, Guzman's model is less independent from normativity than he purports. If he asserts that the foundation of his model is a State's reputation, i.e. how its behavior is perceived and thus evaluated by other States, it is hard to think of reputation without any kind of value-based arguments. So, even if Guzman asserts that the particular State's reason to adhere to the rule may be more of a rational and thus political choice, he at the same time assures us that it is not the State's own perception that counts, but the perception of all other States.[355] However, that such perception by others is free from normative considerations is not to be assumed so easily.

Moreover, his approach is rather State-centric and neglects that, if reputation is what counts, a State does not merely hold reputation with its peers, but among the quite diverse international community of IOs, NGOs, multinational enterprises and, in the end, the global public. Hence, eventually, Guzman's reputation model, in order not to contradict itself or exclude constitutive aspects of what "reputation" actually means, is at its core an utterly value-based, i.e. normative, system: there is a sense of a legal obligation, an *opinio iuris*, because the international community, the reputational audience so to speak, thinks so, based on a normative evaluation. This does not mean, I have to reiterate, that every moral obligation automatically triggers the *opinio iuris* and thus a customary rule. It

[354] See on what may constitute State practice Akehurst, "Custom," 1 ff. and A. D'Amato, *The Concept of Customary International Law* (Cornell University Press, 1971), p. 88.

[355] See Guzman, "Saving," 153.

merely means that, conversely, a customary international law rule often is underpinned by a normative evaluation.

(b) The emergence of general principles

General principles of law – which ought not to be confused with general principles of international law[356] – are usually identified as a subsidiary source[357] of public international law. In any legal system, whether domestic or international, a situation may well arise where a court is confronted with a case in which it is unable to find a law, neither statutory nor case law, covering exactly the issue before it. Moreover, there might emerge challenges pertaining to questions such as how to reconcile two legal rules with one another or how to give voice to perceptions of utter injustice that are not enshrined in an express rule.[358] As is the case on the domestic level, also on the international plane those lacunae and those lacks are to be filled with and compensated by general principles of law. Those general principles of law that form part of the sources of public international law derive from a comparative analysis of the fundamental principles that are common or at least very similar among all or at least the vast majority of States.[359] To name but one – famous – example, in the *Chorzów Factory* case of 1928, dealing with the legal consequences of Poland seizing a nitrate factory in Upper Silesia, the Permanent Court of International Justice found that "it is a general conception of law that every violation of an engagement involves an obligation to make reparation."[360]

[356] Which actually are a special offshoot of customary international law; see *Heintschel* v. *Heinegg*, in Ipsen, *Völkerrecht*, p. 227, and which Cassese describes as "sweeping and loose standards of conduct that can be deduced from treaty and customary rules by extracting and generalizing some of their most significant common points." (*International Law*, p. 188.)

[357] However, there is some discussion about that. While most authors understand Art. 38(1) lit. c of the Statute of the International Court of Justice as identifying general principles as a source of public international law, some rather regard them as mere interpretative standards; see M. Koskenniemi, "General Principles: Reflexions on Constructivist Thinking in International Law," *Oikeustiede-Jurisprudentia (Yearbook of the Finnish Law Society)*, 18 (1985), p. 120 at pp. 127 f. Since both follow the normative understanding of principles that I ground my thoughts on, such differentiation is rather futile, for eventually it is not much more than a "manner of speaking"; *ibid.*

[358] See Shaw, *International Law*, p. 98.

[359] See H. Bokor-Szegö, "General Principles of Law" in M. Bedjaoui (ed.), *International Law: Achievements and Prospects* (Unesco/Martinus Nijhoff Publishers, 1991), p. 213 at p. 213; Nguyen Quoc Dinh, P. Daillier and A. Pellet, *Droit International Public*, 6th edn. (Librairie Générale de Droit et de Jurisprudence, 1999), p. 347.

[360] PCIJ, Series A, No. 17, 1928, 29 at para. 258.

When hence general principles' pedigree is to be found in the distilled gist of common domestic principles, conditions for their extraction are not so different from those that constitute customary international law:[361] Making use of them must be widespread or at least generally accepted and thereby evince a pervasive perception that their character is inherently legal and thus binding – only that determining a general principle focuses on a comparison of such domestic analyses, whereas customary international law examines State practice and *opinio iuris* exclusively from an international perspective.[362]

Moreover, deriving from shared fundamental principles of domestic legal orders, general principles of law may be regarded as the expression of core values underpinning every legal system. Many of them enshrine basic considerations of justice or fairness like *ius non orit ex iniuria*, *nemo iudex in sua re*, good faith, *venire contra factum proprium* or the aforementioned *Chorzów Factory* principle that "every violation of an engagement involves an obligation to make reparation."[363,364] Differently put, general principles epitomize part of what the world community perceives as its core interests as cast in law.[365]

(c) General principles and customary international law as legal translations of the Global Public Interest

Hence it follows from the analysis at (a) and (b) that both aforementioned sources of public international law derive their very existence from a consensus among the international stakeholders, arguably the constituency of the world community, i.e. that those norms that deal with individual or collective concerns of human beings enshrine the most valuable concerns of the international community. *Arguendo*, customary international law and general principles of law encapsulate the Global Public Interest in the international investment law realm – equivalent to the domestic public interest in a domestic public law situation.

361 See *supra* 4 C. 6. (a).

362 For similar approaches see H. Waldock, "General Course on Public International Law," *Recueil des Cours*, 106 (1962), 1 at 54 ff.; B. Vitanyi, "Les Positions Doctrinales Concernant le Sens de la Notion de 'Principes Généraux de Droit Reconnus par les Nations Civilisé'," *Revue Générale de Droit International Public*, 86 (1982), 48 at 55.

363 PCIJ, Series A, No. 17, 1928, 29 at para. 258.

364 For references on the mentioned principles in ICJ and PCIJ case law see Cassese, *International Law*, p. 192.

365 Note Waldock, "General Course," 54, who calls general principles "the 'Common Law' of the international community."

Customary international law, as I have argued above, nowadays mostly focuses on the *opinio iuris* as the international community's perception, i.e. its normative evaluation, of what it regards as law. General principles are the condensed consensus of common domestic perceptions of what belongs to the core values and funding principles of a legal order. Thus, customary international law is based on what the international community regards as their shared interests on the international plane, whereas general principles root in what domestic societies regard as the shared interests on the domestic plane that is common among all or most of them worldwide. In other words, both sources of international law hinge on the shared, i.e. public, interest on a global scale. It plays into the hands of such view that "there will always be a tendency for a general principle of national law recognized in international law to crystallize into customary law."[366] This "transitory nature" of general principles, i.e. "that their repeated use at the international level transforms them into custom,"[367] epitomizes the similar core of general principles and the *opinio iuris*.

Since the said public interest permeates the domestic and the international levels, for it similarly touches upon common values of the international community and domestic societies, it is identical with the Global Public Interest I have described at 5. above. As I have argued in the said subsection, what I call the Global Public Interest theory inheres the notion that every public law system, as international investment law arguably is, founds on the balancing of the individual with the public interest. Consequently, I argue that customary international law and general principles of law may serve as defenses against an infringement of investor rights that the host State may raise as the agent and prism of the Global Public Interest.

Such reasoning is echoed in the above-mentioned *Inceysa* award. The third general principle of international law the Tribunal relies on in order to make its case that El Salvador's consent did not comprise fraudulently gained investments, was what it called "international public policy."[368] According to the Tribunal, "the essential function of [international public policy] is to preserve the values of the international legal system against actions contrary to it."[369] Fraudulent conduct in order to gain an investment and thus the protection of ICSID and the BIT qualifies in that respect,

366 Waldock, "General Course," 62.

367 A. Pellet, in Zimmermann, Tomuschat and Oellers-Frahm (eds.), *The Statute of the ICJ*, Art. 38/Mn. 294.

368 *Inceysa* v. *El Salvador*, para. 245.

369 *Ibid.*

the Tribunal held. Whether there exists a general international principle of "international public policy" may be open to debate and is not to be addressed here. However, what is noteworthy here is that by referring to "the values of the international legal system" and by accepting a worldwide concept of "public policy," the *Inceysa* Tribunal implicitly acknowledged the existence and relevance of a Global Public Interest.

Since we have characterized the investor–host State relationship under international law as a public law type relationship on the global level, the public interest that may serve as the underlying rationale for a justification of infringing investor rights cannot be confined to the domestic realm. Instead, only such legal rules that reflect the interest of the world community as the relevant constituency of the global realm encapsulate the Global Public Interest relevant for the considerations at hand.

Again, customary international law and general principles *per definitionem* fulfill such requirement. They evolve from consensus and practice among States, still the most important actors in the international arena. As a matter of fact, States are not the only stakeholders of the world community, and this book has undertaken a considerable effort to argue for prying open the hieratic State-centric concept of classical public international law. Thus, hinging on the classical instruments of general public international law may seem unsatisfactory or even contradictory, if one refers to the public interest of the world community in an international regulatory régime of global governance that consists of the enmeshment of State and non-State actors. However, as I have argued earlier, although we are currently witnessing a paradigm change in international relations, a shifting focus from a State-centric to a human-centric system, it is undeniable that the State is still the central actor of international relations.[370] That it is the agent of Global Public Interest and hence is entitled[371] to raise defenses against investor rights infringements is the only answer reconcilable with the present state of public international law.

(d) The non-State actor caveat

To conclude, it is hence the Global Public Interest enshrined in customary international law and general principles of law that provides an adequate basis for defenses against and thus (possible) justifications for infringements on investor rights in the public law type system of international

[370] A. Wendt, *Social Theory of International Politics* (Cambridge University Press, 1999), pp. 167 ff.; Armstrong/Farrell/Lambert, *International Law and International Relations*, pp. 10 ff.

[371] Why it is entitled, although not obligated, to raise Global Public Interest concerns will be addressed in Chapter 5.

investment law. However, some limitations to this statement are necessary in order not to overload international investment law with those customary international law rules and general principles that are unfit for the investor–host State relationship.

As has been pointed out on several occasions in this book, most prominently in the sections on Global Public Law and the case law on the state of necessity,[372] investor–State arbitration bestows the investor with the capacity to introduce international law claims directly against the host State on the basis of its own rights separately and distinctly from the relationship of its host and its home State. Hence, views that tie the scope of investor rights to the scope of the bilateral relationship of the investor's host and its home State are out of place. Investor rights neither are accessory to the rights of the home State, nor is the investor automatically bound to the same limitations as its home State. The NAFTA case law concerning Mexico's countermeasures claim as justification of its Chapter XI infringements following measures adopted in response to a trade dispute with the USA, as described in section C. 1. (b) above, provides excellent evidence of this notion: The *CPI* Tribunal as well as the concurring opinion in *ADM* equally underlined that countermeasures were not applicable vis-à-vis the investor, "depend[ing] in large part on the nature of the rights and obligations that arise under Chapter XI."[373] Indeed, the rationale of countermeasures is deeply rooted in the reciprocal relationship of States requiring that they must be directed against the State that has committed the internationally wrongful act.[374]

The Global Public Interest theory, therefore, must find its limits in those customary international law rules and general principles which by their very nature are confined to an inter-State relationship. Such norms

[372] See *supra* 4 A. and 4 C. 1. (b).
[373] *CPI* v. *Mexico*, para. 162.
[374] Article 49 ILC provides:

> "***Article 49***
>
> *Object and limits of countermeasures*
>
> 1. An injured State may only take countermeasures against a State which is responsible for an internationally wrongful act in order to induce that State to comply with its obligations under part two.
> 2. Countermeasures are limited to the non-performance for the time being of international obligations of the State taking the measures towards the responsible State.
> 3. Countermeasures shall, as far as possible, be taken in such a way as to permit the resumption of performance of the obligations in question."

inhere the rationale that the other side, against which they are raised, is also a sovereign State. Excluding them from the scope of the Global Public Interest theory is not only doctrinally sound but makes perfect sense within the framework of the theory itself: No public law system coerces the individual to accept defenses against infringements of its rights that premise that the State' (organ')s counterpart is vested with public authority. Hence, the applicability of customary international law and general principles of law as defenses against investor rights infringements under the Global Public Interest theory is limited to what I call the non-State actor caveat: Only recourse to those of the aforementioned norms may be appropriate that do not presuppose the counterpart, against which they are applied, being vested with sovereign authority.

After such last clarification of the Global Public Interest theory the question remains, however, how to make the notion legally operable that customary international law and general principles – under the non-State actor caveat – may be raised as defenses against investor rights infringements? How should conflicting interests that are enshrined in investor rights in BITs on the one hand and in limitations to those rights in customary international law and general principles of law on the other be addressed? And finally, how can we provide an effective balancing of those conflicting interests that gives enough voice to Global Public Interest concerns but at the same time does not undermine the very purpose of international investment law, i.e. to enhance economic development by effectively protecting foreign investments? It is the goal of the next chapter to delineate a proposal of how to tackle those issues.

5 How to balance the conflicting interests

Proportionality analysis

This chapter will argue for reconciling the investor interest with the Global Public Interest by drawing on proportionality analysis as developed in domestic as well as international contexts. After discussing doctrinal entry points of proportionality analysis in international investment law (A.) as well as some skepticism towards such approach (B.), I will subsequently engage in a thorough comparative analysis of its application in domestic constitutional orders as well as by the European Court of Justice and international Tribunals (C.). From such analysis I will extract the main elements and subprinciples of proportionality analysis (D. and E.) and then undertake the effort of seeking to operationalize it for the balancing of investor rights with host State defenses as enshrined in general principles of law and customary international law (F.). Eventually, it must be kept in mind that well-meant considerations as to giving voice to the Global Public Interest, as crucial as they are, might get easily abused by a ruthless and cunning host State, if there do not exist any restraints to bridle malevolent governments that might be tempted to take, for example, the environment or human rights hostage in pursuit of their protectionist policies. So the last part of this chapter, before H. 1 *et seq.* complete the three hypotheticals from Chapter 2,[1] is addressed at this issue and seeks to find institutional/procedural solutions to that challenge (G.).

A. Doctrinal avenues of proportionality analysis in international investment law

The subsequent analysis will show proportionality's viability as the proper tool to balance investor rights with Global Public Interest defenses and moreover will demonstrate its validity as an emerging general principle

[1] See *supra* 2 C. 5.

of law. Before I engage in such argumentation – and before I, even prior to that, induce (at B.) some skepticism as to the impeccability of proportionality as an analytical instrument – in this short section I will discuss possible doctrinal avenues for proportionality analysis in international investment law.

For first consideration, I recall two provisions that are of relevance for the role of public international law norms in international investment law. I have extensively elaborated on the first, Article 42(1) ICSID,[2] in Chapter 2. Quintessentially, this provision sets two main standards as to the role of international law. Firstly, it defines a hierarchical structure of integration between domestic and international law and places the latter on the top of such structure. This is the much more revolutionary part of Article 42 that I will no longer dwell on in this section, for it has been dealt with considerably and is not of much relevance for the issue at hand. The second standard Article 42(1) second sentence ICSID sets, however, is to declare "such rules of international law" of relevance in an ICSID dispute "as may be applicable." This is not very spectacular, admittedly. However, what it means is that if we seek to apply proportionality in international investment law, we have to (a) establish that it is a "rule of international law" – for if we use it as a balancing tool for BIT investor rights and Global Public Interest defenses that are both of a public international law nature, proportionality must display that same feature – and (b) demonstrate that it "may be applicable." As regards (a), the analysis at C. will make proof of such assertion.

The question of applicability (b) leads me to the second provision relevant here, Article 31(1) and (3)(c) of the Vienna Convention on the Law of Treaties. According to such customary rule of treaty interpretation, which hence is applicable in the interpretation of a BIT,

> 1. A treaty shall be interpreted in good faith in accordance with the ordinary meaning to be given to the terms of the treaty in their context and in the light of its object and purpose.
>
> . . .
>
> 3. There shall be taken into account, together with the context:
>
> . . . (*c*) any relevant rules of international law applicable in the relations between the parties.[3]

[2] As has been mentioned in Chapter 2, most BITs basically emulate the wording enshrined in Art. 42(1) second sentence ICSID, so that what will subsequently be said regarding the ICSID provision holds true in case of BIT arbitration outside the ICSID realm, e.g. UNCITRAL.

[3] Vienna Convention on the Law of Treaties, Art. 31.

Regarding the principle of good faith interpretation enshrined in Article 31(1), Kingsbury and Schill rightly point out that:

> [a] particular feature of most investment treaties is that they make provisions for investor rights without addressing in a comprehensive fashion the relationship of these to continuing powers of State regulation. It is likely that States parties typically did not intend a severe occlusion of these regulatory powers, and a good faith reading of the text of the applicable treaty in context and in light of the object and purpose of the treaty may well indicate that interpretation calls for a balance to be struck between investor protection and State regulatory powers.[4]

Couched in slightly different terms when viewed through the lens of the Global Public Interest theory, the State's authority to regulate in the Global Public Interest as conferred on it by the international community on behalf of whom it acts as an agent, is a basic assumption of any good faith interpretation of a BIT. Thus, in the light of Article 31(1) Vienna Convention any investor right must find its balance in a Global Public Interest defense legitimately raised by the host State. Proportionality analysis is, so my argumentation below will contend, the emerging general principle of law to implement such balancing.

Furthermore, Article 31(3)(c) allows for taking account of relevant rules of international law applicable between the parties to the treaty. "Rules" is not meant in a strict doctrinal sense here, i.e. it refers to the entire set of sources of international law as catalogued in Article 38(1) of the ICJ Statute. Thus, it also includes, among others, general principles of law.[5] These, by their very nature as "general" principles of law, are also "relevant" and "applicable in the relations between the parties [to a BIT]."[6]

[4] B. Kingsbury and S. Schill, "Investor-State Arbitration as Governance: Fair and Equitable Treatment, Proportionality and the Emerging Global Administrative Law," New York University School of Law, Public Law & Legal Theory Research Paper Series, Working Paper No. 09-46, September 2009, p. 23.

[5] See M. K. Yasseen, "L'interprétation des traités d'après la Convention de Vienne sur les Droit des Traités," *Recueil des Cours*, 151 (1976), 1 at 63. Also note what the ICJ observed in this regard in *Gulf of Maine*:

> "[T]he association of the terms 'rules' and 'principles' is no more than the use of a dual expression to convey one and the same idea, since in this context 'principles' clearly means principles of law, that is it also includes rules of international law in whose case the use of the term 'principles' may be justified because of their more general and more fundamental character."

ICJ, *Case Concerning the Delimitation of the Maritime Boundary Limitation in the Gulf of Maine Area (Canada* v. *United States of America)*, Judgment of October 12, 1984, *ICJ Reports*, (1984), 246 at 288–290, para. 79.

[6] See B. Simma and T. Kill, "Harmonizing Investment Protection and International Human Rights: First Steps Towards a Methodology" in C. Binder *et al.* (eds.), *International Investment*

Consequently the proportionality principle, if such general principle of law, applies in international investment law.

B. Some skepticism regarding proportionality analysis

Kicking off a chapter that eventually argues strongly for a prominent role of proportionality in international investment law by challenging the principle's viability as an analytical tool of judicial decision-makers may surprise or even appear awkward. However, while I will seek to demonstrate subsequently why, in my view, proportionality analysis is the instrument most suitable to find optimal solutions of reconciliation of conflicting interests, I am aware that it is neither the only nor an absolutely impeccable response to the challenges mentioned. Hence, this short passage is intended to underline this fact and to maintain awareness of alternative solutions.[7]

The main reason why one should preserve a healthy amount of skepticism vis-à-vis proportionality analysis is its susceptibility to broad policy considerations and thus to a perversion of the role of a judge or arbitrator as an independent third party decision-maker. It is a truism that – particularly, albeit not exclusively, in the domestic realm – judges assume a position beyond a mere arbiter adjudicating a dispute between two parties. Since his or her task is to create and maintain consistency and thus reliability and legal certainty in the judgment – warranted, among others, through precedents and *stare decisis* and/or through several instances and the institute of cassation – the judge reviewing political decisions enshrined in laws, who is called upon to reconcile conflicting interests, cannot ignore that his or her function is also a law-making one. She or he must, by interpreting the law, pronounce what the law actually is. Particularly when fundamental principles of the respective legal order clash, the independent decision-maker determines whether the law is unconstitutional, or the State conduct violates fundamental human rights, etc. In any event, his or her decision is political in the sense that it will either

Law for the 21st Century – Essays in Honour of Christoph Schreuer (Oxford University Press, 2009), p. 687 at p. 698.

[7] In particular see W. Burke-White and A. von Staden, "Private Litigation in a Public Law Sphere: The Standard of Review in Investor-State Arbitration," *University of Pennsylvania Law School, Public Law and Legal Theory Research Paper Series, Research Paper* No. #09–23, 48 ff., considering different standards of review in both domestic and international régimes and arguing eventually for a margin-of-appreciation-like standard similar to the standard of review as employed by the ECtHR.

permit or prohibit a policy adopted by the legislative or executive branch of government.

While this is an inevitable position any independent third-party decision-maker is placed in when called upon to decide a conflict of fundamental interests, proportionality analysis arguably is particularly prone to aggrandize the dangers that inhere in a law-making judge. While most commentators acknowledge proportionality's ability to resolve intra-constitutional or similarly tailored tensions,[8] it is its openness that is criticized in particular.[9] Two traits of proportionality analysis stand out as most suspicious in this regard: The flexibility that the judge is granted in considering alternative solutions or even inventing new ones (necessity) and the level of scrutiny and choice of emphasis on the one or the other principle in the balancing process (proportionality *stricto sensu*).

Admittedly, the creativity that proportionality allows in coming up with new solutions and alternatives to the paths chosen by the government is a very appealing characteristic, for it enables the judge to effectively work towards the optimization of State conduct.[10] However, this asset is also its detriment. Considering alternatives to legislative or executive measures automatically means interfering with legislative and executive competencies – possibly even with their very core. A judge deciding that a law was too intrusive and thus violated, say, a fundamental right because he (*sic!*) could think of an alternative less infringing but equally effective, may easily become a dangerous pattern, for the independent third party decision-maker assumes the role of a super-legislator with questionable legitimacy.

Secondly, on the third step of proportionality analysis, the proportionality *stricto sensu*, the outcome of the balancing process depends heavily on two determinants: the level of scrutiny chosen and the amount of emphasis the judge allocates to either of the conflicting interests at stake. Hence, the argument runs, while given the two factors are determined, the outcome of the balancing is predictable and thus conforms with adequate standards of legal analysis, setting these determinants – and thus

[8] A. Stone Sweet and J. Mathews, "Proportionality Balancing and Global Constitutionalism," *Colum. J. Transntl. L.*, 47 (2008–09), 72 at 89; Burke-White and von Staden, "Private Litigation in a Public Law Sphere," 52.

[9] Burke-White and von Staden, "Private Litigation in a Public Law Sphere," 53; T. J. Gunn, "Deconstructing Proportionality in Limitations Analysis," *Emory Int'l L. Rev.*, 19 (2005), 465 at 477 ff.

[10] R. Alexy, *A Theory of Constitutional Rights*, trans. J. Rivers (Oxford University Press, 2002), p. 399.

eventually deciding the outcome of the balancing – does not follow a reliable pattern but is rather arbitrary according to the political preferences of the judge.[11] He or she may easily twist a decision towards an outcome he or she prefers by choosing a higher or lower level of scrutiny or by determining from the outset that one interest is more important than another.

Such criticism, I have to admit, is not completely unfounded. There are a plethora of judgments by, for example, the German Constitutional Court that lack a discernible explanation and line of argument as to why it chose the specific level of scrutiny or why it considers one principle more important than another.[12] Nonetheless, while sometimes the choice of the level of scrutiny as well as the allocation of emphasis on one or another interest may seem somewhat murky, there are subprinciples of the proportionality analysis guaranteeing a certain level of predictability, which I will elaborate at E. and F. 4. Moreover, as will be demonstrated at F. 1., despite this aforementioned caveat that incites preserving a certain amount of skepticism vis-à-vis proportionality analysis' viability as an analytical tool, its advantages outweigh its detriments.

C. Comparative insights

Following the introductory remarks at A. and B., the ensuing section strives to unveil the roots of proportionality in domestic (German) administrative and constitutional law, how it has spread from those origins to a myriad of different jurisdictions with both Civil Law and Common Law backgrounds, and eventually its impact on international law as evinced by the jurisprudence of international Tribunals. The main goal of such exercise is to demonstrate that we may currently be witnessing the emergence of a general principle of law. However, I am aware that drawing on a multitude of different orders and jurisdictions inheres the risk of falling prey to premature conclusions and transpositions. It is essential to emphasize that fundamental differences exist between both the institutional settings and the legal documents underlying the orders or systems from which I will draw in this analysis. Nonetheless, I argue that there is a common thread to be found when unraveling the case law of domestic and international courts and Tribunals.

11 See Gunn, "Deconstructing Proportionality," 482, pointing at similar criticism.

12 See E. Grabitz, "Der Grundsatz der Verhältnismäßigkeit in der Rechtsprechung des Bundesverfassungsgerichts," *Archiv des Öffentlichen Rechts*, 98 (1973), 568 at 605 f.

1. The German pedigree of proportionality analysis and its reception in other domestic constitutional orders

The principle of proportionality, at least if it is understood as constituting more than a primitive balancing, has its origins in German administrative law. Early roots may be found in the writings of late-eighteenth-century German jurist Carl Gottlieb Svarez, according to whom "it is only the achievement of a preponderant interest for the benefit of the whole that enables the State to ask of the individual to sacrifice a minor interest."[13] While it became established practice in late-nineteenth-century jurisprudence of Prussian administrative courts,[14] it was not until the 1950s, when the German Federal Constitutional Court adopted it for reconciling conflicts between constitutional principles, that it gained both the prominence and the sophistication that so distinctly characterize it nowadays.[15]

The German Constitution, the *Grundgesetz* of 1949, was intended to mark a stark breach with the atrocities and injustices of the Nazi era and create a value-oriented legal framework of society based on a canon of fundamental rights that bind all branches of government.[16] Thus, it was generally agreed upon from its very beginning that as an underlying rationale of the modern German constitutional system, government action infringing upon those fundamental rights could only be justified in exceptional circumstances, which required a highly differentiated complex of scrutiny mechanisms. As Peter Lerche recognized in his 1961 dissertation "Übermaß und Verfassungsrecht,"[17] the technical and regulatory possibilities open to the modern State for intruding in an individual's everyday and private life call for a response in sophisticated legal balancing. Thus, many scholars in the early days of the modern German democracy called for elevating the proportionality principle to constitutional status. As Rupprecht von Krauss argued in 1955, proportionality must apply as a check on State action:

13 H. Conrad and G. Kleinheyer (eds.), *Carl Gottlieb Svarez, Vorträge über Recht und Staat* (Westdeutscher Verlag, 1960), p. 39 (my translation).

14 See R. Zippelius and T. Würtenberger, *Deutsches Staatsrecht*, 32nd edn. (C. H. Beck, 2008), p. 123.

15 On an overview of the development of the principle of proportionality in German legal theory in practice from the late eighteenth century until the 1950s see Stone Sweet and Mathews, "Proportionality Balancing," 97 ff.

16 See D. Willoweit, *Deutsche Verfassungsgeschichte – Vom Frankenreich bis zur Wiedervereinigung Deutschlands*, 6th edn. (C. H. Beck, 2009), pp. 361 ff. On the value-orientation of the *Grundgesetz* see German Federal Constitutional Court, Judgment of January 15, 1958, 1 BvR 400/51, BVerfGE 7, 198 at 205 ff.

17 P. Lerche, *Übermaß und Verfassungsrecht. Zur Bindung des Gesetzgebers an die Grundsätze der Verhältnismäßigkeit und der Erforderlichkeit* (Carl Heymanns Verlag, 1961).

[I]t would be a contradiction to raise personal freedom to the leading State principle and at the same time to permit unnecessary restrictions of this freedom by the State to be considered lawful. It is consequently simply irreconcilable with the system of the Basic Law [*Grundgesetz*] that the executive could be permitted to make incursions into the private sphere of individuals that go farther than is absolutely necessary to the reaching of a permissible end.[18]

With this theoretical foundation in mind, the German Federal Constitutional Court issued its seminal *Apothekenurteil* ("Pharmacy Judgment"). In this case, the Court had to rule on the interference with pharmacists' freedom of profession by a licensing system that limited the number of pharmacy licenses and thus the admission to practice as a pharmacist in order to warrant the population's safe and competent supply with pharmaceuticals.[19] For the first time, the Constitutional Court differentiated between a least-restrictive-measures-test and a balancing between the means and the ends of the measure adopted. Particularly with this latter test, what Krauss had called "proportionality *stricto sensu*,"[20] the judges sought to resolve the conflict between individual rights and public goals – including the protection of third party individual rights – and thus to achieve an optimization of government action. In the words of the German Federal Constitutional Court:

The [purpose of] the constitutional right should be to protect the freedom of the individual [while the purpose of] the regulation should be to ensure sufficient protection of societal interests. The individual's claim to freedom will have a stronger effect... the more his right to free choice of a profession is put into question; the protection of the public will become more urgent, the greater the disadvantages that arise from the free practicing of professions. When one seeks to maximize both... demands in the most effective way, then the solution can only lie in a careful balancing [*Abwägung*] of the meaning of the two opposed and perhaps conflicting interests.[21]

18 R. von Krauss, "Der Grundsatz der Verhältnismäßigkeit in seiner Bedeutung für die Notwendigkeit des Mittels im Verwaltungsrecht," Abhandlungen aus dem Seminar für Öffentliches Recht der Universität Hamburg (Hamburg, 1955), 25. Translation cited from Stone Sweet and Mathews, "Proportionality Balancing," 105.

19 See Kingsbury and Schill, "Investor-State Arbitration as Governance," 24.

20 Krauss, "Grundsatz der Verhältnismäßigkeit," 15. A literal translation would be "proportionality in the narrower sense."

21 German Federal Constitutional Court, Judgment of June 11, 1958, 1 BvR 596/56, BVerfGE 7, 377 at 404 f. Translation cited from Kingsbury and Schill, "Investor-State Arbitration as Governance," 24 f.

Krauss, "Grundsatz der Verhältnismäßigkeit," 25. Translation cited from Stone Sweet and Mathews, "Proportionality Balancing," 107 f.

In subsequent judgments, the Court refined its proportionality analysis by developing an impressive case law and declared that the principle possessed constitutional status.[22] However, while proportionality analysis was gaining prominence in German constitutional law, it spread to domestic constitutional orders in the Americas, Israel and South Africa and thus entered constitutional jurisprudence in both Common Law and Civil Law countries.

Among those, it is Canada in particular that stands out as an early and very influential example of adopting proportionality in the Common Law world.[23] In 1982, after fierce debate and decades of political haggling, Canada enacted the Charter of Rights and Freedoms, which contains an extensive catalog of rights and provides courts with the competence of constitutional review of government action. According to Section 1, the protection of rights is "subject only to such reasonable limits prescribed by law as can be demonstrably justified in a free and democratic society."[24] While thus the Charter sets express, albeit restricted limitations to individual rights protection, courts were called upon to give life to such general formulation and to pronounce what to understand by "reasonable limits . . . demonstrably justified in a free and democratic society." In *Regina* v. *Oakes*, dealing with a provision of the Canadian Narcotics Act, which established a rebuttable presumption that a person found to be in possession of drugs was trafficking drugs and therefore criminally liable, the Canadian Supreme Court – without citing any authority – stated the following:

> First, the measures adopted must be carefully designed to achieve the objective in question. They must not be arbitrary, unfair or based on irrational considerations. In short, they must be rationally connected to the objective. Second, the means, even if rationally connected to the objective in this first sense, should impair 'as little as possible' the right or freedom in question. Third, there must be a proportionality between the effects of the measures which are responsible for limiting the Charter right or freedom, and the objective which has been identified as of 'sufficient importance.'[25]

[22] German Federal Constitutional Court, Judgment of December 15, 1965, 1 BvR 513/65, BVerfGE 19, 342 at 348.

[23] Albeit it must not be forgotten that Canada has a mixed Common Law/Civil Law system; see G.-A. Beaudoin, *La Constitution du Canada – Institutions, Partage des pouvoirs, Droit et libertés*, 2nd (revised) edn. (Wilson & Lafleur Itée, 1991), pp. 24 ff.

[24] Canadian Charter of Rights and Freedoms, § 1, available at http://laws.justice.gc.ca/en/charter/.

[25] Canadian Supreme Court, *Regina* v. *Oakes* [1986] 1 SCR 103, 139.

The three-step proportionality analysis – (1) suitability; (2) necessity; and (3) proportionality *stricto sensu* – as established in German doctrine and case law is unmistakably recognizable.[26] In particular, the description of the third element appears merely to paraphrase the *Apothekenurteil*. However, as Stone Sweet and Mathews point out,[27] *Oakes* does not cite the German Constitutional Court – or any other court – when setting the standard. This demonstrates that the Court was eager to present proportionality analysis as an approach inherent in Canadian law and not as a principle with distinct foreign pedigree.[28] The *Oakes* case had a strong impact on other Common Law countries adopting or flirting with proportionality analysis, such as Ireland[29] and New Zealand.[30]

Moreover, the Israeli Supreme Court, most prominently in the *United Mizrahi Bank Ltd* v. *Migdal Cooperative Village* case, heavily draws on both *Oakes* and German scholarly writings in order to buttress its adoption of proportionality analysis.[31] Chief Justice Barak, writing for the majority of the Court, acknowledged proportionality's burgeoning in administrative law in some European countries, particularly Germany, and went on to note that "from there it spread to the constitutional law of most countries in Europe and outside of it,"[32] specifically mentioning Canada and South Africa.

The latter has also proven very prone to proportionality analysis. After decades of racial discrimination by the apartheid régime, a new Interim Constitution came into force at the end of 1993, delineating a catalog of fundamental rights including a limitations clause similar to the Canadian Charter of Rights and Freedoms and vesting the newly established South African Supreme Court with the power of judicial review. Hence, in 1995, when the Court had to rule on the constitutionality of the death penalty

26 See *infra* 5 D. 27 Stone Sweet and Mathews, "Proportionality Balancing," 117.

28 *Ibid.*

29 See Irish High Court, *Heaney* v. *Ireland* [1994] 3 IR 593 (Ir.), expressly citing *Oakes*; and Irish High Court, *Rock* v. *Ireland* [1997] 3 IR 484 (Ir.), 500.

30 See New Zealand High Court, *Ministry of Transport* v. *Noort* [1992] 3 NZLR 260 (CA) adopting the *Oakes* test; New Zealand High Court, *Hansen* v. *The Queen* [2007] 3 NZLR 1 (SC); P. A. Joseph, "The New Zealand Bill of Rights Experience" in P. Alston (ed.), *Promoting Human Rights Through Bills of Rights: Comparative Perspectives* (Oxford University Press, 1999), p. 283 at p. 305.

31 See Israeli Supreme Court, CA 6821/93 *United Mizrahi Bank Ltd.* v. *Migdal Cooperative Village* [1995] IsrSC 49(4), 436 f. See also A. Barak, *Interpretation in the Law (Vol. III: Constitutional Interpretation)*, 1994, laying the doctrinal foundations for proportionality analysis in Israeli constitutional law, which Chief Justice Barak included in the judgment delivered by himself a year later.

32 *Ibid.*, p. 436.

in its famous decision in *State* v. *Makwanyane*, it turned to proportionality analysis to seek to reconcile the opposing arguments for and against capital punishment:

In the balancing process, the relevant considerations will include the nature of the right that is limited, and its importance to an open and democratic society based on freedom and equality; the purpose for which the right is limited and the importance of that purpose to such a society; the extent of the limitation, its efficacy, and particularly where the limitation has to be necessary, whether the desired ends could reasonably be achieved through other means less damaging to the right in question.[33]

It is no coincidence that this reads very much like *Oakes* or the proportionality analysis employed by the German Federal Constitutional Court, since the justices of the newly constituted South African Supreme Court spent a week in Germany meeting with the judges of the Federal Constitutional Court only very recently before delivering the findings in *Makwanyane*.[34] The fact that the Court refers to proportionality as a single-step multifaceted balancing is only of minor relevance, given that the *Makwanyane* test includes all elements of suitability, necessity and proportionality *stricto sensu* and thus in practice does reach results fundamentally different from a three-step test. In 1996, the new permanent South African Constitution elevated proportionality to express constitutional status, fleshing out the factors as developed in *Makwanyane*. Thus, in 2003, Justice Albie Sachs noted that "[p]roportionality and balancing are at the heart of constitutional litigation in our country."[35]

2. *Proportionality analysis in the European legal order – ECJ jurisprudence*

Therefore the influence of the German proportionality analysis expanded beyond the domestic sphere and has had considerable impact on foreign domestic (constitutional) orders. Maybe the most prominent example of extensive proportionality analysis beyond the domestic realm is to be found in the European legal order, i.e. in the jurisprudence of the ECJ and the European Court of First Instance.[36] Starting from the 1970s, the European courts refer to the typical three-step test of proportionality:

[33] South African Supreme Court, *State* v. *Makwanyane & Another*, 1995 (3) SA 391, 436 (CC).

[34] See C. Smith, "An American's View of the Federal Constitutional Court: Karlsruhe's Justices," *German L.J.*, 2 (2001), Issue 9, available at www.germanlawjournal.com/index.php?pageID=11_artID=17.

[35] A. L. Sachs, "The Challenges of Post-Apartheid South Africa," *Green Bag*, 7 (2003), 63 at 67.

[36] J. Steiner, L. Woods and C. Twigg-Flesner, *EU Law*, 9th edn. (Oxford University Press, 2006), p. 128.

(1) suitability; (2) necessity; and (3) proportionality *stricto sensu*.[37] They employ the principle in basically three situations of conflicts of laws: Firstly, in order to reconcile domestic measures by a Member State conflicting with European law, both primary and secondary; secondly, in order to resolve a conflict between secondary and primary European law; and thirdly, in case a fundamental freedom conflicts with a fundamental right.[38] What is remarkable in European law is that the ECJ developed a proportionality analysis additional to the limitations clauses expressly enshrined in the treaty, deriving it from general principles of European law. In its seminal 1979 *Cassis de Dijon* judgment the ECJ held that while on the one hand the free movement of goods could not only be violated by discriminatory, but also by non-discriminatory, regulations by a Member State, on the other Member States were able to limit fundamental freedoms in the public interest if such interest constituted a so-called "mandatory requirement":[39]

> Obstacles to movement within the Community resulting from disparities between the national laws relating to the marketing of the products in question must be accepted in so far as those provisions may be recognized as being necessary in order to satisfy mandatory requirements relating in particular to the effectiveness of fiscal supervision, the protection of public health, the fairness of commercial transactions and the defence of the consumer.[40]

Whereas it sounds more like a least-restrictive-measures test, the way the ECJ and the Court of First Instance have applied it subsequently has corroborated the aforesaid three-step analysis. In later years, the European courts often added the passage "the disadvantages caused must not be disproportionate to the aims pursued" to the above-cited formulation.[41]

3. *Proportionality in the jurisprudence of international Tribunals*

In the classical public international law sphere of inter-State relations as arbitrated before the International Court of Justice, proportionality analysis also serves to reconcile conflicting interests and to find proper balancing of means–ends relationships – albeit admittedly with much less

[37] Jans, "Proportionality Revisited," 2 ff.

[38] For an overview of funding principles of European law and the relationship of Union law and domestic law of a Member State see *supra* 4 B. 2.

[39] See Kingsbury and Schill, "Investor-State Arbitration as Governance," 26.

[40] European Court of Justice, *Cassis de Dijon*, ECJ 120/78, Judgment of February 20, 1979 – see [1979] ECR 649, para. 8.

[41] European Court of First Instance, Case T-13/99, Judgment of November 23, 2002 – *Pfizer Animal Health SA* v. *Commission* [2002] ECR II-3305, para. 411.

prominence as in the aforementioned domestic and European contexts.[42] The main playground here is the law of countermeasures. In the 1986 *Nicaragua* case,[43] rejecting the legality of US tactical military actions inside Nicaragua, the World Court held:

The acts of which Nicaragua is accused, even assuming them to have been established and imputable to that State, could only have justified proportionate counter-measures . . . They could not justify . . . intervention involving the use of force.[44]

Consequently, it found that it could not:

regard the United States activities . . . relating to the mining of the Nicaraguan ports and the attacks on ports, oil installations, etc. as satisfying [the criterion of proportionality]. Whatever uncertainty may exist as to the exact scale of the aid received by the Salvadorian armed opposition from Nicaragua, it is clear that these latter United States activities in question could not have been proportionate to that aid.[45]

In the 2005 *Congo* v. *Uganda* case, again ruling on military matters and the legality of the use of force as a countermeasure, the ICJ – however, merely in an *obiter dictum* – stated that "the taking of airports and towns many hundreds of kilometers from Uganda's border would not seem proportionate . . . nor to be necessary to that end."[46] Moreover, the *Gabcíkovo-Nagymaros* case of 1997 stressed that "the effects of a countermeasure must be commensurate with the injury suffered, taking into account of the rights in question."[47] Hence, in the field of countermeasures, the most important stage for proportionality analysis in inter-State relations in public international law, proportionality limits both the means and scope of the countermeasures applied.[48]

In the context of the WTO, another inter-State treaty body, panels are frequently called upon to balance public interest with rules promoting

[42] See T. M. Franck, "On Proportionality of Countermeasures in International Law," *Am. J. Int'l L.*, 102 (2008), 715 at 718 f.

[43] On facts, etc. see *supra* 4 C. 6. (a).

[44] ICJ, *Nicaragua Case*, Merits, para. 249.

[45] *Ibid.*, para. 237.

[46] ICJ, *Armed Activities on the Territory of the Congo (Dem. Rep. Congo* v. *Uganda)*, Judgment of December 19, 2005, *ICJ Reports* (2005), 168 at 223, para. 147.

[47] ICJ, *Gabcíkovo-Nagymaros Project (Hungary* v. *Slovakia)*, Judgment of September 25, 1997, *ICJ Reports* (1986), 7, para. 85.

[48] E. Cannizzaro, "The Role of Proportionality in the Law of International Countermeasures," *Eur. J. Int'l L.*, 12 (2001), 889 at 898 f. See also Art. 51 of the ILC Articles on State Responsibility and the commentary on this provision in J. Crawford, *The International Law Commission's Articles on State Responsibility – Introduction, Text and Commentaries* (Cambridge University Press, 2002), p. 294.

free trade. The entry point of proportionality analysis is Article XX of the General Agreement on Tariffs and Trade (GATT) that permits exceptions in the public interest, if the measures undertaken are "necessary" to pursue the alleged purpose. In the pre-WTO dispute *US – Section 337 of the Tariff Act of 1930*, the then European Communities successfully challenged a US measure treating patent infringement litigation differently according to the site of production of the good.[49] The US pleaded that the measure was "necessary to secure compliance with laws . . . relating to . . . the protection of patents,"[50] as provided by GATT Article XX(d). The panel found that:

> a contracting party cannot justify a measure inconsistent with another GATT provision as 'necessary' in terms of Article XX(d) if an alternative measure which it could reasonably be expected to employ and which is not inconsistent with other GATT provisions is available to it. By the same token, in cases where a measure consistent with other GATT provisions is not reasonably available, a contracting party is bound to use, among the measures reasonably available to it, that which entails the least degree of inconsistency with other GATT provisions.[51]

Moreover, in 2001, the WTO Appellate Body in *Korea – Beef* had to rule on a case concerning the labeling and sale of beef depending on its origins: as Korean or non-Korean. While South Korea purported that such measure was "necessary" to protect the public health, the Appellate Body held that:

> [t]he more vital or important . . . common interests or values are, the easier it would be to accept as 'necessary' a measure designed as an enforcement instrument. There are other aspects of the enforcement measure to be considered in evaluating that measure as 'necessary.' One is the extent to which the measure contributes to the realization of the end pursued, the securing of compliance with the law or regulation at issue. The greater the contribution, the more easily a measure might be considered to be 'necessary' . . . [The] [d]etermination of whether a measure, which is not 'indispensable,' may nevertheless be 'necessary' within the contemplation of Article XX(d), *involves in every case a process of weighing and balancing* a series of factors which prominently include the contribution made by the compliance measure to the enforcement of the law or regulation at issue, the importance of the common interests or values protected by that law or regulation, and the accompanying impact of the law or regulation on imports or exports.[52]

[49] Stone Sweet and Mathews, "Proportionality Balancing," 155.

[50] General Agreement on Tariffs and Trade; see *supra* 3 B. 1. (a), Art. XX(d).

[51] GATT Panel Report, *United States – Section 337 of the Tariff Act of 1930*, November 7, 1989, GATT BISD (L/6439–36S/345 36th Supp.) at 345, recital 5.26.

[52] WTO Appellate Body Report, *Korea – Measures Affecting Imports of Fresh, Chilled and Frozen Beef*, December 11, 2000, WT/DS161/AB/R para. 164 (emphasis added).

In both cases, the panel or Appellate Body reduced proportionality analysis basically to a least-restrictive-measures test and thus focused on the second step, i.e. the necessity principle – not very surprisingly so, given the express wording in the GATT ("necessary"). However, the borrowing from European and German law experience is unmistakable, particularly as regards the balancing of a multitude of different factors, which invites the creative problem-solving so typical of proportionality analysis with German pedigree. Considering that in *US – Section 337*, one of the three panelists, Pierre Pescatore, was a former long-serving judge at the ECJ and in *Korea – Beef*, the chairman, Claus-Dieter Ehlermann, was a German senior official of the European Commission, such observation comes as rather unsurprising.[53]

Before briefly glancing at what role proportionality analysis already plays in international investment law, I want to make a last stop in order to quickly assess proportionality's relevance in an international law régime that focuses on the protection of individuals against the exercise of public authority and thus – as I have demonstrated above[54] – exhibits some striking similarities with investment law: the European Convention on Human Rights and Fundamental Freedoms (ECHR) system in the jurisprudence of the ECtHR.

The ECtHR nowadays subjects all rights enshrined in the ECHR to some sort of balancing,[55] most prominently as regards Articles 8 to 11 and 14, where it actually engages in a proportionality analysis very close to the German approach. In *Handyside* v. *the United Kingdom* – involving the censorship of a book on grounds of alleged public morals violations – the Court held that:

> the adjective 'necessary,' within the meaning of Article 10 para. 2 is not synonymous with 'indispensable' [and] neither has it the flexibility of such expressions as ... 'admissible' ... 'useful,' 'reasonable,' or 'desirable.'[56]

In a later case, *Dudgeon* v. *the United Kingdom*, the ECtHR struck down a measure criminalizing homosexual practices as "disproportionate" and

[53] Stone Sweet and Mathews, "Proportionality Balancing," 156 and 159 draw attention to that fact.

[54] See *supra* 4 B. 3.

[55] J. Rivers, "Proportionality and Variable Intensity of Review," *Cambridge L.J.*, 65 (2006), 174 at 182.

[56] European Court of Human Rights, *Handyside* v. *United Kingdom*, App. No. 5493/72 (Eur. Ct. HR December 7, 1976), para. 48.

hence violating the right to privacy as enshrined in Article 8.[57] However, the Court gives some leeway to the Member States as to "mak[ing] the initial assessment of the pressing social need implied by the notion of 'necessity' in this context."[58] Therefore, the Court confines its level of scrutiny to the frame that sets the "margin of appreciation" it grants the Member States. While it is for them to determine in the first place what they consider "necessary in a democratic society,"[59] the judges may only assess the measure adopted within the frame the Member State chooses – with the margin varying according to several factors such as, among others, the specific right involved, the specific alleged government purpose pursued and the degree of interference.[60]

4. A glimpse into investment arbitration jurisprudence vis-à-vis proportionality

Without anticipating detailed analyses of several specific aspects in the chapters below,[61] I will now turn to fleshing out the gist of proportionality approaches to be found in international investment case law, which might serve – jointly with the assessment of the preceding case law of domestic and international courts and Tribunals – to foreshadow how a more thorough proportionality analysis in international investment law could potentially look like. There currently exists a triad of thematic entry points where proportionality analysis is creeping into the investment realm: (1) indirect expropriation; (2) the fair and equitable treatment standard; and (3) the necessity defense as raised in the Argentine cases ensuing from the 2001/2002 economic crisis.

As regards indirect expropriations, in recent awards investment arbitration Tribunals came to use proportionality analysis in order to determine whether the actual host State conduct amounted to a compensable (indirect) expropriation. Hence, the *Tecmed*[62] Tribunal employed a comprehensive weighing and balancing of the competing interests and held the following:

[57] European Court of Human Rights, *Dudgeon* v. *United Kingdom*, App. No. 7525/76 (Eur. Ct. HR October 22, 1981), para. 24.

[58] European Court of Human Rights, *Handyside* v. *United Kingdom*, para. 22.

[59] See Arts. 8–11 ECHR.

[60] Kingsbury and Schill, "Investor-State Arbitration as Governance," 28.

[61] See *infra* Chapters 6–8.

[62] For a detailed analysis of the *Tecmed* decision, including its reasoning on proportionality see *infra* 6 C. 4.

[T]he Arbitral Tribunal will consider, in order to determine if they are to be characterized as expropriatory, whether such actions or measures are proportional to the public interest presumably protected thereby and to the protection legally granted to investments, taking into account that the significance of such impact has a key role upon deciding the proportionality.[63]

Furthermore, in *LG&E* the Tribunal endorsed the *Tecmed* approach and stated:

It is this Tribunal's opinion that there must be a balance in the analysis both of the causes and the effects of a measure in order that one may qualify a measure as being of an expropriatory nature.[64]

Similarly, vis-à-vis fair and equitable treatment (FET) clauses Tribunals draw on proportionality analysis in order to resolve conflicts between investor and legitimate host State interests via balancing a wealth of principles for the purpose of animating the umbrella-like, albeit blurry, legal standard.[65] For example, the Tribunal in *Saluka* v. *Czech Republic* reasoned:

No investor may reasonably request that the circumstances prevailing at the time the investment is made remain totally unchanged. In order to determine whether frustration of the foreign investor's expectations was justified and reasonable, the host State's legitimate right subsequently to regulate domestic matters in the public interest must be taken into consideration as well . . . The determination of a breach of Article 3.1 by the Czech Republic therefore requires a weighing of the Claimant's legitimate and reasonable expectations on one hand and the Respondent's legitimate regulatory interests on the other.[66]

Finally, proportionality analysis plays a role in the reasoning of those Argentine crisis Tribunals that affirmed Argentina's necessity defense.[67] In the above-cited *LG&E* case, seeking to reconcile the found FET violation with the necessity defense, the Tribunal made brief mention of the proportionality principle, though in the negative:

With respect to the power of the State to adopt its policies, it can generally be said that the State has the right to adopt measures having a social or general welfare

63 *Tecmed* v. *Mexico*, para. 122.

64 *LG&E* v. *Argentina*, para. 194, quoting *Tecmed* v. *Mexico*, para. 115.

65 A. Stone Sweet, "Investor-State Arbitration: Proportionality's New Frontier," *Law and Legal Ethics of Human Rights* (2009), available at: http://works.bepress.com/alec_stone_sweet/31.

66 *Saluka* v. *Czech Republic*, paras. 304–306.

67 For a detailed analysis of the necessity defense in the Argentine cases and their relevance vis-à-vis the Global Public Interest theory see *supra* 4 C. 1. (b).

purpose. In such a case, the measure must be accepted without any imposition of liability, except in cases where the State's action is obviously disproportionate to the need being addressed.[68]

By contrast, the *Continental Casualty* award drew extensively on proportionality analysis:

[A]ctions properly necessary by the central government to preserve or to restore civil peace and the normal life of society (especially of a democratic society such as that of Argentina), to prevent and repress illegal actions and disturbances that may infringe such civil peace and potentially threaten the legal order, even when due to significant economic and social difficulties, and therefore to cope with and aim at removing these difficulties, do fall within the application under Art. XI [the necessity clause in the US–Argentina BIT].[69]

In order to illuminate the murky and contentious concept of "necessity" in international law, the arbitrators heavily relied on WTO jurisprudence dealing with the interpretation of "necessary" in Article XX GATT.[70] Citing *EC – Tyres*,[71] a leading WTO case, the Tribunal embraced the following standard:

The necessity of a measure should be determined through 'a process of weighing and balancing of factors' which usually includes the assessment of the following three factors: the relative importance of interests or values furthered by the challenged measures, the contribution of the measure to the realization of the ends pursued by it and the restrictive impact of the measure on international commerce.[72]

While the reasoning in *Continental Casualty* – as in many of the cases cited in this section – may be highly disputable,[73] it is undeniable that the importance of proportionality analysis spreading from German origins to a myriad of domestic legal orders and international régimes is constantly growing – in public international law in general and in international investment law in particular. I will now extract the constituting elements and relevant subprinciples of proportionality analysis before subsequently seeking to operationalize it for balancing investor rights with defenses of the host State enshrining the Global Public Interest.

[68] *LG&E* v. *Argentina*, para. 195. [69] *Continental Casualty* v. *Argentina*, para. 152.

[70] On Art. XX GATT see this section, above.

[71] *EC-Tyres*, WTO Appellate Body, *Brazil Measures Affecting Imports of Retreaded Tyres*, WT/DS332/AB/R, adopted December 17, 2007, para. 7.104.

[72] *Continental Casualty* v. *Argentina*, para. 194. [73] See *supra* 4 C. 1. (b) (ii).

D. Elements of proportionality analysis

As has already been presupposed in earlier sections, proportionality analysis consists of three basic elements: (1) suitability; (2) necessity; and (3) proportionality *stricto sensu*. For a better overview, the ensuing section will briefly summarize the basic content of these three prongs.

1. *Suitability*

Being the first element[74] of the typically three-pronged proportionality test,[75] the suitability principle consists of two interrelated subtests: The judge, arbitrator or other independent decision-maker must determine whether the measure under scrutiny as adopted by any branch of the government, firstly, serves a legitimate government purpose and, secondly, is generally suitable for achieving such purpose. Hence, the suitability test means a proviso of judicial restraint in a double sense.[76]

The government is bestowed with a considerable margin of appreciation ("*Beurteilungsspielraum*"[77]) as to setting the purpose it wants to pursue. Only illegitimate purposes are not permitted and thus constitute a disproportionate interference with the right or interest protected. A purpose is illegitimate only in marginal cases. Applied to the international investment law realm, this would usually only play a role in cases of *ius cogens* violations, such as slavery or if the purpose pursued is of a mere private nature such as corruption for the personal benefit of a State official or his or her cronies.[78] Thus, only in very rare circumstances would the adopted measures fail to fulfill the "legitimate government purpose" requirement.

74 As regards terminology, Georg Nolte rightly notes – pertaining to the European administrative law realm – that the German "'Geeignetheit' [only] means that a particular measure must be theoretically capable of contributing to achieving its aim" and hence proposes to call this first step of the proportionality analysis "capacity of furthering an aim" in order to avoid misunderstandings; see G. Nolte, "General Principles of German and European Administrative Law – A Comparison in Historical Perspective," *Mod. L. Rev.*, 57 (1994), 191 at 193. Since the term "suitability" is used and understood among most scholars in the said meaning, for the sake of avoiding further confusion, I will not change terminology and thus subsequently refer to the first step of proportionality analysis as "suitability" or "the principle of suitability."

75 Of a different opinion in this regard is P. Lerche, *Übermaß und Verfassungsrecht*, pp. 21 ff., who excludes the suitability test from the core of the principle of proportionality and merges the necessity and the proportionality *stricto sensu* test to what he calls "prohibition of excessive measures" ("*Übermaßverbot*").

76 See Grabitz, "Verhältnismäßigkeit," 572. 77 *Ibid.*

78 Kingsbury and Schill, "Investor-State Arbitration as Governance," 29.

Moreover, what makes this threshold even easier to pass is that it is not necessary for the measure under scrutiny to actually be suitable for pursuing that purpose eventually. While the second element of the suitability principle requires establishing "a causal relationship of the measure and its object,"[79] it is sufficient if such relationship existed from an *ex ante* perspective.[80] It is an automatic companion of the margin of appreciation vis-à-vis the legitimate purpose that the government exhausts its duties, if it undertakes an assessment of the situation as possible at the time of the adoption of the measure.[81] Thus, a good faith misjudgment does not fail the suitability test. All the judge, arbitrator or other independent decision-maker has to assess is whether – from an *ex ante* position – the measure taken furthered the (legitimate) purpose as set by the government.

Therefore, from the decision-maker's viewpoint, the suitability principle is merely a very rough grid to exclude obviously disproportionate measures. From the government's perspective, however, it is a safeguard for judicial restraint and against excessive judicial activism that grants considerable leeway in making policy decisions.

2. *Necessity*

As the second step of proportionality analysis, the principle of necessity is often referred to as a least-restrictive-measure-test. However, while such description is not defective in itself, some more precision is helpful. What this level of the proportionality analysis seeks to ascertain is that the specific measure may only be chosen if there is no *relatively* less restrictive measure available. Thus, a measure does not automatically fail the necessity test if there is another measure imaginable that is less restrictive than the one adopted by the government.

Here, again, the (legitimate) government purpose comes into play, for the measure is merely unnecessary if there is no less restrictive measure that is equally effective in achieving the legitimate government purpose pursued. The means are put in relation to the ends and must conform to them. Consequently, as Kingsbury and Schill rightly state, "[t]his step requires answering two questions: first, is there a less restrictive measure, and secondly, is this measure equally effective (and reasonably

[79] J. H. Jans, "Proportionality Revisited," *Legal Issues of Economic Integration*, 27 (2000), 239 at 240.

[80] Grabitz, "Verhältnismäßigkeit," 572.

[81] German Federal Constitutional Court, Judgment of December 18, 1968, 1 BvL 5, 14/64, BVerfGE 25, 1 at 12.

feasible)?"[82] Whether a measure is equally effective or not can hardly be determined *in abstracto*.[83] Furthermore, the government is not limited to choosing only one specific measure but may employ several or plenty of them – provided, of course, they are all equally effective.

Such governmental leeway can be traced back to the optimization ratio inherent in any situation of balancing of conflicting principles.[84] Despite such relative freedom granted to the government in choosing the measures to pursue the legitimate purpose, the necessity test is somewhat stricter than the suitability principle in that in the latter case the test also fails if from an *ex post* perspective the measure undertaken turns out to be more restrictive than another equally effective one.[85]

3. *Proportionality* stricto sensu

The proportionality *stricto sensu*, the third and last step of proportionality analysis, is arguably its heart and soul. Not only is it, as again Schill and Kingsbury stress, "apposite because an analysis that stops at the necessity-stage would allow restricting a right severely in order to protect a negligible public interest."[86] It draws its central role in proportionality analysis from its normative content, for only the proportionality *stricto sensu* allows consideration of, among other relevant factors, the importance of the interests involved, and weighs and hence evaluates them. It focuses on the relationship of means and ends, i.e. adopted measures and pursued legitimate government purpose, and regards – different to the necessity test that only takes the measure(s) as a variable, but the purpose as a constant – both measures and purpose as variables.[87] Only this concept pries open the door for balancing, i.e. comparing means and ends in their respective importance.

Here, it becomes even more apparent than in the context of the necessity principle that proportionality analysis is targeted at optimization of governmental action, for it requires the judge, arbitrator or other decision-maker to undergo "an exercise in creative problem-solving."[88]

82 Kingsbury and Schill, "Investor-State Arbitration as Governance," 29.
83 Grabitz, "Verhältnismäßigkeit," 574.
84 R. Alexy, *Theorie der Grundrechte*, 1st edn. (Suhrkamp, 1986), p. 399.
85 Grabitz, "Verhältnismäßigkeit," 575.
86 Kingsbury and Schill, "Investor-State Arbitration as Governance," 30, citing Krauss, "Grundsatz der Verhaltnismäßigkeit," 15.
87 Grabitz, "Verhältnismäßigkeit," 575.
88 Kingsbury and Schill, "Investor-State Arbitration as Governance," 30.

E. Principles relevant in proportionality analysis

While the said standards constitute the *noyau dur* of proportionality analysis, over the course of years, if not to say decades, of its application, several subprinciples have crystallized providing interpretative guidance. Three of these, which I regard most relevant for proportionality analysis in an investment dispute, are singled out below.

1. *Standards of review (*Kontrolldichte*), margin of appreciation and standards of scrutiny*

The concept of varying levels of review or scrutiny in (constitutional or human) rights analysis is common to nearly all legal systems. It is an achievement of liberal democracy and the rule of law that while judges usually assume the position and competency to control State conduct by independent legal review, they acknowledge their role as judicial bodies and hence their limited competences and legitimacy as political decision-makers. Whether we call it standards of review or *Kontrolldichte* (German Federal Constitutional Court),[89] margin of appreciation (ECtHR)[90] or levels of scrutiny (US Supreme Court),[91] all those instruments aim at adequate allocation of competencies in a separation of power and thus a functional context. Whether such separation is horizontal – between the three branches of government within a State – or a vertical – between the State and an international Tribunal – is of no relevance in this regard. The underlying rationale of either of these standards of review is that the judge has to exercise judicial self-restraint in cases where political, cultural and moral core questions are at stake that the State or a particular branch of government is much more competent to evaluate. On the other hand, review grows stricter the more intense and the more suspicious the intrusion on the individual interest is.[92]

89 Zippelius and Würtenberger, *Deutsches Staatsrecht*, p. 520. Similarly vis-à-vis ECJ jurisprudence, F. Schwab, *Der Europäische Gerichtshof und der Verhältnismäßigkeitsgrundsatz: Untersuchung der Prüfungsdichte* (Peter Lang, 2002), pp. 269 ff.

90 Burke-White and von Staden, "Private Litigation in a Public Law Sphere," 20.

91 B. A. Ackerman, "Beyond Carolene Products," *Harv. L. Rev.*, 98 (1985), 713.

92 For the German realm see H.-J. Papier, "Das Bundesverfassungsgericht als 'Hüter der Grundrechte'" in M. Brenner, P. M. Huber and M. Möstl (eds.), *Der Staat des Grundgesetzes – Kontinuität und Wandel, Festschrift für Peter Badura zum siebzigsten Geburtstag* (Mohr Siebeck, 2004), p. 411 at p. 425. As for the US, in *United States* v. *Carolene Products Co.*, 304 US 144 (1938) the Supreme Court famously stated in a footnote: "[M]ore searching judicial inquiry [is appropriate when the law in question] interferes with individual rights . . . restricts the ability of the political process to repeal undesirable legislation, or . . . discriminates against a 'discrete or insular minority'."

However, while their functional rationale is similar, it must be kept in mind that the doctrinal structure and context of review mechanisms may vary. While *Kontrolldichte* and margin of appreciation are basically subprinciples of proportionality analysis, the levels of scrutiny as developed by the US Supreme Court starting from *Carolene Products*[93] are an independent standard for assessing the violation of a constitutional right. Over the course of time the Court has created three different levels of scrutiny. Under rational basis review it suffices if the relevant statute, etc. is rationally related to a legitimate government purpose.[94] By contrast, strict scrutiny applies where legislation draws distinctions based on suspect classifications, such as race or national origin, alienage, fundamental rights, and content-based restrictions on freedom of speech.[95] To pass this test, the statute must be narrowly tailored to meet a compelling government interest, i.e. it must use the least restrictive or least discriminatory measures to achieve the respective goal.[96] This standard is often characterized as "strict in theory, fatal in fact."[97] More deferential than strict scrutiny but less so than rational basis review, intermediate scrutiny inquires whether the legislation furthers an important governmental purpose and is substantially related to that purpose.[98]

By contrast, in ECtHR jurisprudence, the margin of appreciation does not by itself constitute the review test, but is merely part of it. It is embedded in proportionality analysis, limiting the level of review on both the necessity as well as the proportionality *stricto sensu* stage. For example, vis-à-vis necessity it held that it is "for the national authorities to make the initial assessment of the reality of the pressing social need implied by the notion of 'necessity' in [such] context[s]."[99] The scope of the margin of appreciation "will vary according to the context . . . Relevant factors include the nature of the Convention right at issue, its importance for the individual and the nature of the activities concerned."[100]

Similarly, the German Federal Constitutional Court exercises judicial self-restraint and confines itself to striking down evident violations of

93 US Supreme Court, *United States* v. *Carolene Products Co.*, 304 US 144 (1938).

94 See US Supreme Court, *Railway Express Agency, Inc.* v. *New York*, 336 US 106 (1949).

95 Burke-White and von Staden, "Private Litigation in a Public Law Sphere," 33.

96 *Ibid.*, 34.

97 F. Winkler, "Fatal in Theory and Strict in Fact: An Empirical Analysis of Strict Scrutiny in the Federal Courts," *Van. L. Rev.*, 59 (2006), 793 at 798 ff.

98 See US Supreme Court, *Craig* v. *Boren*, 429 US 190, 197 (1976).

99 European Court of Human Rights, *Handyside* v. *United Kingdom*, para. 48.

100 European Court of Human Rights, *Buckley* v. *United Kingdom*, Judgment of September 25, 1996, 1996-I Eur. Ct. H R, para. 74.

constitutional principles, if the legislature or executive possess more expertise to assess the viability of the adopted policy or if the measure to be assessed is inherently political in nature. For example, the Court confirmed the Federal Chancellor's decision to pose the question of confidence to the *Bundestag*, the German parliament, where his coalition held the majority, in order to dissolve the legislature before the official end of its term. Although the founders of the *Grundgesetz* explicitly sought to avoid a situation in which the parliamentary majority – by initiative of the executive – was enabled to dissolve parliament in order to seek new general elections, the Court granted the Federal Chancellor a considerable prerogative in the assessment whether he was still able to govern properly or whether he had lost parliamentary support. The Court found that such decision was inherently political and hence upheld the measure despite a plethora of serious doubts and fierce opposition in academia.[101] On the other hand, while it allows such prerogative in case of political nature of the decisions, the Court claims the authority to scrutinize the factual basis on which such decisions are made.[102]

2. *"Praktische Konkordanz"*

A second subprinciple of proportionality analysis, or more precisely, of the proportionality *stricto sensu*, is what the German doctrine refers to as "*Konkordanz*" or "*praktische Konkordanz*."[103] It was developed to reconcile

101 German Federal Constitutional Court, Judgment of August 25, 2005, 2 BvE 4/05 and 2 BvE 7/05, BVerfGE 114, 121 at 162 ff. For critique of such view see T. Herbst, "Die auflösungsgerichtete Vertrauensfrage," *Der Staat*, 45 (2006), 45; J. Ipsen, "Zur Regierung verurteilt? – Verfassungsrechtliche Probleme der Vertrauensfrage nach Art. 68 GG," *Neue Juristische Wochenschrift*, 68 (2005), 2201; "Auflösung des 15. Deutschen Bundestages – eine Nachlese," *Neue Zeitschrift für Verwaltungsrecht*, **24** (2005), 1147; R. Dickmann, "Das Kappen der historisch-systematischen Taue einer Verfassungsnorm – Eine kritische Betrachtung der Entscheidung des Bundesverfassungsgerichts zur Bundestagsauflösung 2005," *Bayerische Verwaltungsblätter*, 137 (2006), 72; V. Epping, "'Gefühltes Misstrauen' – die inszenierte Vertrauensfrage vom 1. Juli 2005 – Eine Nachbetrachtung der zweiten Bundestagsauflösungsentscheidung des Bundesverfassungsgerichts," *Recht und Politik*, 41 (2005), 197.

102 German Federal Constitutional Court, Judgment of October 24, 2002, 2 BvF 1/01, BVerfGE 106, 62 at 144 and 150.

103 The term was coined by Konrad Hesse; see K. Hesse, *Grundzüge des Verfassungsrechts der Bundesrepublik Deutschland*, 20th edn. (C. F. Müller Juristischer Verlag, 1995), at MN 72. While its strongest theoretical influences are Kant and Hegel (see in particular I. Kant, *Metaphysik der Sitten*, in W. Weischedel (ed.), *Kant, Immanuel: Werkausgabe in 12 Bänden* (Suhrkamp, 1968), Vol. VIII, 337: "Das Recht ist Inbegriff der Bedingungen, unter denen die Willkür des einen mit der Willkür des anderen nach einem allgemeinen Gesetz der Freiheit in Einklang gebracht werden"), its roots may be traced back to medieval

conflicts between two or more competing fundamental rights.[104] Since fundamental rights enjoy pivotal importance within a legal (constitutional) order, such importance must be reflected in the balancing exercise. Hence, no fundamental right may be considered superior to any other such right *in abstracto*. As a consequence all competing rights have to be reconciled in a differentiated manner that aims at the optimal outcome for every such right.[105] Such optimization imperative is inherent in the idea of rights themselves: Their relevance as encapsulations of fundamental individual interests make it indispensable to seek to give effective protection to any of them as far as is possible.[106]

3. *Limits to the balancing test (*ius cogens*)*

Brief mention has to be made that the balancing test of proportionality analysis is not an infinite exercise without limits. Proportionality is not a utilitarian device to merely find the most effective result. Since it is founded on the idea of rights as normative categories the importance of which for the entire (constitutional) legal order requires seeking optimization through *Konkordanz*,[107] balancing must be reconsidered when *ius cogens* violations are at stake. It would be an oxymoron if the cogent and thus absolute character of such norms was subject to balancing and thus relativized. Hence, if an *ius cogens* norm conflicts with another right that does not display such character, the former must prevail.[108]

canonic law, in particular to the scholars Gratian (*Concordia discordantium canonum*, c. 1140) and Nikolaus von Kues (*De concordantia catholica*, 1433); see A. Winroth, *The Making of Gratian's Decretum* (Cambridge University Press, 2000), pp. 146 ff.; S. G. Kuttner, *Harmony from Dissonance: An Interpretation of Medieval Canon Law* (Latrobe, 1960), pp. 9 ff.

104 It has also found its way into the jurisprudence of the German Federal Constitutional Court and is considered established practice; see German Federal Constitutional Court, Decision of December 17, 1975, 1 BvR 63/68, BVerfGE 41, 29, and recently German Federal Constitutional Court, Judgment of May 31, 2006, 2 BvR 1693/04. In the doctrine, however, the principle is not entirely undisputed. For a critique of *praktische Konkordanz* see A. Fischer-Lescano, "Kritik der praktischen Konkordanz," *Kritische Justiz*, 41 (2008), 166; E.-W. Böckenförde, "Grundrechtstheorie und Grundrechtsinterpretation," *Neue Juristische Wochenschrift*, 38 (1974), 1529 at 1534; E. Hoffmann, *Abwägung im Recht* (Mohr Siebeck, 2007), pp. 377 ff.

105 See Kingsbury and Schill, "Investor-State Arbitration as Governance," 34. See also Hesse, *Grundzüge*, and similarly Lerche, *Übermaß und Verfassungsrecht*, p. 153.

106 See Alexy, *Theory of Constitutional Rights*, p. 152.

107 See *supra* 5 E. 2. and *infra* 5 F. 1.

108 See R. Kolb, "Théorie Du Ius Cogens International," *Revue belge de droit international*, 36 (2003), 5 at 22 ff.

F. Operationalizing proportionality analysis in international investment law

Hence, after the above rather theoretical and abstract examination of proportionality analysis as an interpretative tool for reconciling conflicting interests, it remains to consider the best avenues for making it operable within the realm of international investment law. This necessitates first of all an answer to the still open question raised at B. of why proportionality analysis is actually the instrument most suitable for such undertaking (1.). Moreover, after responding to several unresolved doctrinal questions (2., 3. and 5.), I seek to discuss an open list of factors to be considered when applying proportionality analysis and in particular the proportionality *stricto sensu* in an actual investment case (4.), and analyze how the outcome of proportionality analysis may be translated into monetary terms on the level of compensation and damages (6.).

1. *Why proportionality analysis?*

In Chapter 4 I identified investor rights, inter alia, as trump cards the investor can raise to pierce the sovereignty shield of the host State. On the other hand, I have previously argued for the emergence of a Global Public Interest in international investment law as expressed in general principles of law and customary international law. Again, my argument is that since international investment law is a public law type system, both investor interest as enshrined in investor rights and the Global Public Interest as enshrined in general principles and customary international law and placed in the hands of the host State must be given voice in this system that displays certain constitutional characteristics. Hence, conflicts between investor interests and the Global Public Interest raised by the host State will obviously arise and call for the search for the best legal tool to optimally reconcile them. Given the importance of either interest – the importance of protecting investor interests for the promotion of economic development through foreign direct investment, and the importance of Global Public Interest for fostering the growing normative foundations of public international law – none can prevail *in abstracto* in every case. Even if *in concreto* the one or the other will, effectiveness calls for finding a solution that gives optimal space to both interests.

Proportionality analysis is predestined for such a task. Reconciling conflicting interests while seeking the optimal solution for both of them is at the very core of this legal principle.[109] The aforementioned *Konkordanz* is the most visible among an entire bouquet of subprinciples and mechanisms targeted at achieving the optimal outcome for all interests considered.[110] The said importance of both investor interests and the Global Public Interest calls for a detailed consideration of either of them. True, the Global Public Interest theory as I have developed it above places the host State in the position of an agent of such interest that has discretion to raise it or not. However, while this leeway vis-à-vis introducing Global Public Interest concerns must remain in the hands of the host State, also granting it leeway regarding the level of scrutiny, as Burke-White and von Staden argue for,[111] would corrupt the main purpose of ICSID or most BITs, i.e. fostering economic development through investment protection, and would not do justice to the importance of investor interests.

Burke-White and von Staden promote using the margin of appreciation as an independent standard of scrutiny.[112] They regard it a better standard than proportionality due to the sensitive policy issues investment disputes touch upon and which investment Tribunals, so they assert, lack legitimacy to judge upon.[113] Admittedly there is something to the criticism of using proportionality analysis to resolve conflicts between investor interests and the Global Public Interest in the international investment realm, particularly given proportionality's susceptibility to law-making through judges and arbitrators.[114] However, the double leeway the Burke-White/von Staden proposal entails would be too much to take for the rather young international investment law system. The reason the margin of appreciation approach works in the ECtHR context is that it is not an entirely independent standard of scrutiny opposed to proportionality, as Burke-White and von Staden describe it, but is embedded in proportionality analysis. The double leeway as intended by these two authors would likely open up the investment system to vast abuse by the host State, which could not merely decide whether to raise the Global Public Interest concern but could define the frame for its scrutiny by the Tribunal as well.

109 Alexy, *Theory of Constitutional Rights*, p. 399. 110 See *supra* 6 E. 1. and 2.; *infra* 6 F. 4.

111 Burke-White and von Staden, "Private Litigation in a Public Law Sphere," 51 ff.

112 By contrast, what I have referred to as *Kontrolldichte* – see *supra* 5 E. 1. – is not an independent standard of scrutiny but merely a means of fine-tuning the assessment of the second and third steps of proportionality analysis.

113 Burke-White and von Staden, "Private Litigation in a Public Law Sphere," 53.

114 See *supra* 5 B.

The sensitivity of the policy issue involved, however, is sufficiently addressed by granting discretion whether to raise it or not. Once the host State decides to raise it to defend itself against the investor claim, however, it must accept that the Tribunal will analyze its policies. Only such scrutiny mechanism warrants the optimization of both the investor interest and the Global Public Interest and thus accommodates the prominence and importance of both interests in international investment law. Finally, it has to be mentioned that the margin of appreciation does not play a role at all. There may well be instances in which the nature of the policy issue requires a limited level of scrutiny or *Kontrolldichte*. However, the margin of appreciation's place should be as a subprinciple to fine-tune the necessity and proportionality *stricto sensu* on a case-by-case basis, not as an independent standard of scrutiny in every case.

Hence, it is only proportionality analysis that is able to optimally reconcile individual with public interest in a public law type system displaying certain constitutional features.[115]

2. *Doctrinal structure: Three-tier analysis*

Considering proportionality as the best tool to reconcile conflicting interests on the merits stage raises the question as to how it should be embedded in the overall doctrinal structure of a potential rights violation analysis. For doctrinal clarity, a few words need to be added in this regard. While in the US tradition civil liberties analysis in US Supreme Court jurisprudence is basically a single uniform process,[116] assessment of a fundamental rights violation in German doctrine or in the jurisprudence of the ECtHR or the ECJ follows a three-tier analysis.[117] In the US, limitations analysis is part of the assessment of whether the government has intruded the space protected by the respective freedom. Three levels of

115 Similarly J. Krommerdijk and J. Morijn, "'Proportional' by What Measure(s)? Balancing Investor Interests and Human Rights by Way of Applying the Proportionality Principle in Investor-State Arbitration" in P.-M. Dupuy, F. Francioni and E.-U. Petersmann (eds.), *Human Rights in International Investment Law and Arbitration* (Oxford University Press, 2009), p. 422.

116 See N. C. Johnson, "Vereinigte Staaten von Amerika" in E. Grabitz (ed.), *Grundrechte in Europa und USA*, Vol. I (N. P. Engel Verlag, 1986), p. 885 at p. 937; T. A. Aleinikoff, "Constitutional Law in the Age of Balancing," *Yale L.J.*, 96 (1987), 943.

117 J. Kokott, "Grundrechtliche Schranken und Schrankenschranken" in D. Merten and H.-J. Papier (eds.), *Handbuch der Grundrechte*, vol. I (C. F. Müller Verlag, 2004), p. 853 at pp. 856 ff.

scrutiny – rational basis, intermediate and strict scrutiny[118] – define the level of review and if the Court finds for an intrusion by the government this automatically means the violation of the right. While a sort of balancing also finds its way into Supreme Court jurisprudence,[119] the USA is still far from wholeheartedly endorsing proportionality analysis, which would generally cause problems fitting into the uniform approach of the US system.

By contrast, German doctrine – and many domestic and international orders inspired by it – created a three-tier analysis in order to adequately integrate proportionality in a consistent doctrinal structure: Firstly, the judge must assess the protected sphere (*Schutzbereichsebene*), i.e. the scope of the respective right. In a second step, the particular State conduct constitutes an infringement or intrusion (*Eingriffsebene*) if it touches upon the protected sphere and thereby limits the free exercise of the right in question. However, such infringement does not necessarily mean a violation, for in a third step the judge must analyze whether there is any basis for justification of the infringement (*Rechtfertigungsebene*). Limitations to rights (*Schranken*) must have statutory pedigree (*Gesetzesvorbehalt*) and are themselves limited (*Schrankenschranken*) – most importantly, albeit not exclusively – by proportionality analysis.[120]

While the difference to the US system is more in structure than in actual substance[121] – except, of course, for the role of proportionality – the three-tier analysis is more flexible in distinguishing between the interests at stake and their role as either claim or defense and enables a better accommodation of those interests and their balancing through proportionality analysis. The Global Public Interest theory relies on general principles and customary international law as encapsulations of the Global Public Interest, and their function is to serve as limitations to investor rights. Hence,

118 E. Chemerinsky, *Constitutional Law: Principles and Policies*, 3rd edn. (Aspen Publishers, 2006), p. 539; see also US Supreme Court, *United States* v. *Carolene Products Co.*, 304 US 144 (1938).

119 See Aleinikoff, "Constitutional Law," 943.

120 See P. Lerche, "Grundrechtlicher Schutzbereich, Grundrechtsprägung und Grundrechtseingriff" in J. Isensee and P. Kirchhof (eds.), *Handbuch des Staatsrechts*, Vol. V, 2nd edn. (C. F. Müller Juristischer Verlag, 2000), p. 739 and "Grundrechtsschranken" in J. Isensee and P. Kirchhof (eds.), *Handbuch des Staatsrechts*, Vol. V, 2nd edn. (C. F. Müller Juristischer Verlag, 2000), p. 775.

121 Eventually, it is often no more than a minor difference to distinguish three tiers instead of a uniform assessment, since also under the US system limitations to rights exist, particularly in case of conflicting freedoms; see Johnson, "Vereinigte Staaten," 944.

as for doctrinal structure, a Tribunal has to undergo the three-tier analysis as follows: (1) defining and assessing the scope of the investor right in question (sphere of protection); (2) determining whether the relevant State conduct infringes the right, i.e. touches upon its sphere of protection; and (3) finding whether the State conduct in question meets the requirements of the alleged general principle or customary international law norm and balancing such expression of the Global Public Interest against the investor right by way of proportionality analysis.

3. "Obligations" *vs.* "defenses"

The assessment in the preceding section foreshadowed the dogmatic classification the legal expressions of Global Public Interest concerns take under the Global Public Interest theory. As has been mentioned earlier, under my theory general principles and customary international law serve as limitations to – and thereby justifications of infringements of – investor rights. Therefore some clarifying remarks need to be made regarding the legal character of what I will call "limitations" and "justifications" and what consequences derive from such qualifications. I want to start with what I think legal translations of the Global Public Interest are not: *obligations*. They are not obligations the investor owes to the host State or the international community, nor do they, in turn, obligate the host State to claim them. By "obligation" I refer to legal duties that directly entitle someone to a claim. If the customary international law and general principles norms were in fact "obligations" in the defined sense, the question would arise, how and whether those obligations – originally created in the horizontal context of equal and sovereign States – can be transposed on non-State actors such as investors. One might well consider in this context that where international law principles rely on the rationale of international law as a coordinative system between sovereign equals, a direct or even indirect transfer to non-State actors proves both inappropriate and logically impossible.[122] Thus, the principle of sovereign equality of States,[123] to name but the most obvious example, might not be transposed onto non-State actors – along with any other principle that is rooted in the concept of State sovereignty.[124] An investor, i.e. a non-State actor, cannot owe duties as understood above, the rationale of which is rooted in the concept of sovereignty.

[122] See *supra* 3 A. 2. (a). [123] Art. 2(1) of the United Nations Charter.

[124] On state sovereignty generally see Brownlie, *Principles of Public International Law*, 7th edn. (Oxford University Press, 2008), pp. 289 ff.; H. Kelsen, *Principles of International Law* (Rinehart, 1952), pp. 108 ff.; Shaw, *International Law*, p. 26.

I deem it futile and misleading, however, to engage in such considerations for the sake of the present analysis. The rationale of the legal translations of Global Public Interest lies in the public interest of the world community. Therefore, the question before us is not transferability as such, but whether the particular customary international law rule or general principle encapsulates the Global Public Interest. Dogmatically, the most appropriate denomination for such expressions of the Global Public Interest on the third step of our three-tier structure[125] are *defenses*. Such terminology underlines the role the host State plays: It has the discretion to raise Global Public Interest concerns in order to defend itself against a claimed investor right infringement, because it – in its role as the agent of Global Public Interest – acted in pursuit of a legitimate purpose and in a proportionate manner. The leeway[126] to raise or not to raise the defense reflects the (host) State's position as still the most important and capable actor in public international law. However, it must be kept in mind that it is not enabled to defend itself because it pursued its own interests but because it acted as an agent of the Global Public Interest, a normative concept focused on the wellbeing and promotion of the human being.[127]

4. *Factors to be considered while balancing on the proportionality* stricto sensu *level*

After having delineated the potential doctrinal structure of both the proportionality analysis itself and its embedment in a three-tier test, I will now briefly give a list and explanation of the factors to be considered while balancing on the proportionality *stricto sensu* stage. This last step of proportionality analysis, as I have asserted earlier,[128] is both its spine and its potential handicap, for the flexibility it offers may easily turn into an arbitrary exercise. Hence, it is pivotal to develop certain criteria to invigorate an otherwise somewhat murky concept.

(a) Gravity of the infringement

One of the most obvious factors to be considered is the gravity of the infringement. This pertains both to the investor right and the Global Public Interest enshrined in general principles or customary international law. The more intense the intrusion on the investor interest or the Global Public Interest, the more this fact has to find reflection in the balancing

[125] See *supra* 5 F. 2. [126] See *supra* 5 F. 1. [127] See *supra* 4 A. 2. (b). [128] See *supra* 5 B.

exercise. In this context it must be kept in mind that in case of expropriation Tribunals let suffice a substantial deprivation of property, i.e. if the host State makes it impossible to generate any income from the use of the property.[129] Total deprivation is not necessary. However, on the proportionality *stricto sensu* balancing, such different level of infringement may well play a role in the overall outcome and assessment of the amount of compensation.[130]

(b) Legitimate expectations

In international investment law, the recourse to the investor's legitimate expectations as an argumentative *topos* is quite a familiar exercise. For example in *SPP* v. *Egypt*, the Egyptian government asserted that the actions of Egyptian officials the investor relied on in its claim were null and void because they did not follow the established rules of procedure under Egyptian law and were in conflict with the nature of the public domain.[131] The Tribunal rejected that argument and held that the investor could rely on the government's official representations:

> It is possible that under Egyptian law certain acts of Egyptian officials including even Presidential Decree No. 475, may be considered legally nonexistent or null and void or susceptible to invalidation. However, these acts were cloaked with the mantle of Government authority and communicated as such to foreign investors who relied on them in making investments... Whether legal under Egyptian law or not, the acts in question were acts of Egyptian authorities, including the highest executive authority of Government. These acts, which are now alleged to have been in violation of the Egyptian municipal legal system, created expectations protected by established principles of international law.[132]

However, such pedigree in international investment law is related to interpretations of the fair and equitable treatment standard – as, for example, was the case in *SPP* v. *Egypt* – or indirect expropriations.[133] Nonetheless,

[129] For an elaborate analysis of this issue see W. M. Reisman and R. D. Sloane, "Indirect Expropriation and its Valuation in the BIT Generation," *Brit. Yb. Int'l L.*, 74 (2004), 115.

[130] See U. Kriebaum, *Eigentumsschutz im Völkerrecht – Eine Untersuchung zum internationalen Investitionsrecht sowie zum Menschenrechtsschutz* (Duncker & Humblot, 2008), p. 555.

[131] Dolzer and Schreuer, *Principles of International Investment Law* (Oxford University Press, 2008), p. 135.

[132] *SPP* v. *Egypt*, paras. 82, 83.

[133] See for example the 2004 Canadian Model BIT (FIPA), Annex B.13(1) that mentions as a factor to determine an indirect expropriation "(ii) the extent to which the measure or series of measures interfere with distinct, reasonable investment-backed expectations ... " See www.dfait-maeci.gc.ca/tna-nac/documents/2004-FIPA-model-en.pdf.

the concept of legitimate expectations as an argumentative tool is not foreign to proportionality analysis, with a very similar content and factors considered as in the international investment context vis-à-vis fair and equitable treatment and indirect expropriations. In *Pine Valley* v. *Ireland*, the ECtHR stated upon the lack of legitimate expectations of the investor:

> The applicants were engaged in a commercial venture which, by its very nature, involved an element of risk... and they were aware not only of the zoning plan but also of the opposition of the local authority, Dublin County Council, to any departure from it... This being so, the Court does not consider that the annulment of the permission without any remedial action being taken in their favour can be regarded as a disproportionate measure.[134]

The similarity in the concept and use of legitimate expectations as argumentative *topos* facilitates the transfer to proportionality analysis. Hence, an investment Tribunal assessing the proportionality *stricto sensu* could make use of the case law already developed in international investment law vis-à-vis the concept of legitimate expectations.

(c) Importance of the Global Public Interest

Furthermore, a prominent factor to be considered must also be the importance of the public interest (allegedly) pursued. Admittedly, a Global Public Interest enjoys considerable importance *per definitionem*, for it enshrines pivotal concerns of the world community.[135] However, while any Global Public Interest entails high importance *in abstracto*, its importance may well vary *in concreto*. Therefore, it must be considered whether the interest in the particular case at hand mostly serves exclusively the host State – such fact would also often be an indicator for camouflage (see (d) below) – or whether it has particular importance for individuals or a group of individuals other than the investor or for the international community as a whole.

(d) Seriousness (in pursuit) of the Global Public Interest (camouflage)

As has been foreshadowed, there might be instances in which the host State would simply raise a Global Public Interest argument in order to camouflage less laudable goals, e.g. protectionism or simply an otherwise unjustifiable investor right violation. In order to prevent abuse of the

[134] European Court of Human Rights, *Pine Valley Developments Ltd. and Others* v. *the Republic of Ireland*, Judgment of November 29, 1991, Series A, No. 222.

[135] See *supra* 4 C. 4.

Global Public Interest theory by the host State, the Tribunal must take account of the seriousness – or lack thereof – of the Global Public Interest defense of the host State. This is most obvious in cases where there is no ground for such claim in the first place, because the host State has shown no previous inclination to make any effort in this regard. However, such clear cases will probably be rare compared to instances in which there is mixed evidence – the mere fact itself that the host State changes its policies cannot thwart its recourse to Global Public Interest defenses. In such cases it must be found out whether the Global Public Interest concerns asserted are merely peripheral or whether there is convincing evidence as to the seriousness of the pursuit by the host State. Indicators are the actual factual background, i.e. whether the Global Public Interest concern is imminent,[136] the actual and not the proclaimed purpose of the measure undertaken, whether the host State introduced similar policies in comparable domestic circumstances or whether it treated domestic investors similarly in other such cases.[137]

(e) Importance of the investor right

Similar to the importance of the Global Public Interest, an assessment must also be made as to the importance – *in abstracto* and *in concreto* – of the investor interest, i.e. the investor right. What has been said regarding Global Public Interest generally applies, *mutatis mutandis*, vis-à-vis the investor right's importance as well. Regarding the importance *in concreto*, what the right and the amount of compensation mean for the particular investor is of certain relevance. The importance of the right for the overall investment protection régime is an issue to be considered vis-à-vis the importance *in abstracto*.

(f) Particular public interest in reduced compensation

The circumstances of the case may point to a particular (public) interest in a reduced compensation for an investor right infringement beyond the mere consideration that a Global Public Interest is – naturally – involved. Such circumstances may arise in case of fundamental change in the political system of the host State[138] or in case of imminent economic or social crisis.[139] It must be underlined, again, that such

[136] See also *supra*. [137] See Kriebaum, *Eigentumsschutz im Völkerrecht*, pp. 565 ff.

[138] See the European Court of Human Rights case on the expropriation claim of the former Greek King, *Former King of Greece* v. *Greece*, Judgment of November 23, 2000, ECHR 2000-XII.

[139] In the Argentine cases this issue was a matter of fierce debate; see *supra* 4 C. 1. (b).

factor goes beyond the rationale inherent in my entire Global Public Interest theory that the public law type system of international investment law must reflect its inherent balance between the investor interest and the Global Public Interest, which usually will mean a reduction in compensation.[140]

(g) Involvement of the host State

Furthermore, if the host State is somehow involved in the infringement of the Global Public Interest, this would naturally be a reason to diminish the viability of its defense.[141] This issue is connected to the legitimate expectations factor, for if the host State participated in the infringement or even encouraged it, it has only very limited claim to raise the Global Public Interest afterwards. Such kind of situation is most obvious in case of corruption:[142] It takes two to tango here, so the public official taking the bribe often contributes as much to the infringement[143] as does the investor offering it.

(h) Intentional or incidental infringement?

Finally, the balancing must reflect the fact of whether the infringement of the Global Public Interest was intentional or incidental. An investor, which, for example, accidentally harms the environment or intentionally forces indigenous people into slave labor in order to build a pipeline, displays a different level of respect vis-à-vis the Global Public Interest. Consequently, intentional infringement would usually be an indicator for a lower amount of compensation.

5. *Some doctrinal challenges*

Before eventually considering how the aforesaid may actually be translated into a (limited) amount of compensation and damages, a few challenges must be addressed subsequently, arising from both general public international law and particular features of international investment law.

[140] See *infra* 5 F. 6.

[141] See L. E. Peterson and K. R. Gray, "International Human Rights in Bilateral Investment Treaties and in Investment Treaty Arbitration," IISD Research Paper, April 2003, 22 ff. available at www.iisd.org.

[142] See *infra* 8.

[143] Of course, the official's conduct must be attributable to the host State according to the ILC Articles on State Responsibility; see *infra* 8 D. 1.

(a) Balancing "customary international law" and "general principles" against "treaty law"? The dilemma with Article 38(1) ICJ Statute

Being based on the notion that certain norms of customary international law and general principles enshrine the Global Public Interest and thus may serve as doctrinal avenues for defenses to be balanced against the investor right(s), the Global Public Interest theory must respond to a doctrinal challenge inherent in the sources of law doctrine as put forward by Article 38(1) ICJ Statute. In 1920, Baron Descamps delineated a proposal to the Committee of Jurists that defined a clear-cut order in which international Tribunals should resort to sources of international law: (1) treaty law; (2) custom; (3) general principles of law; and (4) international jurisprudence.[144] In his eyes:

> there was a natural classification. If two States concluded a treaty in which the solution of the dispute could be found, the Court must not apply international custom and neglect the treaty. If a well known custom exists, there is no occasion to resort to a general principle of law. We shall indicate an order of natural *précellence*, without requiring in a given case the agreement of several sources.[145]

However, while this citation appears to imply a formal hierarchy of sources, in the practice of the ICJ there is no such hierarchy discernible, yet the Court considers the formulation in Article 38(1) of its Statute – very largely reflecting Baron Descamps' proposal – as setting forth a "successive order of consideration."[146] However, the reason for such order is practicality rather than logic or compelling legal argument. As Roberto Ago put it:

> Le droit de formation spontanée n'est ni moins réellement existant, ni moins certain, ni moins valable, ni moins observé, ni moins efficacement garanti que celui qui est créé par des faits normatifs spécifiques; au contraire, justement la spontanéité de son origine est plutôt la cause d'une observation plus spontanée et par consequent, plus réelle.[147]

Even more so, the concept of *ius cogens* exemplifies that a formal hierarchy of sources with treaty law on the top is irreconcilable with the modern

[144] See Procès-Verbaux of the Proceedings of the Advisory Committee of Jurists (1920), Annex No. 3, 306.

[145] *Ibid.*, 337.

[146] A. Pellet, in Zimmermann, Tomuschat and Oellers-Frahm, *The Statute*, Art. 38/Mn. 267.

[147] R. Ago, "Droit positif et droit international," *Annuaire Français de Droit International*, 3 (1957), 14 at 62.

state of public international law. While I am aware that the question of a hierarchy of sources ought not to be confused with the question of a hierarchy of norms of international law – *ius cogens* being an issue of the latter question – it is a truism that *ius cogens* norms, by their very nature, are a natural law concept and thus often exist, or at least pre-exist, in the form of unwritten sources of international law.[148] Hence, if Article 38(1) ICJ Statute were to define a hierarchy of sources, i.e. forbade resort to a source of lower rank in case there existed a norm derived from a source of higher rank, a treaty rule eventually could, for example, supersede a peremptory norm of "mere" customary character.

Given the aforesaid, as regards the relationship of treaty law and custom, complex as it may be,[149] for the sake of our present analysis I cannot identify any compelling reservations against balancing customary norms against investor rights derived from BIT provisions. However, vis-à-vis general principles, making such assessment is slightly more complicated. Whereas, as Ian Brownlie rightly stresses,[150] Article 38(1) ICJ Statute identifies general principles as a main, not a subsidiary source of international law,[151] the ICJ has usually only resorted to general principles in order to corroborate an interpretation already derived from analyzing treaty law or custom.[152]

This pattern could invite dispute as to general principles' viability as Global Public Interest defenses to be balanced against BIT provisions. However, the good faith interpretation as set forth in section 5 A. vis-à-vis a balance to be struck in BIT interpretation between the investor interest and the Global Public Interest arguably stands in the tradition of the aforementioned ICJ jurisprudence. Moreover, 5 A. has pointed at

148 L. Alexidze, "Legal Nature of Jus Cogens in Contemporary International Law," *Recueil des Cours*, 172 (1982), 219; see G. M. Danilenko, "International Jus Cogens: Issues of Law-Making," *Eur. J. Int'l L.*, 2 (1991), 42; G. Gaja, "Jus Cogens Beyond the Vienna Convention," *Recueil des Cours*, 172 (1982), 271; A. Gómez Robledo, "Le jus cogens international: sa genèse, sa nature, ses fonctions," *Recueil des Cours*, 172 (1982), 9.

149 On this issue see A. Pellet, in Zimmermann, Tomuschat and Oellers-Frahm, *The Statute*, Art. 38/Mn. 283 ff.

150 Brownlie, *Principles*, p. 16.

151 Cassese appears to entertain the latter view; see Cassese, *International Law*, p. 188.

152 See, e.g., Sir Hersch Lauterpacht in the *Certain Norwegian Loans* case:

> "International practice on the subject [of separability of an invalid condition from the rest of an instrument] is not sufficiently abundant to permit a confident attempt at generalization and some help may justifiably be sought in applicable general principles of law as developed in municipal law."

ICJ Reports (1957), 34 at 56, cited from A. Pellet, in Zimmermann, Tomuschat and Oellers-Frahm, *The Statute*, Art. 38/Mn. 293.

Article 31(3)(c) of the Vienna Convention on the Law of Treaties allowing for taking account of relevant rules of international law applicable between the parties to a treaty, including customary law and general principles. Interpreting the BIT provisions along the lines of further "context" is hence well in conformity with classical public international doctrine.[153]

Additionally, if we take a look into international investment case law, general principles have served to thwart investor rights claims. To name but the examples of *Inceysa* and *Fraport* as discussed above,[154] the respective Tribunals resorted, among others, to the principles of *nemo audiatur propriam turpitudinem allegans* and international public policy in order to assert that the investors had failed to fulfill their "reciprocal if not identical obligations"[155] and thus could not claim a violation of the BIT.[156]

Considering that principles are, to paraphrase Robert Alexy, optimization precepts,[157] the structure of proportionality analysis aiming at achieving the optimal outcome of either interest considered is well suited to accommodate the balancing of investor rights enshrined in treaty law with general principles of law. It will remain a task to be undertaken in section H. to illustrate such exercise by means of environmental, human rights and corruption issues.

(b) Proportionality analysis and expropriation

Without anticipating here a detailed analysis of this issue in Chapter 6,[158] I will just touch on two issues problematic vis-à-vis the relationship of proportionality (and the Global Public Interest theory) on the one hand and expropriation on the other. Firstly, as a matter of general principle, any expropriation requires, as one prerequisite in order to be considered legal, a public purpose being pursued.[159] Whereas not any such domestic "public purpose" will qualify as a Global Public Interest, vice versa, any Global Public Interest can be regarded such "public purpose." Hence, the mere existence of such public purpose pursued can hardly justify per se a balancing on the merits stage resulting in a reduced amount of compensation.[160] What will be necessary in this regard, however, is to determine a specific reason, or as I have called it earlier, a particular public

153 See also on this issue S. W. Schill, "International Investment Law and Comparative Public Law – An Introduction" in S. W. Schill (ed.), *International Investment Law and Comparative Public Law* (Oxford University Press, 2010), p. 3 at pp. 26 ff.

154 And below, see *infra* 8 C. 2. (c) and (d).

155 *Fraport* v. *Philippines*, para. 402.

156 See *supra* 4 C. 1. (a).

157 See Alexy, *Theory of Constitutional Rights*, p. 49.

158 See *infra* 6 D. 1. (b).

159 See Dolzer and Schreuer, *Principles*, p. 88.

160 See *infra* 5 F. 6.

interest in reducing the amount of compensation. Only if the host State paying the full amount of compensation would result in undermining the Global Public Interest as such, will a reduction be justified. Consequently, a Tribunal would – after having affirmed that an expropriation took place – have to engage in an analysis whether there exists a particular interest in reducing the amount of compensation integrated into the balancing exercise.

Secondly, there is a tendency discernible among several investment arbitration Tribunals to assess whether an indirect expropriation occurred by employing proportionality analysis.[161] While this issue will be dealt with mostly in a later section, at this stage it remains to be stressed that a three-tier analysis with proportionality as the last step after a determination of a rights infringement is, for the reasons stated above,[162] the preferable solution.

(c) Proportionality analysis and the fair and equitable treatment standard

The fair and equitable treatment (FET) standard is the chewing-gum provision of international investment law. To be found in almost any investment treaty, whether bilateral or multilateral, it allows including – or at least investment Tribunals have interpreted it that way – such different issues as transparency, predictability and the investor's legitimate expectations, compliance with contractual obligations, procedural propriety and due process, good faith or freedom from coercion and harassment.[163] Therefore, it is no surprise that FET allegedly has become the most popular and most important standard in investment protection.[164]

However, with elasticity comes elusiveness. Many attempts have been made to date at defining what exactly "fair and equitable"[165] means – none of which, however, has eventually succeeded in being generally accepted. Some voices tried to limit FET to the international minimum standard of treatment of aliens as contained in customary international law.[166] While even the scope of the customary international minimum standard

161 *Infra* 6 D. 1. (b). 162 See *supra* 5 F. 2.

163 See Dolzer and Schreuer, *Principles*, pp. 133 ff. with extensive reference to case law.

164 C. Schreuer, "Fair and Equitable Treatment in Arbitral Practice," *J. World Inv. & Trade*, 6 (2005), 357 at 357.

165 The most often-cited definition stems from the *Tecmed* award, *Tecmed* v. *Mexico*, para. 154.

166 See the NAFTA Free Trade Commission (FTC) Note of Interpretation of July 31, 2001: "Minimum Standard of Treatment in Accordance with International Law:

is highly disputed,[167] it must be considered that the wording "fair and equitable" was most likely deliberately selected to mean something different from "customary minimum standard," a formulation that could have been easily adopted instead. Moreover, many investment treaties, such as the US–Argentina BIT, add to the FET clause that investments shall "in no case be accorded treatment less than that required by international law."[168] In this context the Tribunal in *Azurix* v. *Argentina* held:

> The clause, as drafted, permits to interpret fair and equitable treatment... as [a] higher standard than required by international law. The purpose of the third sentence [i.e. the passage quoted above] is to set a floor, not a ceiling, in order to avoid a possible interpretation of these standards below what is required by international law.[169]

Hence, the FET clause inheres the potential of imbuing investment law with broader concepts of public international law. Among the issues currently being considered by investment Tribunals, one displays a distinct potential susceptibility for Global Public Interest considerations

> Article 1105(1) prescribes the customary international law minimum standard of treatment of aliens as the minimum standard of treatment to be afforded to investments of investors of another Party.

The concepts of 'fair and equitable treatment' and 'full protection and security' do not require treatment in addition to or beyond that which is required by the customary international law minimum standard of treatment of aliens.

A determination that there has been a breach of another provision of the NAFTA, or of a separate international agreement, does not establish that there has been a breach of Article 1105(1)."

Available at www.international.gc.ca/trade-agreements-accords-commerciaux/disp-diff/NAFTA-Interpr.aspx?lang=en.

167 While it is fairly established that the 1926 *Neer* case, *Neer* v. *Mexico*, Opinion, US-Mexico General Claims Commission, October 15, 1926, *Am. J. Int'l L.*, 21 (1927), 555, and the *ELSI* decision of the ICJ, *Elettronica Sicula SpA (ELSI) (United States of America* v. *Italy)*, Judgment of July 20, 1989, *ICJ Reports* (1989), 15, are expressions of such standard, it is highly disputed whether the customary guarantees reach beyond such case law; see Dolzer and Schreuer, *Principles*, pp. 128 f. As a NAFTA Tribunal has noted in *ADF* v. *United States*:

> "[T]he customary international law referred to in Article 1105(1) is not 'frozen in time' and... the minimum standard of treatment does evolve... [W]hat customary international law projects is not a static photograph of the minimum standard of treatment of aliens as it stood in 1927 when the Award in the *Neer* case was rendered. For both customary international law and the minimum standard of treatment of aliens it incorporates, are constantly in a process of development."

ADF Group Inc. v. *United States*, Award, January 9, 2003, *ICSID Review – FILJ*, 18 (2003), 195, *ICSID Reports*, 6 (2004), 470, para. 179.

168 Art. II 2. a) of the Argentina–US BIT.

169 *Azurix* v. *Argentina* (ICSID Case No. ARB/01/12), Award, July 14, 2006, para. 361.

enshrined in customary international law and general principles: the investor's legitimate expectations.

In section 5 F. 4. (b) I have already made reference to this concept. Its gist is to warrant a certain level of predictability and security on the basis of what the investor could expect from the perspective of an objective observer taken into account at the time when the investment was made. In the words of the *Tecmed* Tribunal:

> The foreign investor expects the host State to act in a consistent manner, free from ambiguity and totally transparently in its relations with the foreign investor, so that it may know beforehand any and all rules and regulations that will govern its investments, as well as the goals of the relevant policies and administrative practices or directives, to be able to plan its investment and comply with such regulations.[170]

One might well argue that such interpretation of the FET standard provides a good avenue for Global Public Interest considerations, for, *arguendo*, if we consider such Global Public Interest a characteristic feature of international investment law, the investor cannot legitimately expect, at the time it makes its investment, that the host State shield it from measures undertaken in pursuit of such interest. In other words, adopting regulations, say, for the sake of protecting the environment, would then usually not amount to a violation of the FET standard.

While this would – at least doctrinally – fit smoothly into the current international investment law jurisprudence, I prefer a different approach. As the aforementioned has foreshadowed, a broad concept of Global Public Interest considerations via legitimate expectations in order to *define* the fair and equitable treatment standard is likely to turn into a fairly murky concept. It would, in order to prevent arbitrariness, require a proportionality-style balancing at the definition stage. However, if already engaging in such exercise, the much more preferable approach is to also employ the three-tier analysis (see 5 F. 2.) in the context of FET. This would require leaving the concept of FET intact as it is currently interpreted without inferring Global Public Interest considerations on this step. In case the Tribunal finds that the host State has infringed the FET provision, the Global Public Interest considerations will then be dealt with at the third step – justification – by way of the usual proportionality analysis as elaborated in this chapter.

170 *Tecmed* v. *Mexico*, para. 154.

6. *Consequence: Reduced amount of compensation and damages*

Eventually, we arrive at the ultimate question: What should be the actual consequence of introducing defenses by the host State and balancing them with the investor rights according to proportionality analysis? The simple answer is: The – legitimate – defense must find reflection in the amount of compensation and damages.[171] They are by far the most important remedies international investment law provides for and thus they are the ultimate goal every investor seeks. There usually is no reinstatement of the *status quo ante* in the case of expropriation or any other investor right violation[172] – and for good reason: A Tribunal bestowed with the competency to order any remedy other than compensation or damages would be too intrusive on the host State's sovereignty and hence would be in blatant disregard of the current state of public international law, for compliance would be very poor and enforcement mechanisms beyond monetary interests do not exist.[173] Even the ECHR – a system with a much more highly developed network of legal (and moral)[174] compliance mechanisms – basically relies on monetary damages as sanction for Charter rights violations.[175] Since therefore (the amount of) compensation or damages as the chief remedy in international investment law is the only platform for factual consequences of the legal considerations following the application of the Global Public Interest theory and its realization

[171] For the sake of dogmatic clarity, I refer to "compensation as the remedy for a lawful taking or termination of contract and damages as the remedy for an unlawful taking or termination" or any other kind of investor rights violations. See D. Bowett, "Claims between States and Private Entities: The Twilight Zone of International Law," *Catholic U. L. Rev.*, 35 (1986), 929 at 938; see also I. Marboe, *Calculation of Compensation and Damages in International Investment Law* (Oxford University Press, 2009), pp. 8–17.

[172] However, in rare circumstances investment Tribunals have ordered restitution and specific performance: *Goetz and others* v. *Republic of Burundi*, Award, September 2, 1998 and February 10, 1999, *ICSID Reports*, 6 (2000), 5, paras. 132 f.; *Enron* v. *Argentina*, para. 79; *ADC* v. *Hungary*, para. 77. See also C. Schreuer, "Non-Pecuniary Remedies in ICSID Arbitration," *Arbitration International*, 20 (2004), 325.

[173] Contrary to such assessment Anne van Aaken promotes primary remedies in international investment law; see A. van Aaken, "Primary and Secondary Remedies in International Investment Law and National State Liability: A Functional and Comparative View" in S. W. Schill (ed.), *International Investment Law and Comparative Public Law* (Oxford University Press, 2010), p. 721. Given the aforementioned I am rather skeptical whether this integrates well in the current state of the investment régime.

[174] R. Ryssdal, "The Conscience We Need" in R. St. J. Macdonald, F. Matscher and H. Petzold (eds.), *The European System for the Protection of Human Rights* (Kluwer Academic Publishers, 1993), p. xxv.

[175] Art. 50 ECHR; see M. E. Mas, "Right to Compensation under Article 50" in R. St. J. Macdonald *et al.* (eds.), *The European System*, p. 775.

through balancing via proportionality analysis, in this section I will seek to develop certain criteria for translating the outcome of proportionality analysis into a reduced level of compensation or damages.

Before doing so, however, let me note here that recent investment arbitration indicates that Tribunals tend to start taking into account the public law character and Global Public Interest concerns when measuring the amount of compensation or damages. A first example that has already been mentioned in a different context is Article 27 ILC, which several Tribunals referred to as a consequence of a successful state of necessity defense in reaction to the 2001–02 Argentine financial crisis – that, however, failed in most of the cases.[176] Properly applied – which, unfortunately, it was not in most of the Argentine crisis Tribunals – Article 27 ILC may permit the investor recovering its "material loss," but disallows claiming lost profits.[177] While thus Article 27 ILC inheres a balance between the State's and the investor's interest – the former does not have to pay full compensation or damages and the latter does not have to suffer from the consequences of a situation completely beyond its control or influence[178] – its application in investment case law by the Argentina crisis Tribunals was rather defective and hence only provides limited, albeit notable, evidence for investment Tribunals reducing the amount of compensation or damages according to Global Public Interest considerations.

In this regard, *Himpurna* v. *PLN*[179] and Ian Brownlie's Separate Opinion in *CME* v. *Czech Republic*[180] prove much more instructive. In *Himpurna*, Indonesia refused to fulfill its contractual obligations owed to the investor, since the 1997 Asian crisis had made the contract economically unviable. In the eyes of the Tribunal, while the crisis could not justify the breach, the investor's entitlement to *lucrum cessans* was considerably limited for, so

[176] See *supra* 4 C. 1. (b).

[177] See Bjorklund, "Economic Security Defenses" in K. P. Sauvant (ed.), *Yearbook on International Investment Law & Policy 2008–2009* (Oxford University Press, 2009), p. 502; Crawford, *The ILC's Articles on State Responsibility*, p. 190, Art. 27, para. 4; Reinisch, "Necessity in International Investment Arbitration," 207 f.; Ripinsky and Williams, *Damages*, p. 343. See also *supra* 4 C. 1. (b) (iii).

[178] See *supra* 4 C. 1. (b) (iii).

[179] *Himpurna California Energy Ltd* v. *PT (Persero) Perusahaan Listruik Negara (PLN)*, Final Award, May 4, 1999, *Yearbook of Commercial Arbitration*, Vol. XXV (2000), 13 (hereinafter: *Himpurna* v. *PLN*).

[180] *CME Czech Republic BV (The Netherlands)* v. *Czech Republic*, UNCITRAL, Final Award, Separate Opinion by Ian Brownlie, March 14, 2003 (hereinafter: *CME* v. *Czech Republic*, Separate Opinion Brownlie).

the arbitrators held, claiming the full amount of lost profits would have constituted an abuse of rights:

> The respondent did not seek actively to dispossess the claimant of valuable contractual rights; it has suffered helplessly from a precipitate deterioration in the macroeconomic value of the project with respect to which it had accepted the entire market risk.
>
> ...
>
> [T]he issue of *lucrum cessans* has so often come up in the context of cases where the defending State entity has acted to evict the foreign investor from a healthy on-going profitable venture. Thus the notion of the victim's lost profits has gone hand in glove with that of the breaching party's gain.[181]

In contrast to the latter scenario, Indonesia in the present case did not intend to enrich itself by appropriating Himpurna's benefits and hence the Tribunal concluded that this fact must have a "moderating effect" on the recovery of *lucrum cessans*.[182] In other words, the *Himpurna* Tribunal emphasized the limiting influence of the crisis and the pressure that thus was put on the host State on the calculation of compensation and damages.

Along those lines, Professor Brownlie acknowledged the distinct challenges that outflow from the public nature of the State, owing myriads of obligations to its citizens. In his Separate Opinion in *CME* v. *Czech Republic* he held that:

> [a]ny assessment of the commercial approach to compensation in these proceedings must involve an adequate appreciation of the character of a bilateral investment treaty ...
>
> In this context, it is simply unacceptable to insist that the subject-matter is exclusively commercial in character or that the interests at issue are, more or less, those of the investor. Such an approach involves setting aside a number of essential elements in a Treaty relation. The first element is the significance of the fact that the Respondent is a sovereign State, which is responsible for the well-being of its people. This is not to confer a privilege on the Czech Republic but only to recognize its special character and responsibilities. The Czech Republic is not a commercial entity.
>
> ...
>
> The resources of a corporation entail considerable flexibility in changing the location of assets and in changing the organization of assets. The resources of a country, its human and natural resources, are a given: they are necessarily fixed.[183]

[181] *Himpurna* v. *PLN*, 93, para. 332 and 94, para. 335.
[182] *Ibid.*, 96, para. 342.
[183] *CME* v. *Czech Republic*, Separate Opinion Brownlie, paras. 73, 74, 76.

In Brownlie's opinion, such limited flexibility is due to the host State's special role as a sovereign entity obligated to serve the wellbeing of its citizens. He maintains that such role requires a careful balancing of the investor's interest with the interest of the host State, which represents the interest of its population, resting on considerations of fairness that must find reflection in the eventual calculation of compensation and damages.[184,185]

Having thus exhibited that limiting the amount of compensation or damages due to Global Public Interest considerations is a pattern not entirely unfamiliar in international investment law, I will now delineate a non-exhaustive list of factors according to which their impact may be measured. To start with the most obvious, in case of both the host State and the investor being involved in conduct affecting the Global Public Interest – a scenario that might occur quite frequently and is virtually always present regarding corruption – the amount of damages and compensation should be limited according to the host State's contribution. The level of such contribution may be determined by the Tribunal on the basis of the factual matrix, particularly by an assessment that the actions of the host State or the investor had the strongest impact on the impairment of the Global Public Interest. Secondly – also a quite straightforward case – if the Global Public Interest finds expression in a *ius cogens* norm, since, as indicated above, there is no room for balancing, compensation or damages would usually be entirely excluded – except if, again, the host State itself contributed to the *ius cogens* violation itself or if the *ius cogens* allegation lacks any serious ground.

184 *Ibid.*, paras. 72, 79. Furthermore, Brownlie notes the extremely high amount of compensation granted (more than US$ 500 million) in relation to the Czech Republic's annual GDP (about US$ 54 billion). With the damages thus amounting to 1 percent of the Czech Republic's annual GDP, Brownlie asserts by reference to the *Gulf of Maine* case (*Canada* v. *United States*, *ICJ Reports* (1984), 342, para. 237) that signing a BIT must not result in liabilities "likely to entail catastrophic repercussions for the livelihood and economic well-being of the population." See also Ripinsky and Williams, *Damages*, p. 357.

185 Also note *SPP* v. *Egypt*, paras. 190 f., holding that the fact that the claimant's business activities would have become internationally unlawful starting from the date of Egypt ratifying the UNESCO World Cultural Heritage Convention "had 'significant consequences' in terms of determining the quantum of compensation." See L. Liberti, "The Relevance of Non-Investment Treaty Obligations in Assessing Compensation" in P.-M. Dupuy, F. Francioni and E.-U. Petersmann (eds.), *Human Rights in International Investment Law and Arbitration* (Oxford University Press, 2009), p. 557 at pp. 562 ff. On the said UNESCO Convention see Convention Concerning the Protection of the World Cultural and Natural Heritage, Adopted in Paris, November 16, 1972, available at http://whc.unesco.org/en/conventiontext.

Beyond these comparatively simple cases, and as a general principle, the amount of damages and compensation should be determined along the lines of the outcome of the proportionality *stricto sensu* assessment. In particular, the factors as set out in section 6 F. 4. above provide guidance in how much of the original damages or compensation due to the investor rights infringements the investor should actually be entitled to reap. This requires a two-stage test of assessing the investor's damages or compensation: In a first step, the Tribunal must determine the amount exclusively considering the investor rights infringements by the host State. Thereinafter, in a second step, the Tribunal will limit the thus determined amount of damages or compensation according to the outcome of the proportionality *stricto sensu* assessment. Taking account of the actual influence either party exerts on the overall context of the dispute – which, naturally, presupposes a preponderance of the host State as a sovereign entity vested with *puissance publique*[186] – reducing the amount of compensation or damages to zero will constitute a fairly rare scenario beyond *ius cogens* violations without the host State's contribution. However, the more important and imminent the Global Public Interest effectively protected by the measure infringing the rights of the investor, the less the latter may expect to reap as eventual compensation or damages. On the other hand, the investor having no influence on and no relevant connection to the Global Public Interest concerned represents an indicator for a comparatively high level of compensation or damages.[187]

G. Potential safeguards against abuse

As has been alluded to on several occasions, while I have underlined the importance of the Global Public Interest and how it can be translated into legal categories, I am aware that one should not have one's head in the clouds and fall prey to erroneously underestimating the cunning of certain host States in abusing the delineated theory for less laudable purposes. Placing the defense of the Global Public Interest in the hands of the

[186] However, this does not always need to be the case. If the investor exerts control – maybe even by way of a private militia, etc. – over a certain territory in a politically unstable or even failing State, the upper assumption of the host State's preponderance in this regard will be out of place.

[187] This will often be the case regarding measures taken in response to economic emergency. See, e.g., the Argentine crisis as described and analyzed *supra* 4 C. 1. (b). The solution I promote in this regard, i.e. limiting the amount of compensation and damages to the "material loss" suffered, that is *damnum emergens*, according to Art. 27 ILC, seems a good example for such compromise.

host State may well transform into a dangerous concept that inheres the potential to thwart the entire system of international investment law and to turn investment protection into a farce. Without any safeguards – substantive and procedural – such corruption of the investment system is not a very unlikely consequence. A host State would generally raise even absolutely unfounded Global Public Interest concerns in order to defend itself and – most likely – to delay the already quite time-consuming investment arbitration procedures. Therefore, in the following I will elaborate which kind of substantive safeguards the proportionality analysis potentially offers to prevent such scenario, and subsequently delineate a proposal for the introduction of an effective procedural mechanism to counter extensive abuse.

1. *Substantive safeguards: Recap*

Less effective in countering delay tactics and a potential attempt by the host State to thwart the investment protection system as a whole, substantive safeguards are nevertheless a crucial instrument to prevent the host State from succeeding with an unfounded Global Public Interest defense. The entire proportionality principle is – by its very purpose as described earlier[188] – specifically tailored to meet that aim. While this would basically lead to a reiteration of the aforesaid, I will focus on how four particular aspects of proportionality analysis may be applied as safeguards against abuse by the host State. These four aspects are: (1) necessity; (2) gravity of the infringement of the Global Public Interest; (3) legitimate expectations; and (4) seriousness in pursuing the Global Public Interest.

To start, the least-restrictive-measures-test inherent in the necessity step of proportionality analysis is a very effective tool to prevent the host State from adopting excessive measures to meet the Global Public Interest. The State conduct only passes the necessity test if it constitutes the least restrictive equally effective means to reach the purpose pursued by the host State. Thus, any measure that does not fulfill such condition is not a valuable defense against an investor right infringement. This excludes a great number of measures that pursue other, less laudable purposes and which the host State retroactively seeks to camouflage as fostering the Global Public Interest.

The second aspect to be mentioned here is, as are the two other remaining ones, part of the proportionality *stricto sensu* analysis. The gravity of the Global Public Interest infringement naturally is an effective safeguard

[188] See *supra* 5 C. and D.

against abuse, for a minor and negligible intrusion finds its reflection in the balancing exercise and would usually have much resonance in the ultimate outcome, i.e. no or very limited reduction of compensation. Similarly, the legitimate expectations consideration may serve as a means to ensure effective and inabusive use of the Global Public Interest defense: A host State that has pursued a certain policy may not change it and seek excuse in the disguise of Global Public Interest, if the investor could legitimately expect that this policy would remain in place.

This leads to the final aspect, the seriousness in pursuing the Global Public Interest. Considerable change of established policy at the instance of another issue arising which the new policy coincides in promoting makes a Global Public Interest defense highly suspicious, if there is no good reason why the paradigm change occurs at this very moment in time. The host State is under the obligation to justify its behavior and to explain why the situation has fundamentally changed and why the Global Public Interest and not the other "coincidental" result is the ultimate goal of the measure adopted.

2. *Procedural safeguards: Provisional measures*

Despite such sophisticated structure of proportionality analysis specifically tailored to prevent substantial abuse of the ability to raise a defense for justification, I suggest an additional procedural safeguard to be included in the relevant provisions. In my opinion, an effective instrument to counter an attempt of the host State to take the Global Public Interest hostage for dishonest purposes would be to make use of the provisional measures device in Article 47 ICSID. The host State could be barred from abusing the Global Public Interest by being required to raise them as a prima facie defense through the procedural device of provisional measures before undertaking any actual actions in this regard and before alleging those defenses on the merits stage. The Tribunal – or, to accelerate the process, only its president – would then in a cursory assessment determine whether the prima facie case the host State purports to have vis-à-vis the Global Public Interest defense is sufficiently sound or whether it is unfounded. If it is sufficiently sound, i.e. if the allegation passes the first two steps of the three-tier analysis,[189] the host State is entitled to elaborate the detailed argumentation on the merits stage of the main proceedings – naturally, only if the Tribunal has jurisdiction. In case the Tribunal or its president rejects the soundness of the prima facie

[189] See *supra* 5 F. 2.

case vis-à-vis the Global Public Interest defense, the host State is barred from making any allegations regarding such defense on the merits stage. This – admittedly quite strict – mechanism would, so I argue, effectively warrant a sensible use of the host State's authority to raise the Global Public Interest defense and prevent it from abusing laudable concerns for less laudable purposes.

The question remains, however, of how to implement such safeguard through the means of the provisional measures mechanism. To start with, provisional measures are a very common feature in international arbitration, both in commercial and in investment arbitration.[190] Under any adjudication system, be it domestic litigation or international arbitration, their purpose "is to induce behaviour by the parties that is conducive to a successful conduct of the proceedings."[191] However, while this means that provisional measures have to be taken when the dispute's outcome remains still in the dark, the challenge is not to prejudge the case. Thus, central principles are urgency and necessity of the order for provisional measures,[192] which result in basically five prerequisites for obtaining provisional measures from an arbitral Tribunal:

...

2. *prima facie* jurisdiction of the arbitral Tribunal to rule on the merits of the case;

3. reasonable chance of success on the merits (*prima facie* case);

4. urgency or impending injury to the rights of the applicant;

[190] On international commercial arbitration see M. W. Bühler and T. H. Webster, *Handbook of ICC Arbitration*, 2nd edn. (Sweet & Maxwell, 2008), pp. 333 ff.; G. Petrochilos, *Procedural Law in International Arbitration* (Oxford University Press, 2004), p. 218; Poudret and Besson, *Comparative Law of International Arbitration*, pp. 518 ff.; P. Schlosser, *Das Recht der internationalen privaten Schiedsgerichtsbarkeit*, 2nd edn. (Mohr Siebeck, 1989), pp. 305 ff. On ICSID see Dolzer and Schreuer, *Principles*, pp. 262 ff.; C. Schreuer, L. Malintoppi, A. Reinisch and A. Sinclair, *The ICSID Convention – A Commentary*, 2nd edn. (Cambridge University Press, 2009), Art. 47/Mn. 1.

[191] Dolzer and Schreuer, *Principles*, p. 262.

[192] *Ibid.*, p. 263. In ICSID arbitration it is somewhat dubious as to whether the Tribunal may issue binding "orders" for provisional measures, given the wording of Art. 47 ICSID and of Art. 39 Arbitration Rules ("recommend"). However, pursuant to the holding in *Maffezini* v. *Spain*, ICSID Tribunals have concluded that decisions on provisional measures are binding upon the parties: "The Tribunal does not believe that the parties to the Convention meant to create a substantial difference in the effect of these words. The Tribunal's authority to rule on provisional measures is no less binding than that of a final award. Accordingly, for the purposes of this Order, the Tribunal deems the word 'recommend' to be of equivalent value as the word 'order'." See *Maffezini* v. *Spain*, Procedural Order No. 2, October 28, 1999, *ICSID Review – FILJ*, 16 (2001), 207, *ICSID Reports*, 5 (2000), 393 at para. 9.

5. risk of substantial harm in the absence of protection;

6. the forthcoming decision on the merits must not be prejudiced;

. . .[193]

Regarding the third and fourth prerequisites (4. and 5.), the urgency and risk of substantial harm in the absence of protection would result from the bar to raise the Global Public Interest defenses on the merits stage if the host State failed to allege them on the provisional measures stage. I am well aware that this proposed mechanism differs somewhat from the original purpose of provisional measures and requires an amendment of at least the Arbitration Rules,[194] if not the ICSID Convention.[195] However, while there are some differences, the situation does not vary very much from a potential aggravation of the dispute, which is a typical instance in which provisional measures are granted in (ICSID) investment arbitration:[196] Here, the aggravation would lie in the potential obstruction of the proceedings by unfounded Global Public Interest defenses. If the host State raises such defenses without a sound basis, the proceedings are in danger of being thwarted or at least delayed, which is in effect very similar to what the aggravation situation is usually focused on.

H. What this means: Completing the three hypotheticals

At the end of the theoretical part of my book, in which I have undertaken the effort to delineate a theoretical and doctrinal foundation for Global Public Interest defenses of the host State against investor rights infringements, and before I proceed to three case studies exemplifying current international investment law practice vis-à-vis Global Public Interest considerations, let me briefly back-pedal and complete the three hypotheticals laid out at the end of Chapter 2.[197] Their solution according to the Global Public Interest theory is intended to illustrate the impact my theory

[193] Poudret and Besson, *Comparative Law*, p. 536. Similarly Bühler and Webster, *Handbook of ICC Arbitration*, p. 337.

[194] Which may be amended any time by the Administrative Council of the Centre according to Art. 6(1)(c) ICSID.

[195] Which requires a recommendation of a two-thirds majority of Administrative Council and then each Member State must ratify and accept or approve such amendment; Art. 66(1) ICSID.

[196] See Schreuer *et al.*, *The ICSID Convention*, Art. 47/Mn. 135 ff.; *Amco* v. *Indonesia*, Decision on Provisional Measures, December 9, 1983, *ICSID Reports*, 1 (1993), 410.

[197] See *supra* 2 E. 5.

potentially entails on the outcome of actual investment disputes facing a public interest challenge.

1. *Environment*

Returning to our investor that claims compensation after having violated domestic legislation implementing the Stockholm Convention on Persistent Organic Pollutants, we recall that one of its major arguments was that the toxicity of the chemical could not be established definitively.[198] Moreover, environmental protection was merely guaranteed by domestic law, whereas it appeared that on the international law level, investors did not and in fact could not have any environmental obligations. The public interest environmental protection thus had legal relevance only as a *domestic* public interest of the host State and consequently was superseded by the BIT international law rights of the investor.

According to the Global Public Interest theory, the picture changes considerably: The provisions of the Stockholm Convention, though itself not binding upon the investor, have their foundation in the precautionary principle.[199] Assuming the precautionary principle has already accrued to customary international law status,[200] it represents the expression of an international, i.e. *Global* Public Interest. In the regulatory and administrative law type system of international investment law, such Global Public Interest must be balanced against the international individual interest of the investor enshrined in the respective BIT provisions. It is obvious that the pendulum will not necessarily always swing in the direction of the investor's interest – in contrast to the picture we have drawn for a system without host State defenses. Considering my assessment regarding the relationship of the Global Public Interest and expropriation as outlined at F. 5. (b), what is necessary for the precautionary principle to exert any effect on the amount of compensation is a special interest of the host State implementing this Global Public Interest consideration in paying a lower amount of compensation. In other words, this latter maxim must be integrated into the proportionality analysis: A lower amount of compensation must be suitable and the least restrictive measure to address the Global Public Interest, and it has to be assessed whether limiting the amount of compensation due to the pursuit of the Global Public Interest adequately relates to the end of effectively achieving the Global Public

[198] *Ibid.* [199] See Preamble, para. 8 and Art. 1 of the Stockholm Convention.
[200] Which is, in fact, subject to serious debate; see *infra* 6 A. 3.

Interest in the light of, inter alia, the importance of the Global Public Interest and the infringed investor right *in concreto*.

As regards suitability, there is not much doubt that limiting the amount of compensation enables the government to uphold measures furthering the precautionary principle that are at the same time leading to infringements of the expropriation clause. Similarly, without limiting the amount of compensation the government would de facto not be able to implement them, or would at least be severely impeded in doing so since it would always have to face full compensation for any foreign investor affected, which would be so costly that it would lead to considerable regulatory chill. Given these above considerations, full compensation is out of place. However, on the level of proportionality *stricto sensu*, it must be taken into account that the investor, albeit not having a protected interest that the regulatory framework remained unchanged, invested in country B in good faith in the first place and mostly because the country had relatively lax environmental regulation – with the government of B being well aware of that latter fact. Moreover, if the investor were to accept B's measures without any compensation at all, it would face bankruptcy in a scenario that it – except for the US$ 20 million fine – had no influence on. According to the above considerations, an adequate outcome of the proportionality analysis, in my view, would represent B paying 40 percent of compensation for the investor's investment that is not economically feasible any more. However, no compensation should be paid for B imposing the US$ 20 million fine on the investor.

2. *Human rights*

No doubt, leaving the reason for withdrawing the mining license aside, D is obliged to pay compensation representing the fair market value of the gold mine, taking into account its potential to generate considerable future profits. On the other hand, there equally is little doubt that the ban on forced labor constitutes a peremptory (customary) norm of public international law and hence represents a Global Public Interest. The question to be answered, however, is whether the latter assessment bears influence on the former.

Entering the three-tier proportionality analysis, we have to recall the specific shape it takes in case of expropriation, i.e. it necessitates a particular interest in a reduced amount of compensation.[201] As for the easy part, the withdrawal of the license without paying compensation without

[201] See *supra* 5 F. 5. (b) and 5 H. 1.

question meets the suitability requirement: Punishing our investor I by effectively bereaving it of its investment demonstrates the government's determination to oust forced labor and deters future offenses. However, is it necessary not to pay compensation in order to effectively ban forced labor? This requires that paying no compensation is the least restrictive means to achieve this said goal. While one might consider arguing that this represents the only way of effective deterrence, it is very doubtful why consequent criminal prosecution of the subjects responsible combined with a compensable expropriation does not constitute an equally effective way to stop forced labor in D. Hence, in the present case proportionality analysis must halt at the necessity step.

However, one should not be too disconcerted by this result, even though the *ius cogens* violation cannot bear consequence on the level of proportionality. As a matter of fact, when it comes to assessing the amount of compensation, i.e. measuring the fair market value of the investment, the fact that I violated a peremptory norm is of relevance: No reasonable economic actor could expect to reap profits as high as I did, for they accrued from forced labor and thus from the violation of a *ius cogens* norm – a practice that no reasonable business professional can expect to continue. Therefore, the profits I has made in the years preceding the rescission of the license cannot represent viable indicators as to assessing the fair market value. Refraining from fumbling with numbers, there is little doubt that it must be considerably lower. Such result mirrors my findings regarding the principle expressed in Article 27 ILC limiting the amount of compensation or damages to *damnum emergens*.[202] Consequently D must pay compensation to I, however based on an assessment of the fair market value that acknowledges the considerably lower profits if I had not engaged in forced labor.

3. *Corruption*

While on first glance our investor I appears to have a strong case, on second glance the question arises whether its debatable good faith prevents it from successfully pleading violation of the fair and equitable treatment (FET) standard. While one might consider this issue forming part of the assessment of whether or not the FET clause applies, in subsection F. 5. (c) I have promoted a different path preferring a three-tier analysis. Hence, while in the case at hand the principle of good faith constitutes the doctrinal translation of the Global Public Interest – here effectively

[202] See *supra* 5 F. 6.

combating corruption – we again have to assess whether the measure undertaken by the host State, i.e. the presidential decree, passes the three steps of proportionality analysis: suitability, necessity and proportionality *stricto sensu*. Whereas a reasonable connection may be established between measures dispossessing investors that have paid bribes and the combat against corruption, it is highly debatable whether they also represent the least restrictive means to achieve the said goal. However, if we opine that only very harsh treatment of bribers effectively warrants prevention of future perpetrations and thus actually necessitates the punishment of I, we arrive again at the proportionality *stricto sensu* level. Here, given the fact that E only targets the supply side but does not undertake any measures against the corrupt behavior of its officials, the seriousness of pursuit of the Global Public Interest by the presidential decree may be doubted. It may be true that it should play a role in the balancing exercise and thus in assessing the amount of damages that investor I was ruthless enough to pay (the "personal donation") to the economy minister of E and thus to put its economic interest first regardless of the consequences. However, it should equally be taken into account that it was the minister who actually requested the bribe and thus incited I to corruption in the first place.[203] Consequently, as the result of the balancing exercise, the damages E should pay to I should only be marginally reduced, e.g. by 15 percent, meaning that the host State would have to pay US$ 850 million in damages to I.

203 The minister's conduct is attributable to E according to Arts. 4 and 7 of the ILC Articles on State Responsibility.

Part II Global Public Interest in international investment case law

6 International investment law and the environment

This chapter introduces the second part of my book. While the book's main focus – and hence the larger part – has been concentrated on developing and elaborating a new theoretical and doctrinal underpinning towards Global Public Interest in international investment law, the three ensuing chapters nonetheless play an important role. After having delineated my Global Public Interest theory and how to legally translate it in the investment realm, Part II is intended to present case studies of how the current investment arbitration practice grapples with three exemplary Global Public Interest issue areas, i.e. the environment, human rights and corruption. This chapter strives to present how investment arbitration Tribunals have dealt with environmental challenges and considerations in ICSID, NAFTA and disputes arbitrated within other international arbitration frameworks. Before engaging in a thorough analysis of the case law (C.), from which several conclusions derive that relate to the Global Public Interest theory (D.), I will briefly provide an overview of the guiding principles of international environmental law (A.) and discuss the relevance of international environmental law treaties under the Global Public Interest theory and for the scrutiny at hand (B.).

A. Principles of international environmental law

To start with, I reach out to describe in a nutshell the legal substance and status of those most important principles of international environmental law which I deem relevant for the analysis below.[1] Those principles comprise: the polluter pays principle (1.), the principle of preventive action

[1] See *infra* 6 C.

(2.), the precautionary principle (3.), and the common but differentiated responsibility principle (4.).

1. *The polluter pays principle*

Until fairly recently, people understood the environment – the ground, the atmosphere and the oceans – as an enormous receptacle for the disposal of waste. Since the world appeared almost infinite, its receptivity seemed to be equally infinite. However, in the 1970s, eventually, it became obvious that the environment's ability to absorb all the waste was much more limited than expected and that the prevalent attitude had led to the environmental challenges which would persist for generations to come.[2]

The polluter pays principle, first introduced by the OECD in 1972,[3] seeks to tackle the problem by a quite pragmatic economic approach. In its most recent form, enshrined in Principle 16 of the Rio Declaration on Environment and Development,[4] it reads as follows:

> National authorities should endeavour to promote the internalization of environmental costs and the use of economic instruments, taking into account the approach that the polluter should, in principle, bear the costs of pollution, with due regard to the public interest and without distorting international trade and investment.[5]

In other words, the polluter pays principle requires the person responsible for the pollution to bear its costs. According to Gaines, it "strives for the twin goals of efficiency in using economic resources to achieve environmental standards and equity between nations in uniformly allocating the costs of compliance to the polluter sources."[6] Its rationale is thus to protect the environment by making the polluter internalize the environmental costs economically: If I have to pay for something, I instantly become aware of the scarcity of resources. Therefore, the polluter pays

[2] See S. A. Atapattu, *Emerging Principles of International Environmental Law* (Transnational Publishers, 2006), pp. 437 f.

[3] Organization for Economic Cooperation and Development, Recommendation of the Council on Guiding Principles Concerning International Economic Aspects of Environmental Policies, C(72) 128, May 26, 1972, available at www.olis.oecd.org/horizontal/oecdacts.nsf/linkto/C(72)128.

[4] Adopted at the United Nations Conference on Environment and Development, June 14, 1992.

[5] Rio Declaration on Environment and Development, *ILM*, 31 (1992), 874.

[6] S. Gaines, "The Polluter Pays Principle: From Economic Equity to Environmental Ethos," *Tex. Int'l L.J.*, 26 (1991), 463 at 481.

principle seeks to achieve an educational goal as well.[7] Moreover, it pursues a general notion of equity by making nations pay their share of the economic costs accruing from pollution according to their particular contribution.

Having long been confined only to the OECD and EU realms, the polluter pays principle is gaining grip in other regional contexts.[8] However, despite its impressive proliferation in recent years, most authors hesitate to attribute to it the status of customary international law.[9] While, they contend, the argument may be fairly made under the OECD and EU realms respectively,[10] leaving the regional context and evaluating the principle's status at the global level, its customary nature is at best a nascent one. Compared with the principle of preventive action and the precautionary principle, the customary international law nature of which, by the way, is far from being undisputed,[11] the polluter pays principle has received a lesser degree of attention or support.[12]

Nonetheless, arguably it is on the verge of becoming customary international law in not too remote a future. It has been implemented in many domestic jurisdictions all over the world and even such developing countries observing its emergence and proliferation with an attentive skepticism have not been entirely immune from its growing force, for their judiciaries have referred to it on several occasions.[13] However, to the present day, the polluter pays principle lacks a firm and definable legal status as a principle of customary international law, both regarding *opinio iuris* and sufficient practice.

2. *The principle of preventive action*

Being an outflow of Principle 2 of the Rio Declaration – confirming a State's sovereignty over its national resources – the principle of preventive action, however, seeks to minimize environmental damage as an objective in itself rather than as a mere consequence of sovereignty.[14] According to the ICJ in the *Gabcíkovo-Nagymaros* case:

[7] Atapattu, *Emerging Principles*, pp. 438 f.

[8] See, e.g., Art. 5(6)(b) of the Convention for Cooperation in the Protection and Sustainable Development of the Marine and Coastal Environment of the North-East Pacific (The Antigua Convention), done February 18, 2002.

[9] Atapattu, *Emerging Principles*, p. 484; P. Sands, *Principles of International Environmental Law*, 2nd edn. (Cambridge University Press, 2003), p. 280.

[10] *Ibid.* [11] See *infra* 6 A. 2., 6 A. 3. [12] Sands, *Principles*, p. 280.

[13] See Atapattu, *Emerging Principles*, p. 454; see also C. S. Pearson, "Testing the System: GATT+PPP=?," *Cornell In'l L. J.*, 27 (1994), 553 at 553 f.

[14] Sands, *Principles*, p. 246.

> in the field of environmental protection, vigilance and prevention are required on account of the often irreversible character of damage to the environment and of the limitations inherent in the very mechanism of reparation of this type of damage.[15]

Thus, the preventive principle requires States to take action against measures harmful to the environment at an early stage; if possible before damage has actually occurred.[16] If an action or measure is about to cause damage to the environment in violation of rules of international law, the State on the territory of which the crucial action or measure occurs is obliged to prevent the environmental damage to unfold. Instead of taking only reactive steps to repair an environmental crisis or damage, under the principle of preventive action States are required to take active measures in advance.

The principle of preventive action is enshrined in or endorsed by a plethora of international environmental treaties, covering subject areas ranging from the extinction of species of flora and fauna to biodiversity and air pollution and dangerous anthropogenic interference with the climate system.[17] Despite such widespread recognition in international legal instruments, the principle has not yet achieved the status of customary international law.[18] The passage cited above from the ICJ's judgment in the *Gabcíkovo-Nagymaros* case is, as welcome and valuable as it is, not much more than a rather cursory statement that may acknowledge a development but falls way short of lifting the principle up to the pantheon of customary international law.[19]

3. *The precautionary principle*

Principle 15 of the Rio Declaration reads as follows:

> In order to protect the environment, the precautionary approach shall be widely applied by States according to their capabilities. Where there are threats of serious or irreversible damage, lack of full scientific certainty shall not be used as a reason for postponing cost-effective measures to prevent environmental degradation.[20]

15 *ICJ Reports*, (1997), 7 at 78, para. 140. 16 See Sands, *Principles*, p. 280. 17 *Ibid.*, p. 248.

18 See P.-M. Dupuy, "Formation of Customary International Law and General Principles" in D. Bodansky, J. Brunnée and E. Hey (eds.), *The Oxford Handbook of International Environmental Law* (Oxford University Press, 2007), p. 449 at p. 551.

19 J. Vessey, "The Principle of Prevention in International Law," *Austrian Review of International & European Law*, 3 (1998), 181 at 199.

20 Rio Declaration on Environment and Development, *ILM*, 31 (1992), 874.

The aim of the precautionary principle seems to be an oxymoron: It seeks to provide guidance in case of uncertainty.[21] But its purpose is to protect the environment by barring the invocation of scientific uncertainty as a pretext to continue an environmentally dangerous practice. A prominent example is global warming: While there was sufficient evidence to suggest that global warming was taking place, scientific certainty was lacking.[22]

Having its origins in domestic legal instruments in the 1970s, most notably in West Germany,[23] the precautionary principle, in a nutshell, requires States to take measures to protect the environment in case of evidence of serious environmental damage, even in absence of scientific certainty. Its main rationale is "to provide guidance to environmental decision makers in situations where policymakers face scientific uncertainty."[24]

While sounding somewhat similar to the principle of preventive action it must be kept in mind that the precautionary principle serves a different purpose. Whereas the preventive principle requires States to prevent foreseeable environmental harm, the precautionary principle seeks to prevent environmental degradation by disallowing States to invoke scientific uncertainty as justification for inaction. Thus, the former requires action in case harm is certain; the latter seeks to prevent harm where there is scientific uncertainty.

Given that it has only evolved in the international arena as late as the 1980s, the thriving dynamic of the precautionary principle is undeniable. However, considering this short time period, has it already accrued to customary international law status? Such has been alleged by several scholars and even by States in international disputes. Trouwborst, for example, asserts:

> In short . . . a balancing of all preceding considerations on state practice, *opinio juris* and expert opinion allows for the final conclusion that the assumption that nowadays the precautionary principle is a principle of customary international law is much better defensible than the contrary.[25]

[21] Sands, *Principles*, p. 267. [22] Atapattu, *Emerging Principles*, p. 204.

[23] See K. von Moltke, "The Vorsorgeprinzip in West German Environmental Policy" in Twelfth Report, *Royal Commission on Environmental Pollution* (UK, HMSO, Cm. 310, 1988), 57; P. Muchlinski, *Multinational Enterprises and the Law*, 2nd edn. (Oxford University Press, 2007), p. 540.

[24] Atapattu, *Emerging Principles*, p. 205.

[25] A. Trouwborst, *Evolution and Status of the Precautionary Principle in International Law* (Kluwer Law International, 2002), p. 275.

Similar statements were made by the European Communities in the *Beef–Hormones* case[26] before the WTO Appellate Body and by Hungary and Slovakia in the *Gabcíkovo-Nagymaros* case.[27]

However, the World Court and the World Trade Court did not share such enthusiasm. While the ICJ avoided any specific reference to the principle or its rationale overall, the WTO Appellate Body expressed its skepticism regarding the precautionary principle's customary international law status:

Whether it has been widely accepted by Members as a principle of general or customary international law appears less than clear. We consider, however, that it is unnecessary, and probably imprudent, for the Appellate Body in this appeal to take a position on this important, but abstract, question. We note that the Panel itself did not make any definitive finding with regard to the status of the precautionary principle in international law and that the precautionary principle, at least outside the field of international environmental law, still awaits authoritative formulation.[28]

Most scholars share this caution vis-à-vis granting the precautionary principle customary international law status. According to Atapattu, "the better view is that . . . it has entered into the realm of international environmental law, not as a binding principle but rather as a guiding principle."[29] However, it is gaining ground and being acknowledged way beyond the European system.[30] Therefore, it seems appropriate to regard it at least as an evolving or even emerging norm. *In conclusio*, to quote de Chazournes:

Even if it has not yet acquired an unambiguous status in general international law, one should nonetheless consider the precautionary principle as an emerging customary norm. Its conclusion in numerous legal instruments of international and national law, and the fact that it has been taken into consideration by the European Court of Justice as well as by national Tribunals bear witness to this.[31]

26 European Communities – Measures Concerning Meat and Meat Products (Hormones), WT/DS26/AB/R, WT/DS48/AB/R, February 13, 1998 (Hereinafter: *EC – Hormones*).

27 *ICJ Reports* (1997), 7.

28 *EC – Hormones*, para. 123.

29 Atapattu, *Emerging Principles*, p. 287; see also P.-M. Dupuy, *supra* n. 18, pp. 451, 462.

30 See, for example, Indian Supreme Court, *Vellore Citizens' Welfare Forum* v. *Union of India and Others*, Writ Petition (C) No. 914 of 1991, Judgment of August 28, 1996, paras. 10, 11, 15.

31 L. B. de Chazournes, *The Precautionary Principle in Precaution from Rio to Johannesburg* (Proceedings of a Geneva Environment Network Roundtable, 2002).

4. Common but differentiated responsibility principle

The common but differentiated responsibility principle aims to strike a balance between the general international law principles of sovereign equality and equity among States. While Article 2(1) of the United Nations Charter underlines the sovereign equality of its Members as one of the cardinal principles of world order, it is universally recognized that this does not mean that all States are equal in substantive terms.[32] On the contrary, the principle of equity requires not asking substantially the same from, say, France and Uganda.[33] Therefore, the common but differentiated responsibility principle seeks to reconcile both principles: States have common (equality) but differentiated responsibilities (equity). Accordingly, Principle 7 of the Rio Declaration states:

> States shall cooperate in a spirit of global partnership to conserve, protect and restore the health and integrity of the Earth's ecosystem. In view of the different contributions to global environmental degradation, States have common but differentiated responsibilities. The developed countries acknowledge the responsibility that they bear in the international pursuit to sustainable development in view of the pressures their societies place on the global environment and of the technologies and financial resources they command.

There are two discernible elements inherent in the principle: (1) That States share the common responsibility of protecting the environment at national, regional and global levels. (2) That the differing circumstances of each State have to be taken into account, regarding both a State's contribution to a particular environmental threat and its ability to prevent, reduce and control it. According to Phillipe Sands, this has two consequences:

> First, [the principle of common but differentiated responsibility] entitles, or may require, all concerned states to participate in international response measures aimed at addressing environmental problems. Secondly, it leads to environmental standards which impose differing obligations on states.[34]

While differential treatment, particularly vis-à-vis developing countries, can well be called "a common feature of international law,"[35] it seems to

32 Atapattu, *Emerging Principles*, p. 379.

33 See D. French, "Developing States and International Environmental Law: The Importance of Differentiated Responsibilities," *Int'l & Comp. L. Q.*, 49 (2000), 35 at 46 ff.

34 Sands, *Principles*, p. 286.

35 P. Cullet, *Differential Treatment in International Environmental Law* (Ashgate, 2003), p. 86.

be at least premature to consider it customary international law,[36] due to a lack of both sufficient State practice and *opinio iuris*. However,

> Despite a rather disjointed history, the practice of granting differential treatment may be slowly finding stronger roots in the specific context of international environmental law.[37]

Thus, although we are not yet at that point, we may well see the emergence of the common but differentiated principle in the future.

B. Do international environmental law treaties bear any relevance for the analysis at hand?

Taking into account the final conclusions of my analysis regarding what I call the Global Public Interest theory, it might seem astonishing that international treaties could play a role at all in my considerations vis-à-vis international investment case law on environmental matters. Indeed, as regards international investment law, under my approach the stage is only open to rules of customary international law and general principles of law. Part A. of this chapter has been dedicated to the substantive gist of the former. The Global Public Interest theory allows consideration of treaty provisions only in one exceptional scenario – if they incorporate rules that already form part of customary international law or represent general principles of law.

International environmental law treaties are of considerable importance, however, in NAFTA investment arbitration cases. Article 104 and its Annex 104.1 NAFTA read as follows:

Article 104: Relation to Environmental and Conservation Agreements

1. In the event of any inconsistency between this Agreement and the specific trade obligations set out in:
    a) the *Convention on International Trade in Endangered Species of Wild Fauna and Flora*, done at Washington, March 3, 1973, as amended June 22, 1979,
    b) the *Montreal Protocol on Substances that Deplete the Ozone Layer*, done at Montreal, September 16, 1987, as amended June 29, 1990,
    c) the *Basel Convention on the Control of Transboundary Movements of Hazardous Wastes and Their Disposal*, done at Basel, March 22, 1989, on its entry into force for Canada, Mexico and the United States, or
    d) the agreements set out in Annex 104.1,

[36] See Atapattu, *Emerging Principles*, pp. 431, 434.
[37] Cullet, *Differential Treatment*, pp. 88 f.

such obligations shall prevail to the extent of the inconsistency, provided that where a Party has a choice among equally effective and reasonably available means of complying with such obligations, the Party chooses the alternative that is the least inconsistent with the other provisions of this Agreement.

2. The Parties may agree in writing to modify Annex 104.1 to include any amendment to an agreement referred to in paragraph 1, and any other environmental or conservation agreement

. . .

Annex 104.1

Bilateral and Other Environmental and Conservation Agreements

1. *The Agreement Between the Government of Canada and the Government of the United States of America Concerning the Transboundary Movement of Hazardous Waste*, signed at Ottawa, October 28, 1986.
2. *The Agreement Between the United States of America and the United Mexican States on Cooperation for the Protection and Improvement of the Environment in the Border Area*, signed at La Paz, Baja California Sur, August 14, 1983.

Thus, these three multilateral and two bilateral international environmental law treaties prevail over NAFTA investor rights in case of inconsistencies, if both the investor's host and its home State are parties to them and if the host State chooses the least restrictive measure to implement the respective international environmental law treaty provision.[38] While ICSID case law will play a pivotal role, particularly as regards environmental matters, NAFTA cases will prove quite instructive. Moreover, it is a widely recognized phenomenon that investment arbitration cases cite other investment arbitration case law indiscriminately, irrespective of whether they derive from the ICSID, NAFTA, UNCITRAL or any other realm.[39]

C. International investment disputes involving environmental issues

After the preceding overview of the international environmental law principles and treaties most relevant in the context of international investment law, this section is dedicated to a detailed analysis of the international investment arbitration case law involving environmental matters.

[38] For an example and a more elaborate analysis in this regard see the *S. D. Myers* case, *infra* 6 C. 3.

[39] For further explanation and references please consult 6 D. 1. (b).

1. Santa Elena *v.* Costa Rica

(a) Facts and issues

The first case under scrutiny, *Santa Elena* v. *Costa Rica*,[40] is rather atypical for the investment arbitration case law involving environmental matters. Compared to monster arbitrations such as *Methanex*[41] or *Biwater*,[42] to name but two examples, the factual matrix is considerably simpler and issues concerning the environment appear to play a rather incidental, at least subsidiary, role.

Compañiá del Desarrollo de Santa Elena (CDSE), a company the majority of whose shares was held by US nationals, purchased a property in the Guanacaste Province of Costa Rica in order to develop large portions as a tourist resort and residential community. "The terrain consists of over 30 kilometers of Pacific coastline, as well as numerous rivers, springs, valleys, forests and mountains. In addition to its geographical and geological features, the Property is home to a dazzling variety of flora and fauna, many of which are indigenous to the region and to the tropical dry forest habitat for which it is known."[43]

On May 5, 1978, the Costa Rican government issued a decree declaring the expropriation of the Santa Elena property. As reason the decree stated as follows:

> 1. . . .
>
> 2. The lands situated to the north of the Santa Rosa National Park [i.e. the Santa Elena property] contain flora and fauna of great scientific, recreational, educational, and tourism value, as well as beaches that are especially important as spawning grounds for sea turtles.
>
> 3. To meet these objectives, the Government of the Republic requires the property that belongs to the Compañiá de Desarrollo Santa Elena S.A. . . .[44]

CDSE did not object to the expropriation as such, however it did contest the amount of compensation attributed by the Costa Rican government. While the decree foresaw US$ 1,900,000 as compensation, CDSE

[40] *Compañiá del Desarrollo de Santa Elena, SA* v. *Costa Rica* (ICSID Case No. ARB/96/1), Award, February 18, 2000 (hereinafter: *Santa Elena* v. *Costa Rica*).

[41] *Methanex Corporation* v. *United States of America*, UNCITRAL (NAFTA), Final Award, August 3, 2005 (hereinafter: *Methanex* v. *US*); see *infra* 6 C. 6.

[42] *Biwater Gauff (Tanzania) Ltd.* v. *United Republic of Tanzania* (ICSID Case No. ARB/05/22), Award, July 24, 2008 (hereinafter: *Biwater* v. *Tanzania*); see *infra* 6 C. 7.

[43] *Santa Elena* v. *Costa Rica*, para. 15.

[44] *Ibid*., para. 18.

claimed US$ 6,400,000.[45] Throughout the following twenty years, the matter remained unresolved, until in 1998 CDSE introduced an ICSID arbitration. In the time period between 1978 and 1998, CDSE remained in possession of the property but did not – apart from a few measures undertaken prior to the expropriation decree – develop the property any further.[46]

Thus, it is rather unsurprising that the two main issues in the Tribunal's award focused on the amount of compensation: (1) as to the relevant date for the valuation of the property according to the fair market value – since after the expropriation the value of the property had dropped considerably; and (2) as to whether the Tribunal should award simple or compound interest – an important issue given the timespan of more than twenty years between the expropriatory act and the Tribunal's decision.

(b) The public purpose does not affect the duty to pay compensation

As regards these two issues, the Tribunal determined that the relevant date for measuring the value of the property should correspond with the date on which the expropriation took place. Hence, Costa Rica had to compensate the fair market value the property possessed *before* the expropriation decree was issued.[47] Since the Tribunal found that it was impossible to assess the fair market value as of 1978 more than twenty years later, it determined the average between the sum requested by the claimant and the sum approved by the respondent in order to constitute the fair market value of the Santa Elena property.[48] Moreover, since CDSE remained in possession of the property, it was, according to the Tribunal, in the position to exploit it to a limited extent and thus was not entitled to full compound interest. The Tribunal hence awarded an overall compensation, i.e. including interest, of US$ 16,000,000 – instead of more than US$ 41,000,000 as requested by the claimant.[49]

While assessing the expropriation claim of CDSE, the Tribunal declined to consider any evidence submitted by the respondent as to its international obligations to preserve the environment.[50] Furthermore, it

45 *Ibid.*, paras. 17, 19. 46 *Ibid.*, para. 20. 47 *Ibid.*, para. 83.

48 I.e. US$ 4,150,000; the claimant requested US$ 6,400,000, the respondent offered US$ 1,900,000; see *Santa Elena* v. *Costa Rica*, para. 95.

49 *Ibid.*, para. 107.

50 *Ibid.*, para. 32; see M. Hirsch, "Interactions Between Investment and Non-Investment Obligations" in P. Muchlinski, F. Ortino and C. Schreuer, *The Oxford Handbook of International Investment Law* (Oxford University Press, 2008), p. 154 at p. 169.

purported that as regards expropriation the mere fact that the host State pursues a public interest does not change its obligation to compensate, for every expropriation requires a public purpose. In the words of the Tribunal:

71. While an expropriation or taking for environmental reasons may be classified as a taking for a public purpose, and thus may be legitimate, the fact that the Property was taken for this reason does not affect either the nature or the measure of the compensation to be paid for the taking. That is, the purpose of protecting the environment for which the Property was taken does not alter the legal character of the taking for which adequate compensation must be paid. The international source of the obligation to protect the environment makes no difference.

72. Expropriatory environmental measures – no matter how laudable and beneficial to society as a whole – are, in this respect, similar to any other expropriatory measures that a state may take in order to implement its policies: where property is expropriated, even for environmental purposes, whether domestic or international, the state's obligation to pay compensation remains.[51]

Hence, according to the Tribunal, the reason why the host State undertook the measure does not at all affect the legal assessment as an expropriatory measure.

(c) A conservative decision

At first glance, the Tribunal's reasoning regarding expropriation sounds appealing: Every expropriation requires a public purpose, thus public interest concerns such as preserving the natural diversity of flora and fauna may well serve as such public purpose but do not affect the host State's obligation to pay compensation. Indeed, if a host State was able to allege public interest concerns in general as a basis for justification of expropriation, the investor's protection in this regard would simply render void given the myriad of public purposes possible.[52] However, as Moshe Hirsch points out,[53] recent investment arbitration case law has shattered the foundation of such reasoning. In the *Saluka*[54] and *Methanex*[55] awards the Tribunals stated that general regulatory practice that pursued a public purpose should not even be considered an expropriation and thus

[51] *Santa Elena* v. *Costa Rica*, paras. 71, 72.

[52] See also *supra* 5 F. 5. (b).

[53] Hirsch, "Interactions," 170, n. 80.

[54] *Saluka Investments BV* v. *Czech Republic*, Partial Award, March 17, 2006, PCA, available at www.pca-cpa.org/showpage.asp?pag_id=1149 (hereinafter: *Saluka* v. *Czech Republic*), para. 262.

[55] *Methanex* v. *US*, Pt. IV, Ch. D, para. 7.

not entail any obligation to compensate, if the measure is enacted with due process and in a non-discriminatory manner, unless specific commitments had been given to the investor. The *Saluka* Tribunal even claimed this as forming "part of customary international law today."[56] Moreover, as will be described in detail below, the Tribunal in the *Tecmed* case chose an interpretation of the expropriation clause that also allowed for a wide range of environmental – and other public interest – considerations.[57] While it is true for the case at hand that the measure under scrutiny was targeted directly at the investor and did not merely affect it, inter alia, under a general regulatory scheme, at the very least the complete ignorance that the *Santa Elena* award demonstrates vis-à-vis such argumentation is remarkable. It is hardly surprising that such ignorance extends to not considering any international environmental obligations that might burden the host State.

2. Metalclad *v.* Mexico

(a) Facts and issues

Waste disposal is always a delicate issue, for everybody agrees that it is necessary, but nobody wants to have a site on his or her doorstep. The following case, *Metalclad* v. *Mexico*, of August 30, 2000,[58] is the first in a line of cases that arose out of disputes about waste disposal and/or the construction and operation of waste landfills.

In 1993, the federal government of Mexico granted Confinamiento Tecnico de Residuos Industriales, SA de CV (COTERIN), a Mexican company, a permit to construct and operate a transfer station for hazardous wastes and, shortly after, to construct and operate a station and landfill for the

[56] *Saluka* v. *Czech Republic*, para. 262. See also Dolzer and Schreuer, *Principles of International Investment Law* (Oxford University Press, 2008), pp. 109 ff.; C. N. Brower and E. R. Hellbeck, "The Implications of National and International Environmental Obligations for Foreign Investment Protection Standards, Including Valuation: A Report from the Front Lines" in The International Bureau of the Permanent Court of Arbitration, *International Investments and Protection of the Environment – The Role of Dispute Resolution Mechanisms*, Papers emanating from the Second PCA International Law Seminar, May 17, 2000, The Permanent Court of Arbitration/Peace Palace Papers (Kluwer Law International, 2001), p. 19 at p. 22.

[57] See *infra* 6 C. 4., 6 D. 1. (b). To be sure, and as has been argued in Chapter 5, my doctrinal preference lies with balancing public interest issues such as environmental concerns with investor rights on the compensation stage rather than addressing them when asking whether the measure amounts to an expropriation, i.e. with the secondary rather than the primary level.

[58] *Metalclad Corporation* v. *United Mexican States* (ICSID Case No. ARB(AF)/97/1), Award, August 30, 2000 (hereinafter: *Metalclad* v. *Mexico*).

waste. When COTERIN received the permit, Metalclad, a US corporation of Delaware, purchased COTERIN including all its licenses. Metalclad alleged that immediately after it had purchased COTERIN, the local government of San Luis Potosi (SLP), the region where the transfer station and landfill were supposed to be located, started a campaign to denounce and prevent the operation of the landfill. However, as the Tribunal found, the federal government of Mexico assured Metalclad that the latter was entitled to build and operate the landfill.[59]

In early 1995, the Autonomous University of SLP and the Mexican Federal Attorney's Office for the Protection of the Environment issued a study confirming earlier findings that, although the landfill site raised some concerns, with proper engineering it was geographically suitable for a hazardous waste landfill.[60] Shortly after the beginning of its operation, demonstrators opposing the landfill blocked the site so that Metalclad was effectively prevented from operating the landfill. Subsequently, following intense negotiations, Metalclad and the federal government of Mexico entered into an agreement (*Convenio*) that provided for and allowed the operation of the landfill. However, the municipal government of SLP declined to grant the permit for operation of the landfill. In September 1997, the governor of SLP, three days before the expiry of his term, by Ecological Decree declared the region in which the landfill was situated a Natural Area for the protection of cactus.[61] According to Metalclad, the decree "definitely cancelled any possibility that exists of opening the industrial waste landfill."[62] Metalclad contended violation of NAFTA Articles 1105 ("fair and equitable treatment") and 1110 ("measures tantamount to expropriation").

(b) Transparency as part of FET?

The Tribunal found that the municipality's actions were attributable to Mexico and thus that it had violated both the fair and equitable treatment and the (indirect) expropriation clauses of NAFTA.[63] In relation to NAFTA Article 1105, referring to the provision's object and purpose, the Tribunal inferred a transparency element as alluded to in Article 102(1) of NAFTA. Hence it stated that the contradictory conduct of the federal government on the one hand and the municipal government on the other, including the Ecological Decree, was inconsistent with the fair and equitable

59 *Metalclad* v. *Mexico*, paras. 35 ff. 60 *Ibid.*, para. 44. 61 *Ibid.*, paras. 47 ff., 59.
62 *Ibid.*, para. 60. 63 *Ibid.*, paras. 101, 112.

treatment standard.[64] Refraining from considering any national environmental or administrative competence regulations and laws, according to the Tribunal Metalclad additionally suffered an indirect taking, for the Ecological Decree de facto – though not expressly – did not allow for any possibility of continuing to operate the landfill.[65]

(c) A controversial award

The *Metalclad* award is a much-disputed and controversial decision in several different regards.[66] Since it is of minor interest for the questions before us, I will refrain from commenting on the doctrinal challenges of both the fair and equitable treatment and indirect expropriation clauses the Tribunal's reasoning entails.[67] Suffice it to say that reading a transparency obligation into Article 1105 NAFTA is a rather precarious path that most subsequent Tribunals did not follow, at least not with the pervasiveness as applied in *Metalclad*.[68]

Regarding Mexico's allegations of internal separation of administrative powers the Tribunal was certainly right to stress that domestic laws may never serve as justification for breaching international obligations.[69] However, it is remarkable how prone the Tribunal was to inferring as applicable law pro-investor considerations such as the transparency requirement, and did not even consider international environmental instruments as possible applicable law or even the health and environmental risks pointed at in the party submissions. Additionally, considering the well-known and longstanding opposition of the local and regional community to the landfill, it is hard to argue, as the Tribunal did however, that Metalclad could claim legitimate expectations that the permit to operate and the operation of the landfill itself would run smoothly and without setbacks.[70] Moreover, the award does not even address allegations of extensive bribery of public officials by Metalclad that might have influenced decisions to grant permission to construct the landfill in the

[64] *Ibid.*, para. 99. [65] *Ibid.*, paras. 108, 110.

[66] See, e.g., M. Sornarajah, *The International Law on Foreign Investment*, 3rd edn. (Cambridge University Press, 2010), p. 350.

[67] For a detailed analysis of these questions see Dolzer and Schreuer, *Principles*, pp. 133 ff.

[68] See *ibid.*, p. 134 and the fierce critique in Schneiderman, *Constitutionalizing Economic Globalization*, pp. 83 f. See also *The United Mexican States* v. *Metalclad Corporation*, 2001 BCSC 664, Judgment, Supreme Court of British Columbia, Tysoe J, May 2, 2001, para. 68.

[69] See Art. 27 of the Vienna Convention on the Law of Treaties; *Metalclad* v. *Mexico*, para. 100.

[70] See Schneiderman, *Constitutionalizing Economic Globalization*, p. 84.

first place despite the potentially precarious impact of a waste landfill on the environment in the region.[71]

3. S. D. Myers *v.* Canada

(a) Facts and issues

While the *Metalclad* award was much criticized for its alleged myopia vis-à-vis environmental issues and international environmental instruments as potential justifications for investor rights' violations, and *Santa Elena* revealed a similar pattern, *S. D. Myers* v. *Canada*, decided on November 13, 2000,[72] appears to mark somewhat of a shift of the tide in this regard. In fact, it is one of the most prominent decisions to date dealing with the relationship of investment and environmental matters.

S. D. Myers is a US company incorporated in Ohio that specializes in the process of PCB[73] remediation. By the early 1970s, many countries started to recognize the high toxicity and thus the potential risk to human life and health of PCB. Therefore, Canada and the United States, following an OECD decision as of 1973, effectively banned both the production of PCB and the export of PCB waste – with the exception of PCB export to each other. Moreover, in 1986 the two countries concluded the Transboundary Agreement, which contemplated the possibility of cross-border activity, recognizing that the long common border engendered opportunities for a generator of hazardous waste to benefit from using the nearest appropriate disposal facility.[74] Then, in 1989, Canada acceded to the Basel Convention,[75] whereas the United States signed it but had not ratified it

[71] See H. Raeschke-Kessler and D. Gottwald, "Corruption" in P. Muchlinski, F. Ortino and C. Schreuer (eds.), *The Oxford Handbook of International Investment Law* (Oxford University Press, 2008), p. 584.

[72] *S. D. Myers, Inc.* v. *Canada*, UNCITRAL (NAFTA) Partial Award, November 13, 2000 (hereinafter: *S. D. Myers* v. *Canada*).

[73] As the Tribunal explains, "[t]he term 'PCB' is an abbreviation for a synthetic chemical compound known as polychlorinated biphenyl. This compound consists of chlorine, carbon and hydrogen and has a combination of properties that provide an inert, fire-resistant and insulating material. This makes the compound suitable for insulation. PCBs were used mainly in electrical equipment and to a lesser extent in other products. PCBs biodegrade slowly and remain in the environment for a long time. To eliminate them from the environment, PCBs must be disposed of through either a process of thermal destruction at high temperatures or by chemical processing. Landfilling is also used as a means of disposal, but this method merely contains the material in a relatively safe manner and does not result in the removal of the substance from the environment."; *S. D. Myers* v. *Canada*, para. 94.

[74] See *ibid*, paras. 98–103 and Hirsch, "Interactions," 163 f.

[75] Basel Convention on the Control of Transboundary Movements of Hazardous Wastes and their Disposal, done March 22, 1989; see www.basel.int/text/documents.html.

at the time the dispute arose. Regarding the obligations a State member to the Basel Convention undertakes, the Tribunal explicates:

106. State parties to the Basel Convention accept the obligation to ensure that hazardous wastes are managed in an environmentally sound manner. The Basel Convention establishes rules and procedures to govern the transboundary movement of hazardous wastes and their disposal. Amongst other things, it prohibits the export and import of hazardous wastes from and to states that are not party to the Basel Convention (Article 4(5)), unless such movement is subject to bilateral, multilateral or regional agreements or arrangements whose provisions are not less stringent than those of the Basel Convention (Article 11).

107. The Basel Convention also requires appropriate measures to ensure the availability of adequate disposal facilities for the environmentally sound management of hazardous wastes that are located within it (Article 4(2)(b)). It also requires that the transboundary movement of hazardous wastes be reduced to the minimum consistent with the environmentally sound and efficient management of such wastes and be conducted in a manner that will protect human health and the environment (Article 4(2)(d)).[76]

Canada adopted corresponding legislation in order to transform its international obligations into domestic law. In a parliamentary address ensuing the signing of the Convention and the adoption of the legislation, the then Canadian Minister for the Environment stated: "It is still the position of the government that the handling of PCBs should be done *in Canada by Canadians*."[77]

In 1990, S. D. Myers began its efforts to obtain the necessary approvals to import electrical transformers and other equipment containing PCB wastes into the USA from Canada. By this time S. D. Myers had become one of the most prominent operators in the PCB disposal industry in the USA.[78] In 1993, S. D. Myers prepared to expand its business to Canada and incorporated Myers Canada under the Canadian Business Corporation Act. In the meantime, Canadian PCB waste disposal operators launched an eventually successful lobbying campaign to ban commercial export of PCB for waste disposal – Canadian authorities closed the common border with the US for cross-border movement of PCB waste for about one-and-a-half years.[79] While S. D. Myers claimed violation of Canada's obligations under NAFTA Chapter 11, among others of the national and fair and equitable treatment standards, Canada asserted its obligations under other international instruments, including the Transboundary Agreement and the

[76] *S. D. Myers* v. *Canada*, paras. 106 f. [77] *Ibid.*, para. 116 (emphasis added by the Tribunal).
[78] *Ibid.*, para. 109. [79] *Ibid.*, paras. 118–124.

Basel Convention, as grounds for its conduct and argued that S. D. Myers' interpretation of Chapter 11 was inconsistent with these treaties.[80]

(b) Generally open for environmental considerations, but distrusting Canada in the case at hand

The Tribunal showed considerable distrust towards Canada's allegations that its complete PCB export ban was necessary to perform its obligations under the Basel Convention. By contrast, it relied on the Minister's statement that "the handling of PCB should be done in Canada by Canadians," culling Canada's discriminatory intent. Hence, the Tribunal concluded:

> that there was no legitimate environmental reason for introducing the ban. Insofar as there was an indirect environmental objective – to keep the Canadian industry strong in order to assure a continued disposal capability – it could have been achieved by other measures.[81]

Having discerned the actual motivation behind the ban, the Tribunal set the hermeneutic frame by citing Article 102(2) and Article 1131(1) of the NAFTA.[82] These provisions refer to "applicable rules of international law" as the law to be applied by the Tribunal. Consequently, it examined both the Transboundary Agreement and the Basel Convention according to potential inconsistencies with the provisions of NAFTA Chapter 11. The NAFTA seeks to reconcile inconsistencies by way of the rules enshrined in Article 104, which I cite again:

Article 104: Relation to Environmental and Conservation Agreements

1. In the event of any inconsistency between this Agreement and the specific trade obligations set out in:
   a) the *Convention on International Trade in Endangered Species of Wild Fauna and Flora*, done at Washington, March 3, 1973, as amended June 22, 1979,
   b) the *Montreal Protocol on Substances that Deplete the Ozone Layer*, done at Montreal, September 16, 1987, as amended June 29, 1990,
   c) the *Basel Convention on the Control of Transboundary Movements of Hazardous Wastes and Their Disposal*, done at Basel, March 22, 1989, on its entry into force for Canada, Mexico and the United States, or
   d) the agreements set out in Annex 104.1,

[80] *Ibid.*, paras. 148–150. [81] *Ibid.*, para. 195.

[82] Art. 102(2) provides: "2. The Parties shall interpret and apply the provisions of this Agreement in the light of its objectives set out in paragraph 1 and in accordance with applicable rules of international law." Art. 1131(1) reads: "1. A Tribunal established under this Section shall decide the issues in dispute in accordance with this Agreement and applicable rules of international law."

> such obligations shall prevail to the extent of the inconsistency, provided that where a Party has a choice among equally effective and reasonably available means of complying with such obligations, the Party chooses the alternative that is the least inconsistent with the other provisions of this Agreement.

. . .[83]

Thus, as already briefly mentioned in part B. of this chapter, Article 104 specifies that the Basel Convention should prevail in case it was ratified by the NAFTA parties involved in the dispute.[84] The Tribunal stressed that while Article 11 of the Basel Convention allows for the contracting parties to conclude bilateral or multilateral agreements regarding the cross-border movement of waste, Canada was in no position to assert the Basel Convention or the Transboundary Agreement as justification for violating Chapter 11:

> [W]here a state can achieve its chosen level of environmental protection through a variety of equally effective and reasonable means, it is obliged to adopt the alternative that is most consistent with open trade.[85]

Put differently, whereas in case of inconsistencies between Chapter 11 and the treaties specified in Article 104 a NAFTA party may well rely on these treaties' provisions to justify violations of investment protection rules, in the dispute at hand Canada did not undertake to seek for reconciliation with the NAFTA goals of free trade and investment. Drawing on a similar argumentation, the Tribunal denounced Canada's allegations vis-à-vis NAFTA Chapter 3 that refers to the GATT's General Exception clause.[86] The Tribunal acknowledged that Chapter 3 may justify what otherwise would be a violation of Chapter 11, but rejected Canada's contentions in this case for its measures had not met the conditions of Article XX GATT, particularly the provision's chapeau.[87]

(c) A progressive award

As already alluded to, the *S. D. Myers* case marks a shift of the tide regarding the role of international environmental agreements in investment

[83] Emphasis in the original. [84] *S. D. Myers* v. *Canada*, para. 214.

[85] *S. D. Myers* v. *Canada*, para. 221.

[86] Art. XX of the General Agreement on Tariffs and Trade; see *supra* 3 B. 1.

[87] *S. D. Myers* v. *Canada*, para. 298. On the extensive case law and literature regarding the chapeau of Art. XX GATT, see M. Matsushita, T. J. Schoenbaum and P. C. Mavroidis, *The World Trade Organization – Law, Practice, and Policy* (Oxford University Press, 2003), pp. 456 ff; S. Gaines, "The WTO's Reading of the GATT Article XX Chapeau: A Disguised Restriction on Environmental Measures," *U. Pa. J. Int'l Econ. L.*, 22 (2001), 739.

disputes. While the host State did not succeed with any of its contentions in this regard, the paradigm change is nonetheless remarkable. Note what the Tribunal found. It did not reject Canada's allegations as such, in fact it acknowledged that the NAFTA treaty provides for cases in which international environmental instruments such as the Basel Convention may trump Chapter 11. Moreover, it applied the same rationale vis-à-vis the application of the GATT Article XX exceptions. In both instances, Canada's claim eventually failed – because it did not choose the least trade- and investment-restrictive measure regarding the first one and since the requirements of Article XX GATT's chapeau were not met concerning the second one. However, this merely demonstrates that invoking justifications depends on fulfilling certain requirements– a criterion that Canada did not meet in the case at hand. Nonetheless, if these requirements are met – if there is an irreconcilable inconsistency with the Basel Convention and if the host State may invoke GATT Article XX – a host State may infringe upon investors' rights with only very limited entitlement of the latter to compensation.[88]

Another issue needs mention here that will gain more prominence later in my analysis[89] but that should not be neglected entirely at this stage. The final part of Article 104(1) NAFTA reveals elements of a proportionality test, which the Tribunal internalized to a quite remarkable degree. To quote again Article 104(1) of the NAFTA:

> such obligations shall prevail to the extent of the inconsistency, provided that where a Party has a choice among *equally effective and reasonably available* means of complying with such obligations, the Party chooses the *alternative* that is the *least inconsistent* with the other provisions of this Agreement.[90]

Of the proportionality test as established in the continental European tradition and in the case law of the ECJ and ECHR,[91] this provision employs at least two of the three factors to be considered, i.e. suitability for a legitimate purpose and necessity.[92] While a measure can only be considered suitable for a legitimate purpose if the party employing it chooses equally effective and reasonably available means, the least-restrictive-measure test is the *noyau dur* of the necessity factor.[93]

[88] If we follow the *Santa Elena* pattern that the expropriatory purpose is irrelevant for triggering the obligation to compensate; see *supra* 6 C. 1.

[89] See *infra* 6 D. 1. (c). [90] Emphasis added.

[91] For references in this regard see *supra* 5 C. 3. and *infra* 7 C.

[92] See *supra* Chapter 5, particularly 5 D. On proportionality in the international investment law context, see Kingsbury and Schill, "Investor-State Arbitration as Governance," 21 ff. The third factor is the proportionality *stricto sensu*; see *ibid.*, 29.

[93] See J. H. Jans, "Proportionality Revisited," *Legal Issues of Econ. Integration*, 27 (2000), 239 at 240.

Admittedly, as remarkable as they are, those findings are direct consequences of the inbuilt mechanics and framework of the NAFTA régime that are not transferable interchangeably to other investment treaties. However, while caution is needed to prevent hasty conclusions, the extent to which those considerations drive or inform the reasoning of investment arbitration Tribunals outside the NAFTA context is something to keep in mind.

4. Tecmed *v.* Mexico

(a) Facts and issues

Similarly to *Metalclad*,[94] the dispute in *Tecmed* v. *Mexico*,[95] a BIT case between a Spanish investor and the United Mexican States, arose out of the operation of a waste landfill in Mexico, the respondent in the case. Tecmed, the claimant, was awarded a waste landfill located in the State of Sonara, Mexico in a public auction held in 1996. Although the landfill had been built in 1988, the community living next to it showed continuing opposition to its operation when Tecmed took over the facility. The claimant sought damages, including compensation for damage to reputation, and interest in connection with damage allegedly having accrued as of November 25, 1998, on which date an agency of the Mexican Ministry of the Environment rejected the application for renewal of the authorization to operate the landfill, expiring on November 19, 1998, pursuant to a Ministry resolution on the same date, whereby the Ministry through its agency further requested it submit a program for the closure of the landfill.[96]

Mexico sought to draw the Tribunal's attention to several shortcomings by Tecmed that led to the community's unrest and ongoing unfavorable attitude towards the landfill. Furthermore, the respondent listed several circumstances that triggered the withdrawal of the license:

> 1) the site of the Landfill did not comply with applicable Mexican regulations in terms of its location and characteristics;
> 2) in 1998, Cytrar [which operated the landfill for Tecmed] had committed a number of irregularities while operating the Landfill, mainly related to the transportation of waste from Alco Pacífico, and such irregularities triggered strong community pressure against the Landfill;
> 3) Mexican authorities, mainly from the Municipality of Hermosillo, expressed their doubts as to the Landfill's operations;

94 See *supra* 6 C. 2.

95 *Tecnicas Medioambientales Tecmed SA* v. *The United Mexican States* (ICSID Case No. ARB (AF)/00/2), Award, May 29, 2003 (hereinafter: *Tecmed* v. *Mexico*).

96 *Ibid.*, para. 39.

4) there was the risk that community pressure might increase if operation of the Landfill continued; and
5) since 1997 Cytrar had reportedly been aware that community pressure suggested that the operation of the Landfill was not feasible due to its location, and that is why it agreed to relocate it at its own cost.[97]

(b) A reference to the European Court of Human Rights

The award, dated May 29, 2003, focused in particular on indirect expropriations in case of regulatory administrative actions and thus seized the opportunity to elaborate on the findings in the *Santa Elena* case. It stated:

121. After reading Article 5(1) of the Agreement and interpreting its terms according to the ordinary meaning to be given to them (Article 31(1) of the Vienna Convention), we find no principle stating that regulatory administrative actions are *per se* excluded from the scope of the Agreement, even if they are beneficial to society as a whole – such as environmental protection – , particularly if the negative economic impact of such actions on the financial position of the investor is sufficient to neutralize in full the value, or economic or commercial use of its investment without receiving any compensation whatsoever.[98]

The Tribunal then cited the *Santa Elena* passage stating that a laudable environmental purpose for the expropriation does not affect the obligation to compensate[99] and continued:

122. After establishing that regulatory actions and measures will not be initially excluded from the definition of expropriatory acts, in addition to the negative financial impact of such actions or measures, the Arbitral Tribunal will consider, in order to determine if they are to be characterized as expropriatory, *whether such actions or measures are proportional to the public interest presumably protected thereby and to the protection legally granted to investments, taking into account that the significance of such impact has a key role upon deciding the proportionality*. . . . There must be a *reasonable relationship of proportionality between the charge or weight imposed to the foreign investor and the aim sought to be realized by any expropriatory measure*. To value such charge or weight, it is very important to measure the size of the ownership deprivation caused by the actions of the state and whether such deprivation was compensated or not. On the basis of a number of legal and practical factors, it should be also considered that the foreign investor has a reduced or nil participation in the taking of the decisions that affect it, partly because the investors are not entitle[d] to exercise political rights reserved to the nationals of the State, such as voting for the authorities that will issue the decisions that affect such investors.[100]

[97] *Ibid.*, para. 105. [98] *Ibid.*, para. 121. [99] See *supra* 6 C. 1.
[100] *Tecmed v. Mexico*, para. 122 (emphasis added).

Such considerations as to the reason for a more preferable treatment of foreign investors vis-à-vis nationals of the host State mirror case law by the European Court of Human Rights (ECtHR), which the Tribunal cites:

Not only must a measure depriving a person of his property pursue, on the facts as well as in principle, a legitimate aim 'in the public interest,' but there must also be a *reasonable relationship of proportionality between the means employed and the aim sought to be realised*... The requisite balance will not be found if the person concerned has had to bear 'an individual and excessive burden'... The Court considers that a measure must be both appropriate for achieving its aim and not disproportionate thereto.

...

... *[N]on-nationals are more vulnerable to domestic legislation*: unlike nationals, they will generally have played no part in the election or designation of its authors nor have been consulted on its adoption. Secondly, although a taking of property must always be effected in the public interest, different considerations may apply to nationals and non-nationals and there may well be legitimate reason for requiring nationals to bear a greater burden in the public interest than non-nationals.[101]

(c) A dubious take on challenging *Santa Elena*

Surprising if not astonishing in the Tribunal's reasoning is the extensive consideration of the principle of proportionality to define the boundaries of the indirect takings clause of Article 5 of the Mexico–Spain BIT, particularly since the provision – in stark contrast to Article 1 of the Additional Protocol No. 1 to the European Convention on Human Rights[102] – does not contain any reference to a proportionality element. While, again, a detailed analysis of the findings in this regard remains reserved for a later part of this chapter,[103] let me highlight that the Tribunal ran on the

[101] *Ibid.*, cited from European Court of Human Rights, *In the case of James and Others* v. *United Kingdom*, Judgment of February 21, 1986, 50 (hereinafter: *James* v. *UK*), 19 f., 24; http://hudoc.echr.coe.int (emphasis added).

[102] European Convention on Human Rights, Protocol No. 1, Enforcement of certain Rights and Freedoms not included in Section I of the Convention, done at Paris on March 20, 1952, Art. 1:

> "Every natural or legal person is entitled to the peaceful enjoyment of his possessions. No one shall be deprived of his possessions except in the public interest and subject to the conditions provided for by law and by the general principles of international law.
>
> The preceding provisions shall not, however, in any way impair the right of a State to enforce such laws as it deems necessary to control the use of property in accordance with the general interest or to secure the payment of taxes or other contributions or penalties."

[103] See *infra* 6 D.

tracks of the *Santa Elena* award by determining that the *nature* of the public interest has no effect on the obligation to compensate. Rather, it reasoned that the *fact* of a public interest being pursued may well serve as justification for treating the foreign investor more favorably than the domestic one, since the former – in contrast to the latter – is neither part of the constituency in the host State nor is part or benefactor of the domestic "public" that is supposed to profit from the interest pursued.[104] In other words, in the Tribunal's view, the public interest is a domestic one that serves the interest of those who are part of the domestic community, i.e. citizens and domestic investors. Since foreign investors are by definition not domestic, they take no share in the benefit of the – domestic – public interest, but do not, in turn, have to carry as heavy a burden as domestic investors.

What incites some skepticism vis-à-vis such on first glance rather appealing reasoning is that the picture the Tribunal attempts to paint of the role of a foreign investor does not reflect the reality in most host States. To start with, a democratic process of decision-making may exist in most Member States to the European Convention on Human Rights; in many capital importing States, however, it does not exist at all or is merely a farce. But even leaving this premise of the above reasoning aside, the Tribunal completely neglects the fact that foreign investors frequently engage in considerable lobbying campaigns before they finally decide to invest. To assume that they have no say in shaping the regulatory framework is far from being true. Furthermore, in a globalized economy, the legal status of where a company is incorporated is no longer the sole indicator for this company's ties to a specific country. While it may be incorporated in one country and thus may be a "foreign" investor in another, it might nonetheless have very close ties to the latter, being deeply embedded in its economy and thus also impacted by measures undertaken in the "public interest": It is hard to understand why, say, hypothetical US legislation to only produce hybrid cars as of 2030 would affect Ford more than Honda, a Japanese and thus "foreign" car manufacturer that has possessed factories in the US since the mid-1980s and employs tens of thousands of people in the United States. Finally, limiting the public interest to the domestic sphere is myopic as regards the progressing internationalization or globalization of regulatory issues. As I have contended earlier,[105] investment disputes can be described as (Global) Public Law disputes that display features of Global Administrative as well as Constitutional

[104] *James* v. *UK*, 24. [105] *Supra* 4 A. 3.

character. Particularly if the domestic measure has an international pedigree, e.g. is based on legislation that simply transforms obligations undertaken under public international law into domestic law, it is difficult to grasp why the public interest pursued should be considered to be merely domestic.

5. Waste Management *v.* Mexico

(a) Facts and issues

Waste Management v. *Mexico*,[106] the next case to be scrutinized, stands in the line of disputes involving waste landfills and/or waste disposal.[107] With the events unfolding against the backdrop of the Mexican financial crisis of 1994 to 1996,[108] Acaverde, a wholly owned subsidiary of Waste Management, a Delaware corporation, concluded on February 9, 1994 a Concession Agreement with the City of Acapulco for the provision of waste disposal services. Almost immediately, Acaverde encountered difficulties in enforcing the exclusivity arrangements contained in the Concession Agreement, and there was strong customer resistance to paying for waste disposal services, either at all or at the published rate. As the Tribunal specified, "[t]he cast of resisters included the pig-farmers (*porcicultores*) who took waste food from restaurants as food for their animals; the 'pirates' (*piratas*) who ran unauthorised pick-up trucks looking for (and also dumping) waste, and the hawkers or barrow-men (*carretilleros*) who would do small jobs, including waste disposal, for a tip. Acaverde eventually reached an agreement with the pig-farmers association, but the *piratas* and the *carretilleros* were a continuing source of difficulty."[109]

Moreover, Acaverde encountered difficulties in securing regular monthly payments by the city for its services. Of twenty-six monthly invoices, the City of Acapulco only paid one in full and another two

[106] *Waste Management, Inc.* v. *United Mexican States* (ICSID Case No. ARB(AF)/00/3), Award, April 30, 2004 (hereinafter: *Waste Management* v. *Mexico*).

[107] See *supra* 6 C. 2.

[108] The Tribunal specifies the chief aspects of the crisis as follows: "[T]he Mexican financial crisis . . . started in December 1994 with a substantial devaluation of the currency and continued for several years. During that period the value of the peso was approximately halved, the rate of inflation reached 38 per cent, and federal revenues to the States and municipalities were greatly affected. The effects on the City [of Acapulco] were numerous: tourist numbers declined, its financial obligations under the Concession Agreement (which were indexed to inflation) were substantially increased and the federal revenues it received were substantially reduced." (*Waste Management* v. *Mexico*, para. 101.)

[109] *Ibid.*, para. 54.

in part.[110] In its defense, the City claimed failures in performance of Acaverde's obligations under the Concession Agreement: Acaverde did not collect waste from households that had not contracted with it, in order to induce them to do so, which led to so-called "black spots (*puntos negros*),"[111] where waste accumulated and the hygiene situation grew precarious.

Then, on October 9, 1997 a massive hurricane struck the city of Acapulco with devastating consequences: hundreds of citizens died and many areas of the city were entirely destroyed or severely damaged. Only about two weeks later – with, as the Tribunal called it, "unhappy timing given that the City was still reeling from the hurricane"[112] – Acaverde informed the city that it would suspend its services with effect from November 12, 1997. Waste Management, as mother of Acaverde, claimed damages for violation of the fair and equitable treatment and expropriation clauses of NAFTA, Articles 1105 and 1110.

(b) Public interest having an impact on the Tribunal's finding

Unsurprisingly to the careful reader, Waste Management's claims failed regarding both Article 1105 and 1110 of the NAFTA. Since it is not relevant for the analysis at hand, I will not recapitulate most of the Tribunal's findings. In respect of the fair and equitable treatment standard, however, the Tribunal's reasoning attracts some interest. Its chief argument in declining Waste Management's claim in this regard was asserting public interest considerations:

> 111. Against this background of breaches of contract and allegations of non-performance, two facts are evident. The first is that the Concession Agreement was unpopular with a significant proportion of the residents of the concession area, many of whom were not permanently resident in Acapulco but maintained holiday apartments there . . .
>
> 112. The second fact is that the financial plans of the City, and thus of the Claimant, were severely affected by the Mexican financial crisis, which lasted well into 1996 and severely affected the City's capacity to perform its obligations . . . [113]

Although the Tribunal was anxious to stress that it did "not suggest that financial stringency or public resistance are, as such, excuses for breaches of contractual commitments on the part of a municipality,"[114] contending that such public interest considerations made the difference was

[110] See *ibid.*, para. 58. [111] *Ibid.*, para. 63. [112] *Ibid.*, para. 68.
[113] *Ibid.*, paras. 111 f. [114] *Ibid.*, para. 114.

exactly what it did. Admittedly, legitimate expectations and thus the circumstances a company finds itself in can have considerable impact on the interpretation of the fair and equitable treatment standard.[115] The prominence of the public interest considerations in declining Waste Management's claim is remarkable nonetheless.

6. Methanex *v.* United States

(a) Facts and issues

Before getting (in 7. below) to one of the more recent ICSID awards involving environmental matters, let me briefly present *Methanex* v. *United States*, a NAFTA dispute that has already been mentioned earlier.[116] As regards the facts, the award is very elaborate and extensive and hence contains a myriad of information that is not relevant for the analysis here. So I will limit both the presentation of facts and issues and the Tribunal's findings to those necessary to understand the dispute's importance to the questions before us.

At the time of proceedings, Methanex was the world's largest producer of methanol, a feedstock for the gasoline additive MTBE.[117] MTBE is interchangeable with ethanol. Archer Daniels Midland (ADM), a US corporation and the world's largest producer of ethanol, heavily lobbied for the State of California's ban on the sale and use of MTBE, which was intended to become legally effective on December 31, 2002. The ban effectively meant that MTBE was replaced entirely by ethanol. Methanex claimed compensation from the USA, resulting from losses caused by the ban on MTBE.[118]

Methanex claimed violation of the national treatment, fair and equitable treatment and expropriation provisions of the NAFTA.[119]

(b) A right to regulate?

The Tribunal dismissed all of Methanex's claims. In particular, as already referred to above, it found that general regulatory schemes such as the Californian ban on MTBE usually could not be considered expropriatory measures:

115 Most prominently argued in R. Dolzer, "Fair and Equitable Treatment: A Key Standard in Investment Treaties," *Int'l L.*, 39 (2005), 87.

116 See *supra* 6 C. 1.

117 MTBE (methyl tertiary-butyl ether) is a synthetic, volatile, colorless and organic ether, with a turpentine-like taste and odor.

118 *Methanex* v. *US*, Pt. I, para. 1.

119 NAFTA Articles 1102, 1105 and 1110.

[A]s a matter of general international law, a non-discriminatory regulation for a public purpose, which is enacted in accordance with due process and, which affects, inter alios, a foreign investor or investment is not deemed expropriatory and compensable unless specific commitments had been given by the regulating government to the then putative foreign investor contemplating investment that the government would refrain from such regulation.[120]

Such finding conforms with a widespread view in public international law.[121] State sovereignty has often been alleged to constitute its main argumentative source. It is considered an outflow of the State's sovereign authority to set the general regulatory standards and thus an investor is not entitled to any kind of compensation, provided that the host State enacts the measures with due process and in a non-discriminatory manner. However, the *Methanex* Tribunal appears to suggest an additional facet to this reasoning. In its Decision on Petitions of Third Persons to Intervene as Amici Curiae,[122] the Tribunal stated: "There is an undoubtedly public interest in this arbitration."[123] Hence, the Tribunal acknowledged the host State's role as the prism for the public interest. While the reason for the State assuming such role is the principle of State sovereignty, the reason for not granting compensation in case of general regulatory schemes, if we take the Tribunal's statement seriously, appears to be the public interest as such rather than the sovereignty reserve as under classical public international law.

7. Biwater *v.* Tanzania

(a) Facts and issues

Biwater v. *Tanzania*[124] is the most recent ICSID decision discussing environmental issues that I will analyze here. The award – 250 pages strong – is rooted in an intricate and highly complex factual matrix that I will now attempt to unravel. It additionally sparks considerations vis-à-vis the relationship of human rights and investment law and arbitration that I will analyze further in Chapter 7.[125]

In 2003, the Republic of Tanzania was awarded World Bank, African Development Bank and European Investment Bank loans in the amount

[120] *Methanex* v. *US*, Pt. IV, Ch. D, para. 7.
[121] See Dolzer and Schreuer, *Principles*, pp. 109 ff.
[122] *Methanex Corporation* v. *United States of America*, Decision on Petitions of Third Persons to Intervene as Amici Curiae, January 15, 2001.
[123] *Ibid.*, para. 49.
[124] *Biwater Gauff (Tanzania) Ltd.* v. *United Republic of Tanzania* (ICSID Case No. ARB/05/22), Award, July 24, 2008 (hereinafter: *Biwater* v. *Tanzania*).
[125] See *infra* 7 B. 2. (b) (iv).

of US$ 140 million for the purpose of commissioning a comprehensive program of repairs and upgrades to, and the expansion of, what was called "the Dar es Salaam Water and Sewerage Infrastructure: the Dar es Salaam Water Supply and Sanitation Project."[126] As a condition of the funding, the three development banks obliged Tanzania to appoint a private operator to manage and operate the water and sewerage systems, and carry out some of the works associated with the project.[127]

The Republic therefore invited tenders for the project in 2002 and eventually chose Biwater Gauff Tanzania (BGT) to carry it out. Biwater, a British company, held 80 percent and Gauff, a German company, held 20 percent of the shares in their joint venture BGT.[128] Upon their successful tender, the investors cooperated with a Tanzanian-owned company, Super Doll Trailer Manufacture Co. Ltd. (STM), as required by the procurement laws of Tanzania.[129] Moreover, Biwater and Gauff incorporated City Water Services Limited (City Water) under the laws of Tanzania on December 17, 2002 as the company operating the water and sewerage infrastructure. STM subsequently agreed to acquire a minority shareholding in City Water. At the time of the proceedings, BGT held 51 percent of the shares in City Water, and STM held the remaining 49 percent.[130]

On February 19, 2003 City Water, as the operating company, entered into three key contracts with the Dar es Salaam Water and Sewerage Authority (DAWASA) for the implementation of the project:

- the Water and Sewerage Lease Contract;
- the Supply and Installation of Plant and Equipment Contract (SIPE); and
- the Contract for the Procurement of Goods (POG).[131]

The incidents leading to the dispute started to unfold when City Water failed to considerably improve the dire water supply situation in Dar es Salaam, even taking into account DAWASA's prior failures and shortcomings.[132] Additionally, City Water experienced serious financial distress due to miscalculations, performance shortcomings and considerably lower tariffs compared with DAWASA's prior to the takeover by City Water.[133] Regarding the subsequent events, the Tribunal elaborates:

> Between 13 May 2005 and 1 June 2005, a series of events took place which, according to BGT, constituted breaches by the Republic of its obligations under international and domestic law. By way of overview:
>
> – on 13 May 2005, the Minister of Water and Livestock Development purported to terminate the Lease Contract;

[126] *Biwater* v. *Tanzania*, para. 3. [127] *Ibid.* [128] *Ibid.*, para. 4. [129] *Ibid.*, para. 5. [130] *Ibid.* [131] *Ibid.*, para. 6. [132] *Ibid.*, para. 147. [133] *Ibid.*, para. 178.

- on 16 May 2005, a call was made on the entire amount of the Performance Bond established by City Water in connection with the Lease Contract;
- on 17 May 2005, DAWASA issued a cure notice for the reinstatement of the Performance Bond under Article 50.1 of the Lease Contract;
- on 24 May 2005, the Tanzania Revenue Authority withdrew a VAT exemption;
- on 25 May 2005, DAWASA issued a Notice to Terminate under Article 51.3 of the Lease Contract, on the ground of failure to remedy the alleged breach notified in the cure notice of 17 May 2005; and finally
- on 1 June 2005, City Water's senior management were deported, and representatives of the Republic and DAWASA seized the company's assets, installed a new management (representatives of DAWASCO, a newly formed Government entity) and took over City Water's business.[134]

Biwater and Gauff jointly claimed violation of their right to fair and equitable treatment as well as prompt, adequate and effective compensation upon alleged expropriation under the Agreement between the United Kingdom of Great Britain and Northern Ireland and the United Republic of Tanzania for the Promotion and Protection of Investments of August 2, 1996.[135]

(b) Amicable towards environmental issues

While deciding on the viability of *amicus curiae*[136] briefs, the Tribunal stated that it "[was] mandated to resolve claims as between BGT and the Republic, but also recognized that this arbitration raise[d] a number of issues of concern to the wider community in Tanzania."[137] Having been admitted to set out their opinions, the *amici* underlined that the environmental issues[138] the dispute entailed required the investors to attain "the highest level of responsibility to meet their duties and obligations as foreign investors before seeking protection under international law." According to the *amici*, the investors' breach of their responsibility was

134 *Ibid.*, para. 15. 135 *Ibid.*, para. 16.

136 On *amicus curiae* briefs generally as practiced under the Anglo-American doctrine see S. Krislov, "The Amicus Curiae Brief: From Friendship to Advocacy," *Yale L. J.*, 72 (1962–63), 694; G. A. Caldeira and J. R. Wright, "Amici Curiae before the Supreme Court: Who Participates, When, and How Much?," *J. of Pol.*, 52 (1990), 782.

137 *Biwater* v. *Tanzania*, para. 358. To corroborate its point, the Tribunal also cited the *Methanex* dictum: "there is an undoubtedly public interest in this arbitration." See *Methanex* v. *US*, para. 141 and *supra* 6 C. 6.

138 On the human rights issues in this case, particularly the right to water, see *infra* 7 B. 2. (b).

to be found in their miscalculations and other shortcomings,[139] for given the importance of their investment for the population from an environmental perspective, they should have acted with more due diligence in order to warrant the water supply.[140] In a nutshell: The higher the public interest concerns, the higher the threshold the investor has to pass in order to claim compensation.

At the beginning of the Tribunal's subsequent analysis it seemed as if the Tribunal was proving immune to the *amici*'s reasoning: BGT succeeded with all its claims regarding breaches of its investor rights – the Tribunal found violations of the fair and equitable treatment as well as the expropriation clauses of the UK–Tanzania BIT. However, and here comes the intriguing part of the award, BGT was eventually not awarded any kind of compensation, for the Tribunal declined to find for any monetary damages caused by the aforementioned violations.[141] According to the arbitrators, the damages and financial setbacks from which BGT suffered were due to BGT's own miscalculations, and thus its investment was already lacking any economic value when its rights under the BIT were violated.

Considering this finding, it appears the Tribunal proved much more sympathetic to the *amici*'s allegations than it was ready to admit. It is notable that the standard for causation, derived from a thorough analysis of established customary international law rules, turned out to be applied very strictly – one could say much more strictly than might have been anticipated.[142] Though it did refrain from making any specific reference to the environmental issues involved, it is hard to ignore that there remains a smack of the acknowledged public interest concerns as the actual driving force in the Tribunal's considerations – at least as regards the standard-setting for causation of monetary damages and its application.[143]

8. Chemtura *v.* Canada

(a) Facts and issues

The NAFTA dispute *Chemtura* v. *Canada*[144] centers on the continuous process of Canada's attempt to change its policy vis-à-vis lindane, an

139 See *Biwater* v. *Tanzania*, para. 358. 140 *Biwater* v. *Tanzania*, paras. 380 f.
141 *Ibid.*, para. 807. 142 See *ibid.*, paras. 790 ff. 143 See *ibid.*, paras. 787 ff.
144 *Chemtura Corporation (formerly Crompton Corporation)* v. *Government of Canada*, Ad Hoc NAFTA Arbitration under UNCITRAL Rules, Award, August 2, 2010 (hereinafter: *Chemtura* v. *Canada*).

allegedly toxic pesticide. According to several independent scientific studies, including that of the WHO,[145] lindane causes serious health risks and may even lead to death.[146] As Canada asserted in its Counter-Memorial, lindane use is banned in fifty-two countries and severely restricted in another thirty-three. Lindane is currently being considered for a full international ban under the UN Convention on Persistent Organic Pollutants.[147] Thus, Canada introduced a policy to reduce and eventually ban the use of lindane.

According to Canada, in 1997 Gustafson, a US subsidiary of Chemtura, a US corporation and the claimant in the present dispute, launched a lobbying campaign to ban the import of canola products grown with lindane. Gustafson sells a lindane substitute called Gaucho. Since Canadian canola producers sold mostly to the US and mostly still used lindane at that time, a ban on lindane-produced canola allegedly would have put all canola and all lindane producers in Canada out of business.[148] From 2002 onwards, the US EPA, Chemtura's home regulator, introduced a new initiative to further restrict the use of lindane.[149]

Chemtura purported that Canada's regulation vis-à-vis lindane, and particularly the manner in which it enacted such restrictions and bans, was contrary to its obligations under NAFTA Chapter 11:

More particularly, Canada failed to meet the minimum standard of treatment in Article 1105 of NAFTA by:

- Improperly demanding a 'voluntary' withdrawal of lindane products based on irrelevant considerations, (i.e. trade rather than scientific concerns); and deregistering products without a sufficient evidentiary basis;
- failing to abide by promised conditions of Crompton Canada's withdrawal of lindane products from the Canadian market, which gave rise to legitimate expectations and on which Crompton Canada had reasonably relied;
- denying Crompton Canada a right to be heard prior to the suspension of its lindane product registrations;
- failing to maintain a transparent regulatory process;
- suspending Crompton Canada's lindane registrations without evidence or lawful authority;

[145] World Health Organization; for further information on the WHO see www.who.int.
[146] *Chemtura* v. *Canada*, Counter-Memorial of the Host State, October 20, 2008, para. 28.
[147] United Nations Convention on Persistent Organic Pollutants; Stockholm Convention.
[148] *Chemtura* v. *Canada*, Counter-Memorial of the Host State, October 20, 2008, paras. 5 ff.
[149] *Ibid.*, para. 14.

- acting in an arbitrary, grossly unfair and unjust manner in dealings with Crompton Canada; and
- failing to act in good faith in respect of the treatment accorded to Crompton Canada.[150]

(b) A chutzpah not rewarded

What is most surprising in this dispute is the boldness of Chemtura, the investor. According to Canada's allegations – which the Tribunal deemed correct – Chemtura sought compensation for Canada enacting a policy that: (1) is in conformity with international environmental initiatives; and (2) the investor itself – through its subsidiary – lobbied for in the US and thus caused Canada to do so as well.

As regards the first issue, it appears that "Chemtura [sought] to hold [Canada] responsible for the fact that it can no longer profit from the sale of a toxic chemical that has been internationally banned based on demonstrated health and environmental concerns."[151] While it is true that the USA has neither ratified the Stockholm Convention nor that its provisions are applicable by way of NAFTA Article 104 or Annex 104.1,[152] it is nonetheless hard to grasp why such general environmental regulatory scheme should amount to a violation of the fair and equitable treatment standard.[153] Indeed, the international restrictions and the incremental ban of lindane use in combination with the internal US regulations over the course of the past decade established a regulatory framework under which Chemtura was in no position to legitimately expect to continue producing and selling lindane in Canada as it did before.[154] Additionally, recent investment arbitration case law suggests that Tribunals show a tendency not to regard general regulatory schemes as expropriation if they are enacted for a public purpose, with due process and in a non-discriminatory manner.[155]

Secondly, Chemtura was unable to eliminate the suspicion that it sought to claim damages for a conduct by Canada for which it itself, through its subsidiary, lobbied in the US. Considering that NAFTA pursues the creation of a harmonious framework of rules on trade and investment among its members, one might well argue that such conduct amounts to a *venire contra factum proprium*, in other words triggers the international law

[150] *Chemtura* v. *Canada*, Memorial of the Investor, para. 2.
[151] *Chemtura* v. *Canada*, Counter-Memorial of the Host State, October 20, 2008, para. 16.
[152] See *supra* 6 C. 4. [153] See *Chemtura* v. *Canada*, para. 163. [154] *Ibid.*, paras. 159 ff.
[155] See *Methanex* v. *US*, Pt. IV, Ch. D, para. 7; *Saluka* v. *Czech Republic*, para. 262.

principle of estoppel.[156] The Tribunal also found no violation of the fair and equitable treatment standard in this regard, holding that Chemtura's allegations were "not sufficient to prove bad faith or lack of fairness."[157] Accordingly, the arbitrators declined Chemtura's claims as to breaches of the national treatment most favored nation and expropriation clauses of NAFTA on similar accounts.[158]

D. Analysis of the case law

1. *Preliminary conclusions*

The task of the ensuing analysis is to detect and trace the scrutinized cases' leitmotivs. How did the Tribunals treat (Global) Public Interest considerations pertaining to the environment? Are there any recurring themes as to how they involved international environmental law instruments in their reasoning? And is there a consistent application vis-à-vis the proportionality principle? All these are questions to be asked and answered throughout this part, which seeks to draw preliminary conclusions from the relevant ICSID and NAFTA jurisprudence.

(a) Hesitancy to refer to international environmental law instruments

Let me start my conclusions with a brief observation: Investment arbitration Tribunals, whether established under ICSID, NAFTA, or any other arbitration mechanism, exhibit a sweeping reluctance to refer to international environmental law instruments. Consideration of soft law instruments such as the Rio Declaration is absent, as is any discussion of the possible relevance of international environmental law principles; and even international environmental law treaties do not usually play a decisive role in the Tribunals' reasoning, even if matters are discussed that would invite them to do so. The *Santa Elena* and *Metalclad* awards, to name but two examples, declined to analyze the potential relevance of the

[156] For a general overview of this principle of international law see Shaw, *International Law*, pp. 102 f. See also ICJ, *Cameroon* v. *Nigeria*, *ICJ Reports* (1998), 275 at 303:

> "An estoppel would only arise if by its acts or declarations Cameroon had consistently made it fully clear that I had agreed to settle the boundary dispute submitted to the Court by bilateral avenues alone. It would further be necessary that, by relying on such an attitude, Nigeria had changed position to its own detriment or had suffered some prejudice."

[157] *Chemtura* v. *Canada*, para. 224.

[158] *Ibid.*, paras. 237, 250, 267.

Convention on Biological Diversity,[159] although the host States asserted their obligation and concern to protect endangered species – the "dazzling variety of flora and fauna"[160] in the case of *Santa Elena* and the protection of rare species of cactus in *Metalclad*. The host State's allegations might have proven unfounded.[161] However, not even considering them demonstrates a deeply entrenched skepticism about making reference to non-investment treaties.[162]

While I do not want to neglect *S. D. Myers*, which is exemplary – and actually to date the only example – of a Tribunal carefully considering international environmental treaties,[163] it appears – at least for now – that it is a rare outlier among a yet very hesitant large majority of Tribunals which do not see the need to refer to such instruments. This is, just as a side note, very well in line with the Global Public Interest theory focusing on customary international law and general principles and hence leaving treaties outside the body of norms applicable as defenses of the host State against investor rights infringements.

159 Convention on Biological Diversity, concluded at Rio de Janeiro on June 5, 1992; www.cbd.int/convention/. However, it should be mentioned that in 1978, when the dispute initially arose, this Convention was not yet concluded.

160 *Santa Elena* v. *Costa Rica*, para. 15. See also Convention on the Conservation of Migratory Species of Wild Animals, done at Bonn on June 23, 1979; www.cms.int/documents/convtxt/cms_convtxt.htm. Moreover, as C. N. Brower and E. R. Hellbeck point out, the *Santa Elena* Tribunal also did not consider the World Heritage Convention (Convention for the Protection of the World Cultural and Natural Heritage, Paris, November 16, 1972, 1037 United Nations Treaty Series, 151), which would have had a strong effect on the amount of compensation, as the *SPP* award evinces; see *SPP* v. *Egypt*, para. 190 ("The Implications of National and International Environmental Obligations for Foreign Investment Protection Standards, Including Valuation: A Report from the Front Lines" in The International Bureau of the Permanent Court of Arbitration, *International Investments and Protection of the Environment – The Role of Dispute Resolution Mechanisms*, Papers emanating from the Second PCA International Law Seminar, May 17, 2000, The Permanent Court of Arbitration/Peace Palace Papers (Kluwer Law International, 2001), p. 19 at pp. 25 f.).

161 Particularly in *Metalclad*, the local government declaring the region in which the landfill was located an area for the protection of cactus only after any other means to prevent the construction and operation of the site failed, incites skepticism.

162 Here, I differ sharply in my analysis from Moshe Hirsch's conclusions; cf. M. Hirsch, "Interactions Between Investment and Non-Investment Obligations," *supra* n. 50, at pp. 173 f. While Hirsch finds that "[m]ost investment Tribunals that faced arguments regarding inconsistencies between investment obligations and non-investment treaties did not hesitate to examine carefully the non-investment treaty's provisions," he can only cite two cases in his support and actually refers himself to three that refute his contention.

163 I.e. the Basel Convention on the Control of Transboundary Movements of Hazardous Wastes and their Disposal.

(b) Global Public Interest concerns

Despite the Tribunals' skepticism towards making direct reference to international environmental law considerations or instruments, their endorsement of Global Public Interest concerns – at least in the majority of the reviewed case law – is remarkable indeed. Such endorsements differ considerably in strength and nature, ranging from mere acknowledgment in *Methanex*[164] to granting Global Public Interest a rather distinctive doctrinal role as potential justifications of NAFTA Chapter 11 infringements in *S. D. Myers*.[165] Let me start by briefly recapitulating what the arbitrators found in the four decisions that expressly or implicitly embraced public interest as an argumentative *topos* in order to infer limitations on investor rights.

Both the *Methanex* and *Biwater* cases acknowledged that the outcome of the award was going to have an impact far beyond the bilateral relationship of the foreign investor and the host State. By stating that "[t]here is an undoubtedly public interest in this arbitration,"[166] the Tribunals accepted that the respective dispute leaves the private sphere of a mere controversy between two parties over contractual matters and touches upon challenges which concern third persons or even society as a whole. Whether an investor can construct and operate a landfill, whether its rights are violated by a host State banning the export or import of chemical substances, or whether a city's withdrawal of the concession to provide water services triggers the investor's claim to damages all constitute questions that are just one flipside of a coin: They foreshadow that, viewed from the opposite angle, the questions pertaining to the very same issue are also whether the investor is permitted to construct the landfill and how it operates it in the vicinity of a local community, whether a host State may ban the export or import of chemical substances potentially harmful to the environment or human health, or whether an investor has fulfilled its obligations under the concession agreement to provide clean water and other water and water sewage services. In the domestic realm, private contracts and disputes that exhibit such public interest relevance are usually embedded in a framework of public rules and regulations.

164 See *Methanex Corporation* v. *United States of America*, Decision on Petitions of Third Persons to Intervene as Amici Curiae, January 15, 2001, para. 49.

165 *S. D. Myers* v. *Canada*, para. 298.

166 *Methanex Corporation* v. *United States of America*, Decision on Petitions of Third Persons to Intervene as Amici Curiae, January 15, 2001, para. 49; *Biwater* v. *Tanzania*, para. 358.

Public procurement laws govern the tender, and shortcomings in providing the service or operating the site encounter responses by public law remedies, e.g. a fine or the rescission of the contract, usually administered by the executive. The *Methanex* and *Biwater* Tribunals expressly recognizing the "public interest" hence indicates the growing tendency in investment arbitration to acknowledge parallel needs in the international investment law realm, i.e. embedding the investor–host State dispute in a public law framework.

While at least in *Methanex*, the public interest relevance did not go much further than acknowledgement per se, the *S. D. Myers* case is much more explicit and prominent in effectively drawing consequences from such – here rather implicit – acknowledgement of (Global) Public Interest concerns. The Tribunal did not strike down Canada's contention to embark on NAFTA's Third Chapter General Exceptions Clause for justification of investor rights infringements because it did not see viability in making the legal argument. While Canada's assertion failed in the end, the Tribunal carefully considered its argumentation and acknowledged that "[t]he NAFTA Parties properly wanted to ensure that Chapter 11 could not be used to impugn government measures that are protected by other specific aspects of the NAFTA"; it then referred to the General Exceptions clauses.[167] Hence, the arbitrators accepted environmental and other Global Public Interest considerations enshrined in measures and regulations adopted by the host State as possible justifications of violations of investor rights. The fact that Canada eventually fell short of establishing that it had fulfilled the requirements of GATT Article XX – the General Exceptions Clause that NAFTA Chapter 3 incorporates – does not decrease the importance of this quite remarkable finding in *S. D. Myers*. Having said that, due to most BITs lacking a General Exceptions Clause, the *S. D. Myers* case is not identically transferable to ICSID or other investment arbitration. Investment arbitration Tribunals cite prior decisions quite indiscriminately, irrespective of whether those are arbitrated under the NAFTA or ICSID or UNCITRAL (or any other) realm.[168] While this does not mean, of course, that they are blind vis-à-vis inbuilt systemic differences of the investment and arbitration treaties on the basis of which they were established, the similarity of the matter and also – not to forget – the similarity, if not identity, of the arbitrators in NAFTA, ICSID or other investment disputes encourages drawing comparisons and inspires the

[167] *S. D. Myers* v. *Canada*, para. 298. [168] See Schill, *Multilateralization*, pp. 362 ff.

search for similar solutions between and among the different investment treaties.[169]

A good example of such internalization of investment jurisprudence by Tribunals established under different arbitration treaty realms, the *Biwater* award exhibits the thriving force of Global Public Interest considerations in ICSID cases. Citing the *Methanex* reference to public interest,[170] the Tribunal rejected the Global Public Interest concerns raised by the *amici* in the first place.[171] However, regarding the damages – the very core of any investment arbitration proceeding, for monetary reparation is the ultimate goal of any investment dispute[172] – it found for the host State adopting basically the same argumentation as employed by the *amici* to justify the investor rights infringements.[173] Similarly, in *Waste Management*, public interest considerations led the Tribunal to decline the investor's claim regarding the violation of the fair and equitable treatment standard, for it asserted the unfavorable public opinion vis-à-vis the landfill and the host State's dire financial situation as decisive factors.[174]

While thus the majority of the case law – to a lesser or stronger degree – endorsed Global Public Interest considerations, three cases stand out as proponents for skepticism vis-à-vis their viability as limitations to investor rights: *Metalclad*, *Santa Elena* and *Tecmed*. Whereas *Metalclad* does not even address any contentions such as environmental concerns or allegations of corruption and thus reconciles the challenge simply by ignoring it, *Santa Elena* and *Tecmed*, after a thorough analysis, expressly decline allowing the raising of environmental concerns as justification for investor rights infringements. Both disputes, dealing mainly with expropriation claims, deny (Global) Public Interest justifications basically on the argument that since every legal expropriation requires a public purpose, the treaty clause would render void if environmental issues and other

169 See Dolzer and Schreuer, *Principles*, p. 36. See also *AES Corp.* v. *Argentina*, Decision on Jurisdiction, April 26, 2005, *ICSID Reports*, 12 (2007), 312, para. 30; *Saipem* v. *Bangladesh*, Decision on Jurisdiction, para. 67; also on the notion that the similarity of BITs and the MFN clause leads to a "multilateralization" of international investment law generally see Schill, *Multilateralization*, pp. 278 ff.; O. K. Fauchald, "The Legal Reasoning of ICSID Tribunals – An Empirical Analysis," *EJIL*, 19 (2008), 301.

170 See *Biwater* v. *Tanzania*, para. 358; see also *Methanex Corporation* v. *United States of America*, Decision on Petitions of Third Persons to Intervene as Amici Curiae, January 15, 2001, para. 49.

171 *Biwater* v. *Tanzania*, para. 380.

172 For not a single investment treaty grants restoration of the factual situation *ex ante*; all are targeted at monetary recovery only.

173 *Biwater* v. *Tanzania*, para. 804.

174 *Waste Management* v. *Mexico*, paras. 111 f.

public interest considerations allowed compensation to be declined. To cite *Santa Elena* again:

72. Expropriatory environmental measures – no matter how laudable and beneficial to society as a whole – are, in this respect, similar to any other expropriatory measures that a state may take in order to implement its policies: where property is expropriated, even for environmental purposes, whether domestic or international, the state's obligation to pay compensation remains.[175]

This statement is as straightforward as it is defective. True, due to incorporating "public purpose" as a precondition, the expropriation clause does require a special approach. However, this does not mean that expropriation claims disallow Global Public Interest considerations as a matter of logic. The *Methanex* and *Saluka* Tribunals in fact employed Global Public Interest considerations – not as justifications in the strict doctrinal sense, but nonetheless as the basis for refusing to apply the expropriation clause in the first place.[176] General regulatory practice, those two Tribunals held, is not to be considered an expropriation, if the measure is enacted with due process and in a non-discriminatory manner, unless specific commitments had been given to the investor.[177] Interestingly, if we carefully scrutinize the *Tecmed* award, we find considerations quite similar to those conditions in the passage on proportionality elements in the expropriation clause:

the Arbitral Tribunal will consider, in order to determine *if they are to be characterized as expropriatory*, whether such actions or measures are *proportional to the public interest presumably protected* thereby and to the protection legally granted to investments, taking into account that the significance of such impact has a key role upon deciding the proportionality.[178]

Seen from that angle, the – at first glance – odd construction that the proportionality test is employed as a precondition of the expropriation attempts to tackle the very same challenge as in *Methanex* and *Saluka*, i.e. how to give relevance to (Global) Public Interest considerations in expropriation claims. The core doctrinal answer is surprisingly similar in all three awards: Upon certain conditions, measures involving (Global) Public Interest concerns are not to be considered an expropriation. This marks

175 *Santa Elena* v. *Costa Rica*, para. 72. 176 See *supra* 6 C. 1. (c).

177 *Saluka* v. *Czech Republic*, Partial Award, March 17, 2006, PCA, para. 262; *Methanex* v. *US*, Pt. IV, Ch. D, para. 7.

178 *Tecmed* v. *Mexico*, para. 122 (emphasis added).

the fundamental difference between the *Santa Elena* and the *Tecmed* decisions. I do not want to neglect that, dogmatically, the *Methanex/Saluka* solution differs from the *Tecmed* solution in that the first establishes *absolute* conditions upon the fulfillment of which the measure is not considered expropriatory, while the latter requires a balancing between "the public interest presumably protected" and "the protection legally granted to investments" and thus sets a *relative* rather than an absolute standard. Considering that very laudable general regulatory measures aiming at a public purpose might well entail hardships and sacrifice for the proprietor in the interest of society, and which require compensation,[179] and also considering that the investment arbitration case law on indirect expropriations provides us with only a very elusive standard which bears striking resemblance to a balancing test, the *Tecmed* solution appears to be more appealing due to its greater flexibility. However, while both solutions still exist – and actually the *Methanex/Saluka* solution appears to prevail for now[180] – they are targeted at the same challenge and require very similar factors to be considered, since the balancing of the *Tecmed* solution would mainly consider the factors mentioned in the *Methanex/Saluka* solution, i.e. non-discrimination, general application, due process and special commitments.[181]

Moreover, there lies another dimension of Global Public Interest considerations in the *Tecmed* solution. Establishing the proportionality test in order to discern whether the measure undertaken was in fact an (indirect) expropriation or not, the *Tecmed* Tribunal cites the European Court of Human Rights (ECtHR) as authority for such standard.[182] In the cited decision, *Matos e Silva, Lda., and Others* v. *Portugal*, the ECtHR – in conformity with its well-established case law – acknowledged that in order to evaluate whether an expropriation has occurred, the Court has to "determine whether a fair balance was struck between the demands of the general interest of the community and the requirements of the protection of the

[179] See *ADC Affiliate Limited and ADC & ADMC Management Limited* v. *Republic of Hungary* (ICSID Case No. ARB/03/16), Award, October 1, 2006 (hereinafter: *ADC* v. *Hungary*), paras. 423 f.

[180] See Dolzer and Schreuer, *Principles*, pp. 109 ff.

[181] The aforesaid, including my preference of the *Tecmed* over the *Methanex/Saluka* solution, is not meant to reverse my general statement arguing for a separation of the proportionality test and the assessment of an investor right infringement as established in Chapter 5; see *supra* 5 F. 5. (b). I prefer the latter approach over the *Tecmed* solution. However, I opine that among two defective approaches currently existent in ICSID jurisprudence, I deem the *Tecmed* solution the better one.

[182] *Tecmed* v. *Mexico*, para. 122.

individual's fundamental rights."[183] The *ratio* behind this statement is to be found in the "Belgian Linguistics" case of 1968[184] by tracing back the references in *Matos e Silva*. There the Court, called upon to define the right to education, stated the following:

> 5. The right to education guaranteed by the first sentence of Article 2 of the Protocol (P1–2) *by its very nature calls for regulation by the State, regulation which may vary in time and place according to the needs and resources of the community and of individuals.* It goes without saying that such regulation must never injure the substance of the right to education nor conflict with other rights enshrined in the Convention.
>
> The Court considers that the *general aim* set for themselves by the Contracting Parties through the medium of the European Convention on Human Rights, was to provide effective protection of fundamental human rights, and this, without doubt not only because of the historical context in which the Convention was concluded, but also of the social and technical developments in our age which offer to States considerable possibilities for regulating the exercise of these rights. *The Convention therefore implies a just balance between the protection of the general interest of the Community and the respect due to fundamental human rights while attaching particular importance to the latter.*[185]

The Court recognizes that the right to education, as the right to property, is normatively determined in that it can only be given a meaning if the State defines its overall scope and limits. Such normative determination (*Normgeprägtheit*) is a common phenomenon in German constitutional law doctrine vis-à-vis the right to property.[186] What it means is that since the State defines the overall scope and limits of the right "according to the needs and resources of the community and of individuals,"[187] public interest considerations and their balance with individual rights form an integral part of what defines the right to property in its very core. The *Tecmed* Tribunal, by adopting such reasoning under reference to the ECtHR case law, therefore acknowledged that public interest considerations lie at

[183] *In the case of Matos e Silva, Lda., and Others* v. *Portugal*, European Court of Human Rights, Judgment of September 16, 1996, 19, para. 86 (hereinafter: *Matos e Silva* v. *Portugal*).

[184] European Court of Human Rights, *Case "Relating to Certain Aspects of the Laws on the Use of Languages in Education in Belgium,"* Merits (Application Nos. 1474/62; 1677/62; 1691/62; 1769/63; 1994/63; 2126/64), Judgment of July 23, 1968 (hereinafter: Belgian Linguistics case).

[185] *Ibid.*, I. A., para. 5 (emphasis added).

[186] See M. Appel, *Entstehungsschwäche und Bestandsstärke des verfassungsrechtlichen Eigentums* (Duncker & Humblot, 2004), pp. 88 ff.

[187] Belgian Linguistics case, I. A., para. 5.

the very core of the expropriation clause in Article 5 of the Spain–Mexico BIT.

Finally, while I deem the *Tecmed* solution preferable to the *Saluka/Methanex* approach, I want to emphasize once more that I oppose what the Tribunal makes of it subsequently. To recall, the Tribunal continues:

> On the basis of a number of legal and practical factors, it should be also considered that the foreign investor has a reduced or nil participation in the taking of the decisions that affect it, partly because the investors are not entitle[d] to exercise political rights reserved to the nationals of the State, such as voting for the authorities that will issue the decisions that affect such investors.[188]

I have mentioned earlier that limiting public interest considerations to the domestic realm, to name but the most important of a couple of caveats,[189] blatantly misrepresents the Global Public Law features international investment law in general displays.[190]

(c) Elements of proportionality

However, the *Tecmed* solution to public interest considerations in (indirect) expropriation cases is of interest to my analysis also because it bears the potential to inform the role the principle of proportionality might play as means to reconcile investor rights and public interest justifications. Having already scrutinized its inherent public interest focus,[191] here it suffices to point out that the proportionality test the Tribunal applies is limited to the proportionality *stricto sensu*, i.e. the mere balancing between several indicators the Tribunal considers relevant for the analysis.[192] While thus the *Tecmed* Tribunal only considers the third factor of the proportionality test,[193] *S. D. Myers*, by referring to NAFTA Article 104, limits itself to the necessity or least restrictive measures test, the second factor. Hence, while the case law appears to commence giving credit to

188 *Ibid.*, para. 122.
189 See *supra* 6 C. 4. (c).
190 See *supra* 6 C. 4. (c).
191 See *supra* 6 D. 1. (b).
192 The Tribunal elaborates as follows: "There must be a reasonable relationship of proportionality between the charge or weight imposed to the foreign investor and the aim sought to be realized by any expropriatory measure. To value such charge or weight, it is very important to measure the size of the ownership deprivation caused by the actions of the state and whether such deprivation was compensated or not." (*Tecmed* v. *Mexico*, para. 122.)
193 The proportionality test consists of three factors: (1) suitability for a legitimate government purpose; (2) necessity; (3) proportionality *stricto sensu*. See Kingsbury and Schill, "Investor-State Arbitration as Governance," pp. 29 f. and *supra* 5 D.

the proportionality analysis and test, Tribunals seem not ready to apply the entire three-factor test.

2. The case law on environment in the light of the Global Public Interest theory

Looking at the case law on environment, as has been mentioned earlier, we can identify two patterns: Either the Tribunal simply ignores – expressly or implicitly – the Global Public Interest concerns the dispute before it implicates[194] (this is only the case, however, in a minority of the decisions I have scrutinized here); or (as is the pattern in the majority of disputes) the Tribunal rejects or ignores legal arguments pertaining to the environment on the level of the merits, but considerably reduces or even completely denies damages or compensation based on reasoning severely influenced by the very same argumentation the Tribunal has just declined to consider. I draw two conclusions from this assessment. Firstly, such divide shows that while Tribunals are commencing to acknowledge the existence and relevance of Global Public Interest concerns, i.e. in the present case the environment, international investment law in this regard is still in a formative period. Secondly, in case Tribunals give voice to environmental concerns, they do not really know how to handle them. Tribunals fall short of developing a thorough and coherent approach of how to integrate those considerations into the investment régime, absent an underpinning theoretical and doctrinal foundation. The only thing those Tribunals allocating relevance to the environment appear to implicitly agree on is that the Global Public Interest considerations should bear consequences on the amount of damages or compensation. While the Global Public Interest theory eventually arrives at the same result, I think its advantages become strikingly apparent when viewing it against the backdrop of the case law described and analyzed. It provides a thorough theoretical underpinning, rooted in current general public international law theory as well as a thorough doctrinal structure giving clear-cut advice on how to integrate Global Public Interest considerations into the investment régime and on how to strike a fair balance with the investor rights.

Let me pick just one case in order to illustrate how environmental concerns should be resolved according to the Global Public Interest theory.

[194] For a similar conclusion, albeit claimed for the majority of the case law, see K. Tienhaara, *The Expropriation of Environmental Governance – Protecting Foreign Investors at the Expense of Public Policy* (Cambridge University Press, 2009), pp. 204 ff.

The Tribunal in *Biwater* found for violations of the fair and equitable treatment as well as the expropriation clauses of the UK–Tanzania BIT. So far, the decision is in line with the Global Public Interest theory, albeit with a minor doctrinal adjustment, for at this stage it speaks of "infringements" rather than "violations."[195]

Now, while the *Biwater* award moves from the merits to the damages stage, the Global Public Interest theory rests with the former by asking, after the assessment whether an investor right has been infringed, if such infringement may be justified by a Global Public Interest defense the host State was entitled to raise. Hence, we must enquire whether the Global Public Interest assertion that BGT, given the importance of its investment for the population from an environmental perspective, should have acted with more due diligence in order to warrant the water supply – which eventually led the Tribunal to decline damages – finds a legal translation in a customary law norm or a general principle of law.

Since the said allegation – rightfully – contends that BGT could not in good faith expect to reap benefits from an ineffective water system that it was unable to improve, the host State can rely on the principle of good faith as a Global Public Interest defense. Without going into detail as to the differentiation between the two investor rights vis-à-vis the proportionality test,[196] the measures undertaken by Tanzania were suitable, constitute the least restrictive means – the withdrawal of the license was in order given the inability of BGT to fix the problem and the importance of warranting general water supply in Dar es Salaam – and due to the same reason also meet the requirements of the proportionality *stricto sensu* test. Therefore, translating such outcome of the proportionality test in terms of damages and compensation, we arrive at the same result as in the *Biwater* Tribunal. However, what constitutes the major difference is that such result does not rest on a dubious reasoning concealing the actual impetus for declining damages to the investor. Instead, it founds on the Global Public Interest theory as elaborated in Chapter 4, applied according to a thorough doctrinal structure translating the theory into legal categories as described in Chapter 5.

195 See *supra* 5 F. 2.

196 Note that the expropriation clause requires a specific modification of the proportionality analysis; see *supra* 5 F. 5. (b).

7 Human rights and investment – friends or foes?

A. Doctrinal approaches in a nutshell

Over the course of the past couple of years, the relationship and potential points of conflict between investment law and human rights have caught the attention of international lawyers from both international economic law and human rights law backgrounds. The debate revolves mostly around an analysis of the investment arbitration case law involving human rights issues – a task that I too will tackle, at (B.) below. However, several scholars have recently undertaken the effort of stretching the discourse beyond mere descriptive models and have sought to delineate approaches on how to reconcile international investment law with human rights.[1] The ensuing brief overview does not purport to be exhaustive and, for example, deliberately leaves out the authors advocating proportionality balancing in investment law,[2] for since I have given it considerable space and thought earlier,[3] I seek to avoid repetition in this regard.

To start with, those authors with a general public international law background, having a fresh look at the issue – and maybe a first look at international investment law – take refuge in classical means of treaty interpretation according to customary international law as enshrined in the VCLT. According to those voices, ICJ practice evinces that rules external to those laid down in the treaty to be interpreted may be taken

[1] See in particular on this issue the two collections of essays, P.-M. Dupuy, F. Francioni and E.-U. Petersmann (eds.), *Human Rights in International Investment Law and Arbitration* (Oxford University Press, 2009) and C. Binder *et al.* (eds.), *International Investment Law for the 21st Century – Essays in Honour of Christoph Schreuer* (Oxford University Press, 2009).

[2] E.g. see Petersmann, "Constitutional Theories."

[3] See *supra* Chapter 5.

into account, as states Article 31(3)(c) VCLT. Thus, they argue, BIT clauses such as those guaranteeing free and equitable treatment, full protection and security or prohibiting discrimination and arbitrariness should be interpreted in the light of human rights as one of the most important obligations of the host State.[4] However, Simma and Kill stress that:

> [q]ualification of any treaty obligation by employing a presumption in favour of existing rules of law . . . presupposes that of two possible interpretations of a treaty, one coheres with existing law while another conflicts with it. It will therefore be necessary to demonstrate that a particular interpretation of an investment treaty would be in conflict with international human rights law before presumption in favour of human rights law could be employed.[5]

Leaving this last issue aside, some scholars favor a slightly similar approach, however with an exclusive focus on the fair and equitable treatment standard. Such treaty standard, so they argue, is the (exclusive) entry point of human rights law – the investor's legitimate expectations that this clause allegedly protects or comprises the host State's human rights obligations the investor must take due notice of.[6] According to such view, if it could have foreseen – from the standpoint of a reasonable average entrepreneur – that the host State was under the obligation to abide by a human rights provision potentially hampering its entrepreneurial freedom, the investor would be in no position to claim a violation of the fair and equitable treatment standard.[7]

Finally, Steven Ratner's "theory of legal responsibility" deserves some brief mention here.[8] Though not particularly directed at investment law, his theory dealing with multinational corporations' responsibility for human rights violations also relates to the complex before us. The theory rests on four elements, each asserted by Ratner as doctrinal

[4] See Simma and Kill, "Harmonizing Investment Protection," 682, 703 ff.; Dupuy, "Unification Rather than Fragmentation," 62, albeit with several reservations (see 58). Article 31(3)(c) requires that "any relevant rules of international law applicable in the relations between the parties" shall be taken into account when interpreting a treaty.

[5] Simma and Kill, *ibid.*, 706.

[6] Dupuy, "Unification Rather than Fragmentation," 54; I. Knoll-Tudor, "The Fair and Equitable Treatment Standard and Human Rights Norms" in P.-M. Dupuy *et al.* (eds.), *Human Rights*, p. 310 at p. 338; P. Muchlinski, "Caveat Investor? The Relevance of the Conduct of the Investor under the Fair and Equitable Treatment Standard," *Int'l & Comp. L. Q.*, 55 (2006), 527. However, Knoll-Tudor asserts that human rights considerations should not be employed to eradicate FET violations but rather to lower the amount of compensation the host State has to pay; see 342.

[7] For a different view see Knoll-Tudor, *ibid.*

[8] S. R. Ratner, "Corporations and Human Rights," 443.

pillars of potential corporate responsibility for human rights: (1) corporate responsibility via State responsibility, i.e. corporations as agents or accomplices of a State violating an international legal norm;[9] (2) "the nexus factor," i.e. how close the ties are between the corporation and the affected individuals;[10] (3) the nature of the substantive right at issue, i.e. is this a right that a non-State actor can infringe as easily as a State, or does the right flow from the specific nature of sovereign authority or any other feature exclusive to the State?;[11] (4) the structure of the enterprise as an actor and the place of the human rights violator within that structure.[12] However, Ratner falls short of laying out a clear-cut opinion as to the application of what he calls his "theory of legal responsibility." While he offers several possibilities of implementation ranging from a non-binding code of conduct to a multilateral treaty, his theory, though potentially instructive, unfortunately lacks the specificity for direct implementation in the investment context.

B. Human rights issues in investment disputes

After this quick glance at selected approaches by other authors, the chief part of my analysis – as in the previous as well as the ensuing chapter – will be dedicated to a thorough evaluation of investment arbitration case law revolving around human rights issues as an example for Global Public Interest considerations. While, occasionally, investors invoke human rights issues as basis or corroboration of their claims against the host State (1.), the main focus is on instances in which the host State sought salvation in human rights arguments in order to justify alleged BIT violations asserted by the investor (2.). Section C. will eventually put together the observations made regarding each case and will undertake to find common ground and similar patterns in the approaches of ICSID and other investment Tribunals.

1. *Alleged violations of the investor's human rights*

Albeit not in the primary focus of my inquiries here, brief mention should be made that the parallelism of human rights and investor rights, as already alluded to in Chapter 4,[13] might potentially entail the investor invoking violations of its human rights by the host State as opposed to

[9] *Ibid.*, 497 ff. [10] *Ibid.*, 506 ff. [11] *Ibid.*, 511 ff. [12] *Ibid.*, 518 ff.
[13] See *supra* 4 B. 2.

human rights violations by the investor – allegations of which in investment arbitration case law will be dealt with extensively below. While investor rights and human rights, as Professor Moshe Hirsch and Professor Pierre-Marie Dupuy rightly point out, differ somewhat in their normative concepts and origin – the one rooted in the law of aliens linked to the State of their nationality, the other deriving from the inherent nature of the human being itself[14] – their similarities clearly preponderate. Both deal with the individual – or private actor – being confronted with the exercise of public authority by the (host) State. In both cases, international law has elevated the dispute to the international level and stripped it of the domestic constraints and thus of the bias and potential oppression of domestic jurisdiction. Hence, human rights law and international investment law are characterized by an asymmetrical relationship[15] between the actors involved: As opposed to the classical concept of public international law, non-State actors are provided with direct rights (and claims) against a sovereign State.[16]

Given such similar features, it cannot be too surprising that, at least occasionally, investors have attempted to resort to human rights in investment disputes in order to extend or corroborate their claim. In *Biloune* v. *Ghana*,[17] an UNCITRAL case of the late 1980s, a Syrian investor, Mr. Biloune, contended that the government of Ghana, by among others, arresting him, holding him in custody for thirteen days and eventually deporting him to Togo substantially interfered with his investment, which basically amounted to his de facto expropriation. The claimant asserted that the arrest, detention and deportation constituted human rights violations and thus required compensation independent from the alleged forfeiture of the investment that resulted therefrom. The Tribunal concluded its jurisdiction vis-à-vis the alleged expropriation but simultaneously found that it lacked jurisdiction with regard to the human rights claims. Its competence was limited, so it argued, to commercial disputes arising under the contract concluded between the government of Ghana and Mr. Biloune exclusively in respect of foreign investment issues.[18] In other

14 Dupuy, "Unification Rather than Fragmentation," 47; Hirsch, "Investment Tribunals and Human Rights," 107.

15 Hirsch, *ibid.*, 98.

16 On this issue see also Chapter 4 B. pertaining to similarities with the ECHR and the European law systems in this regard.

17 *Biloune and Marine Drive Complex Ltd.* v. *Ghana Investments Centre and the Government of Ghana*, Ad-Hoc Awards on Jurisdiction and Liability, October 27, 1989 and on Damages and Costs, June 30, 1990, UNCITRAL, *ILR*, 95 (1993), 184 (hereinafter: *Biloune* v. *Ghana*).

18 *Ibid.*, 203.

words, the Tribunal declined jurisdiction to hear allegations of human rights violations as an independent basis for a compensation claim.

Similarly, in the case of *Patrick Mitchell* v. *Democratic Republic of Congo*,[19] the published annulment decision cites the unpublished award referring to, inter alia, the incarceration of the claimant's lawyers while his firm was closed and a vast number of important documents were seized by Congolese authorities.[20] While it is obvious that such conduct raises human rights issues, neither the Tribunal nor the ad hoc Committee even make mention of them.

A little outlier in this line of cases dealing with allegations of compensable human rights violations of the investor, the Tribunal in *Desert Line Projects* v. *Yemen* awarded moral damages in the amount of US$ 1 million to the claimant for harassment, threatening and detention of its executives.[21] According to the arbitrators:

> the violation of the BIT by the Respondent, in particular the physical duress exerted on the executives of the Claimant, was malicious and is therefore constitutive of a fault-based liability. Therefore, the Respondent shall be liable to reparation for the injury suffered by the Claimant, whether it be bodily, moral or material in nature. The Arbitral Tribunal agrees with the Claimant that its prejudice was substantial since it affected the physical health of the Claimant's executives and the Claimant's credit and reputation.[22]

Although the Tribunal thus did not base its findings exclusively on issues pertaining to human rights of natural persons, but on matters of economic relevance as well (credit and business reputation), *Desert Line Projects* v. *Yemen* dares to move one step further where the other Tribunals shied away[23] – however, in a quite limited fashion and to a rather limited degree.

Furthermore, three cases that involved reference to ECtHR jurisprudence in order to corroborate the findings of investor rights violations – alleged either by the claimant or relied upon by the Tribunal – deserve

19 *Patrick Mitchell* v. *Democratic Republic of Congo* (ICSID Case No. ARB/99/7), Decision on the Application for Annulment of the Award, November 1, 2006.

20 *Ibid*., para. 1, citing para. 23 of the Award of February 9, 2004.

21 *Desert Line Projects LLC* v. *The Republic of Yemen* (ICSID Case No. ARB/05/17), Award, February 6, 2008 (hereinafter: *Desert Line Projects* v. *Yemen*).

22 *Ibid*., para. 290.

23 See also S. Wilske and M. Raible, "The Arbitrator as Guardian of International Public Policy?" in C. A. Rogers and R. P. Alford (eds.), *The Future of Investment Arbitration* (Oxford University Press, 2009), p. 249 at pp. 268 ff. on the policy implications of introducing human rights and further public policy considerations to the investment régime.

a quick glance. The first of these, the NAFTA arbitration *Mondev* v. *US*,[24] pertained to a commercial real estate development contract concluded between the City of Boston, the Boston Redevelopment Authority (BRA) and a Massachusetts subsidiary of Mondev International, a Canadian company. In a lawsuit ensuing from a dispute between the parties, the Massachusetts courts dismissed Mondev's claim because, among others, a Massachusetts statute granted the BRA judicial immunity for intentional torts. Mondev submitted the case to NAFTA arbitration claiming violation of NAFTA Chapter 11 investor rights (inter alia national and fair and equitable treatment as well as expropriation) by the said court decisions and the city's and the BRA's conduct. The Tribunal considered in this context the denial of access to a court as a human rights issue informing the interpretation of the minimum treatment standard, Article 1105(1) NAFTA.[25] It analyzed case law of the ECtHR on Article 6(1) of the ECHR – a provision dealing with access to the courts in civil rights disputes – and stated the following:

> [T]he Court [i.e. the ECtHR] recognises that it 'may not create by way of interpretation of Article 6(1) a substantive civil right which has no legal basis in the State concerned.' By parity of reasoning, there are difficulties in reading Article 1105(1) so as in effect to create a new substantive civil right to sue BRA for tortious interference with contractual relations.[26]

Moreover, it expressed skepticism as to the viability and relevance of drawing on ECtHR case law in NAFTA arbitration:

> These decisions concern the 'right to a court,' an aspect of the human rights conferred on all persons by the major human rights conventions and interpreted by the European Court in an evolutionary way. They emanate from a different region, and are not concerned, as Article 1105(1) of NAFTA is concerned, specifically with investment protection. At most, they provide guidance by analogy as to the possible scope of NAFTA's guarantee of 'treatment in accordance with international law, including fair and equitable treatment and full protection and security.'[27]

Hence, the Tribunal dismissed Mondev's claim in this regard and concluded that the immunity granted to the BRA and the Massachusetts courts' decisions upholding such immunity amounted to a violation of Article 1105(1) of the NAFTA.

In *Tecmed* v. *Mexico*, analyzed extensively above,[28] the Tribunal relied on *James* v. *UK* and further ECtHR jurisprudence to support its findings

[24] *Mondev International Ltd* v. *United States of America* (ICSID Case No. ARB(AF)/99/2 (Award)), Award, October 11, 2002 , *ILM*, 42 (2003), 85.

[25] *Ibid*., para. 141. [26] *Ibid*., para. 143. [27] *Ibid*., para. 144. [28] See *supra* 6 C. 5.

pertaining to the interpretation of the expropriation clause in the Mexico–Spain BIT.[29] Here, the Tribunal did not make any reservation as to the viability of citing ECtHR decisions in order to determine whether an (indirect) expropriation had occurred.

Finally, in the third case deserving brief mention, *Channel Tunnel* v. *France and the United Kingdom*,[30] the relevance of the ECHR and the ECtHR's jurisprudence was again under scrutiny. The dispute involved the investors' claim that both France and the United Kingdom had failed to grant protection of the investment against clandestine migration occurring through the so-called Eurotunnel linking France and the United Kingdom with a direct train and transportation connection below the English Channel.[31] According to the claimants, the obligations undertaken by France and the United Kingdom in the 1986 Concession Agreement had to be read in conjunction with, inter alia, Article 14 of the ECHR and Additional Protocol I of the Convention providing for the protection of property. The Tribunal regarded the application of international law as limited to the confines of the Concession Agreement itself and declined jurisdiction to consider such allegations pertaining to the ECHR, holding that:

> the Concession Agreement does not contain any contractual commitment by the States Parties that they will comply with their own or with European law . . . In short, national and European law claims against the States are to be the subject of proceedings before the appropriate national and European forums. By contrast it is for the Tribunal to deal with disputes involving the application of the Concession Agreement.[32]

As this short overview succintly exhibits, investment Tribunals – irrespective of which institutional pedigree they derive from – are reluctant to embrace human rights arguments in favor of the investor with too much enthusiasm. The investor seeking to corroborate its claim on human rights grounds or claiming human rights violations as an independent basis for compensation usually[33] fails in its zealous quest to expand the gamut of compensable investor rights violations to the human rights sphere.[34]

29 *Tecmed* v. *Mexico*, para. 122.

30 *Channel Tunnel Group Ltd. and France-Manche SA* v. *Governments of the United Kingdom and France*, Partial Award, January 30, 2007, PCA, available at www.pca-cpa.org/upload/files/ET_PAen.pdf.

31 *Ibid.*, paras. 48 ff.

32 *Ibid.*, para. 148.

33 With the rare exception of *Desert Line Projects* v. *Yemen*, paras. 289 ff.

34 See *Biloune* v. *Ghana* and *Channel Tunnel* v. *United Kingdom and France*.

However, human rights considerations are not entirely absent in investment arbitration. As the *Mondev* and *Tecmed* cases demonstrate – and as I have already pointed out at 4 B. 3. – investment Tribunals making reference to human rights and human rights cases, above all the ECHR and the ECtHR case law, to buttress or test their scrutiny of the investor rights provisions are a more and more familiar occurrence in ICSID and other investment arbitration jurisprudence. To conclude, the role of human rights and human rights jurisprudence, albeit considerably limited at the present state, is expanding – however, mostly within the confines of an established investor right enshrined in an investment treaty; much more rarely[35] as an independent basis for compensation.

2. *Alleged violations of human rights* by *the investor*

After such brief mention of the – rare – instances in which investors themselves invoked human rights as basis for compensable violations of their rights or in which the Tribunal referred to human rights (jurisprudence) to find for or corroborate violations of investor rights, I will now concentrate (at (a) and (b)) on the much more frequent cases that involve alleged human rights violations by the investor on which the host State relies as a defense against asserted investor rights violations.

(a) General human rights cases

(i) Siemens *v.* Argentina

The ensuing two cases, *Siemens*[36] and *Sempra*,[37] revolve around – to a lesser or greater degree – the Argentine crisis of 2001–02, one aspect of which has already been dealt with extensively above.[38] While the latter award mostly focuses on the viability of the necessity defense under the specific circumstances of the Argentine crisis, the *Siemens* case actually originates in a dispute that dates back to before the crisis unfolded.

(1) Facts, issues and the Tribunal's findings

In the late 1990s, Siemens, through its Argentine subsidiary SITS, won a tender as to the development of a national identification and immigration control system that also comprised supervising the production of national identity cards.[39] All prices in the Concession Contract concluded between the Argentine Republic and SITS were denominated in Argentine pesos. At the time, pesos were convertible into dollars at par pursuant to

[35] See *Desert Line Projects* v. *Yemen*, paras. 289 ff.
[36] *Siemens* v. *Argentina*.
[37] *Sempra* v. *Argentina*.
[38] *Supra* 4 C. 1. (b).
[39] *Siemens* v. *Argentina*, paras. 81 ff.

the Argentine Convertibility Law. The execution of the project had two stages: a system engineering stage, which consisted of designing the system specifications and acquiring the computer hardware, software and telecommunications networks necessary for its implementation; and a system operation stage, to be managed by the government. SITS would receive compensation only during this second stage.[40] In August 1999, Argentina requested SITS to postpone production of the identity cards, allegedly due to an extraordinary increase in demand given the upcoming election in October 1999.[41] After several postponements and delays, on February 24, 2000 Argentina suspended the production, printing and distribution of all new DNIs because, in the case of foreigners' DNIs, the RNP subsystem printed the left thumbprint at the place reserved for the right thumbprint. Argentina prohibited SITS from introducing any modification to the system to correct this problem.[42] In November 2000, at the dawn of the unfolding economic crisis, the Argentine Congress approved the Economic–Financial Emergency Law, which empowered the President to renegotiate public sector contracts.[43] Eventually, in May 2001, the Argentine Ministry of the Interior submitted an altered, much less favorable contract to SITS stressing that its terms were non-negotiable.[44] Following administrative appeal, Siemens submitted the dispute to ICSID arbitration.

Siemens claimed violation of, inter alia, the umbrella, expropriation and fair and equitable treatment clauses of the Argentina–Germany BIT. Relevant for the present analysis, however, are Argentina's allegations regarding human rights as the applicable law to the dispute[45] and as a factor to be considered while determining the amount of compensation.[46] As to the applicable law issue, Argentina underlined that under its Constitution human rights treaties assume constitutional status and thus trump ordinary legislation. In its view, "human rights so incorporated in the Constitution would be disregarded by recognizing the property rights asserted by the Claimant given the social and economic conditions of Argentina."[47] The Tribunal, however, somewhat laconically merely observed that Argentina had not developed this argument any further and thus without further evidence or elaboration such allegations did not amount to any relevance regarding the merits of the case.[48]

[40] *Ibid.*, para. 87. [41] *Ibid.*, para. 89. [42] *Ibid.*, para. 92. [43] *Ibid.*, para. 96.
[44] *Ibid.*, para. 97. [45] *Ibid.*, paras. 74 f. [46] *Ibid.*, para. 346. [47] *Ibid.*, para. 75.
[48] *Ibid.*, para. 79.

Moreover, Argentina purported that when an expropriation – as the Tribunal found had occurred vis-à-vis Siemens' investment – is necessitated by social policy reasons, the compensation must not always reflect the fair market value. In this regard, Argentina stressed its dire financial situation when the expropriation took place, a situation that practically compelled it to alter the conditions of the contract with SITS in order to warrant basic governmental functions and social services, and cited the ECtHR case *James* v. *UK*[49] to further corroborate its argumentation.[50] However, the Tribunal also declined Argentina's argument in this regard, underlining that the *Tecmed* case, on which Argentina relied as citing *James* v. *UK*, mentioned the above consideration in the context of determining whether an expropriation had occurred and not as part of the subsequent assessment of the level of compensation, which, so the Tribunal emphasized, are two distinct issues in international law.[51]

(2) Half-effort and full skepticism

The aforementioned exhibits the Tribunal's reluctance to infer any human rights considerations in the dispute before it – a pattern already observable vis-à-vis the case law on human rights contentions in favor of the investor.[52] While it is too early at this stage to speculate whether this is in fact also the leitmotiv regarding human rights allegations as defenses by the host State, it deserves mention that Argentina appears to have made only a half-effort to sustain its human rights argumentation. It must be conceded to the Tribunal that merely saying that there are human rights out there that need to be protected is no sufficient claim. In fact, Argentina merely purported that "human rights . . . would be disregarded by recognizing the property rights asserted by the Claimant given the social and economic conditions of Argentina."[53] This murky and cryptic reference to broad human rights considerations appears to be somewhat of a pattern in Argentina's argumentation in several disputes involving the 2001–02 financial crisis. In the *CMS* award, for example, Argentina

[49] *James* v. *UK*, European Court of Human Rights, *EHRR*, 8 (1986), 123, para. 48, Respondent's Legal Authorities No. AL RA 86, quotation in Argentina's Rejoinder, para. 577. In this decision the ECtHR held that Art. 1 of the First Protocol does not "guarantee a right to full compensation in all circumstances. Legitimate objectives of 'public interest' such as pursued in measures of economic reform or measures designed to achieve greater social justice, may call for less than reimbursement of full market value." See also *supra* 6 C. 4. and D. 2.

[50] *Siemens* v. *Argentina*, para. 346. [51] *Ibid.*, para. 354. [52] See *supra* 7 B. 1.

[53] *Siemens* v. *Argentina*, para. 75.

contended "that, as the economic and social crisis that affected the country compromised basic human rights, no investment treaty could prevail as it would be in violation of such constitutionally recognized rights."[54] Here, again, the Tribunal brushed such allegations away by reprehending Argentina's cursory reference to "human rights" without any further specification and elaboration.[55]

(ii) Sempra *v.* Argentina

(1) Facts, issues and the Tribunal's findings

Similarly to the *Siemens* award, *Sempra* v. *Argentina* involved human rights defenses of the Argentine government against investor rights violations contended by the investor, albeit with a stronger emphasis on the relationship of the state of necessity[56] and the host State's purported responsibility to guarantee basic human needs. The dispute concerns the investment of Sempra Energy International, a US corporation, in two Argentine companies, Sodigas Pampeana SA and Sodigas Sur SA, which in turn are the owners of two such distribution companies, Camuzzi Gas Pampeana (CGP) and Camuzzi Gas del Sur (CGS), which obtained licenses as a result of the effort of privatization of the Argentinian gas sector in the early 1990s.[57] Those licenses foresaw, among others, the calculation of tariffs in US dollars and their semiannual adjustment according to changes in the US Producer Price Index (PPI).[58] According to the claimant, in the period 2000 to 2002, the Argentine government adopted, inter alia, measures prohibiting PPI adjustments of tariffs, the derogation of the calculation of tariffs in US dollars, the unilateral modification of the license by the government without payment of compensation, and the failure to reimburse subsidies owed.[59] Such measures, so Sempra argued, resulted in the permanent abrogation and repudiation of most of the rights it had under the regulatory framework and the license.[60] Argentina countered that its responsibility vis-à-vis the alleged expropriation was excluded by the public international law rules on State responsibility pertaining to the state of necessity and by similar provisions in the US–Argentina BIT.[61] In this context, the respondent asserted that the cataclysmic events and imminent peril of the 2001–02 economic crisis also necessitated the measures undertaken from a human rights perspective, for international human rights obligations such as the Inter-American Convention on Human Rights require

[54] *CMS* v. *Argentina*, para. 114. [55] *Ibid.*, para. 121.
[56] On the *Sempra* case see also *supra* 4 C. 1. (b). [57] *Sempra* v. *Argentina*, para. 83.
[58] *Ibid.*, para. 85. [59] *Ibid.*, para. 93. [60] *Ibid.* [61] *Ibid.*, para. 98.

preserving the institutional survival and constitutional order of a State.[62] In this context, the Tribunal observed that:

> [t]he discussion about institutional survival and preservation of the constitutional order has also been related to the provisions of the Inter-American Convention on Human Rights, to which Argentina is a party. At the hearing, Counsel for the Respondent put the following question to a legal expert: '[W]ould Argentina have been compelled because of the Inter-American Convention to maintain its constitutional order towards the end of 2001, 2002, and afterwards?' The answer from Professor Reisman was '[y]es.'[63]

The Tribunal, while acknowledging Argentina's dire financial situation in the relevant time period, concluded that the constitutional order was not imperiled to such a degree as to assume a state of necessity, neither according to customary international law, nor the relevant treaty provisions. Hence, so the Tribunal reasoned, "[e]ven if emergency legislation became necessary in this context, legitimately acquired rights could still have been accommodated by means of temporary measures and renegotiation."[64] In other words, the Tribunal denied that the measures adopted were the least-restrictive equally effective alternative in order to warrant the human rights obligations Argentina was allegedly obliged to preserve.

(2) Skepticism continued

As in most Argentine crisis cases,[65] the crux of the matter was whether the factual circumstances of the economic breakdown met the conditions of the necessity defenses as set forth in Article 25 ILC Articles on State Responsibility or the respective BIT provision. Similar to most – however, not all – awards on the matter, the *Sempra* Tribunal found that the crisis was grave, but not grave enough for accepting the necessity defense.[66] While Argentina's human rights allegations in the *Siemens* case could rightly be blamed as being cursory, similar replenishment is in place vis-à-vis the *Sempra* Tribunal's consideration of the human rights implications of the necessity defense. True, it acknowledged that the dispute "raises the complex relationship of investment treaties, emergency and

[62] *Ibid.*, paras. 328 ff. [63] *Ibid.*, para. 331. [64] *Ibid.*, para. 332. [65] See *supra* 4 C. 1. (b).

[66] Similarly, again the *CMS* Tribunal; see *CMS* v. *Argentina*, para. 331: "In the present case there are, as concluded, elements of necessity partially present here and there; when the various elements, conditions and limits are examined as a whole it cannot be concluded that all such elements meet the cumulative test. This in itself leads to the inevitable conclusion that the requirements of necessity under customary international law have not been fully met so as to preclude the wrongfulness of the acts."

the human rights of both citizens and property owners."[67] However, with one simple stroke it brushed away Argentina's extensive elaborations on both the factual grounds of the necessity defense and its consequences on human rights obligations without providing any compelling reasoning. It succinctly held:

> The Tribunal *believes* that the constitutional order was not on the verge of collapse, as evidenced by, among many examples, the orderly constitutional transition that carried the country through *five different Presidencies in a few days' time*, followed by elections and the reestablishment of public order.[68]

Interestingly enough, what the Tribunal considers compelling and sufficient evidence for the stability of the system – five different presidencies within ten days – may well be interpreted to corroborate the opposite conclusion, i.e. that the constitutional order was in a state of grave instability and on the verge of collapse. Whatever one considers the correct conclusion to be drawn from the evidence presented in the *Sempra* case, there is little doubt as to the Tribunal's eagerness to avoid considering human rights implications.

(iii) Glamis *v.* US[69]

(1) Facts, issues and the Tribunal's findings

Glamis Gold, Ltd. "was a publicly held Canadian corporation engaged in the exploration, development and extraction of precious metals in the United States and Latin America"[70] that, in 2006, merged with another Canadian company named Goldcorp, Inc. Starting from 1987, through its US subsidiary, Glamis had been acquiring mining claims and mill sites in the Imperial Desert in Southeastern California and attained full ownership of what it called "The Imperial Project" site in 1994. According to the factual summary:

> [t]hrough open-pit mining techniques, [Glamis] planned to mine gold and silver with the expectation of removing 150 million tons of ore, and 300 million tons of waste rock, from three large open pits during the Project's projected 19-year life (from 1998 to 2017).[71]

The regulatory landscape mining developers have to maneuver in in California is highly complex. However, three statutes may be identified as

[67] *Sempra* v. *Argentina*, para. 332. [68] *Ibid.* (emphasis added).

[69] *Glamis Gold, Ltd.* v. *United States of America*, Award, June 8, 2009, NAFTA, available at www.state.gov/s/l/c10986.htm (hereinafter: *Glamis* v. *US*).

[70] *Glamis* v. *US*, Memorial of Claimant Glamis Gold, Ltd., para. 19.

[71] *Glamis* v. *US*, para. 33.

the most relevant relating to the dispute at hand: Firstly, the 1872 Mining Law bestows any US citizen with the right to enter federal public lands and acquire ownership of a limited area of land, if he or she is able to prove the valuable and marketable discovery of hardrock minerals. Secondly, the 1976 Federal Law Policy and Management Act enables the US Department of the Interior to impose and to manage specific protections regarding the federal public land within the California Desert Conservation Area (CDCA), a zone created by the Act and designed to preserve areas of significant scenic and biological importance and surrounding the Imperial Project site.[72] The Bureau of Land Management (BLM) is competent to prepare and implement a comprehensive plan for operation, development and protection of the public land.[73] Thirdly, according to the California Desert Protection Act of 1994 (CDPA), mining or development is prohibited on a vast area in the neighborhood of the Imperial Project.[74]

Glamis claimed to have been assured by BLM, which approved the Project in 1996, that its investment would remain "comfortably outside of the wilderness areas designated by the CDPA."[75] However, the Quechuan Indian Nation, the organization representing the indigenous Indian tribe of the Quechuans, would soon intervene and allege that the Imperial Project's proximity to its sacred ancestral sites would put the Quechuans' spiritual and ceremonial practices, by which they transmit their culture to new generations, in grave peril.[76] According to their Non-Party Supplemental Submission, the Quechuans claimed that, inter alia, due to several provisions of the International Covenant on Civil and Political Rights (ICCPR) as well as the UN Declaration on the Rights of Indigenous Peoples,[77] the Imperial Project could not be executed.[78] Thus, in January 2001, the BLM reversed its decision and the US Secretary of the Interior denied the mining permit. Moreover, subsequently, the California legislature adopted several additional measures that Glamis later on asserted as having further obstructed its investment.[79] On December 9, 2003, Glamis filed a Notice of Arbitration against the United States under NAFTA

[72] *Ibid.*, paras. 41–43. See also J. Cantegreil, "Implementing Human Rights in the NAFTA Regime – The Potential of a Pending Case: Glamis Corp v. USA" in P.-M. Dupuy *et al.*, *Human Rights in International Investment Law and Arbitration*, p. 367 at p. 371.

[73] *Ibid.* [74] *Glamis* v. *US*, paras. 65 ff. [75] *Glamis* v. *US*, Notice of Arbitration, para. 6.

[76] *Glamis* v. *US*, Counter-Memorial of Respondent United States of America, paras. 50 ff.; *Glamis* v. *US*, Non-Party Supplemental Submission of the Quechuan Indian Nation, 1.

[77] UN Declaration on the Rights of Indigenous Peoples, UN GA Res. 61/295, September 13, 2007, available at http://issuu.com/karinzylsaw/docs/un_declaration_rights_indigenous_peoples.

[78] *Ibid.*, 5 f. [79] Cantegreil, "Implementing Human Rights," 372.

Chapter 11, "claim[ing] that the United States, through both the federal and state actions, expropriated the mining rights possessed by Glamis in violation of Article 1110 of the NAFTA and that the United States, through both the federal and state actions, denied Glamis the fair and equitable treatment required by Article 1105 of the NAFTA."[80]

In turn, the Quechuans countered in their Non-party Supplemental Submission that:

under NAFTA Article 1131(1) [providing that a Tribunal adjudicating a claim under Chapter 11 'shall decide the issues in dispute in accordance with [the NAFTA] and applicable rules of international law'], the Tribunal is required to be mindful of how it construes the provisions at issue in this claim, Articles 1105 and 1110, so that they do not require or authorize State conduct of the kind that would conflict with international norms protecting indigenous people generally, and the citizens of the Quechuan Tribe in particular. Such an approach is the only way to ensure consistency in wider public international law and is also mandated in the customary international law rules on treaty interpretation, as restated in Article 31(3)(c) of the *Vienna Convention on the Law of Treaties*.[81]

The Tribunal, in a very elaborate and lengthy award comprising 362 pages, eventually found no violation of the NAFTA, neither of the expropriation nor of the minimum standard of treatment clauses. As to Article 1110 (expropriation), it held that Glamis' investment was not rendered substantially without value by the measures adopted by the US government and the Californian legislature.[82] In its view:

the first factor in any expropriation analysis is not met: the complained of measures did not cause a sufficient economic impact to the Imperial Project to effect an expropriation of Glamis' investment.[83]

Furthermore, the Tribunal also struck down Glamis' claim regarding a breach of the international minimum standard enshrined in NAFTA Article 1105. Defining the crucial threshold along the lines of the 1926 *Neer* case,[84] the Tribunal did not see any grounds for the adopted measures and legislation violating the said standard. Rather, it opined that given the location of the Imperial Project next to the CDCA and in the proximity of the Quechuan Indians, Glamis was not entitled to compensation for the BLM revising its decision and the subsequent

[80] *Glamis* v. *US*, para. 11.

[81] *Glamis* v. *US*, Non-Party Supplemental Submission of the Quechuan Indian Nation, 8 (emphasis in the original).

[82] *Glamis* v. *US*, paras. 328 ff. [83] *Ibid.*, para. 17 citing paras. 534–536.

[84] *Neer* v. *Mexico*, October 15, 1926, 4 R. Int'l Arb. Awards, 60.

measures by the US Department of the Interior and the California state legislature.[85] However, the Tribunal expressly declined to consider the human rights arguments as brought forward by the Quechuan Indian Nation.

(2) A clandestine role of human rights?

When reading the *Glamis* award – which is, indeed, a very time-consuming exercise – it is more than apparent that the extremely long decision never directly addresses human rights considerations per se. Admittedly, elaborate passages, particularly vis-à-vis the claimant's allegations regarding the international minimum standard in Article 1105 of the NAFTA, deal with the US and California measures targeted at protecting the interests of the Quechuan Indians. However, the Tribunal treats them as any other legislation or administrative decisions the effect of which it has to consider in light of NAFTA Chapter 11. It does not even mention, let alone assess the validity or viability of, human rights provisions or soft law instruments such as the ICCPR or the UN Declaration on the Rights of Indigenous Peoples. In other words, what the Tribunal seems to implicitly convey is that human rights arguments may exclusively ground in domestic legislation, but lack applicability – despite the quite broad wording of NAFTA Article 1131(1) – as an international law claim. Such limitation to domestic law, however, basically means the marginalization of human rights considerations as an independent argumentative *topos*: For the Tribunal, the content of the measure itself – the public interest, i.e. in the present case the human rights considerations – is rather irrelevant. What interests the Tribunal is exclusively the question whether the measures adopted by the host State meet the conditions as set forth in the *Neer* case, i.e. amount to an "outrage, to bad faith, to wilful neglect of duty, or to an insufficiency of governmental action so far short of international standards that every reasonable and impartial man would readily recognize its insufficiency."[86]

Hence, complete myopia vis-à-vis human rights allegations? It appears so – at least at first glance. However, what is peculiar – and the Tribunal does not entirely succeed in extinguishing such smack of peculiarity – is that the Tribunal chooses to step back to the *Neer* case of 1926, without accepting any other development having occurred since, as the customary international law minimum standard of treatment and apply the *Neer* principles so strictly in the relevant case. True enough, NAFTA Tribunals have been more cautious regarding the interpretation of

[85] *Ibid.*, paras. 824 ff. [86] *Neer* v. *Mexico*.

Article 1105 NAFTA after the Commission interpretation of 2001 ensuing the broad *Metalclad* holding.[87] Nonetheless, the limitedness and strictness with which the Tribunal chooses to apply Article 1105 NAFTA is remarkable. While there is no express indication in the *Glamis* award and thus any consideration in this regard is in the sphere of pure speculation, it does not seem entirely far-fetched that the Quechuan's cultural and ritual heritage being at stake might have influenced the Tribunal's initial standard-setting.

(iv) Piero Foresti, Laura de Carli and others *v.* South Africa

(1) Facts and issues

Finally, before moving (at (b)) to a case study on a specific – and highly disputed – human rights issue, a case arbitrated under the ICSID Additional Facility Rules merits some mention in this analysis.[88] The dispute raises a sensitive human rights question, because it arguably stretches beyond the realm of universal human rights and touches upon issues at the core of the host State's national identity inhering highly explosive societal issues. However, proceedings were eventually discontinued on November 20, 2009.[89]

South Africa, having unfettered the chains of apartheid in the early 1990s, elected a black leadership according to free, equal and universal suffrage free from racial discrimination, which initiated a host of measures to reinvigorate and strengthen the long disadvantaged black majority. Reconciling the conflicts between the former white elite and the former black underprivileged by empowering the latter while avoiding castigating the former has been the primary challenge of the South African constitutional architecture, which is specifically fine-tuned to address this challenge.[90] Among such "affirmative action"[91] was the

[87] See *supra* 6 C. 2.

[88] *Piero Foresti, Laura de Carli and others* v. *Republic of South Africa* (ICSID Case No. ARB(AF)/07/1) (hereinafter: *Foresti et al.* v. *South Africa*).

[89] *Foresti et al.* v. *South Africa*, Award, August 4, 2010, para. 38. A sidenote: As a corollary of the discontinuance the Tribunal noted in the cited award that counsel for claimants had solicited a bribe of ZAR 5 million to achieve a settlement with the respondent over costs and fees, which led to additional oral hearings, etc.; see *ibid.*, para. 31.

[90] C. Guillebeau, "Affirmative Action in a Global Perspective: The Cases of South Africa and Brazil," *Sociological Spectrum*, 19 (1999), 443; F. M. Higginbotham, "Affirmative Action in the United States and South Africa: Lessons from the Other Side," *Temp. Int'l & Comp. L.J.*, 13 (1999), 187.

[91] "Affirmative action is either a voluntarily adopted policy, or a court-ordered or court-approved legal remedy applied in particular cases to redress specific, proven effects of past or current discrimination against women and/or minorities." J. C. Bond, "Affirmative Action at the Crossroads: An Essay," *Guild Prac.*, 53 (1996), 4 at 10. The

so-called Minerals and Petroleum Resources Development Act (MPRDA) that entered into force on May 1, 2004. According to this legislation, private ownership of mining rights is to be replaced by licenses issued by the government. Former rights-holders are entitled to apply for so-called "new order rights."[92] However, those are subject to a bundle of restrictions and conditions foreign to the old rights. To name but the most prominent of those conditions, the MPRDA provides that the "old order" rights will be converted to new order rights only if they comply with South Africa's Mining Charter, which obliges that 15 percent of equity be sold to "historically disadvantaged South Africans (HDSAs)" within five years after the entry into force of the MPRDA, and that 26 percent equity be divested by ten years from that date.[93] In brief, "[t]he MPRD Act is intended to boost the black population's participation in the mining sector, and forms part of a wider effort by the South African government to address the country's racial inequalities rooted in a legacy of apartheid."[94] A group of European investors holding shares in two major South African mining companies, Marli and Red Graniti, initiated an arbitration procedure under the ICSID Additional Facility Rules claiming violations of their rights enshrined in the BITs concluded between South Africa and Italy and the Belgo-Luxembourg Economic Union respectively. In particular, they assert that replacing their mining rights with the "new order rights" amounts to an expropriation due to the several restrictions and conditions mentioned above. Furthermore, the investors maintain that the said equity divestitures constitute a violation of the fair and equitable treatment standard.[95]

(2) A very touchy issue

According to the petition for limited participation as third-party by several human rights and public interest groups, the MPRDA:

terminology varies in different countries: While "affirmative action" derives from the USA, the term "reservation" is used in India and the term "positive discrimination" is used in Europe to address basically the same issue. On compliance with affirmative action obligations in international treaties in the US see M. Cohn, "Affirmative Action and the Equality Principle in Human Rights Treaties: United States' Violation of its International Obligations", *Va. J. Int'l L.*, 43 (2002–03), 249.

92 D. Vis-Dunbar, "South African Court Judgment Bolsters Expropriation Charge over Black Economic Empowerment Legislation in the Mining Sector," *investmenttreatynews*, March 23, 2009, available at www.investmenttreatynews.org/cms/news/archive/2009/03/23/.

93 L. E. Peterson, "More Details Emerge of Miner's Case against South Africa," *investmenttreatynews*, November 30, 2007, 3, available at www.investmenttreatynews.org/cms/news/archive/2009/03/23/.

94 Vis-Dunbar, *supra* n. 92.

95 Peterson, *supra* n. 93, 2 f.

was enacted... for important public policy reasons and in furtherance of constitutionally mandated goals. These include: human rights advancement, and in particular the pursuit of substantive equality; sustainable development; environmental protection; sound and prudent stewardship of the nation's natural resources; and the need to proactively redress the apartheid history of exploitative labour practices, forced land deprivations, and discriminatory ownership policies which previously characterised South Africa's mining sector for decades.[96]

While such elaborate description might quite accurately mirror South Africa's intentions when adopting the Act, it is surprising that the South African judiciary turned out to be much less prone to such considerations than one would have expected given the importance ascribed to the legislation in the petition.[97] In an interim application judgment in a case introduced by other foreign investors but displaying the same factual matrix as in *Foresti*, judge Willie Hartzenberg of the Pretoria High Court fully endorsed the plaintiffs' argumentation vis-à-vis expropriation, being almost identical to the claimants' allegations in *Foresti*. Despite being an interim judgment and thus focusing only on selected issues, it is surprising that judge Hartzenberg did not even make mention of "affirmative action" issues but on the contrary cites the South African Constitution to corroborate his findings[98] – albeit there exist several provisions permitting positive actions to enhance conditions for the underprivileged in South Africa.[99]

"Affirmative action" considerations are not at all foreign to international human rights law. For example, Article 2(2) of the Race Convention provides:

States Parties shall, when the circumstances so warrant, take, in the social, economic, cultural and other fields, special and concrete measures to ensure the adequate development and protection of certain racial groups or individuals belonging to them, for the purpose of guaranteeing them the full and equal enjoyment of human rights and fundamental freedoms. These measures shall in no case entail as a consequence the maintenance of unequal or separate rights for

[96] *Foresti et al.* v. *South Africa*, Petition for Limited Participation as Non-Disputing Parties in Terms of Articles 41(3), 27, 39, and 35 of the Additional Facility Rules, para. 4.1.

[97] *Ibid.*, paras. 4.1 ff.

[98] North and South Gauteng High Court, Pretoria, *Agri South Africa and Annis Möhr van Rooyen* v. *Minister of Minerals and Energy*, Case 55896/2007, Judgment of March 6, 2009, para. 6.

[99] Only see Arts. 9(2), 25(5) and 25(8) of the South African Constitution, available at www.info.gov.za/documents/constitution/index.htm.

different racial groups after the objectives for which they were taken have been achieved.[100]

Considering this, it is not entirely unlikely that South Africa may find itself in a conflict between two international obligations – complying with the South Africa–Italy BIT on the one hand and complying with the provisions of the Race Convention on the other. One might well argue that South Africa's shortcoming as to signing potentially contradictory treaties cannot be to the detriment of the foreign investor. However, if such conflict indeed occurs, it will play out to the detriment of someone – and the same argument applies vis-à-vis the human rights issue, if one does not purport that the host State needs to give preference to the treatment of aliens and that its own citizens can be expected to carry a greater burden.[101] Apart from such potential conflict among international obligations, the most explosive issue the *Foresti* dispute inheres is that it touches upon a question at the very core of South Africa's societal identity, i.e. "affirmative action" or "positive discrimination" as a licit means fundamental to the reconciliation of racial tensions after decades of apartheid.[102] This is not a legal argument and in itself not a legal issue. However, the Tribunal will find itself in a position where it can hardly avoid considering, at least implicitly, the potential effect its decision might have on both South Africa's internal and external policy – internal as to the treatment of foreign investors under its domestic law and external as to the conclusion and framing of future and potential drives for amendment of old BITs.

(b) Specific case study: The right to water

Water has become a prominent subject in investment arbitration over the course of the past decade. Following the wave of privatizations sparked most forcefully by the World Bank in the late 1990s and at the beginning of

[100] International Convention on the Elimination of All Forms of Racial Discrimination, 660 UNTS 13, *ILM*, 19 (1980), 352, open for signature March 7, 1966 (entered into force January 4, 1969) (hereinafter: Race Convention). South Africa ratified the Race Convention on December 10, 1998.

[101] As can arguably be derived from the following holding of the ECtHR in *James* v. *UK*: "[A]lthough a taking of property must always be effected in the public interest, different considerations may apply to nationals and non-nationals and there may well be legitimate reason for requiring nationals to bear a greater burden in the public interest than non-nationals." ECHR, App No. 8793/79, February 21, 1986, *EHRR*, 8 (1986), 123, at para. 50. However, this passage exclusively refers to measures relating to property and thus may encounter difficulties when being directly transposed to other human rights areas.

[102] See Guillebeau, "Affirmative Action," 444 f.

the new millennium, several disputes have arisen particularly regarding investments in the water and sewage systems of major cities in Latin America and Africa.[103] Being a basic human need, vital not only to mere existence and survival but also to a vast gamut of necessities such as cleaning, sewering, washing, cooling, food production, etc., water is a particularly delicate issue. If the population – or at least considerable parts of the population – lack access to clean water, massive health problems, diseases and even death are the consequences that are often very likely to canalize in social turmoil or even upheaval. Hence, it is no surprise that the enthusiastic privatization of the water sector in Third World countries and emerging markets entailed a host of investment arbitration claims where the privatization did not go as planned – which was, in fact, quite frequently the case.

Starting from the 1970s, several political documents have sought to infer a legal meaning to the undoubtedly vital human need for water.[104] While early attempts pertained more to the objective legal character of the importance of water, more recent initiatives are aiming at establishing a subjective right to water and thus granting it status as a human right. The debate on the right to water is a prime example of international human rights law and international environmental law discourse coalescing – in a very coarse summary, its objective character pertaining to environmental law[105] and its subjective character to human rights.

To date the most prominent and most influential attempt to give shape and underscore legal relevance to the right to water certainly represents General Comment No. 15 of the Committee on Economic, Social and Cultural Rights of November 26, 2002.[106] The Committee views the right to water as a penumbral right emerging from ICESCR Articles 11(1) and 12(1). The former deals with "the right of everyone to an adequate standard of living . . . including adequate food, clothing and housing."[107] According

103 P. Thielbörger, "The Human Right to Water Versus Investor Rights: Double-Dilemma or Pseudo-Conflict?" in P.-M. Dupuy *et al.* (eds.), *Human Rights*, p. 487 at pp. 493 ff.

104 See S. McCaffrey, "The Human Right to Water" in E. Brown Weiss, L. Boisson de Chazournes and N. Bernasconi-Osterwalder (eds.), *Fresh Water and International Economic Law* (Oxford University Press, 2005), p. 93 at p. 95.

105 See *Lake Lanoux, Spain* v. *France*, Arbitral Award, November 16, 1957, *Report of International Arbitral Awards*, 12 (1957), 281; *Gabcíkovo-Nagymaros* case; see further C. Tomuschat, *Human Rights – Between Idealism and Realism* (Oxford Unversity Press, 2003), pp. 48 ff.

106 General Comment No. 15, UN Doc. E/C 12/2002/11 of November 26, 2002, available at www.unhchr.ch/tbs/doc.nsf/0/a5458d1d1bbd713fc1256cc400389e94?Open document.

107 International Covenant on Economic, Social and Cultural Rights, Adopted and opened for signature, ratification and accession by General Assembly resolution 2200A (XXI) of December 16, 1966, entry into force January 3, 1976, available at www.ohchr.org/english/law/cescr.htm.

to the Committee, the word "including" indicates that the list of rights comprised in Article 11(1) is not exhausted by those expressly mentioned in the provision:

> The right to water clearly falls within the category of guarantees essential for securing an adequate standard of living, particularly since it is one of the most fundamental conditions for survival.[108]

Article 12(1) focuses on the highest attainable standard of health for everyone. In General Comment No. 15, the Committee reiterates its opinion that the components underscoring the right to health include potable water.[109]

As to the normative content of the right, the Committee identifies three relevant factors applicable under any circumstances: (1) *availability*, i.e. "[t]he water supply for each person must be sufficient and continuous for personal and domestic uses"; (2) *quality*, i.e. "[t]he water required for each personal or domestic use must be safe, therefore free from micro-organisms, chemical substances and radiological *hazards* that constitute a threat to a person's health"; and (3) *accessibility*, i.e. the "[w]ater and water facilities and services have to be accessible to *everyone* without discrimination, within the jurisdiction of the State party."[110]

General Comment No. 15 constitutes a tremendous step forward *en route* to the customary international law status and universal recognition of a right to water. However, leaving aside the contentious debate regarding economic and social rights' justiciability,[111] as evinced by a plethora of skeptical statements rejecting its legally binding status,[112] the right to water cannot yet be regarded a norm of customary international law.[113]

108 General Comment No. 15, para. 3.

109 General Comment No. 14, UN Doc. E/C 12/2002/4 of May 11, 2000, available at www.unhchr.ch/tbs/doc.nsf/%28symbol%29/E.C.12.2000.4.En.

110 General Comment No. 15, para. 12.

111 On this issue see M. Scheinin, "Economic and Social Rights as Legal Rights" in A. Eide, C. Krause and A. Rosas (eds.), *Economic, Social and Cultural Rights – A Textbook* (Martinus Nijhoff Publishers, 1995), p. 41.

112 Only see Summary Reports of the World Water Fora in Mexico City and Istanbul published by the International Institute for Sustainable Development (IISD), available at www.iisd.ca/ymb/water/worldwater5/.

113 S. M. A. Salman and S. McIneray-Lankford, *The Human Right to Water* (The World Bank, 2004), p. 75; Thielbörger, "The Human Right to Water Versus Investor Rights," 491; J. Scanlon, A. Cassar and N. Nemon (eds.), *Water as a Human Right?* (International Union for Conservation of Nature and Natural Resources, 2004), pp. 9 ff.; M. Craven, "Some Thoughts on the Emergent Right to Water" in E. Riedel and P. Rothen, *The Human Right to Water* (Berliner Wissenschafts Verlag, 2006), p. 37 at p. 39.

Therefore, as Pierre Thielbörger put it quite accurately, "the assumption that a right to water derives from the right to an adequate standard of living and the right to health is more of a suggestion by the CESCR than a legal ruling."[114] Thus, having delineated in brief words the current status of the right to water as to its alleged content, normative foundations and customary character as well as its potential relevance in investment arbitrations, I will now analyze four cases pertaining to water privatization and international investment issues.

(i) Compañia de Aguas de Aconquija *v.* Argentina *("the* Vivendi *story")*

Compañia de Aguas de Aconquija v. *Argentina*,[115] also known as "the *Vivendi* story," is one of the longest disputes in ICSID history, stretching over the course of more than eight years with two Tribunal decisions, one annulment award and several requests preceding and ensuing each decision by both of the Tribunals and the ad hoc Committee.[116] After laying out the basic facts underscoring *Vivendi* and the issues it implies, a brief summary of all three awards will be followed by the usual comments – targeted on the overall dispute as well as each of the three rulings.

(1) Facts and issues

Compagnie Générale des Eaux (CGE), which later became Vivendi, held a 36 percent share in a Spanish and an Argentine company respectively, which each held 27 percent of the shares in Compañia de Aguas de Aconquija (AdA).[117] In 1993, Tucumán, one of Argentina's poorest provinces, privatized its dilapidated water and sewage facilities. Following a two-year tender process, CGE – which was the only bidder remaining – won the bid and concluded a Concession Contract with Tucumán; the Argentine government was not involved in the tender or conclusion of the contract at any stage of the procurement process.[118] The contract contained conditions less favorable than indicated in the invitation to tender – a reduced amount of investments required and a raise of consumer prices. Notwithstanding such departure from the invitation to tender, Tucumán

[114] Thielbörger, "The Human Right to Water Versus Investor Rights," 492 f.

[115] *Compañia de Aguas de Aconquija, SA (AdA) & Compagnie Générale des Eaux (CGE)* v. *Argentina (Vivendi)* (ICSID Case No. ARB/97/3) (hereinafter: *Compañia de Aguas de Aconquija* v. *Argentina*, or *Vivendi*).

[116] For a complete list of awards, requests and other documents revolving around the *Vivendi* story consult http://ita.law.uvic.ca/alphabetical_list.htm.

[117] *Compañia de Aguas de Aconquija* v. *Argentina*, para. 24, n. 6.

[118] *Ibid.*, paras. 25 f.

authorities entered into the contract with AdA without undertaking any further negotiations.

Pursuant to the Concession Contract, CGE assumed responsibility for the operation of the water and sewage system of Tucumán on July 22, 1995. It is undisputed that there were serious technical and commercial deficiencies in the structure and operation of the Tucumán water and sewage system at the time of the CGE takeover.[119] From an early point in CGE's performance under the Concession Contract, disputes arose between CGE and the authorities of Tucumán. These disputes became the subject of extensive publicity and controversy.[120] In 1996, after a political turmoil in Tucumán, the governor renegotiated the contract with AdA seeking for additional mandatory investments by AdA and reduced consumer prices. However, despite a compromise being reached, the governor submitted an altered contract to the legislature, which AdA refused to sign. Eventually, AdA rescinded the Concession Contract in 1997.[121] The main issues of the dispute were: (1) whether the Concession Contract's clause referring any dispute exclusively to the local courts of Tucumán excluded the Tribunal's jurisdiction or whether it still had jurisdiction according to Article 8 of the France–Argentina BIT and Article 25 ICSID extending jurisdiction to "any legal dispute" arising out of an investment; (2) whether Argentina violated the expropriation and fair and equitable treatment clauses of the France–Argentina BIT; and (3), as was emerging over the course of the dispute and the Tribunals' and ad hoc Committee's decisions, whether the interpretation of the Concession Contract had any influence on the assessment of whether Argentina breached the BIT.

(2) The awards

The first Tribunal, issuing its award on November 21, 2000, held – and both the Annulment Committee and the second Tribunal endorsed this ruling – that the Concession Contract could not waive the Tribunal's jurisdiction if established under the BIT and Article 25 ICSID, which in the eyes of the Tribunal prevailed over the domestic law contract.[122] Moreover, it regarded the *sedes materiae* of the dispute mainly in the terms of the Concession Contract. Consequently, it held that the question of a breach of the BIT could only be answered after the local Tucumán courts

[119] *Ibid.*, para. 28. [120] *Ibid.*, para. 29. [121] *Ibid.*, paras. 36 f.

[122] *Compañia de Aguas de Aconquija, SA (AdA) & Compagnie Générale des Eaux v. Argentina* (ICSID Case No. ARB/97/3), Award, November 21, 2000, *ICSID Reports*, 5 (2002), 299 (hereinafter: *Vivendi I*), paras. 45 and 53 ff.

had decided upon the performance issues pertaining to the contract – which, according to the Concession Contract, they were the only ones competent to.[123]

This last ruling granting the Concession Contract's jurisdictional clause a considerable relevance through the backdoor met serious criticism by the subsequent Annulment Committee, instituted upon the request of Vivendi. According to the ad hoc Committee, the Tribunal was entitled to base its decision on the Concession Contract and thus failed to decide the claims despite having jurisdiction – which constitutes a ground for annulment (Article 52(1)(b) ICSID). The Committee stated that the Tribunal was called upon to decide whether a breach of the BIT had occurred. If this had required an interpretation of the Concession Contract, the Tribunal would have been obligated to do so.[124]

Hence, a second Tribunal was constituted and eventually delivered its award on August 20, 2007[125] holding that a breach of the treaty and a breach of the Concession Contract are two different issues that are not connected. Thus, the Tribunal did not find it necessary to determine whether a breach of the Concession Contract had occurred.[126] Nonetheless, the Tribunal found for a violation of the fair and equitable treatment standard; Article 3 of the BIT states:

> Under the fair and equitable standard, there is no doubt about a government's obligation not to disparage and undercut a concession . . . that has properly been granted . . . based on falsities and motivated by a desire to rescind or force a renegotiation. And that is exactly what happened in Tucumán.[127]

Moreover, according to the Tribunal, "Claimants were radically deprived of the economic use and enjoyment of their investments," which constitutes a breach of the expropriation clause in Article 5 of the BIT.[128] Consequently, the Tribunal awarded US$ 105 million plus interest to Vivendi as compensation for the breaches of the France–Argentina BIT.[129]

123 *Ibid.*, paras. 77–79.

124 *Compañia de Aguas de Aconquija, SA (AdA) & Vivendi (formerly Compagnie Générale des Eaux)* v. *Argentina* (ICSID Case No. ARB/97/3), Decision on Annulment, July 3, 2002, *ILM*, 41 (2002), 1135 (hereinafter: *Vivendi* annulment), paras. 95, 112.

125 *Compañia de Aguas de Aconquija, SA (AdA) & Vivendi (formerly Compagnie Générale des Eaux)* v. *Argentina* (ICSID Case No. ARB/97/3), Award, August 20, 2007 (hereinafter: *Vivendi II*).

126 *Ibid.*, paras. 7.3.10 f.

127 *Ibid.*, para. 7.4.39.

128 *Ibid.*, para. 7.5.34.

129 *Ibid.*, para. 11.1.

(3) No camouflage permitted

The first striking issue as to the *Vivendi* story is Argentina's, i.e. the Tucumán officials', shortcomings vis-à-vis the right to water, that certainly contributed to the unfolding of the dispute. Local authorities agreed on AdA's terms contrary to their own invitation to tender and although they were aware that they needed to ensure stable water prices and quality, which according to the Concession Contract initially concluded with AdA was not at all warranted. This, arguably, already constitutes a violation of the right to water.[130] When the Tucumán governor realized the consequences of the Concession Contract, he sought to renegotiate and eventually de facto dictate new terms that were more in line with the needs of the Tucumán population and thus in conformity with obligations vis-à-vis the right to water as purported by General Comment No. 15.

Therefore, the *Vivendi* story is a prime example of a not unfamiliar pattern regarding investment disputes involving human rights issues: The host State, while desperately seeking to accommodate the investor, ignores the needs of its population and only afterwards, i.e. after the investment has been made and it thus has assumed responsibility for the investment under the BIT, realizes the fatal consequences of its shortcomings and seeks to revise or amend its decision, which, however, then violates its obligations owed to the investor under the BIT. Depriving CGE, i.e. Vivendi, of (some of) the rights granted in the Concession Contract is a conduct for which the host State must pay compensation. If this was foreseeable – which it obviously was here given the invitation to tender originally providing for most of the content Tucumán eventually requested from AdA – then the host State cannot hide behind a noble cause and must pay compensation.

(ii) Aguas del Tunari *v.* Bolivia

"The Cochabamba Water Wars," as *Aguas del Tunari* v. *Bolivia*[131] was famously dubbed, is somewhat of an oddity in this collection of investment cases related to the right to water, for the dispute was settled before the Tribunal could issue its decision. The reason why I nonetheless mention it here, apart from its prominence in international media,[132] is that it is a prime example of the growing influence of third parties and the

130 Thielbörger, "The Human Right to Water Versus Investor Rights," 495.

131 *Aguas del Tunari, SA* v. *Bolivia* (ICSID Case No. ARB/02/3) (hereinafter: *Aguas del Tunari* v. *Bolivia*).

132 J. Shultz, "The Politics of Water in Bolivia," *The Nation*, January 28, 2005, www.thenation.com/doc/20050214/shultz; "Bolivian Tension Mounts as Roadblock

public opinion on issues going far beyond the mere business concern of the investor.

The facts are as follows: During the late 1990s, the World Bank pressured Bolivia to privatize its water systems, particularly those of big cities. In 1997, it stressed that financial support to improve the canalization and water facilities of Cochabamba, Bolivia's third-largest city, was dependent on the authorities selling the system to a private investor. The local public operator had constantly failed to provide sufficient water services to the population of Cochabamba: Only 57 percent had full access to fresh water and a considerable share of the population had to rely on private wells. Eventually, in September 1999, Bolivia granted a forty-year concession to Aguas del Tunari, a subsidiary of the US corporation Bechtel, following a non-public bidding process. Soon after Aguas del Tunari took over management of the Cochabamba water system prices soared by an average of 35 percent, sparking a city-wide rebellion which the military suppressed with massive force killing a teenager and wounding more than a hundred people. Subsequently, Bechtel abandoned the project and Bolivia terminated the contract and replaced Aguas del Tunari with a public company.[133]

Bechtel claimed US$ 50 million in damages under the Netherlands–Bolivia BIT.[134] Several NGOs and other interest groups requested admission as non-disputing parties applying for third party or at least *amicus curiae* status arguing that they had a direct interest in the matter and that their participation would increase transparency.[135] The president of the Tribunal found that such admission depended on the consent of both parties. Such consent being absent, the Tribunal rejected the petitions for participation in the proceedings, either as party or as *amicus curiae*. In early 2006, following extensive and continuing international pressure from civil society, NGOs and the media, the parties requested discontinuation of the proceedings and subsequently abandoned the dispute.[136]

Deadline Looms," CNN, March 10, 2000, http://archives.cnn.com/2000/WORLD/americas/10/03/bolivia.protests.reut/index.html.

133 Thielbörger, "The Human Right to Water Versus Investor Rights," 499.

134 Bechtel had set up an affiliate in the Netherlands specifically for "BIT shopping," since there was no BIT between the US and Bolivia at the time the dispute arose.

135 See, e.g., Petition of la Coordinadora para la Defense del Agua y Vida, la Federación Departemental Cochabambina de Organizaciones Regantes, Sempa Sur, Friends of the Earth-Netherlands, Oscar Livera, Omar Fernandez, Father Luis Sánchez, and Congressman Jorge Alvarado to the Abitral Tribunal, August 29, 2002.

136 See Statement by Jonathan Marshall, media relations manager for Bechtel, available at www.bilaterals.org/article.php3?id_article=3612>.

Two aspects are relevant as to the right to water. Firstly, General Comment No. 15 stipulates that "services, whether publicly or privately provided, are affordable for all, including socially disadvantaged groups."[137] While this was not even the case before privatization, the situation did not improve in this regard – on the contrary, soaring water prices soon after privatization in September deteriorated the already very dire state of water services in Cochabamba, eventually being the straw that broke the camel's back. Secondly, by not only failing to improve the water system but by granting Aguas del Tunari exclusive rights to provide the water services in Cochabamba, access to alternative water resources that existed before was severely impeded. This pertains to the first factor, i.e. availability of water, referred to in General Comment No. 15 as pivotal to be warranted in all circumstances.[138] Eventually, due to the dispute being abandoned, none of the issues could be considered – or rejected – by the Tribunal. While it is open to debate whether the Tribunal would indeed have engaged in discussing the right to water, it is beyond doubt that – in a factual but no less forceful way – this contentious human right played a very considerable role in *Aguas del Tunari* v. *Bolivia*, for it was the concerns inhering the legal translation the right to water purports to be that incited the turmoil in Cochabamba, led the myriad of NGOs and interests groups to become engaged in the dispute – one way or another – and attracted the interest of international media that eventually pressured the parties, i.e. Aguas' parent company Bechtel in particular, to abandon the dispute.

(iii) Azurix *v.* Argentina

The next dispute under scrutiny, *Azurix* v. *Argentina*,[139] also stretches over a considerable time period resulting in an (however, dismissed) application on annulment[140] of the original award.[141] However, the ad hoc Committee's decision deals with issues not particularly relevant to my analysis here and thus I consider it a venial sin not to further elaborate on the *Azurix* annulment award.

(1) Facts, issues and the Tribunal's decision

As for the facts of the *Azurix* award, in 1999 American corporation Azurix, an Enron spin-off, won the bid for a thirty-year concession to run the water

[137] General Comment No. 16, para. 27. [138] *Ibid.*, para. 12.

[139] *Azurix Corp.* v. *Argentina* (ICSID Case No. ARB/01/12) (hereinafter: *Azurix* v. *Argentina*).

[140] *Azurix Corp.* v. *Argentina* (ICSID Case No. ARB/01/12), Decision on the Application for Annulment of the Argentine Republic, September 1, 2009.

[141] *Azurix Corp.* v. *Argentina* (ICSID Case No. ARB/01/12), Award, July 14, 2006.

and sewage systems in the Argentine province of Buenos Aires, paying US$ 438.6 million as a so-called "canon payment."[142] By March 2000 customers complained about very low water pressure, and local water supply for half a million people was contaminated with bacteria. Customers were advised by authorities to boil tap water, to minimize exposure to water and not to pay their water bills. Eventually, Azurix terminated the Concession Contract in October 2001.[143] The Tribunal summarizes the issues and claims introduced by the parties as follows:

> The Claimant contends that its investment in Argentina has been expropriated by measures of the Respondent tantamount to expropriation and that the Respondent has, in addition, violated its [BIT] obligations . . . of fair and equitable treatment, non-discrimination and full protection and security; that such measures are actions or omissions of the Province or its instrumentalities that resulted in the non application of the tariff régime of the Concession for political reasons; that the Province did not complete certain works that were to remedy historical problems and were to be transferred to the Concessionaire upon completion; that the lack of support for the concession régime prevented ABA [Azurix's subsidiary] from obtaining financing for its Five Year Plan; that in 2001, the Province denied that the canon was recoverable through tariffs; and that 'political concerns were always privileged over the financial integrity of the Concession,' and '[w]ith no hope of recovering its investments in the politicized regulatory scheme, ABA gave notice of termination of the Concession and was forced to file for bankruptcy.'

> The Respondent has disputed the allegations of the Claimant. For the Respondent, the dispute is a contractual dispute and the difficulties encountered by the Concessionaire in the Province were of its own making. In particular, the Respondent has argued that the case presented by the Claimant is intimately linked to Enron's business practices and its bankruptcy; that the price paid for the Concession was excessive and opportunistic and related to the forthcoming IPO of Azurix at the time Azurix bid for the Concession . . . and that the Concessionaire did not comply with the Concession Agreement, in particular its investment obligations, and the actions of the Province, including the termination of the Concession Agreement by the Province, were justified.[144]

Azurix claimed US$ 550 million in compensation alleging, inter alia, expropriation and failure to provide fair and equitable treatment.

The Tribunal's view can be fairly summarized by its following statement: "The Tribunal understands that governments have to be vigilant and protect the public health of their citizens but the statements and

[142] *Ibid.*, para. 41.
[143] Thielbörger, "The Human Right to Water Versus Investor Rights," 496.
[144] *Azurix* v. *Argentina*, paras. 43 f.

actions of the provincial authorities contributed to the crisis rather than assisted in solving it."[145] The Tribunal found that Argentina's actions did not amount to an expropriation,[146] for by applying the *Tecmed* approach, i.e. proportionality analysis in the assessment of whether an expropriation had actually occurred,[147] the arbitrators opined that the degree of impact suffered by Azurix did not pass the relevant threshold in order to be regarded as expropriatory.[148] Furthermore, the Tribunal held that Argentina did not provide fair and equitable treatment, since it engaged in political interference with the tariff régime and failed to complete the repairs that would have been required to avoid the contamination of the water in the first place.[149]

The Tribunal granted compensation in the amount of the fair market value of the concession;[150] however, it refrained from allowing Azurix to recover the entire canon payment of US$ 438.6 million. Instead, it decided that the canon payment should not be considered recoverable through periodic tariff increases; rather, in the Tribunal's view, it was upon the investor to make the appropriate calculation as to the expected earning stream and to bid for the concession accordingly. In the words of the Tribunal:

> [N]o well-informed investor, in March 2002, would have paid for the Concession the price (and more particularly, the Canon) paid by Azurix in mid-1999, irrespective of the actions taken by the Province and of the economic situation of Argentina at that time.[151]

Nonetheless, the Tribunal also stressed Argentina's responsibility as to the loss in value of Azurix's investment.[152]

(2) Concealed relevance again

There are two aspects of the Tribunal's decision relevant vis-à-vis the right to water. Firstly, in their assessment of proportionality according to the *Tecmed* standard[153] the arbitrators could have easily referred to the right to water, e.g. the State's obligation to provide affordable access to clean water,[154] as a factor to be considered in the balancing exercise of the proportionality *stricto sensu*.[155] Admittedly, the Tribunal underlined the public interest implications of the dispute as a general matter. However, it shied away from undertaking a detailed balancing exercise where it

145 *Ibid.*, para. 144. 146 *Ibid.*, para. 322. 147 See *supra* 6 C. 4.
148 *Azurix v. Argentina*, para. 322. 149 *Ibid.*, para. 376. 150 *Ibid.*, para. 424.
151 *Ibid.*, para. 426. 152 *Ibid.*, para. 428. 153 See *supra* 6 C. 4. and D. 3.
154 See General Comment No. 15, para. 12(c)(ii). 155 See *supra* 5 D. 3.

would have been compelled to become more precise, but instead came to its conclusion merely after a very cursory glance at the factors involved.[156]

The second issue worth mentioning regarding the right to water is the arbitrators' reasoning vis-à-vis compensation. The Tribunal held that Azurix merely was entitled to fair market value of the investment and thus could not retain the entire canon payment it had paid in order to obtain the concession. According to the arbitrator, a reasonable businessman could not have expected to recuperate the whole sum but merely a small fraction of the canon payment given the tariff policy agreed upon by Azurix and Argentina in the Concession Contract: "[N]o well-informed investor . . . would have paid for the Concession the price (and more particularly, the Canon) paid by Azurix."[157] Arguably, the Tribunal thus implicitly applied a core principle inhering the right to water, i.e. the right to affordable access to water for everyone.[158] It involves States ensuring that water prices stay at an affordable level even if a private operator provides the water services and hence must adopt necessary measures, including appropriate pricing policies.[159] By holding that Azurix could not expect recuperation of the entire canon payment, since water tariffs had to remain below a certain threshold and thus could not be considered to fully amortize the price paid for the investment, the *Azurix* Tribunal arguably endorsed the right to water as an argumentative *topos* in its assessment of compensation to be granted to the investor.[160]

However, given that the Tribunal did not mention the right to water at all, initial enthusiasm needs to be dampened down. It seems equally plausible that the arbitrators did not even think of the right to water but merely considered it inappropriate to award about half a billion dollars in an investment dispute that exhibited viable claims and defenses on both sides. Nonetheless, to say as much, what this holding undoubtedly demonstrates is the growing impact and importance of Global Public Interest considerations in international investment law.

(iv) Biwater *v.* Tanzania

The last award to be mentioned here is a familiar fellow: As regards the facts, issues and holdings of the *Biwater* award, I refer to my elaborations at 6 C. 7. Hence, let me directly jump to the comments on the case vis-à-vis

156 See Thielbörger, "The Human Right to Water Versus Investor Rights," 498.

157 *Azurix* v. *Argentina*, para. 426.

158 See General Comment No. 15, para. 12(c)(ii).

159 See Thielbörger, "The Human Right to Water Versus Investor Rights," 498.

160 *Ibid.*

the right to water. *Biwater* pairs with the aforementioned *Azurix* award in the impact of Global Public Interest considerations on the Tribunal's holding on compensation. Similarly to the latter, the Tribunal in *Biwater* acknowledged the public interest concerns dominating the dispute: "At least in theory, and viewed at that time, this [water] crisis could have threatened a vital public service and the situation therefore had to be resolved one way or the other in the near future."[161] By finding that the investor was not entitled to any compensation at all, for there was no causal link between the loss in value of the investment and the BIT rights violations by the host State, the *Biwater* award appears to have internalized the relevance of Global Public Interest considerations to an even higher degree than *Azurix*.

C. Analysis of the case law

Hence, I come to the assessment of the case law on human rights issues, which will be devoted – due to its much higher relevance to the questions scrutinized in this book – exclusively to alleged human rights violations by the investor. In this regard, no difference is to be made between what I have called "general human rights cases"[162] and the specific case study regarding the right to water.[163] After having outlined what I consider the observations and conclusions worth mentioning, I will close this chapter with a glance at how human rights issues can be much more satisfyingly resolved according to the Global Public Interest theory (4.).

1. What's wrong with human rights?

Comparable to one of my conclusions regarding environmental issues,[164] we can here observe a similar pattern of reluctance to directly refer to or consider human rights argumentation in the analyzed case law. Sometimes, such reluctance may originate in the host State's lukewarm half-effort of merely referring to human rights issues in an overly broad and cursory manner.[165] Quite understandably, if host States linger in lofty and abstract principles and fail to invoke human rights arguments in instances other than as a last resort, and if all other options have run out, Tribunals display serious skepticism vis-à-vis the sincerity of such allegations by the government. In *Siemens*, Argentina very broadly asserted that

[161] *Biwater Gauff* v. *Tanzania*, para. 654. [162] See *supra* 7 B. 2. (a).
[163] See *supra* 7 B. 2. (b). [164] See *supra* 6 D. 1.
[165] See *Siemens* v. *Argentina*, *supra* 7 B. 2. (a) (i).

the dispute involves human rights issues and that those could be seriously affected in case the Tribunal did not decide in Argentina's favor. Unsurprisingly so, the Tribunal was not very impressed by such argumentation and declined to consider the allegation, underlining Argentina's insufficient elaborations in this regard.[166] As already mentioned earlier while commenting on the *Siemens* case, this pattern is to be found in Argentina's defense pertaining to several cases dealing with or revolving around the 2001–02 financial crisis.[167]

Moreover, as another aspect quite counterproductive to expanding the role of human rights in investment disputes, it needs mention that in some instances host States themselves were involved in or considerably contributed to the situation they later claim as infringing their citizens' human rights. In the *Vivendi* story, a main factor in the escalation of events and the dire position many water consumers found themselves in was that Tucumán officials approved AdA's bid although it did not fulfill the conditions as set out in the invitation to tender.[168] Similarly, in *Azurix*, the drinking water's infestation with bacteria was mostly due to decades of shortcomings in the maintenance and renovation of Buenos Aires' water and sewage system when it was still run by the local government.[169]

However, though admittedly host States frequently give reason for the Tribunals to be very cautious as far as human rights allegations are concerned, quite occasionally arbitrators have to take the blame for being cursory themselves. For example, the *Sempra* award brushes away quite detailed elaborations by Argentina on the human rights implications of the state of necessity. The Tribunal held – I have quoted the passage before:[170]

> The Tribunal *believes* that the constitutional order was not on the verge of collapse, as evidenced by, among many examples, the orderly constitutional transition that carried the country through *five different Presidencies in a few days' time*, followed by elections and the reestablishment of public order.[171]

Leaving aside the quite unconvincing argumentation regarding the inflation of presidencies as an indicator for stability,[172] it must be added that belief is an oddity in legal argument – at least if it entails such weak

166 *Siemens* v. *Argentina*, para. 79.
167 See, e.g., *CMS* v. *Argentina*, para. 114 and *supra* 7 B. 2. (a) (i).
168 See *supra* 7 B. 2. (b) (i) (1).
169 See *supra* 7 B. 2. (b) (iii) (1).
170 See *supra* 7 B. 2. (a) (ii) (2).
171 *Sempra* v. *Argentina*, para. 332 (emphasis added).
172 On this argument see also *supra* 7 B. 2. (a) (ii) (2).

support. In fact, it appears that the Tribunal was very eager to avoid engaging in human rights considerations under any circumstance.

Such hesitancy, if not to say hostility, vis-à-vis human rights arguments cannot be explained by mere skepticism and ignorance. By contrast, more and more eminent public international law scholars, many among them with a longstanding experience in the field of human rights, become arbitrators in investment disputes, both under ICSID as well as NAFTA or other arbitration realms. Abstractly speaking, Tribunals such as *Phoenix* acknowledge – in *obiter dicta* – that:

> nobody would suggest that ICSID protection should be granted to investments made in violation of the most fundamental rules of protection of human rights, like investments made in pursuance of torture or genocide or in support of slavery or trafficking of human organs.[173]

However, beyond such rather hypothetical considerations, investment Tribunals are very reluctant to take account of human rights. Hence, the roots for such reluctance must lie deeper than mere professional bias. As some scholars elucidate, the crux with international human rights considerations lies in the question of the law applicable to an investment dispute.[174] This, so some argue, further leads to the jurisdictional issue that the consent to arbitration is limited to the substance of the request for arbitration.[175] Since international investment law – at least until now – has lacked a solid theoretical and doctrinal foundation for the application of public international law norms beyond those enshrined in BITs, it is understandable that Tribunals shy away from applying human rights or other public interest issues encapsulated in public international law norms, particularly if those may be asserted as defenses against undisputable investor rights infringements. My Global Public Interest theory, prepared, elaborated and further developed and replenished extensively in Chapters 2, 4 and 5, is specifically tailored as a response to such shortcoming.[176]

[173] *Phoenix Action Ltd*. v. *Czech Republic* (ICSID Case No. ARB/06/5), Award, April 15, 2009, para. 78.

[174] Dupuy, "Unification Rather than Fragmentation," 56.

[175] C. Reiner and C. Schreuer, "Human Rights and International Investment Arbitration" in P.-M. Dupuy *et al*. (eds.), *Human Rights*, p. 82 at p. 89.

[176] Also see *infra* 7 C. 4.

2. *Through the back door*

While thus at first sight there is distinguishable myopia discernible among investment Tribunals dealing with human rights issues, on second glance it becomes apparent that their – indirect – influence on the final outcome of the award is much more prominent than one would initially have suggested. The reason for this lies in the fact that the battlefield where human rights actually unfold their force is not to be found on the main stage of the merits – here, as I have demonstrated in 1., Tribunals at least until the present date have hardly accepted any human rights arguments – except when it comes to what the dispute is eventually all about: compensation. This pattern is most obvious in the *Biwater* and *Azurix* cases. While the argumentations revolving around the right to water failed on the merits stage, the arbitrators then considerably reduced compensation (*Azurix*) or denied compensation at all (*Biwater*), basing their argumentation on *topoi* similar to those they had declined to adopt regarding the merits. As a side note, in the end this comes quite close to the result of applying the Global Public Interest theory – albeit without the doctrinal and theoretical underpinning and in a quite contorted manner.

In *Biwater*, the Tribunal found that the loss in value of the investment was not caused by the investor rights violations committed by the host State, for it was BGT's miscalculations that failed taking into account the adjustments necessary in the Dar es Salaam water system and the limits regarding licit increase of water prices.[177] Similarly, the *Azurix* Tribunal denied the investor recouping the US$438.6 million canon payment because a reasonable businessperson would have been in no position to expect recovery of the entire canon given the limits of water price increase and the renovation necessary to guarantee a well-functioning and clean water system.[178] Differently put, in both cases the Tribunals' arguments can be boiled down to the following: The investor is only entitled to compensation within the limits of what it can expect to recoup when warranting a well-functioning, clean water system to affordable prices for everyone, i.e. within the limits of the core principles of the right to water.

However, the *Glamis* award is a good example for demonstrating that the indirect influence of human rights considerations is beginning to stretch beyond the confines of compensation. The Tribunal, strictly harking

[177] *Biwater* v. *Tanzania*, paras. 786 ff. [178] *Azurix* v. *Argentina*, para. 426.

back to the *Neer* case of 1926 to determine the international minimum standard of treatment according to Article 1105 NAFTA, appears to indirectly honor human rights and other public interest considerations as outlined in the Quechuan Non-Party Submission.

Hence, one is tempted to ask: What is all the fuss about? Why do the Tribunals say one thing – explicitly brushing away human rights arguments by the host State – and actually do another – granting them entrance through the back door by choosing overly strict standards or reducing or denying compensation? One reason I have already given: The lack of doctrinal and theoretical foundation for human rights considerations in the Tribunals' argumentation and thus their fear of exceeding their powers by going beyond what the parties have consented to. This, however, merely explains why Tribunals do not explicitly and directly consider human rights. It does not explain why they nonetheless do so implicitly and indirectly. In my opinion, the answer is quite simple: Because they see themselves confronted with deciding Global Public Law disputes involving questions of Global Public Interest they cannot disregard. They start to acknowledge that their role goes beyond that of mere arbiters of private issues.

The second reason why Tribunals start to indirectly adopt human rights considerations is interwoven with the publicness of the dispute and leads me to my last observation.

3. *Growing role of third parties*

With the disputes being arbitrated before investment Tribunals growing in relevance for the public and thus stretching far beyond a private law relationship to Global Public Interest issues of sometimes pivotal importance, it is not only the Tribunals understanding and reacting to such relevance. As several disputes serve as prime examples, for example *Glamis* or the pending *Foresti* cases, third party submissions by private interest groups from civil society or international non-governmental organizations are proliferating.[179] Moreover, even if the Tribunal declines the submission of *amicus curiae* briefs or any other form of statements by non-parties, the public pressure is undeniable as is its influence on both the arbitrators and the parties, as the "Cochabamba Water Wars" give impressive testimony.[180] The stronger such participation – by one way or

[179] See *supra* 7 B. 2. (a) (iii), (iv). [180] See *supra* 7 B. 2. (b) (ii).

another – of third parties grows, the more interdependent the "public" and the conduct of the parties before, during and after the proceedings and the outcome of the arbitral award will become.

4. The case law on human rights in the light of the Global Public Interest theory

The field of human rights is undoubtedly the most controversial Global Public Interest issue in international investment law, mainly – albeit not exclusively – because of its high profile in both the media and public opinion. The rush to, and pressure for, *amicus curiae* submissions and other ways of third party participation bear witness to such fact. However, as holds true in law as in ordinary life, the one making the loudest noise is not always the one with the strongest position. Without question, human rights more than any other issue epitomize the Global Public Interest within the architecture of a value-oriented system of public international law spotlighting the human being.[181] Hence, protection of their core principles is of utmost importance. On the other hand, a too proactive approach risks overstretching the investment régime. Therefore, the Global Public Interest theory deliberately allows only for raising such Global Public Interests that have crystallized into general principles and customary international law.

This is what constitutes the major challenge vis-à-vis the current case law on human rights: There are an impressive number of disputes in which the parties or the Tribunal raised human rights issues or referred to human rights jurisprudence. However, either those human rights allegations were overly broad, unfounded or – as regards the disputes involving the right to water – related to human rights issues that might have found resonance under international human rights treaty régimes but have not (yet) been condensed into customary international law norms or general principles of law.

Again, this might appear highly unsatisfactory, particularly considering the prominence of human rights (contentions) on the global stage. Nonetheless, this does not change the fact that we have not yet encountered an investment dispute involving customary international human rights law or even *ius cogens*, such as indicated in the hypothetical on human rights at 5 H. 2.; or that the right to water lacks both the coherent practice and *opinio iuris* to be considered a norm of customary

[181] See *supra* 4 A. 2. (b), (c).

international law. Thus, surprisingly and to some even disappointingly, the current case law on human rights would not have been decided differently according to the Global Public Interest theory, since no allegation meets its threshold, i.e. that the asserted public interest can be pegged to a customary norm or a general principle.

8 Corruption and other irregularities

A. How bad is corruption?

Nowadays, it has become almost conventional wisdom that corruption[1] is the scourge of economic development.[2] This has not always been the case. Until the 1960s many economists argued that corruption helped to foster efficiency in weak and poorly functioning States.[3] Rightly, such "greasing-the-wheel" arguments belong to the past.[4] A World Bank survey in 2002 estimated that bribes totaling US$ 1 trillion are paid annually.[5] While it is detrimental enough that this enormous sum is lost for the public benefit – particularly in low-income economies – revenue costs are only one of many negative dimensions of corruption. For the sake of the present analysis, I will confine myself to briefly describing those economic and political dimensions which I deem the most important and most relevant.

1 This chapter draws on parts of A. Kulick and C. Wendler, "A Corrupt Way to Handle Corruption? Thoughts on the Recent ICSID Case Law on Corruption," *Legal Issues of Economic Integration*, 37 (2010), 61–86.

2 See the famous quote of Benjamin Franklin, "There is no kind of dishonesty into which otherwise good people more easily and frequently fall, than that of defrauding the government," from "'F. B.': On Smuggling," *The London Chronicle*, November 21–24, 1767 (draft), available at http://franklinpapers.org/franklin/framedVolumes.jsp.

3 See N. Leff, "Economic Development Through Bureaucratic Corruption," *American Behavioral Scientist*, 8 (1964), 8.

4 On the philosophical and ethical dimensions of corruption, particularly the two prevalent models explaining why bribery is ethically wrong, see S. R. Salbu, "Transnational Bribery: The Big Questions," *Nw. J. Int'l L. & Bus.*, 21 (2001), 435 at 439 ff.

5 See S. Rose-Ackerman, "Governance and Corruption" in B. Lornberg (ed.), *Global Crises, Global Solutions* (Cambridge University Press, 2004), p. 301.

New Institutional Economics[6] identifies the transaction costs corruption entails, i.e. "costs that occur as a consequence of exchanging services or goods for a return."[7] First of all, advantages retained from corruption are not legally enforceable and thus always implicate the potential risk of non- or poor performance, which in turn reduces the reliability of the business relationship.[8] A second category of transaction costs are the costs for finding and concealing trustworthy partners for collaboration. Since it is impossible to openly search for public officials that are both reliable and corrupt, considerable sums have to be paid for retaining the information needed.[9] Thirdly, given the illegality of their deal, the partners to a corrupt pact are bound to each other and may easily become mutually dependent, which again may lead to an increase in costs, particularly if the public official decides to blackmail the other side – or vice versa.[10] Those transaction costs are expenses the enterprise has to bear – money that the company could have invested in its facilities or to expand its business. Moreover, reduced predictability in business relationships due to a high level of corruption may slow down investments in the country or even provide an incentive to invest elsewhere.

As regards the political or social dimension of corruption, obviously the most detrimental of effects is inefficiency: A company succeeds in a tender not because it offers the best deal, or it gets approval for its project not because it fulfills the legal conditions required, etc. but because it pays the highest bribe. The social costs of graft pertain to the fact that the bribe induces public officials "to favor those who are willing to pay over the general public."[11] This, in turn, may not only undermine the

[6] See in particular the work of Douglass North: D. C. North, "Understanding Economic Change" in J. M. Nelson, C. Tilly and L. Walker (eds.), *Transforming Post-Communist Political Economies* (National Academy Press, 1997), p. 13; *Understanding the Process of Institutional Change* (Princeton University Press, 2005). For a general overview see C. Menard and M. Shirley (eds.), *Handbook of New Institutional Economics* (Edward Elgar, 2005). On the foundations of New Institutional Economics see H. Demsetz, "Information and Efficiency: Another Viewpoint," *Journal of Law and Economics*, 12 (1969), 1 building on the work of Ronald Coase, particularly the Coase theorem: see R. Coase, "The Nature of the Firm," *Economica*, 4 (1937), 386.

[7] J. Graf Lambsdorff, "What Nurtures Corrupt Deals? On the Role of Confidence and Transaction Costs" in D. Della Porta and S. Rose-Ackerman (eds.), *Corrupt Exchanges: Empirical Themes in the Politics and Political Economy of Corruption* (Nomos Verlagsgesellschaft, 2002), p. 20.

[8] *Ibid.*, p. 21. [9] *Ibid.* [10] *Ibid.*

[11] D. Della Porta and S. Rose-Ackerman, "Corrupt Exchanges: An Introduction" in D. Della Porta and S. Rose-Ackerman (eds.), *Corrupt Exchanges*, 1 at 5.

legitimacy of the government[12] but constitutes a major challenge to the Global Public Interest.

B. Forms of corruption, definitions and international instruments

1. *"Hard corruption" and "influence peddling"*

Before I delve into the analysis of international investment case law on corruption and other irregularities, I have to take a brief glance at the international instruments dealing with corruption and related issues. This requires, at the outset, clarifying the terminology we are dealing with. Quite frequently, international instruments differentiate between so-called "hard corruption" to public officials and "influence peddling." According to Article 1.1 of the OECD Convention on Combating Bribery of Foreign Public Officials in International Business Transactions, "hard corruption" is:

> intentionally to offer, promise or give any undue pecuniary or other advantage, whether directly or through intermediaries, to a foreign public official, for that official or for a third party, in order that the official act or refrain from acting in relation to the performance of official duties, in order to obtain or retain business or other improper advantage in the conduct of international business.[13]

Thus, "hard corruption" requires an intentional act pursued with the purpose of influencing a public official in the performance of his or her official duties, which in turn is directed at gaining an undue business advantage. As detrimental as "hard corruption," "influence peddling" means:

> the promising, giving or offering, directly or indirectly, of any undue advantage to anyone who asserts or confirms that he or she is able to exert an improper influence over the decision-making of any [public official] in consideration thereof, whether the undue advantage is for himself or herself or for anyone else, as well as the request, receipt or the acceptance of the offer or the promise of such an advantage, in consideration of that influence, whether or not the influence is exerted or whether or not the supposed influence leads to the intended result.[14]

12 For a different view that shows deep skepticism vis-à-vis what he calls "the international anti-corruption campaign" see D. Kennedy, "The International Anti-Corruption Campaign," *Conn. J. Int'l L.*, 14 (1999), 455.

13 OECD Convention on Combating Bribery of Foreign Public Officials in International Business Transactions, November 21, 1997 (hereinafter: OECD Convention on Combating Bribery), available at www.oecd.org/document/21/0,3343,en_2649_34859_2017813_1_1_1_1,00.html.

14 See Art. 12, Criminal Law Convention, Council of Europe, January 27, 1999, at http://conventions.coe.int/Treaty/EN/Treaties/Html/173.htm.

Briefly put, "influence peddling" seeks to oust improperly influencing the decision-making process of public officials by offering any undue advantage in exchange. In contrast to "hard corruption," the bribe does not necessarily have to be paid for a specific conduct. While it is nothing else but a variation of "hard corruption," a consensus to criminalize such conduct was more difficult to achieve, at least on the OECD platform, because "influence peddling" is not covered by the OECD Convention on Combating Bribery of Foreign Public Officials in International Business Transactions. However, the subsequent analysis underlies a broader definition of corruption and thus does not merely include "hard corruption" but "influence peddling" as well.

2. *International instruments*

(a) OECD Convention on Combating Bribery of Foreign Public Officials in International Business Transactions

Still the most comprehensive international treaty specifically targeted at corruption, the OECD Convention on Combating Bribery of Foreign Public Officials in International Business Transactions[15] was an ambitious project even at the time of its adoption on November 21, 1997. While corruption and bribery have been on the OECD agenda since the mid-1970s, it was not until 1989 that a working group of legal experts started to convene on the issue, which resulted in the 1994 Recommendation on Bribery in International Business Transactions and in a Revised Recommendation as of May 1997 – which provided the foundation of the said Convention in late 1997.[16] As of July 2009, the Convention has thirty-eight signatories, including all thirty OECD Member States as well as Argentina, Brazil, Bulgaria, Chile, Estonia, Israel, Slovenia, and South Africa.

The approach the Convention takes vis-à-vis fighting corruption is by obliging the contracting parties to criminalize bribery of foreign public officials. It thus only focuses on so-called "active bribery," i.e. the act of bribing officials, and thus does not address "passive bribery" (the act of taking the bribe).[17] Article 1.1 of the Convention reads as follows:

[15] See OECD Convention on Combating Bribery.

[16] See P. Van den Bossche, "A 'Normal' Business Practice Becomes a Criminal Offence – The 1997 OECD Convention on Combating Bribery of Foreign Public Officials in International Business Transactions" in M. Bronckers (ed.), *New Directions in International Economic Law – Essays in Honour of John H. Jackson* (Kluwer Academic Publishers, 2000), p. 441 at p. 443.

[17] See *ibid.*, p. 445.

> Each Party shall take such measures as may be necessary to establish that it is a criminal offence under its law for any person intentionally to offer, promise or give any undue pecuniary or other advantage, whether directly or through intermediaries, to a foreign public official, for that official or for a third party, in order that the official act or refrain from acting in relation to the performance of official duties, in order to obtain or retain business or other improper advantage in the conduct of international business.

Thus, even merely offering or promising an undue pecuniary or other advantage constitutes corruption and needs to be criminalized by the State parties. Such obligation expands to acts of complicity, incitement, aiding and abetting, authorization and attempt as well as conspiracy.[18] What the Convention does not cover are so-called "grease payments," i.e. "small payments made to induce public officials to perform functions that are part of their routine duties,"[19] for they are not directed at obtaining or retaining improper advantages, as Article 1.1 requires.

As regards sanctions, the Convention obliges the parties to provide for punishment of those responsible for or involved in the bribery by effective, proportionate and dissuasive criminal penalties.[20] While it does not stipulate what exactly such penalties should look like, they must correspond to and equal the penalties for bribery of domestic officials. Moreover, the State parties must ensure that the bribe and any improper advantage derived from the payment of the bribe will be seized and confiscated.[21] Finally, investigation and prosecution of bribery shall not be influenced by considerations of national economic interest, the potential effect upon relations with another State or the identity of the persons involved.[22]

The Convention's direct relevance in the investment context is rather limited, given (1) that only a small number of ICSID Members – albeit encompassing the vast majority of investment exporting countries – are also parties to the OECD Convention, and considering (2) that it deals with the criminalization of bribes in the home countries of the investors, whereas investment disputes center on the investor's treatment by the host State. Thus, its relevance is more to be found in its role as an indicator of the growing concern and action of the international community vis-à-vis corruption as an international public policy concern.

[18] See *ibid.*, pp. 445, 446. [19] *Ibid.*, p. 447. [20] Art. 3.1.

[21] Art. 3.3. The Commentary to Art. 3.3 speaks in this regard of "'proceeds' of bribery," i.e. "profits or other benefits derived by the briber from the transaction or other improper advantage obtained or retained through bribery."

[22] Art. 5.

(b) Criminal Law Convention on Corruption of the Council of Europe

Another document that may have such rather indirect effect on international investment law jurisprudence is the Criminal Law Convention on Corruption of the Council of Europe.[23] As the name indicates, the document is regionally limited – however, it should not be forgotten what applies equally to the aforesaid OECD Convention, namely that the Member States constitute the lion's share of capital exporting countries, except of course the USA and Japan.

However, the Criminal Law Convention on Corruption is much broader in scope than the OECD Convention: It extends to domestic public officials as well as officials, judges and members of parliament in international institutions and also criminalizes bribery in the private sector.[24] Moreover, Member States must penalize influence peddling, money laundering and any participatory act.[25] As regards sanctions, the Convention provides for the same mechanisms as the OECD Convention, i.e. effective, proportionate and dissuasive sanctions and measures as well as confiscating or otherwise depriving the instrumentalities and proceeds of criminal offences established in accordance with the Convention, or property the value of which corresponds to such proceeds.[26]

Again, note that the Convention only obliges States to take measures under their domestic law to penalize various forms of corruption, and thus does not establish direct obligations vis-à-vis corruption in the international relationship of the host State and the investor. Nonetheless, as does the OECD Convention, it qualifies as a strong international public policy indicator.[27]

(c) BIT provisions relevant in corruption cases

Before I engage in an analysis of the relevant international investment case law on corruption, I would like – for the sake of a better understanding – to point at provisions in an international instrument the relevance of which for the present analysis is pivotal. BITs are, as the name indicates, bilateral treaties and thus their content may vary.[28] There are, however, a couple of clauses that almost every BIT contains – among them the definition of "investment" and the consent to investment arbitration before

[23] Criminal Law Convention on Corruption of the Council of Europe, Strasbourg, January 21, 1999, at http://conventions.coe.int/treaty/en/Treaties/Html/173.htm.

[24] See *ibid.*, Arts. 2–11. [25] Arts. 12–15. [26] Art. 19. [27] See *supra* 8 B. 2. (a).

[28] See 2 A.

(usually) various fora. Under ICSID arbitration, both clauses relate to each other, for Article 25 ICSID states that the jurisdiction of ICSID extends to any legal dispute arising out of an investment, which the parties consent to submit to a Tribunal. It leaves open what exactly should be deemed an investment – a deliberate decision to give leeway to BIT parties to define the term. Hence, if the share or asset in the dispute does not qualify as "investment" as defined in the BIT, the host State's consent to ICSID arbitration – usually given by way of a general consent in the BIT – does not cover such share or asset.

Most BIT definitions of "investment" include an "accordance with the laws of the host State" clause, which excludes any investment that has been made illegally under the domestic law of the host State. The idea behind such provision is obvious: Host States do not want such investments to benefit from the protections granted under the BIT that they do not permit according to their own laws. Since corruption is illegal under almost any domestic legal order, thus jurisdiction usually constitutes a heavily disputed issue in ICSID (and other international investment law) cases that involve allegations of corruption.

C. Corruption disputes in international investment law

1. *Distinguish two different types of corruption disputes*

Before I enter the analysis of international investment case law on corruption and other irregularities, it has to be noted that we can distinguish two different types of corruption disputes,[29] only one of which is relevant for the present analysis. The first category pertains to the investor–host State relationship, i.e. involves a dispute over the investment contract and/or the protections granted under a BIT. Here, the validity of the investment contract and the applicability of the BIT – including its jurisdiction clause – are the central issues. This analysis will exclusively focus on such type of cases.

To be distinguished from investor–host State arbitration, many disputes arise between the investor and its intermediaries about the validity, application and interpretation of the agency agreement. Such cases occur very frequently, for "[i]nvestors hardly ever commit illicit activities themselves. In the majority of cases they contract intermediaries . . . to

[29] See H. Raeschke-Kessler and D. Gottwald, "Corruption" in P. Muchlinski, F. Ortino and C. Schreuer (eds.), *The Oxford Handbook of International Investment Law* (Oxford University Press, 2008), p. 584 at pp. 591 ff.

act on their behalf. The advantages for the investor are obvious: he does not have to lose face to anyone, and leaves the 'dirty work' to others."[30] However, after the host State has awarded the project to the investor, the investor refuses to pay the commission fee, alleging that the agency agreement was invalid *ab initio* since its objective was illicit, i.e. to bribe foreign officials.[31] Such dispute involves litigation or arbitration between two private parties – hence differing considerably from the first type – and will therefore not be subject matter of the present analysis.[32]

2. *International investment case law pertaining to corruption and other irregularities*

While until very recently corruption did not play a relevant role in international investment law, in the past couple of years it has accrued to considerable prominence. The subsequent analysis does not merely aim at tracing such development but also seeks to critically scrutinize the Tribunals' reasoning and discuss alternatives to the path chosen in the respective cases. I will commence with briefly mentioning two cases, which predate the prominence of corruption (a) and then concentrate on one case that I deem very instructive for the understanding of the complexities of the issues involved (b). The case law following at (c) to (e) will be employed to further illustrate such observations before I enter into my final analysis of the matter in D.

(a) *Wena* v. *Egypt* and *SGS* v. *Pakistan*

For a very long period in investment arbitration, Tribunals have been myopic if not ignorant vis-à-vis allegations of corruption. While it does not find any mention in the vast majority of investment cases, one of the first disputes where it was at least addressed by one of the parties was *Wena* v. *Egypt* in 2002 – a case we have already encountered earlier.[33] However, the Tribunal did not consider it relevant for the issues involved to engage in considerations on the impact of corruption on international investment law.[34]

In *SGS Société Générale de Surveillance SA* v. *Islamic Republic of Pakistan*,[35] decided August 6, 2003, the Tribunal acknowledged the potential legal

30 *Ibid.*, p. 592. 31 *Ibid*, p. 593.

32 On corruption in agency agreement disputes, see M. Scherer, "Circumstantial Evidence in Corruption before International Tribunals," *International Arbitration Law Review*, 5 (2002), 29.

33 See *supra* 2 D. 4. 34 *Wena* v. *Egypt*, para. 46.

35 *SGS Société Générale de Surveillance SA* v. *Islamic Republic of Pakistan* (ICSID Case No. ARB/01/13), Award, August 6, 2003 (hereinafter: *SGS* v. *Pakistan*).

relevance of corruption in an investment dispute, particularly regarding consent to jurisdiction according to Article 25 ICSID and the respective clause in the Swiss–Pakistani BIT. However, it refrained from addressing the issue in a detailed way and left it open given that insufficient evidence prevented exhaustive evaluation of the issue.[36]

(b) *World Duty Free* v. *Republic of Kenya*

(i) Facts and issues

The next case under scrutiny, *World Duty Free* v. *Kenya*, paints the picture of a classical corruption scenario, involving the host country's highest ranking officer, i.e. its President, and unfolding a scandal that eventually led to the incremental erosion of his reputation and eventually to him losing the 2002 elections to Mr. Mwai Kibaki.[37] The facts are quite straightforward:[38] In 1989, Mr. Nasir Ibrahim Ali, a Dubai businessman and owner and general manager of The House of Perfume – which was later renamed World Duty Free – sought to expand his business of selling perfume and other duty free articles in airport facilities in Africa, particularly the airports of Nairobi and Mombasa, the two biggest cities in Kenya. While his offer to the Kenyan authorities foresaw that he would develop the airport facilities to high-class standards, the staff of the office of the President of Kenya insinuated that Mr. Ali's project would only be considered favorably if he made a "personal donation" to the President himself, Mr. Daniel arap Moi. According to the testimony of Mr. Ali – not disputed by Kenya – he was led to believe that such proceeding was required by Kenyan protocol and that without the "donation" he could not meet the President in person, which in return meant that his project would fail. Mr. Ali accordingly made the "personal donation" of US$ 2 million to President Moi and received approval for his project. Subsequently, World Duty Free and the Republic of Kenya, due to the lack of a BIT between the United Arab Emirates and the Republic of Kenya,[39] concluded an investment contract.

After having developed the airport facilities and having run the duty free area for some time, Mr. Ali, beginning in 1992, encountered a series of setbacks. That year it became apparent that Mr. Pattni, close counselor to President Moi and owner of the company Goldenberg International

[36] See *ibid.*, paras. 141–143 and n. 163 of the Award.

[37] "Kenya's Ruling Party is Defeated After 39 Years," *The New York Times*, December 30, 2002, available at www.nytimes.com/2002/12/30/world.

[38] *World Duty Free Company Limited* v. *the Republic of Kenya* (ICSID Case No. Arb/00/7), Award of the Tribunal, October 6, 2006 (hereinafter: *World Duty Free* v. *Kenya*); see paras. 62 ff.

[39] *Ibid.*, para. 24.

Ltd., had committed massive fraud by forging false contracts between Goldenberg and World Duty Free as a consignee of (non-existent) gold and diamonds, in order to raise money for Moi's re-election campaign. The estimated overall sum of this forgery and fraud campaign amounted to approximately US$ 438 million. Allegedly and again not disputed by Kenya, Mr. Ali was neither involved in nor aware of Mr. Pattni's misconduct. When Mr. Pattni's perpetrations began to trickle down to the public, he sought to take control of World Duty Free Kenya – in order to cover up his crimes – supported by judgments of Kenyan courts, which decided in Mr. Pattni's favor based on forged documents. Any appeal was initially declined. Direct evidence, however, that Mr. Pattni acted as the agent of the Kenyan government could not be presented.

(ii) Commercial arbitration rationales in investment arbitration?

First and foremost, the Tribunal determined in abundant clarity that the "personal donation" must undoubtedly be considered a bribe, although the claimant asserted the local Kenyan custom of Harambee, a kind of collective contribution toward individual or communal activities, in order to justify his behavior.[40] Having clarified that matter, the Tribunal went on to identify corruption as a breach of international public policy. While it sought to differentiate between international public policy as (1) a domestic principle of law that is universally accepted in all legal orders but the content of which may vary among the different orders, and (2) a principle of international law, the Tribunal left it somewhat in the obscure on which of the two types of international public policy it founded its reasoning. Relying on several international commercial arbitration awards, the Tribunal specifically cited Judge Lagergren in ICC Case No. 1110:

> After weighing all the evidence I am convinced that a case such as this, involving such gross violation of good morals and international public policy, can have no countenance in any court... nor in any arbitral Tribunal. Thus, jurisdiction must be declined in this case. It follows from the foregoing, that in concluding that I have no jurisdiction, guidance has been sought from general principles denying arbitrators to entertain disputes of this nature rather than from any national rules on arbitrability. Parties who ally themselves in an enterprise of the present nature must realise that they have forfeited any right to ask for assistance of the machinery of justice (national courts or arbitral Tribunals) in settling their disputes.[41]

[40] See *World Duty Free* v. *Kenya*, paras. 131, 134.
[41] ICC Case No. 1110 (1963), *Arbitration International*, (1994), 277.

In other words, corruption violates the *bones mores*, both on the domestic and the international stage, as evinced by several international instruments that sanction corruption,[42] and thus an arbitral Tribunal has to decline jurisdiction, for "assistance of the machinery of justice" shall not be granted to such blatant disregard of decency and good practice in international (commercial) relations. Similarly, English law, being applicable by the choice of the parties according to Article 42(1) first sentence ICSID, denies jurisdiction based on the principle that nobody shall profit from his or her own criminal behavior – *ex dolo malo non oritur actio.*[43]

Moreover, the Tribunal declined to give leeway to World Duty Free's contention that the Kenyan government, by way of its most senior officer, was seriously involved in the corruption malpractice, indeed solicited it in the first place.[44] Declining to balance the perpetrations of Mr. Ali with the actions of President Moi, the Tribunal stated that it "[did] not identify the Kenyan President with Kenya"[45] and thus did not consider any kind of attribution. Consequently, jurisdiction was declined.

(iii) Why the Tribunal got it wrong

While the outcome of the award, denial of jurisdiction, may not be totally surprising, it is the reasoning that provokes some serious skepticism. There are basically four aspects that the Tribunal either neglects or in which its reasoning is rather dubious: (1) the transferability of principles from commercial to investment arbitration; (2) the rules of State responsibility on attribution of actions by State organs; (3) the addressee and overall purpose of international public policy; and (4) the principle of unjust enrichment. I will now address all four issues.

As stated before, the Tribunal rests a major part of its reasoning on drawing on international commercial arbitration awards that identify corruption as a violation of international public policy.[46] While reference to commercial arbitration is quite common among investment Tribunals – and quite naturally so, given that the ICSID Convention built on the international commercial arbitration system,[47] not to mention that many investment disputes come before the fora of UNCITRAL, the ICC, etc. – some major differences between the two systems should not

[42] See, for example, Art. V.2 of the New York Convention of 1958 or Art. 36 UNCITRAL.

[43] See *World Duty Free* v. *Kenya*, para. 161; see also paras. 148 ff.

[44] *Ibid.*, para. 180. [45] *Ibid.*, para. 178. [46] *Ibid.*, para. 161.

[47] See G. Cordero Moss, "Commercial Arbitration and Investment Arbitration: Fertile Soil for False Friends?" in C. Binder *et al.* (eds.), *International Investment Law for the 21st Century – Essays in Honour of Christoph Schreuer* (Oxford University Press, 2009), p. 782 at p. 791.

be overlooked. To name but the most obvious, in commercial arbitration the parties are legal peers, two private entities that must pursue their interests via litigation or arbitration and can or at least shall not act unilaterally. By contrast, the relationship of the two parties in an investment dispute is not horizontal but rather vertical: The investor is a private entity, whereas its arbitral opponent is a sovereign State that at least has the power – even if it may not always have the right – to pursue its own interests unilaterally.[48] Such asymmetry,[49] i.e. the simple fact that the other party is invested with *puissance publique*, changes the relationship among the parties and thus the nature of the dispute entirely: As has been demonstrated above,[50] international investment arbitration describes a (Global) Public Law type claim that aims at controlling the exercise of public authority – which constitutes a fundamental difference to the exclusively private law relationship among the legal peers of a commercial arbitration proceeding.

Therefore, while denying jurisdiction in a commercial arbitration dispute is an effective sanction against both the claimant and the respondent, for very often both sides have interests at stake and since they cannot pursue their interests unilaterally, under investment arbitration the situation is quite the contrary. Here, declining jurisdiction is detrimental exclusively for the investor. It, in contrast to the host State, needs the arbitration proceeding to pursue its interests. In fact, considering Article 27 ICSID prohibiting recourse to diplomatic protection, the arbitral proceeding is its only chance to receive justice. The host State, again,

[48] In this regard, it is nothing but cynical – or misconstrues the main characteristic of an investment dispute – when the *World Duty Free* Tribunal argues that its decision is not specifically directed against World Duty Free but declines to arbitrate a dispute infected by corruption simply because of the fact of the corruption itself rather than who has committed it. Saying "in other words, if Kenya were guilty of bribery and the claimant in this proceeding, it would likewise fall at the same procedural hurdle, to the benefit of the Claimant as Respondent" (*World Duty Free* v. *Kenya*, para. 181) ignores the fact that in investment arbitration – and different to commercial arbitration – the respondent, i.e. the host State, will hardly ever find itself in the position to be the claimant. Other than a private entity, it does not need an arbitral Tribunal to pursue its interests – it simply acts unilaterally in its sovereign capacity. In fact, most investment arbitration mechanisms do not even provide for the host State's access to arbitration.

[49] See on this issue and other features that distinguish investment arbitration from commercial arbitration P. Kahn and T. Wälde, *Les Aspects nouveaux du Droit des Investissements Internationaux/New Aspects of International Investment Law*, Hague Academy of International Law – Centre for Studies and Research in International Law and International Relations 2004 (Martinus Nijhoff Publishers, 2006), pp. 76–91.

[50] See *supra* 4 A. 3.

does not depend on arbitration;[51] it can always use its public authority to achieve its goals and just take what it seeks.

Thus, although – it is most obvious in the case at hand – considerably often both sides will be involved and thus carry responsibility for the corruption, the result of the Tribunal's reasoning in *World Duty Free* is, simply put, that it is exclusively one side, i.e. the investor, that experiences the detrimental effects of declining jurisdiction. As a matter of consequence, the host State on the contrary is rather privileged since given that no arbitration claim is admissible concerning this investment, for the Tribunal regards the investment itself as infected with corruption and thus no licit basis for an arbitration proceeding, the host State gets a carte blanche. It is practically invited to abuse its already strong position as a sovereign power to do as it pleases with the investment. Such consequences, however, are not merely coincidental to the denial of jurisdiction; they lie at the very core of the investment arbitration system itself. Transferring premises and principles from commercial arbitration to investment arbitration, hence, is more than dubious, at least as regards the particular matter before us. In fact, it leads to undermining the spirit and the main purpose of international investment law, which is to provide investors with an effective instrument with which to defend themselves against infringements of their rights by the host State by enabling them to initiate a legalized arbitration procedure before an international and independent Tribunal, or, in other words, to prevent the host State from exploiting its sovereign authority.

Getting to the second issue to be scrutinized, the aforementioned criticism would be less viable if the actions by President Moi could not be linked to the Republic of Kenya. Differently put, if the Tribunal were right that taking the bribe is an action not attributable to Kenya, or in the words of the Tribunal that "the Kenyan President [cannot be identified] with Kenya."[52] Indeed, if Kenya as the host State were not involved in the corruption that led the Tribunal to decline jurisdiction, it would be fair to sanction the sole perpetrator, i.e. the investor. This is basically the line of argumentation followed by the Tribunal. However, such view hardly conforms with the public international law rules on State responsibility.

Applying the ILC Articles on State Responsibility draws a different picture. Article 4 is clear and simple:

[51] As a matter of fact, under most arbitration mechanisms it does not even have access to it.

[52] See *World Duty Free* v. *Kenya*, para. 178.

Article 4: Conduct of organs of State

1. The conduct of any State organ shall be considered an act of that State under international law, whether the organ exercises legislative, executive, judicial or any other functions, whatever position it holds in the organization of the State, and whatever its character as an organ of the central government or of a territorial unit of the State.
2. An organ includes any person or entity which has that status in accordance with the internal law of the State.

The President is head of the Executive, maybe the most prominent, clearly the most powerful State organ under the Kenyan Constitution. States, as all juridical persons by the way, are legal fictions and cannot act themselves, but need to act through organs, the actions of which are generally attributable. While the Tribunal implicitly applies this rule vis-à-vis World Duty Free and Mr. Ali as its agent, it refrains to do the same vis-à-vis the Republic of Kenya and President Moi. Even an excess of authority, as Article 7 ILC makes abundantly clear, does not prevent the attribution, if the organ acts in its official capacity. While taking bribes is not within the authority of a President and the *pot-de-vin* was denominated "personal donation," it was targeted at influencing the President's official decision on a procurement contract – which it obviously did. Thus, it is hard to understand how, under the rules of State responsibility, which are generally applicable in an investor–state dispute – at least vis-à-vis the host State[53] – the Tribunal could come to say that President Moi's actions are not attributable to the respondent, the Republic of Kenya.

As regards the third issue, the Tribunal argues that the purpose of the "laws" and thus the purpose of denying jurisdiction are to protect not the parties but the public.[54] In other words, according to the Tribunal, the purpose of international public policy is to protect the public[55] from the detrimental consequences of illicit activities such as corruption. However, this award does not protect the public, i.e. "the mass of tax-payers and other citizens making up one of the poorest countries in the world,"[56] for

[53] See K. Hobér, "State Responsibility and Attribution" in P. Muchlinski, F. Ortino and C. Schreuer, *The Oxford Handbook of International Investment Law* (Oxford University Press, 2008), p. 549 at p. 554.

[54] See *World Duty Free* v. *Kenya*, para. 181. An interesting dictum, by the way, which is not necessarily the view in international commercial arbitration, which always stresses the prominent role of the principle of party autonomy.

[55] The Tribunal appears to understand "public" as the *polis* of the host State, i.e. basically Kenyan society; see *World Duty Free* v. *Kenya*, para. 181.

[56] *Ibid.*

it actually encourages corrupt officials, which according to these findings do not have to fear any consequences at all from their illicit conduct. This is neither the case internally and personally, at least as long as they are in power, nor internationally and vis-à-vis the host State itself, for the latter de facto receives the investment when the Tribunal denies jurisdiction.[57] Thus, instead of discouraging corruption as a widespread practice by government officials, overall it actually furthers such behavior, for corruption at least from the viewpoint of the host State has no repercussions while it allows reaping of all the benefits of the investment made in consequence of the corruption.

Finally, the award ignores that its findings mean that the host State remains unjustly enriched: Following the Tribunal's line of argumentation, since the corruption infringed the *ordre public*, the investment contract is null and void. This, in turn, would usually trigger the obligation to re-transfer the investment, which, however, cannot be claimed if the Tribunal denied jurisdiction in the first place. Consequently, the Tribunal's reasoning even disregards the principle of unjust enrichment.[58]

(c) *Inceysa* v. *El Salvador*

The next case that deserves some more detailed scrutiny is *Inceysa Vallisoletana, SL* v. *Republic of El Salvador*, some aspects of which I have already discussed in Chapter 4.[59] However, in this part the focus will be put on the way the Tribunal dealt with Inceysa's illicit behavior.

(i) Facts and issues

Regarding the facts in *Inceysa*, while seeking to avoid repeating myself too much, let me recapitulate briefly: In 1999, the El Salvadorian Ministry of the Environment and Natural Resources (MARN) issued an invitation to tender for contracting mechanical inspection services for vehicles throughout El Salvador. Later, it was discovered that Inceysa Vallisoletana, SL, who eventually won the public procurement contract, had committed massive fraud in order to improve its chances in the tender. In particular it had: (1) submitted false financial statements; (2) forged documents

57 See *supra* in this subsection.

58 C. Schreuer, "Unjustified Enrichment in International Law," *Am. J. Comp. L.*, 22 (1974), 281; W. Friedmann, "The Uses of 'General Principles' in the Development of International Law," *Am. J. Int'l L.*, 57 (1963), 279 at 295.

59 *Inceysa Vallisoletana, SL* v. *Republic of El Salvador* (ICSID Case No. ARB/03/26), Award, August 2, 2006. See *supra* 4 C. 1. (a).

regarding the experience of Inceysa's administrator; (3) misrepresented Inceysa's experience and reputation in the field of vehicle inspections; (4) submitted forged documents to prove the existence of multimillion dollar contracts in other countries; and (5) obfuscated the association between Inceysa and ICASUR, another participant in the bidding procedure.[60] Subsequently, (1) El Salvador refused to send the initiation order executing the contract; (2) did not provide access to a crucial database and (3) to the legal framework necessary to make the collection and payment system by Inceysa effective; and (4) eventually terminated the contract, which finally led Inceysa to request constituting an Arbitral Tribunal pursuant to Article 37(2)(b) ICSID based on the arbitration clause of Article 11 of the Spain–El Salvador BIT.

(ii) The Tribunal declines jurisdiction

The crucial issue in the eyes of the Tribunal was whether it had jurisdiction *ratione voluntatis* under Article 25 ICSID and Article 11 of the Spain–El Salvador BIT.[61] In short, the Tribunal reasoned that it lacked jurisdiction on two grounds: Firstly, fraud infringes the laws of El Salvador, which in turn means that the investment was not made "in accordance" with such laws and thus did not represent a protected "investment" as defined by Article 1(1) of the Spain–El Salvador BIT. Since the jurisdiction of the Tribunal covers merely such "investments" as defined under Article 1(1) of the BIT, Inceysa had no claim. Secondly, since both the BIT and the ICSID Convention are international treaties, their interpretation has to consider general principles of law as part of public international law, which is applicable according to Article 42(1) ICSID.[62] Hence, several general principles of law, such as the principle of good faith, the principle *nemo audiatur propriam turpitudinem allegans*, international public policy and the prohibition of unjust enrichment prevent Inceysa from having recourse to ICSID arbitration.

(iii) Setting a bad precedent

Refraining from making comments on the potential role of general principles of law,[63] I will limit myself to a brief analysis of the Tribunal's denial of jurisdiction on the grounds of a lack of consent to ICSID arbitration according to Articles 25 ICSID and 11 and 1(1) BIT.

[60] *Inceysa* v. *El Salvador*, para. 53. [61] See also *supra* 4 C. 1. (a). [62] See *supra* 2 E. 2.

[63] On their role according to the Global Public Interest theory in general see *supra* 4 C. 6. On their specific role regarding corruption see also *infra* 8 D. 2. (b) (iii).

When focusing on consent, the question automatically arises as to its scope. The Tribunal argues that, since fraud violates the laws of El Salvador, Inceysa's investment was not protected under BIT Article 1(1) and thus fell outside the scope of consent to ICSID arbitration as under Article 25 ICSID and Article 11 of the Spain–El Salvador BIT. Admittedly, this is – viewed per se – a consistent reasoning. However, we may ask ourselves, can such reasoning be held up in its generality, i.e. that any violation of the laws of the host State leads to the investment not being made "in accordance" with domestic law and thus being excluded from the scope of consent? I want to recall the grotesque argumentation by Ukraine in *Tokios Tokelés*, where it asserted that the Tribunal lacked jurisdiction because the investor registered its subsidiary under the term "subsidiary private enterprise," which is not a recognized legal form under Ukrainian law, as opposed to "subsidiary enterprise."[64] Is such lack of "accordance with the laws" of the host State really a ground on which jurisdiction to ICSID arbitration should be denied? As the answer can be nothing else but negative, we have to conclude that the phrase "in accordance with the laws of the host State" cannot possibly mean that a Tribunal has to decline jurisdiction in case of *any* violation of domestic law. Otherwise, the very purpose of ICSID and any BIT, i.e. to effectively protect investments, would be forfeit given the tremendous uncertainty such interpretation would entail.

This, however, leads to the next question: What kinds of violations qualify as violations that justify declining jurisdiction? While it is obvious that there is a considerable difference between insufficient denomination of a subsidiary and massive fraud, it is very hard if not impossible to discern where exactly to draw the line between those two extremes in future cases, if one endorses the Tribunal's reasoning in *Inceysa*. Without anticipating a detailed analysis of this question below[65] and by just tipping on the issue, one possible solution could be to consider the illegality and its consequences at the merits stage. Otherwise – as I already hinted at while discussing *World Duty Free* – the investor would be excluded from the only way to pursue its interests against the host State, for the denial of jurisdiction is a very blunt instrument that does not allow for differentiation and balanced allocation of responsibilities. However, it has to be asserted here that in this regard there is a major difference between the factual

[64] *Tokios Tokelés* v. *Ukraine* (ICSID Case No. ARB/02/18), Decision on Jurisdiction, 2004, para. 83.
[65] See *infra* 8 D. 2. (b) (iii).

matrix in *Inceysa* as opposed to that in *World Duty Free*, which, I want to foreshadow as much, must find its reflection in an alternative proposal:[66] While it needs two to tango as regards corruption, in case of fraud the exclusive responsibility lies with the investor. The host State, quite frequently bearing major responsibility itself for the bribery, is usually not involved at all in the fraudulent behavior of the investor, at least not in a case like *Inceysa*.

(d) *Fraport* v. *Philippines*

(i) Facts and issues

The next case on my agenda is *Fraport AG Frankfurt Airport Services Worldwide* v. *Republic of the Philippines*.[67] The complexity of the factual matrix is flabbergasting, so I will seek to extract the essence relevant for our analysis at hand. Starting in 1999, Fraport, a leader in the international airport business and owner of the Frankfurt International Airport, had been involved in plans for the construction and operation of Manila International Airport's Terminal 3. In order to advance this project, it had been acquiring – directly or indirectly through its subsidiaries – the majority of shares in PIATCO, a Philippine company, on which the Philippine government conferred the concession rights for construction and operation of Terminal 3. This, however, violated the Anti-Dummy Law of the Philippines, which prohibits – and sanctions as a criminal offence – foreign control of public utility exceeding 40 percent of the shares. Fraport, by contrast, sought full control of PIATCO, although it was perfectly aware that it was attempting to circumvent the laws of the Philippines. When such conduct came to the knowledge of the Filipino officials, they initiated an expropriation proceeding which eventually led Fraport to abandon its plans and thus its investment regarding the Terminal 3 project.

(ii) Again declining jurisdiction

Analyzing this factual matrix, the Tribunal's majority[68] employed reasoning similar to the argumentation chosen by the *Inceysa* Tribunal,[69] albeit with a slight difference. Similarly to the Spain–El Salvador BIT, the BIT between Germany and the Philippines contained a clause defining an "investment" as "any kind of asset *accepted in accordance with the respective*

[66] See *ibid*.

[67] *Fraport AG Frankfurt Airport Services Worldwide* v. *Republic of the Philippines* (ICSID Case No. ARB/03/25), Award, August 16, 2007 (hereinafter: *Fraport* v. *Philippines*).

[68] Mr. Cremades' dissenting opinion will be addressed *infra*.

[69] See *supra* 8 C. 2. (c).

laws and regulations of either Contracting State ..."[70] Similarly, again, the Tribunal declined jurisdiction on the grounds that the investor had violated domestic law, that its "investment" was not protected under the BIT and thus it was not covered by the Philippines' consent to ICSID arbitration according to Article 9 of the BIT and Article 25 ICSID. However, when the Tribunal referred to the principle of good faith as an argumentative *topos* for denying jurisdiction, it refrained from discussing it as a principle of international law and thus as a means to interpret the BIT, but employed it as a principle of domestic law instead.[71]

Of some interest in this regard is Mr. Cremades' dissent, for he concludes that it is the Filipino government that has acted in bad faith. According to Mr. Cremades, the "Respondent in this arbitration escapes from the agreement to arbitrate by asserting the criminal control of a franchise that for four years it has insisted does not exist."[72] In other words, if the concession contract is null and void, it is legally inexistent and thus cannot amount to any control of a public utility, that is criminally sanctioned under the Anti-Dummy Law.

(iii) Following a bad precedent

Although I do not entirely agree with Mr. Cremades' reasoning, it unveils the very argumentative dilemma a Tribunal is confronted with if it chooses to deny jurisdiction on the grounds of a violation of domestic law. While one might argue that Mr. Cremades' argumentation is defective, for otherwise no violation of domestic law would exclude jurisdiction, this is exactly what should be a cause of concern. The analysis how the domestic law of the host State should be interpreted and thus what exactly amounts to a violation of such law is a question that goes to the merits of the case. It should not be dealt with on the jurisdictional stage.

(e) *Kardassopoulos* v. *Georgia*

(i) Facts and issues

The final decision under scrutiny as regards international investment case law, *Ioannis Kardassopoulos* v. *Georgia*,[73] is of particular interest to the

[70] See *Fraport* v. *Philippines*, para. 300.

[71] Which is in contrast to *Inceysa*, in which the Tribunal discussed the principle of good faith, along with other principles, as principles of international law (see *Inceysa* v. *El Salvador*, para. 248 – a fact that Mr. Cremades criticizes in his dissent).

[72] *Fraport* v. *Philippines*, dissenting opinion of Mr. Cremades, §32.

[73] *Ioannis Kardassopoulos* v. *Georgia* (ICSID Case No. ARB/05/18), Decision on Jurisdiction, July 6, 2007 (hereinafter: *Kardassopoulos* v. *Georgia*).

analysis at hand, for the reasoning employed by the Tribunal calls into question a considerable part of the *World Duty Free* award. Before we enter into such analysis, let me briefly summarize the pertinent facts.

When Georgia became independent in the aftermath of the Soviet Union's collapse in the early 1990s, the newly emergent State sought to develop its natural resources and profit from its favorable geo-strategic position at the Caspian Sea through foreign investments in the oil and gas sector, particularly building pipelines. One of those investors attracted by the business opportunities in this then-transitional economy was the claimant in the present dispute, Ioannis Kardassopoulos, a Greek national. He owned or controlled Tramex USA and Tramex Panama, the two companies that made the investment in the pipeline project. In order to advance the project, Tramex concluded a joint venture agreement (JVA) with two entities, fully owned by the Georgian government, Transneft and SakNavtobi. While both Tramex and Mr. Kardassopoulos were assured by senior Georgian officials, including the then-President and Prime Minister, that the JVA and thus their investment would be protected and legal under Georgian law, Transneft and SakNavtobi were prohibited by Georgian law to enter into the JVA. Thus, since Georgia asserted that as a consequence Kardassopoulos' investment was not made in accordance with Georgian law as required by the Georgia–Greece BIT, the issue before the Tribunal once more was whether it had jurisdiction under Article 25 ICSID and the corresponding provision in the BIT.

(ii) The host State is responsible for the actions of its organs

In brief, the Tribunal rejected Georgia's contentions. According to the arbitrators, while the host State's consent does not cover the investor making an investment in breach of the former's laws, the situation in the case at hand was the reverse: It was merely the State-owned entities that breached the law. Moreover, since Article 7 of the ILC Draft Articles on State Responsibility confirms the attributability of State action that is *ultra vires* and since both the former President and Prime Minister assured the legality and protection of the investment, Georgia was in no position to successfully claim denial of jurisdiction.[74]

(iii) Avoiding World Duty Free's *mistake*

Such reasoning is as simple as it is straightforward. The host State is responsible for its most senior officials' conduct; even if they exceed their

[74] *Ibid.*, para. 190.

authority, i.e. act illegally. Additionally, if the State itself is – or better, its organs themselves are – involved in breaching the law, it is precluded from claiming that the Tribunal should decline jurisdiction. Not very remarkable – however, more or less the contrary to what the *World Duty Free* Tribunal found in its decision less than a year earlier. This observation leads me to my preliminary conclusions regarding the international investment case law on corruption.

D. Analysis of the case law

1. *Preliminary conclusions*

Admittedly, the legal-factual matrix in *World Duty Free* differed to some extent from *Kardassopoulos*. In particular in the former case, no BIT existed between the investor's home and its host State and thus the dispute did not center on Article 25 ICSID and the respective provisions that most BITs contain. The main issues, however, were basically the same: (1) was the Tribunal's jurisdiction excluded because the investor was involved in a serious breach of the law, and (2) did it matter that the host State itself by way of its most senior officials played a considerable if not pivotal role in such irregularities?

As regards the second question, it is – from a legal point of view – very hard to understand why the *World Duty Free* Tribunal refrained from attributing the State organs' conduct to the State – as did the *Kardassopoulos* award. The rules on State responsibility are straightforward in this regard; a conclusion other than affirming attribution is almost impossible to draw.[75] So, why was *World Duty Free* decided otherwise nonetheless? Let me consider several observations from the analysis of international investment case law before I seek to respond to this question, the answer to which may prove very instructive as to what should be the proper way to deal with corruption in international investment law.

First and foremost, the most obvious point is that in all cases[76] discussed here, corruption or other irregularities were dealt with at the jurisdictional stage, i.e. the main issue was whether they amounted to the exclusion of the Tribunal's jurisdiction. While it may appear quite logical that such questions arise at the jurisdictional stage – given the "in accordance with the laws of the host State" clauses in BITs and the longstanding tradition to oust corruption by denying jurisdiction in international

[75] See *supra* 8 C. 2. (b).

[76] That is, all cases that dealt with corruption, etc. in more than a cursory manner; which basically excludes *Wena* and *SGS*.

commercial arbitration cases – it has to be noted that declining jurisdiction is a very blunt instrument. A Tribunal either has jurisdiction or it does not. A compromise or balancing between conflicting interests is not possible. There may be good reasons for excluding such balancing.[77] However, the consequences of such black-and-white approach are far-reaching, particularly considering the fact that investment arbitration very frequently is the only means by which the investor can effectively resist the host State's sovereign authority – a path that is barred if the Tribunal declines jurisdiction.[78]

Secondly, there exist different categories of cases that we have to distinguish in order to properly compare them with each other: As for a first category, most cases – *Inceysa, Fraport, Kardassopoulos* – involved a BIT and thus centered on the question whether the investment made was covered by the host State's consent to investment arbitration. By contrast, *World Duty Free* was a contract arbitration without a BIT between the investor's home and its host State where public policy was the main argument against jurisdiction. Another way to categorize the case law is to distinguish whether the conduct under scrutiny in the respective cases was unilateral or mutual. While corruption is usually mutual, for both sides' conduct is illicit, fraud, for example, is merely unilateral. Here, again, *Inceysa, Fraport* and *Kardassopoulos* are in one group – though it has to be noted that in *Inceysa* and *Fraport*, the investor's unilateral conduct was under scrutiny, whereas *Kardassopoulos* focused on the host State's unilateral actions – and *World Duty Free* stands alone as the only case with mutually illicit conduct.

A third observation pertains to the fact that the Tribunals in all cases discussed above appear to see an element of reciprocity in the investor–host State relationship as regards corruption and other irregularities. While some directly addressed "reciprocal if not identical obligations"[79] of the investor, others at least implicitly endorsed the idea that an investor's illicit conduct may have repercussions in investment arbitration. The stage where such repercussions play out is the Tribunal's jurisdiction – based dogmatically either on a breach of domestic law[80] or general principles such as, among others, public policy.[81]

77 See *infra*. 8 D. 2. (b) (i).

78 For an extensive analysis of the pros and cons of such way to deal with corruption in investment arbitration see *infra* D. 2. (b) (i) and (ii).

79 *Fraport* v. *Philippines*, para. 402.

80 *Inceysa, Fraport* and *Kardassopoulos*.

81 *Inceysa* and *World Duty Free*.

This leads me to the last observation that touches upon an issue I have already pointed at earlier:[82] It appears that investment Tribunals, while grappling with how to deal with such issues of corruption, sometimes tend to cling to conventional wisdom from international commercial arbitration,[83] the unmodified transfer of which misconstrues basic characteristics of international investment law. The (Global) Public Law type character and the asymmetry in the relationship of the host State and the investor create a dynamic inherently different from the interplay between two private entities in international commercial arbitration. Yet in investment arbitration Tribunals refer indiscriminately to principles developed under the latter system.[84]

Putting those four observations together, it becomes apparent both why *World Duty Free* was decided the way it was, and what is entailed in the flaws of the approach chosen by investment Tribunals towards corruption. As I have already alluded to at 8 C. 2. (a) (iii), if jurisdiction is the stage where corruption is given relevance doctrinally, the fact that it is a very blunt instrument has serious consequences. Because it is an all-or-nothing decision, nuanced reasoning appears to be as difficult as nuanced findings. Naturally, the factual question of whether corruption or other irregularities actually occurred plays a prominent role. It obviously runs the risk that the host State might easily exploit it in order to delay and hence to undermine a proceeding. However, the main problem with addressing the issue on the jurisdictional stage lies with the absence of any possibility to balance interests – a doctrinal instrument that is only available on the merits. Let me consider the dilemma the Tribunal would have found itself in, if it had – in accordance with the rules on State responsibility – attributed President Moi's conduct, i.e. taking the bribe, to Kenya. If we deem jurisdiction to be the proper stage on which to deal with such issues, the problem that arises is impossible to resolve: Denying jurisdiction would mean disregarding the legal relevance the Tribunal has just affirmed vis-à-vis the host State's responsibility; granting jurisdiction would do the reverse, i.e. undermining the relevance of the investor's conduct. Apart from the political tremors that affirming State responsibility for corruption would trigger, it is very likely that those former

[82] See *supra* 8 C. 2. (b) (iii).

[83] See Moss, "Commercial Arbitration and Investment Arbitration," 793 ff.

[84] See *World Duty Free* v. *Kenya*, para. 161; *Inceysa* v. *El Salvador*, para. 245 and nn. 66, 67 of the award, which refer to private international law treatises.

considerations may have induced the *World Duty Free* Tribunal to decide the way it did.[85] Thus it is more than likely that the Tribunal was fully aware of the fact that it was pure lip service to stress that such decision was intended to exclude any dispute involving corruption as such and thus was not directed against the investor specifically, who just accidently found itself in the position of the claimant. As I have stated before, declining jurisdiction is *always* directed against the investor, for the latter is the only one that will choose investment arbitration to pursue its interests. The host State, by contrast, will always use its sovereign authority to get what it deems to be in its interest and then, as the case may be, take the risk that the investor might resort to investment arbitration. This is, among many others, a main reason why the thrust of international commercial arbitration is not simply transferable to investment arbitration without modification.[86]

Acknowledging the other observations, i.e. that there exists a certain degree of reciprocity in international investment law and that *World Duty Free* is the prime example of such reciprocal element, since the conduct legally relevant before the Tribunal was mutual, I argue that in case of corruption, declining jurisdiction meets some serious criticism. It exclusively sanctions the investor's conduct and disregards the involvement of the host State. This, however, contravenes the reciprocity component the Tribunals avail themselves of in order to argue for exclusion of jurisdiction. Moreover, it often relies on an ill-placed reference to international commercial arbitration, the underlying rationales of which do not indiscriminately apply to a system that is built on a (Global) Public Law type relationship of the investor and the host State.[87] Finally, addressing the issue on the jurisdictional stage entails an all-or-nothing decision that does not allow for the nuanced balancing a reciprocal relationship usually requires. It must be added that while such balancing and reciprocity is most obvious in cases of mutually illicit conduct, even in case of unilateral action a balanced approach on the merits stage offers a more flexible solution that promises to reconcile rights and obligations of both parties that lie on different levels.

[85] Considering the arbitrators' prominence and outstanding expertise in the field of public international law, the alternative conclusion – ignorance and incompetence vis-à-vis general public international law – can be excluded with absolute certainty.
[86] See *supra* 8 C. 2. (b) (iii) and Moss, "Commercial Arbitration and Investment Arbitration," 793 ff.
[87] *Ibid.*

2. *Alternative approaches*

Having thus arrived at the conclusion that the way investment Tribunals deal with corruption is not satisfying doctrinally, I will now proceed to discuss alternative approaches and their potential advantages, as well as the challenges a solution different to the ICSID Tribunals' current one has to face.

(a) Modification or adaptation of the main contract

Raeschke-Kessler and Gottwald provide an alternative to the solution investment Tribunals currently offer.[88] They argue that corruption also invokes the responsibility of the State for the illicit conduct of its organs and thus, "if the state could easily avoid any obligation resulting from a contract tainted by corruption, it could profit from its own violation of international law."[89] Building on this argument combining considerations from the rules of State responsibility[90] with the principle *nemo audiatur suam turpitudinem allegans*, Raeschke-Kessler and Gottwald hence regard the investment contract between the host State and the investor as valid and propose contractual modification or adaptation instead, which should be decided by the Tribunal.[91]

Such proposal firstly is strongly influenced by German Civil Law doctrine and the case law of the Bundesgerichtshof[92] and secondly fails to answer the question why either side, once the illegal conduct has become public, would be interested in continuing a relationship infected by corruption. This is particularly true if the investor faces a new government that seeks to deviate from its predecessor's misconduct – which very frequently is the situation, as, for example, in the *World Duty Free* case. Moreover, nowadays investors often do not conclude an investment contract any more but rely exclusively on the BIT, which enjoys primacy and supremacy in international investment law.[93] Therefore, seeking

[88] See Raeschke-Kessler and Gottwald, "Corruption," 598 ff.

[89] *Ibid.*, 597.

[90] For a more extensive analysis regarding the rules of State responsibility see *infra* 8 D. 2. (b) (ii).

[91] See Raeschke-Kessler and Gottwald, "Corruption," 598.

[92] It is rather unsurprising that Raeschke-Kessler and Gottwald refer to the Bundesgerichtshof, given that Mr. Raeschke-Kessler is Rechtsanwalt beim Bundesgerichtshof. The fact that they draw on German doctrine is, of course, not a valuable counter-argument in itself. However, inferring domestic doctrine into an international law dispute has to be done with particular care.

[93] See *supra* 2 E. 2.

salvation simply in the modification of the investment contract does not do justice to the complexity of the legal architecture in an investment dispute. Retaining its validity does not automatically resolve the jurisdictional issue, for nonetheless the question remains whether the host State consented to investment arbitration vis-à-vis an investment made by violation of the law of the host State. Consequently, a broader approach would be preferable, one that also responds to issues of jurisdiction and interpretation of the BIT.

(b) Balancing with the investor's rights on the merits stage

(i) Challenges: Consent of the host State, definition of investment in the BIT and nullity of the investment contract

A balanced approach that seeks to take into account infringements of both the investor and the host State on the merits stage meets some serious challenges that have to be addressed before hastily praising its advantages. While, from a policy perspective, it might be preferable to promote a merits solution instead of a jurisdiction alone, so one might well argue, from a legal standpoint it is virtually impossible to enter the merits stage in disputes where corruption is involved. As has been demonstrated before, the argument runs, any Tribunal, in order to establish its jurisdiction, must confirm that the host State has consented to submit the dispute before the Tribunal to ICSID arbitration. Article 25 ICSID, which deals with such consent, requires that "the jurisdiction of the Centre shall extend to any legal dispute arising directly out of an investment." The ICSID Convention does not provide for a definition of what should be considered an "investment"; however, almost every BIT defines "investment" as, among others, "any share or asset that has been made in accordance with the law of the host State." Bribery of domestic public officials being illegal under any domestic legal order – as well as fraud or other comparable illicit conduct – the share or asset under dispute hence does not qualify as "investment." Additionally, any contractual basis for the "investment" is null and void and thus must be treated as legally non-existent under the domestic order of the host State. Finally, treaties laying obligations on States vis-à-vis corruption, such as the OECD Convention on Combating Bribery of Foreign Public Officials in International Business Transactions[94] or the Criminal Law Convention on Corruption of the Council of Europe,[95] require the parties "to confiscate or otherwise deprive the instrumentalities and proceeds of criminal

[94] See *supra* 8 B. 1. [95] *Supra* 8 B. 2.

offences established in accordance with [these] Convention[s], or property the value of which corresponds to such proceeds."[96] Thus, arguably, seeking to introduce a balancing approach is nothing but a pipe dream, for it is impossible for a host State on the one hand to deprive the investor of the "investment" and its proceeds illegally made, and on the other to pay considerable compensation or even return some of the assets – which might well be the outcome of a Tribunal's balancing test. Where, the question arises, is there any room for a balanced approach?[97]

Admittedly, such challenges are considerable. However, as an initial response, let me reconsider the observations made vis-à-vis the *Inceysa* case.[98] The Tribunal's finding that *any* violation of the host State's laws means that the asset or share under dispute does not qualify as "investment" and thus excludes the host State's consent to ICSID arbitration, may lead to absurd results: In *Tokios Tokelés*, Ukraine as respondent contended that the Tribunal lacked jurisdiction merely because the investment's denomination was not in accordance with the terminology provided by Ukrainian law.[99] Thus, if we consequently follow the reasoning of the jurisdictional solution, legal certainty would be put into serious jeopardy. While, hence, such interpretation of the "in accordance with the laws of the host State clause" is unacceptable, there remain but two options to resolve the question of what, then, is the appropriate interpretation.

The first option would be to differentiate between those violations of the laws that do not qualify for exclusion of jurisdiction and those that do. The only reasonable criterion for such differentiation appears to be the gravity of the violation. Gravity, however, is a normative criterion that, without any positive guidelines is utterly murky, for there is no clear demarcation line. Moreover, what should be the decisive factor, the quality or the quantity of the breach? While everybody would agree that corruption and fraud *in abstracto* would well qualify as such grave violations, it is not very easy to answer *in concreto* whether forging just one minor document or paying just a small sum of money that evidently had no influence on the outcome of the governmental decision actually

96 *Ibid.*, Art. 19.3.

97 It must be added that such challenges only arise in case there is a BIT involved. If no BIT exists between the home and the host State of the investor, as e.g., in *World Duty Free*, arguing for a balanced approach meets no serious reservations, if we identify the comparison to international commercial arbitration as misguided in a public law type dispute such as ICSID arbitration; see *supra* 8 C. 2. (b) (iii).

98 See *supra* 8 C. 2. (c).

99 *Tokios Tokelés* v. *Ukraine* (ICSID Case No. ARB/02/18), Decision on Jurisdiction (hereinafter: *Tokios Tokelés* v. *Ukraine*), para. 83.

qualify in this regard. There might be, *mutatis mutandis*, cases where the quantity of – in the abstract – a minor violation of the host State's laws might qualify it as a grave breach. In one word, this option is nothing but arbitrary.

Therefore, only the second option remains: The passage "in accordance with the laws of the host State" must be given relevance not on the jurisdictional stage but in the merits of the case. The path chosen by the ICSID Tribunals in *Inceysa*, *Fraport* and *Kardassopoulos* employed the definition of "investment" in the respective BITs in order to animate the term "investment" in the arbitration clause of the BIT and Article 25 ICSID. Both provisions deal with the host State's consent to allow investors to introduce claims on the investment arbitration stage. What the State parties that include such "in accordance with the law of the host State clauses" into BITs intend is to prevent investments the *nature* of which they oust or resent. No host State wants to protect and thus provide access to arbitration regarding such *types* of foreign "investments" that it itself refuses to protect and hence declares illegal under its domestic law. If I do not want anybody to build, for example, a factory that produces heroin in my country, I have an interest in excluding such kind of "investments" from the scope of protection for FDI under the BIT. What I oust through the instrument of my domestic law should not be arbitrable via ICSID – I simply seek to prevent any heroin factory from being built, either by a domestic or a foreign investor.

This consideration differs from a situation in which the *nature* or *type* of investment is generally legal and welcome under the domestic laws of the host State. If, during the *process* of making such legal *type* of investment, the investor engages into conduct that – separately viewed – is illegal, this cannot change the fact that the type of investment remains itself legal and welcome. A power plant remains beneficial to the host State's economy and population, irrespective of whether the investor respected every law of the host State while the plant was constructed. Such irregularities are rather incidental to the type of investment and do not change their overall nature. Indeed, a domestic investor (or its organs) that engage(s) in illegal conduct during the process of investing may be criminally sanctioned for such conduct. However, it usually does not lose all its rights vis-à-vis the investment itself, in particular the right to access to court.

Considering the foregoing, corruption is usually rather incidental to the investment and does not modify its *nature*. While the *process* of investing hence may be tainted with corruption, the *type* of investment nonetheless remains the same. Thus, the mere fact that corruption occurred cannot be a factor in determining whether the investment is welcome in the host State and whether it therefore is encompassed under the scope of the latter's consent to investment arbitration. Consequently, the "in accordance with the laws of the host State" clause may not serve as a basis for excluding investments from jurisdiction in case of corruption.

A further argument in favor of such an approach would constitute the following: A host State that itself was involved in the illegal activities which led to the investment not having been made "in accordance with the law of the host State" is accountable for its public officials, even the most senior ones, taking bribes – according to the rules on State responsibility. If it now seeks to contend that such "investment" cannot be allowed to constitute licit ground for arbitration, it simply asserts its own illicit conduct in its own interest. Thus, it is fair to argue that the host State is barred from asserting the "in accordance with the law of the host State" clause to exclude the Tribunal's jurisdiction in such a scenario due to the principle of estoppel or *venire contra factum proprium.*[100] While it may seem odd at first glance that a host State consequently is faced with arbitration in a case that it seems never to have consented to, such result is merely the consequence of the host State's involvement in what it alleges to exclude the jurisdiction. It is prevented from arguing that it never wanted such kind of investments if its officials attributably have initiated or fuelled them by requesting or at least taking the bribe. Moreover, in case of unilaterally illegal conduct on the part of the investor, such argumentation still endorses the exclusion of jurisdiction according to the respective treaty clause.

(ii) Arguments in favor of a balanced approach

While those challenges are considerable and some of them are well founded, arguments in favor of a balanced approach are nonetheless myriad. I will limit myself to those four I deem most prominent and most convincing: The solution chosen by the ICSID Tribunals disregards the rules of the law of State responsibility (a); the same is true vis-à-vis the principle of *venire contra factum proprium* or estoppel (b); and considerations of policy (c) make a strong case for a balanced approach.

(a) State responsibility As has been hinted at before, the investment Tribunals' jurisdictional solution neglects or, one may even say, disregards

[100] See M. N. Shaw, *International Law*, 6th edn. (Cambridge University Press, 2008), pp. 102 f.

fundamental rules of State responsibility. A State is a legal fiction, a construct that can only act through organs and other agents the conduct of which, under certain conditions, is attributable to the State. If the conduct of such organs, even of the most senior office-holders such as the President or Prime Minister, influences the application of a legal rule, it triggers the State's responsibility. Even if such organs act in excess of their official authority, their conduct remains attributable to the State, as Article 7 ILC clarifies. Moreover, it should not be forgotten that as much as the State is a legal construct that needs organs to act, in most cases the investor itself is a company and thus also a legal construct whose organs' conduct is then attributable to it. In *World Duty Free*, this principle was so self-evident to the Tribunal that it did not even mention that it was Mr. Ali as agent for the claimant, i.e. *World Duty Free*, who committed the graft. If such attribution is self-evident vis-à-vis the investor, there is no reason why the rules of State responsibility should not equally apply vis-à-vis the host State. It has to be noted, however, that in cases in which unilateral conduct rests on the investor's side,[101] such argumentation is not viable.

However, there remain other doubts as well. Arguing for obligations by the rules on State responsibility, one might say, is flawed, for those rules are secondary, i.e. regulate the responsibility once it has been established that a duty exists. Thus, the argument runs, saying that the rules on State responsibility provide doctrinal ground for an approach balancing with duties on the merits stage means taking the second step before the first. However, it is not licit to draw conclusions from a secondary rule for a primary one.

But such argumentation runs into its own traps. As regards corruption, it is not subject to debate that an obligation lies on the parties not to engage in acts of bribery. The Tribunals themselves talk about "reciprocal . . . obligations."[102] Thus the main question, indeed, is, whether such conduct the illicitness of which is undisputed is attributable to the host State. Such questions of State responsibility are, however, exactly the core of the issues the ILC Articles focus on.

(b) Venire contra factum proprium/estoppel A second set of principles of international law the jurisdictional solution chosen by the ICSID Tribunals does not sufficiently take into consideration is well-known in all legal orders: Nobody shall act in contradiction to his own conduct and thus shall not profit from his own illicit behavior – as enshrined in the Civil

[101] See *supra* 8 D. 1. [102] *Fraport* v. *Philippines*, para. 301.

Law principles of *venire contra factum proprium* or *nemo audiatur suam turpitudinem allegans* and the Common Law principle of estoppel. If the host State alleges that the investor is barred from claiming violation of its rights on the ICSID or any other arbitral platform, because it was engaged in bribery of public officials, the former asserts nothing else but that the Tribunal should disregard the above-stated principles: As demonstrated above, the host State is responsible for the conduct of its public officials who take the bribe or even request it in the first place. Saying that the investor therefore cannot pursue its rights within the investment realm means plainly and simply that the host State seeks to profit from its own illicit conduct.

However, it should not be ignored that those arguments apply – and actually were applied by the Tribunals[103] – vis-à-vis the investor as well. Thus, it would not do justice to the mutually illicit conduct if we applied those principles without modification, i.e. meaning that a Tribunal should give no credit at all to the host State's contention that the investor acted illicitly – as much as it is not preferable that the investor is entirely prohibited to do so vis-à-vis the public official's conduct attributable to the host State. This, however, argues perfectly for a balanced approach that takes those considerations into account by allowing for both sides to allege the illicit conduct of the other.

(c) Policy considerations As regards policy, the first consideration that comes to mind, however, is actually an argument against a balancing approach on the merits stage and in favor of a jurisdictional solution: Arguably, effectively preventing corruption requires ousting it at the earliest stage possible and cutting the supply side. If there is no one paying the bribe, corruption cannot flourish. An investor always has the choice not to invest in a host State that is known as a hotbed of corruption. And the corrupt host State, thus, will very quickly learn that it will not receive any investments if it continues its corrupt practices. Consequently, it is asserted, excluding jurisdiction is the proper way to deal with corruption, for the deterrence it entails for the investor will finally lead to an end to corruption overall.

Reality, however, tells a different story. On the one hand, the threat of sanctions by domestic and supranational supervision institutions in case of corruption are much more of a deterrent, for they quite often are much more detrimental. Thus, there is little need for another harsh sanction to

[103] See *Inceysa* v. *El Salvador*, para. 248.

the investor – if the threat to pay billions of dollars and to be ousted by the international public community is not deterrent enough, the investor will also not care about jurisdictional consequences within the investment realm. On the other hand, corruption, if it once becomes established practice, is a scourge that is widespread and omnipresent and hence not limited to foreign investments. If an administration is corrupt, official decisions will not be made without bribes, indiscriminately, whether they are in favor of a foreign or a domestic enterprise – the bribe requested may be higher in the latter case, but that is about it. Moreover, while thus the jurisdictional solution is inadequate to fight corruption overall, it is quite unlikely that such approach effectively limits corruption vis-à-vis foreign investment either.

As I said before, corruption is endemic and thus will affect any official decision, whether concerning foreign investments or not. Given the fact that according to recent surveys by Transparency International (TI), in more than 40 percent of the countries surveyed corruption was widespread, i.e. even minor official decisions required paying a bribe,[104] it is hard to imagine that an administration in such countries changes its attitude vis-à-vis bribes just as regards foreign investors. The result much more probable to entail the jurisdictional solution is twofold: Firstly, investors will refrain from investing in such countries, while the latter will not make considerable efforts to fight corruption. In other words, poor countries will get even poorer and their economic development comes to a halt. Secondly, I opine that the jurisdictional solution is not merely ineffective; it even *encourages* government officials in their corrupt conduct. If I can take bribes and the only consequence of my behavior on the international (legal) stage is that the investor cannot claim any violation of its rights under the BIT or the investment contract, I get carte blanche: I am virtually invited to take the bribe and afterwards expropriate the investor or otherwise forfeit its influence in the investment for I earn double – I get the bribe money and I get the investment. Particularly in countries with high levels of corruption and reduced levels of democratic accountability of the political elite, where personal and public interests are intermingled or are perceived as virtually the same,[105] such argumentation appears very appealing.

[104] Transparency International is a NGO focusing on the combat against and research into corruption worldwide. See the Corruption Perception Index (CPI), available at www.transparency.org/policy_research/surveys_indices/cpi/2009/cpi_2009_table.

[105] A scenario that, unfortunately, is not very rare in many developing countries.

Taking these considerations into account, a balanced approach offers a better solution as regards policy as well. If corruption is dealt with at the merits stage, the investor retains the possibility of pursuing its interests – for investment arbitration most often will be the only option in this regard. Thus, the host State is barred from illicitly taking or disadvantaging the investment without legal repercussions. A balanced approach that provides consequences for the host State's conduct – or better, the public officials' conduct attributable to the State – deters both the host State and the investor: The host State has to pay compensation for violating the rights of the investor and the investor realises that its illicit conduct can lead to considerable reduction of its compensation.

(iii) Integrating the balanced approach into international investment case law according to the Global Public Interest theory

(a) General principles of law: Good faith, international public policy and nemo audiatur suam turpitudinem allegans. While I thus assert that the jurisdictional solution offered by investment Tribunals is not preferable considering the argumentation above, I opine that my approach could easily be integrated into the international investment case law, which provides sufficient links for such shift. Argumentative linchpins of the jurisdictional solution as regards the interpretation of the BIT are general principles of law that the Tribunals grant prominence to as the point of entry for the "reciprocal obligations" they attempt to lay on the investor. The Tribunals specifically mention the principles of good faith, international public policy and *nemo audiatur suam turpitudinem allegans*.[106] Such general principles of law, under my theory, all qualify for host State defenses as encapsulations of the Global Public Interest. Hence, while my solution seeks to balance the competing interests of investor and host State on the merits stage, the similarity and thus the connecting link to international investment case law rests in those general principles of law as argumentative *topoi*.

(b) The case law on corruption in the light of the Global Public Interest theory. Corruption is somewhat different from the other two exemplary Global Public Interest issues discussed in this book. This is because of two reasons. Firstly, the case law on corruption and other irregularities exhibits the most coherent jurisprudence on legal consequences of

[106] See *Inceysa* v. *El Salvador*, para. 248; *World Duty Free* v. *Kenya*, para. 161; *Fraport* v. *Philippines*, para. 301.

Global Public Interest considerations for the investor. In no other area of the investment régime does the investor encounter repercussions as severe and as stringent as it does if it is involved in corruption, fraud, etc. Secondly, however, such stringency and coherence, as welcome as they may be from the viewpoint of legal certainty, entail serious challenges if the Tribunal's decisions are defective. Large parts of my analysis at D. have addressed this issue and, naturally so, sought to provide solutions. Since therefore much has already been said on how the Global Public Interest theory should be implemented vis-à-vis issues of corruption and irregularities and thus how the existing case law should be modified accordingly, in this final section it merely remains to briefly exemplify how an actual case should have been decided in line with my theory.

As regards *World Duty Free* v. *Kenya*, since the hypothetical on corruption is modeled after it, I refer to the end of Chapter 5 for what I deem a proper solution according to the Global Public Interest theory.[107] The assessment made in the hypothetical, i.e. requiring the host State to pay 85 percent of the claimed compensation and damages, seems to reflect an appropriate outcome for the *World Duty Free* case as well.

The case I want to reconsider here is *Inceysa* v. *El Salvador*. According to my view, the Tribunal has jurisdiction over the matter, for the "in accordance with the laws of the host State" clause rather pertains to the *nature* of the investment and is not concerned with incidental legal infringements regarding the *process* of investing. Hence, the investor's fraudulent conduct is an issue to be resolved on the merits stage. Assuming that El Salvador's conduct amounts to an investor rights violation,[108] it then needs to be established, firstly, whether the Global Public Interest – here, effectively combating corruption and other similar irregularities – has found expression in a customary norm or a general principle and, secondly, whether the host State's measures meet all three requirements of the proportionality test, i.e. suitability, necessity and proportionality *stricto sensu*. In the situation at hand, the legal translation of the Global Public Interest inheres in the principle *nemo audiatur suam turpitudinem allegans*. The legitimate goal pursued here constitutes warranting a fair and transparent procurement procedure leading to the identification of the best and most cost-effective offer. Therefore, it is obvious that offers which

107 See *supra* 5 H. 3.

108 Which is far from sure, considering that the measures undertaken represent a direct reaction to Inceysa's fraudulent behavior, which at least calls into question the viability of a fair and equitable treatment claim, given that Inceysa's legitimate expectations are quite limited.

do not fulfill – but on the contrary seek to undermine – those requirements, must meet serious repercussions. Hence, the measures undertaken by El Salvador, particularly rescinding the contract, are both suitable and necessary vis-à-vis achieving the stated purpose. Moreover, considering on the one hand the importance of the project as such, as well as the pivotal interest of a developing country in particular to identify the best and most cost-effective offer available, and taking into account on the other hand Inceysa's highly abusive conduct in deliberately undermining an efficient procurement, El Salvador's measures also meet the proportionality *stricto sensu* requirement. Hence compensation or damages, considering the aforesaid, are out of place. Therefore, we arrive at a final result similar to the actual *Inceysa* award, albeit with very different reasoning and based on a coherent theoretical foundation.

9 Concluding remarks

Chapter 8 concludes the second part of this book. As has been stated before, while Part I sought to develop both a theoretical underpinning and a doctrinal structure for integrating the Global Public Interest into the investment régime, in Part II I have undertaken the exemplification of my Global Public Interest theory using case law studies from three pivotal issues that epitomize, although do not exhaust, the Global Public Interest. My point of departure in Chapter 2 has been the assessment that the process of "internationalization" and "integration" international investment law is currently undergoing has serious consequences for the understanding of the investment system. I have fleshed out several distinct features of this system and have described it, viewed against the backdrop of the Global Administrative Law and Constitutionalism theories, as Global Public Law.[1]

Following a comparative analysis with two other systems exhibiting public law features in an inter- or supranational context,[2] my core thesis condensing the preceding analyses argues that the inherent rationale of any public law system, and hence of the Global Public Law system international investment law represents, is the equilibrium of the public and the individual interest.[3] In accordance with the current state of public international law – shaping and informing investment law – that spotlights the human being but still relies on States as the main motor of the international community, I have placed the decision whether to raise what I call Global Public Interest issues in international investment law in the hands of the host State. Under my theory, it is the latter that is entitled to rely on general principles and customary international law

[1] *Supra* 4 A. [2] *Supra* 4 B. [3] *Supra* 4 C.

as legal translations of the Global Public Interest constituting defenses against investor rights infringements.[4]

Finally, I have promoted the principle of proportionality as the most suitable and most effective instrument to balance the public with the individual interest and thus to reconcile the Global Public Interest with the protection of investor rights. Several safeguards, substantive as well as procedural, see to avoiding any abuse by the host State.[5] Thereinafter, I have analyzed the investment arbitration case law involving environmental, human rights and corruption issues and come to assess – at the end of the respective analyses – how cases should be solved and how the solution should be doctrinally structured according to my theory.[6] Together with the hypotheticals addressed at the end of Chapter 5 the analysis exhibits the advantages as well as marks the limits of the Global Public Interest theory.

What emerges from this tour d'horizon through my book is a twofold assessment of the Global Public Interest theory that appears to constitute a paradox: It is very expansive and very limited at the same time. On the one hand, it delineates a broad theoretical concept, relying on a progressive and contestable understanding of public international law and thereby inferring norms as the "applicable international law" in investment disputes that before were considered foreign to – if not to say unsuitable for – international investment law. On the other hand, however, hinging on general principles and customary international law arguably exhibits a very doctrinal if not to say legalistic understanding of public international law. Indeed, my Global Public Interest theory leaves no room for soft law and hence completely disregards instruments such as the OECD Guidelines on Multinational Enterprises and the UN Global Compact, to name but two prominent examples.[7] Admittedly, the price to be paid by such limitation is high: Both the hypothetical and the case law on human

[4] *Ibid.* [5] *Supra* 5 G. [6] *Supra* 6, 7 and 8.

[7] See Report of the World Summit on Sustainable Development, Johannesburg, August 26 to September 4, 2002, available at http://daccess-ods.un.org/TMP/7699301.html; Agenda 21, Ch 1: Preamble, Para. 1.1., available at www.un.org/esa/sustdev/documents/agenda21/english/agenda21chapter1.htm; The UN Global Compact, available at www.unglobalcompact.org/AboutTheGC/index.html; on the drafting history of the Compact see E. Morgera, "The UN and Corporate Environmental Responsibility: Between International Regulation and Partnerships," *Eur. Com. & Int'l Env. L. Rev.*, 15 (2006), 93; Millennium Development Goals, adopted at the UN Millennium Summit in New York, September 18, 2000 – see www.un.org/millenniumgoals/; The OECD Guidelines for Multinational Enterprises, Revision 2000, available at www.olis.oecd.org/olis/2000doc.nsf/LinkTo/daffe-ime-wpg(2000)9.

rights have concluded with very sobering results – not meeting the proportionality test in the first case and not even being able to provide for a customary norm or general principle in the second.

As has been asserted before, these results may be seen as severely dissatisfying or even dismaying, particularly considering the boldness of my theory's theoretical underpinnings. However, such Janus-faced feature of the Global Public Interest theory is deliberate and necessary. My survey of current BIT practice in Chapter 3 has revealed that the bilateral treaty system – at least at the present stage – is unable and, in my opinion, inadequate to satisfyingly accommodate the conflicting issues at stake. Moreover, even if some countries were to draft BITs effectively tackling the challenge, the scattered patchwork of bilateralism makes it almost impossible to create a coherent legal framework of almost universal application. Not to speak of a multilateral investment treaty, which seems to be way out of reach after the spectacular failure of the OECD attempt in this regard in 1998.[8] Hence, a conventional solution is not a realistic option in the nearer future; the challenges, however, are imminent. The Global Public Interest theory provides an adequate response to what I have called the public interest challenge particularly because it displays Janus-faced features as described. They warrant the safeguard that international investment law simultaneously opens up to and legally accommodates, theoretically as well as doctrinally, issues of global public concern while it hinders abuse and overstretching of the investment régime with broad considerations of dubious legal pedigree. Admittedly, this may entail discomforting results to those wishing to pry the door wide open for public interest allegations – as demonstrated vis-à-vis human rights. However, I think that the solution presented by the Global Public Interest theory reconciles best the natural tensions between vision and reality. It acknowledges the growing value-orientation in public international law but accepts the State as still the pivotal and indispensable protagonist on the international stage, and thus bestows the latter with the capacity to raise the legal translation of the Global Public Interest as enshrined in custom and general principles as defenses to be balanced with the infringed investor rights.

Despite the said Janus-faced character of the Global Public Interest theory, this book undoubtedly delineates a bold approach. I do not deny that it leaves many questions unanswered and raises even more new ones.

[8] See M. Trebilcock and R. Howse, *The Regulation of International Trade*, 3rd edn. (Routledge, 2005), p. 458.

For example, which of the ILC Articles on State Responsibility are actually applicable as expressions of the Global Public Interest? In case the investor's organs directly violate a Global Public Interest norm, is their conduct attributable according to the domestic (corporate) law of the host State, an analogous application of the ILC Articles or a third régime yet to be established? Moreover, how to effectively and convincingly express the outcome of the proportionality analysis in the amount of compensation or damages eventually to be paid by the host State? These and many more questions are for future scholarly work and above all future investment Tribunals to determine. While I have also sought to provide important practical guidance on implementing the Global Public Interest theory substantively as well as procedurally, this book focuses on providing theoretical and doctrinal answers. Again, some of them are bold. However, challenging and unanswered questions require audacious responses. I would be more than satisfied if they helped to spark the debate on Global Public Interest in international investment law, and even more so if they inspired future research or case law on the topic.

Bibliography

van Aaken, A., "Primary and Secondary Remedies in International Investment Law and National State Liability: A Functional and Comparative View" in S. W. Schill (ed.), *International Investment Law and Comparative Public Law* (Oxford University Press, 2010), p. 721

Ackerman, B. A., "Beyond Carolene Products," *Harv. L. Rev.*, 98 (1985), 713

Addo, M. K. (ed.), *Human Rights Standards and the Responsibility of Transnational Corporations* (Kluwer Law International, 1999)

Ago, R., "Droit positif et droit international," *Annuaire Français de Droit International*, 3 (1957), 14

Akehurst, M., "Custom as a Source of International Law," *Brit. Yb. Int'l L.*, 44 (1976), 1

Aleinikoff, T. A., "Constitutional Law in the Age of Balancing," *Yale L.J.*, 96 (1987), 943

Alexidze, L., "Legal Nature of Jus Cogens in Contemporary International Law," *Recueil des Cours*, 172 (1982), 219

Alexy, R., *A Theory of Constitutional Rights*, trans. J. Rivers (Oxford University Press, 2002)

Theorie der Grundrechte, 1st edn (Suhrkamp, 1986)

Alston, P. (ed.), *Non-State Actors and Human Rights* (Oxford University Press, 2005)

"The 'Not-a-Cat' Syndrome: Can the International Human Rights Regime Accommodate Non-State Actors?" in P. Alston (ed.), *Non-State Actors and Human Rights* (Oxford University Press, 2005), p. 3

(ed.), *Promoting Human Rights Through Bills of Rights: Comparative Perspectives* (Oxford University Press, 1999)

Alvarez, J. E., "A BIT on Custom," *N.Y.U. J. Int'l L. & Pol.*, 42 (2010), 17

"Critical Theory and the North American Free Trade Agreement's Chapter Eleven," *U. Miami Inter-Am. L. Rev.*, 28 (1996–97), 303

and K. Khamsi,"The Argentine Crisis and Foreign Investors – A Glimpse into the Heart of the Investment Regime" in K. P. Sauvant (ed.), *Yearbook on International Investment Law & Policy 2008–2009* (Oxford University Press, 2009), p. 379

D'Amato, A., *The Concept of Customary International Law* (Cornell University Press, 1971)

Appel, M., *Entstehungsschwäche und Bestandsstärke des verfassungsrechtlichen Eigentums* (Duncker & Humblot, 2004)

Armstrong, D., T. Farrell and H. Lambert, *International Law and International Relations* (Cambridge University Press, 2007)

Arts, B., M. Northmann and B. Reinalda (eds.), *Non-State Actors in International Relations* (Ashgate, 2001)

Atapattu, S. A., *Emerging Principles of International Environmental Law* (Transnational Publishers, 2006)

Aust, A., *Modern Treaty Law and Practice*, 2nd edn. (Cambridge University Press, 2007)

Baez, C., M. Dearing, M. Delatour and C. Dixon, "Multinational Enterprises and Human Rights," *Miami Int'l & Comp. L. Rev.*, 8 (1999–2000), 183

Barak, A., *Interpretation in the Law (vol. III: Constitutional Interpretation)*, 1994

Behrens, P., "Towards the Constitutionalization of International Investment Protection," *Archiv des Völkerrechts*, 45N (2007), 153

Bernhardt, R., "The Convention and Domestic Law" in R. St. J. Macdonald, F. Matscher and H. Petzold (eds.), *The European System for the Protection of Human Rights* (Martinus Nijhoff Publishers, 1993), p. 25

(ed.), *The Encyclopedia of Public International Law*, vol. I (North Holland, 1992)

Binder, C. *et al.* (eds.), *International Investment Law for the 21st Century – Essays in Honour of Christoph Schreuer* (Oxford University Press, 2009)

Bindreiter, U., *Why Grundnorm? – A Treatise on the Implications of Kelsen's Doctrine* (Kluwer Law International, 2002)

Bishop, R. D., J. Crawford and W. M. Reisman, *Foreign Investment Disputes* (Kluwer Law International, 2005)

Bjorklund, A., "Economic Security Defenses in International Investment Law" in K. P. Sauvant (ed.), *Yearbook on International Investment Law & Policy 2008–2009* (Oxford University Press, 2009), p. 479

Blanpain, R. (ed.), *Multinational Enterprises and the Social Challenges of the XXIst Century* (Kluwer Law International, 2000)

Böckenförde, E.-W., "Grundrechtstheorie und Grundrechtsinterpretation," *Neue Juristische Wochenschrift*, 38 (1974), 1529

Bodansky, D., J. Brunnée and E. Hey (eds.), *The Oxford Handbook of International Environmental Law* (Oxford University Press, 2007)

A. von Bogdandy, "Constitutionalism in International Law: Comment on a Proposal from Germany," *Harv. Int'l L. J.*, 47 (2006), 223

"The Telos of International Law – Christian Tomuschat's General Course and the Evolution of the Universalist Tradition" in P.-M. Dupuy *et al.* (eds.), *Völkerrecht als Wertordnung – Common Values in International Law: Festschrift für Christian Tomuschat* (N. P. Engel Verlag, 2006), p. 703

and J. Bast (eds.), *Principles of European Constitutional Law* (Hart Publishing, 2006)

Boisson de Chazournes, L., *The Precautionary Principle in Precaution from Rio to Johannesburg*, Proceedings of a Geneva Environment Network Roundtable, 2002

Bokor-Szegö, H., "General Principles of Law" in M. Bedjaoui (ed.), *International Law: Achievements and Prospects* (Unesco/Martinus Nijhoff Publishers, 1991), p. 213

Bond, J. C., "Affirmative Action at the Crossroads: An Essay," *Guild Prac.*, 53 (1996), 4

Van den Bossche, P., "A 'Normal' Business Practice Becomes a Criminal Offence – The 1997 OECD Convention on Combating Bribery of Foreign Public Officials in International Business Transactions" in M. Bronckers (ed.), *New Directions in International Economic Law – Essays in Honour of John H. Jackson* (Kluwer Academic Publishers, 2000), p. 441

Bowett, D., "Claims between States and Private Entities: The Twilight Zone of International Law," *Catholic U. L. Rev.*, 35 (1986), 929

Brenner, M., P. M. Huber and M. Möstl (eds.), *Der Staat des Grundgesetzes – Kontinuität und Wandel: Festschrift für Peter Badura zum siebzigsten Geburtstag* (Mohr Siebeck, 2004)

A. Broches, "The Convention on the Settlement of Investment Disputes between States and Nationals of Other States: Applicable Law and Default Procedure" in P. Sanders (ed.), *International Arbitration: Liber Amicorum Martin Domke* (Martinus Nijhoff Publishers, 1967), p. 12

"The Convention on the Settlement of Investment Disputes between States and Nationals of Other States," *Recueil des Cours*, 136 (1972), II, 329

Bronckers, M. (ed.), *New Directions in International Economic Law – Essays in Honour of John H. Jackson* (Kluwer Academic Publishers, 2000)

Brower, C. N. and E. R. Hellbeck, "The Implications of National and International Environmental Obligations for Foreign Investment Protection Standards, Including Valuation: A Report from the Front Lines" in The International Bureau of the Permanent Court of Arbitration, *International Investments and Protection of the Environment – The Role of Dispute Resolution Mechanisms*, Papers emanating from the Second PCA International Law Seminar, May 17, 2000, The Permanent Court of Arbitration/Peace Palace Papers (Kluwer Law International, 2001), p. 19

Brown Weiss, E., L. Boisson de Chazournes and N. Bernasconi-Osterwalder (eds.), *Fresh Water and International Economic Law* (Oxford University Press, 2005)

Brownlie, I., *Principles of Public International Law*, 7th edn. (Oxford University Press, 2008)

Bühler, M. W. and T. H. Webster, *Handbook of ICC Arbitration*, 2nd edn. (Sweet & Maxwell, 2008)

Burke-White, W., "The Argentine Financial Crisis: State Liability under BITs and the Legitimacy of the ICSID System," *Asian J. WTO & Int'l Health L and Pol'y*, 3 (2008), 199

and A. von Staden, "Investment Protection in Extraordinary Times: The Interpretation and Application of Non-Precluded Measures Provisions in Bilateral Investment Treaties," *Va. J. Int'l L.*, 48 (2007–08), 307

"Private Litigation in a Public Law Sphere: The Standard of Review in Investor-State Arbitration," *University of Pennsylvania Law School, Public Law and Legal Theory Research Paper Series, Research Paper* No. #09–23
Caldeira, G. A. and J. R. Wright, "Amici Curiae before the Supreme Court: Who Participates, When, and How Much?," *J. of Pol.*, 52 (1990), 782
Cannizzaro, E., "The Role of Proportionality in the Law of International Countermeasures," *Eur. J. Int'l L.*, 12 (2001), 889
Cantegreil, J., "Implementing Human Rights in the NAFTA Regime – The Potential of a Pending Case: Glamis Corp v. USA" in P.-M. Dupuy, F. Francioni and E.-U. Petersmann (eds.), *Human Rights in International Investment Law and Arbitration* (Oxford University Press, 2009), p. 367
Cassese, A., *International Law*, 2nd edn. (Oxford University Press, 2005)
Cerexhe, É., *Le Droit Européen* (Bruylant/Nauwelaerts, 1989)
Chemerinsky, E., *Constitutional Law: Principles and Policies*, 3rd edn. (Aspen Publishers, 2006)
Chen, L.-C., *An Introduction to Contemporary International Law*, 2nd edn. (Yale University Press, 2000)
Claassen, C. D. *et al.* (eds.), *"In einem vereinten Europa dem Frieden der Welt zu dienen . . . ,": Liber amicorum Thomas Oppermann* (Duncker & Humblot, 2001)
Coase, R., "The Nature of the Firm," *Economica*, 4 (1937), 386
Cohn, M., "Affirmative Action and the Equality Principle in Human Rights Treaties: United States' Violation of its International Obligations," *Va. J. Int'l L.*, 43 (2002–03), 249
Conrad, H. and G. Kleinheyer (eds.), *Carl Gottlieb Svarez: Vorträge über Recht und Staat* (Westdeutscher Verlag, 1960)
Cordero Moss, G., "Commercial Arbitration and Investment Arbitration: Fertile Soil for False Friends?" in C. Binder *et al.* (eds.), *International Investment Law for the 21st Century – Essays in Honour of Christoph Schreuer* (Oxford University Press, 2009), p. 782
Craig, W. L., W. W. Park and J. Paulsson, *International Chamber of Commerce Arbitration*, 3rd edn. (Oceana Publications, 2000)
Craven, M., "Some Thoughts on the Emergent Right to Water" in E. Riedel and P. Rothen, *The Human Right to Water* (Berliner Wissenschafts Verlag, 2006), p. 37
Crawford, J., "Democracy and the Body of International Law" in G. H. Fox and B. R. Roth (eds.), *Democratic Governance and International Law* (Cambridge University Press, 2000), p. 91
The International Law Commission's Articles on State Responsibility – Introduction, Text and Commentaries (Cambridge University Press, 2002)
and T. Grant, "International Court of Justice" in T. G. Weiss and S. Daws (eds.), *The Oxford Handbook on the United Nations* (Oxford University Press, 2007), p. 193
Cullet, P., *Differential Treatment in International Environmental Law* (Ashgate, 2003)
Danilenko, G. M., "International Jus Cogens: Issues of Law-Making," *Eur. J. Int'l L.*, 2 (1991), 42

Dembour, M.-B., *Who believes in human rights?: Reflections on the European Convention* (Cambridge University Press, 2006)

Demsetz, H., "Information and Efficiency: Another Viewpoint," *Journal of Law and Economics*, 12 (1969), 1

Depenheuer, O. *et al.* (eds.), *Staat im Wort: Festschrift für Josef Isensee* (C. F. Müller Verlag, 2007)

Dickmann, R., "Das Kappen der historisch-systematischen Taue einer Verfassungsnorm – Eine kritische Betrachtung der Entscheidung des Bundesverfassungsgerichts zur Bundestagsauflösung 2005," *Bayerische Verwaltungsblätter*, 137 (2006), 72

van Dijk, P., F. van Hoof, A. van Rijn and L. Zwaak (eds.), *Theory and Practice of the European Convention on Human Rights, 4th edn.* (Intersentia, 2006)

Dolzer, R., "Fair and Equitable Treatment: A Key Standard in Investment Treaties," *Int'l L.*, 39 (2005), 87

and C. Schreuer, *Principles of International Investment Law* (Oxford University Press, 2008)

Douglas, Z., *The International Law of Investment Claims* (Cambridge University Press, 2009)

Dugan, C. F., D. Wallace, Jr., N. D. Rubins and B. Sabahi, *Investor-State Arbitration* (Oxford University Press, 2008)

Dupuy, P.-M., "The Constitutional Dimension of the Charter of the United Nations Revisited" in *Max Planck Y.B. United Nations L.*, 1 (1997), p. 1

"Formation of Customary International Law and General Principles" in D. Bodansky, J. Brunnée and E. Hey (eds.), *The Oxford Handbook of International Environmental Law* (Oxford University Press, 2007), p. 449

"Unification Rather than Fragmentation of International Law? The Case of International Investment Law and Human Right Law" in P.-M. Dupuy, F. Francioni and E.-U. Petersmann (eds.), *Human Rights in International Investment Law and Arbitration* (Oxford University Press, 2009), p. 45

et al. (eds.), *Human Rights in International Investment Law and Arbitration* (Oxford University Press, 2009)

et al. (eds.), *Völkerrecht als Wertordnung – Common Values in International Law: Festschrift für Christian Tomuschat* (N. P. Engel Verlag, 2006)

Dworkin, R., "Rights as Trumps" in J. Waldron (ed.), *Theories of Rights*, 6th impr. (Oxford University Press, 1995), p. 153

Taking Rights Seriously (Harvard University Press, 1977)

Eide, A., C. Krause and A. Rosas (eds.), *Economic, Social and Cultural Rights – A Textbook* (Martinus Nijhoff Publishers, 1995)

Epping, V., "'Gefühltes Misstrauen' – die inszenierte Vertrauensfrage vom 1. Juli 2005 – Eine Nachbetrachtung der zweiten Bundestagsauflösungsentscheidung des Bundesverfassungsgerichts," *Recht und Politik*, 41 (2005), 197

Estreicher, S., "Rethinking the Binding Effect of Customary International Law," *Virg. J. Int'l L.*, 44 (2003–04), 5

Fassbender, B., "Grund und Grenzen der konstitutionellen Idee im Völkerrecht" in O. Depenheuer *et al.* (eds.), *Staat im Wort: Festschrift für Josef Isensee* (C. F. Müller Verlag, 2007), p. 73

Fauchald, O. K., "The Legal Reasoning of ICSID Tribunals – An Empirical Analysis," *Eur. J. Int'l L.*, 19 (2008), 301

Favoreu, L., P. Gaïa, R. Ghevontian, J.-L. Mestre, O. Pfersmann, A. Roux and G. Scoffoni, *Droit constitutionnel*, 9th edn. (Dalloz, 2006)

Fidler, F. D., "Challenging the Classical Concept of Custom: Perspectives on the Future of Customary International Law," *Ger. Yb. Int'l L.*, 37 (1996), 216

Fischer-Lescano, A., "Kritik der praktischen Konkordanz," *Kritische Justiz*, 41 (2008), 166

Fitzmaurice, G., "General Course on Public International Law," *Recueil des Cours*, 92 (1957), II, 68

Fox, G. H. and B. R. Roth (eds.), *Democratic Governance and International Law* (Cambridge University Press, 2000)

Franck, T. M., "Is the UN Charter a Constitution?" in J. A. Frowein *et al.* (eds.), *Verhandeln für den Frieden – Negotiating for Peace: Liber Amicorum Tono Eitel* (Springer, 2003), p. 95

"On Proportionality of Countermeasures in International Law," *Am. J. Int'l L.*, 102 (2008), 715

Franklin, B., "'F. B.': On Smuggling," *The London Chronicle*, November 21–24, 1767 (draft), available at http://franklinpapers.org/franklin/framedVolumes.jsp

French, D., "Developing States and International Environmental Law: The Importance of Differentiated Responsibilities," *Int'l & Comp. L. Q.*, 49 (2000), 35

Friedmann, W., *The Changing Structure of International Law* (Columbia University Press, 1964)

"The Uses of 'General Principles' in the Development of International Law," *Am. J. Int'l L.*, 57 (1963), 279

Frowein, J. A. *et al.* (eds.), *Verhandeln für den Frieden – Negotiating for Peace: Liber Amicorum Tono Eitel* (Springer, 2003)

Fry, J. D., "International Human Rights Law in Investment Arbitration: Evidence of International Law's Unity," *Duke J. Int'l & Comp. L.*, 18 (2007), 77

Gaillard, E. and Y. Banifatemi, "The Meaning of 'and' in Article 42(1), Second Sentence, of the Washington Convention: The Role of International Law in the ICSID Choice of Law Process," *ICSID Review – FIJL*, 18 (2003), 375

Gaines, S., "The Polluter Pays Principle: From Economic Equity to Environmental Ethos," *Tex. Int'l L.J.*, 26 (1991), 463

"The WTO's Reading of the GATT Article XX Chapeau: A Disguised Restriction on Environmental Measures," *U. Pa. J. Int'l Econ. L.*, 22 (2001), 739

Gaja, G., "Jus Cogens Beyond the Vienna Convention," *Recueil des Cours*, 172 (1982), 271

Goldman, B., *Le droit applicable selon la Convention de la BIRD, du 18 mars 1965, pour règelement des différends relatifs aux investissements entre États et ressortissants d'autres États, in Investissements Étrangers et abitrage entre États et personnes privées*, La Convention BIRD du 18 mars 1965 (1969)

Goldsmith, J. L. and E. A. Posner, "A Theory of Customary International Law," *U. Chic. L. R.*, 66 (1999), 1113

"Understanding the Resemblance between Modern and Traditional Customary International Law," *Virg. J. Int'l L.*, 40 (1999–2000), 640
Gómez Robledo, A., "Le jus cogens international: sa genèse, sa nature, ses fonctions," *Recueil des Cours*, 172 (1982), 9
Gonzales, G., "EC Fundamental Freedoms v. Human Rights in the Case C-112/00 Eugen Schmidberger v. Austria [2003] ECR I-5659," *Legal Issues of Economic Integration*, 31 (2004), 219
Grabitz, E., "Der Grundsatz der Verhältnismäßigkeit in der Rechtsprechung des Bundesverfassungsgerichts," *Archiv des Öffentlichen Rechts*, 98 (1973), 568
Grimm, D., "Does Europe Need a Constitution?," *Eur. L. J.*, 1 (1995), 282
Guillebeau, C., "Affirmative Action in a Global Perspective: The Cases of South Africa and Brazil," *Sociological Spectrum*, 19 (1999), 443
Gunn, T. J., "Deconstructing Proportionality in Limitations Analysis," *Emory Int'l L. Rev.*, 19 (2005), 465
Guzman, A. T., "Saving Customary International Law," *Mich. J. Int'l L.*, 27 (2005), 115
and T. L. Meyer, "Customary International Law in the 21st Century" in R. A. Miller and R. M. Bratspies (eds.), *Progress in International Law* (NV, 2008), p. 197
Haase, M., *Grundnorm – Gemeinwille – Geist* (Mohr Siebeck, 2002)
Habermas, J. (ed.), *Der gespaltene Westen – Kleine Politische Schriften X* (Suhrkamp, 2004)
"Hat die Konstitutionaliseriung des Völkerrechts noch eine Chance?" in J. Habermas (ed.), *Der gespaltene Westen – Kleine Politische Schriften X* (Suhrkamp, 2004), p. 113
"Remarks on Dieter Grimm's 'Does Europe Need a Constitution?'," *Eur. L. J.*, 1 (1995), 303
Haltern, U., *Europarecht – Dogmatik im Kontext* (Mohr Siebeck, 2005)
"Tomuschats Traum: Zur Bedeutung von Souveränität im Völkerrecht" in P.-M. Dupuy *et al.* (eds.), *Völkerrecht als Wertordnung – Common Values in International Law: Festschrift für Christian Tomuschat* (N. P. Engel Verlag, 2006), p. 867
Hannikainen, L., "The Collective Factor as a Promoter of Customary International Law," *Baltic Yb. Int'l L.*, 6 (2006), 125
Peremptory Norms (Jus Cogens) in International Law – Historical Development, Criteria, Present Status (Finnish Lawyers Publishing Company, 1988)
Van Harten, G., *Investment Treaty Arbitration and Public Law* (Oxford University Press, 2007)
and M. Loughlin, "Investment Treaty Arbitration as a Species of Global Administrative Law," *Eur. J. Int'l L.*, 17 (2006), 121
Hartley, T. C., *The Foundations of European Community Law*, 6th edn. (Oxford University Press, 2007)
Hartwig, M., "Much Ado About Human Rights: The Federal Constitutional Court Confronts the European Court of Human Rights," *German Law Journal*, 5 (May 1, 2005), available at www.germanlawjournal.com/index.php?pageID=11_artID=601

Herbst, T., "Die auflösungsgerichtete Vertrauensfrage," *Der Staat*, 45 (2006), 45
Hesse, K., *Grundzüge des Verfassungsrechts der Bundesrepublik Deutschland*, 20th edn. (C. F. Müller Juristischer Verlag, 1995)
Higginbotham, F. M., "Affirmative Action in the United States and South Africa: Lessons from the Other Side," *Temp. Int'l & Comp. L.J.*, 13 (1999), 187
Higgins, R., *Problems and Procedures – International Law and How We Use It* (Clarendon Press, 1994)
Themes and Theories – Selected Essays, Speeches, and Writings in International Law, vol. I (Oxford University Press, 2009)
Hirsch, M., "Interactions between Investment and Non-Investment Obligations" in P. Muchlinski, F. Ortino and C. Schreuer, *The Oxford Handbook of International Investment Law* (Oxford University Press, 2008), p. 154
"Investment Tribunals and Human Rights: Divergent Paths" in P.-M. Dupuy, F. Francioni and E.-U. Petersmann (eds.), *Human Rights in International Investment Law and Arbitration* (Oxford University Press, 2009), p. 97
Hobér, K., "State Responsibility and Attribution" in P. Muchlinski, F. Ortino and C. Schreuer, *The Oxford Handbook of International Investment Law* (Oxford University Press, 2008), p. 549
Hoffmann, E., *Abwägung im Recht* (Mohr Siebeck, 2007)
Hoogh, A., "The Relationship between Jus Cogens, Obligations Erga Omnes and International Crimes: Peremptory Norms in Perspective," *Austrian Journal of Public International Law*, 42 (1991), 183
Ipsen, J., "Auflösung des 15. Deutschen Bundestages – eine Nachlese," *Neue Zeitschrift für Verwaltungsrecht*, 24 (2005), 1147
"Zur Regierung verurteilt? – Verfassungsrechtliche Probleme der Vertrauensfrage nach Art. 68 GG," *Neue Juristische Wochenschrift* 68 (2005), 2201
Ipsen, K., *Völkerrecht*, 5th edn. (C. H. Beck, 2004)
Isensee, J. and P. Kirchhof (eds.), *Handbuch des Staatsrechts*, vol. V, 2nd edn. (C. F. Müller Juristischer Verlag, 2000)
Jägers, N., "The Legal Status of Multinational Corporations Under International Law" in M. K. Addo (ed.), *Human Rights Standards and the Responsibility of Transnational Corporations* (Kluwer Law International, 1999), p. 259
Janis, M. W., R. S. Kay and A. W. Bradley, *European Human Rights Law*, 3rd edn. (Oxford University Press, 2008)
Jans, J. H., "Proportionality Revisited," *Legal Issues of Economic Integration*, 27 (2000), 239
Johnson, N. C., "Vereinigte Staaten von Amerika" in E. Grabitz (ed.), *Grundrechte in Europa und USA*, vol. I (N. P. Engel Verlag, 1986), p. 885
Jones, R., "The 1999 Review of the OECD Guidelines for Multinational Enterprises" in R. Blanpain (ed.), *Multinational Enterprises and the Social Challenges of the XXIst Century* (Kluwer Law International, 2000), p. 141
Joseph, P. A., "The New Zealand Bill of Rights Experience" in P. Alston (ed.), *Promoting Human Rights Through Bills of Rights: Comparative Perspectives* (Oxford University Press, 1999), p. 283

Joseph, S., "An Overview of the Human Rights Accountability of Multinational Enterprises" in M. T. Kamminga and S. Zia-Zarifi (eds.), *Liability of Multinational Corporations under International Law* (Kluwer Law International, 2000), p. 75

Kahn, P. and T. Wälde, *Les Aspects nouveaux du Droit des Investissements Internationaux/New Aspects of International Investment Law*, Hague Academy of International Law – Centre for Studies and Research in International Law and International Relations 2004 (Martinus Nijhoff Publishers, 2006)

Kamminga, M. T. and S. Zia-Zarifi (eds.), *Liability of Multinational Corporations under International Law* (Kluwer Law International, 2000)

Kapeteyn, P. J. G., A. M. McDonnell, K. J. M. Mortelmans and C. W. A. Timmermans, *The Law of the European Union and the European Communities*, 4th (rev.) edn. (Kluwer Law International, 2008)

Kelsen, H., *Introduction to the Problem of Legal Theory* (Clarendon Press, 1996)

Principles of International Law (Rinehart, 1952)

Reine Rechtslehre, 1st edn. (F. Deuticke, 1934)

Kennedy, D., "The International Anti-Corruption Campaign," *Conn. J. Int'l L.*, 14 (1999), 455

Kingsbury, B., N. Krisch and R. B. Stewart, "The Emergence of Global Administrative Law," *Law & Contemporary Problems*, 68 (2005), 15

Kingsbury, B., N. Krisch, R. B. Stewart and J. B. Wiener, "Foreword: Global Governance as Administration – National and Transnational Approaches to Global Administrative Law," *Law & Contemp. Probs.*, 68 (2004–05), 1

Kingsbury, B. and S. Schill, "Investor-State Arbitration as Governance: Fair and Equitable Treatment, Proportionality and the Emerging Global Administrative Law," New York University School of Law, Public Law & Legal Theory Research Paper Series, Working Paper No. 09–46, September 2009

Knoll-Tudor, I., "The Fair and Equitable Treatment Standard and Human Rights Norms" in P.-M. Dupuy, F. Francioni and E.-U. Petersmann (eds.), *Human Rights in International Investment Law and Arbitration* (Oxford University Press, 2009), p. 310

Koh, H. H., "Transnational Legal Process" in G. Simpson (ed.), *The Nature of International Law* (Ashgate, 2001), p. 311

Kokott, J., "Grundrechtliche Schranken und Schrankenschranken" in D. Merten and H.-J. Papier (eds.), *Handbuch der Grundrechte*, vol. I (C. F. Müller Verlag, 2004), p. 853

Kolb, R., "Théorie Du Ius Cogens International," *Revue belge de droit international*, 36 (2003), 5

Koskenniemi, M., "General Principles: Reflections on Constructivist Thinking in International Law" in M. Koskenniemi (ed.), *Sources of International Law* (Ashgate, 2000), p. 359

"The Pull of the Mainstream," *Mich. L. Rev.*, 88 (1990), 1946

(ed.), *Sources of International Law* (Ashgate, 2000), Introduction, p. xi

Krauss, R. von, "Der Grundsatz der Verhaltnismäßigkeit in seiner Bedeutung für die Notwendigkeit des Mittels im Verwaltungsrecht," Abhandlungen aus dem Seminar für Öffentliches Recht der Universität Hamburg (Hamburg, 1955)

Kriebaum, U., *Eigentumsschutz im Völkerrecht – Eine Untersuchung zum internationalen Investitionsrecht sowie zum Menschenrechtsschutz* (Duncker & Humblot, 2008)

"Is the European Court of Human Rights an Alternative to Investor-State Arbitration?" in P.-M. Dupuy, F. Francioni and E.-U. Petersmann (eds.), *Human Rights in International Investment Law and Arbitration* (Oxford University Press, 2009), p. 219

Krisch, N. and B. Kingsbury, "Symposium: Global Governance and Global Administrative Law in the International Legal Order – Introduction: Global Governance and Global Administrative Law in the International Legal Order," *Eur. J. Int'l L.*, 17 (2006), 1

Krislov, S., "The Amicus Curiae Brief: From Friendship to Advocacy," *Yale L. J.*, 72 (1962–63), 694

Krommerdijk, J. and J. Morijn, "'Proportional' by What Measure(s)? Balancing Investor Interests and Human Rights by Way of Applying the Proportionality Principle in Investor-State Arbitration," in P.-M. Dupuy, F. Francioni and E.-U. Petersmann (eds.), *Human Rights in International Investment Law and Arbitration* (Oxford University Press, 2009), p. 422

Kühling, J., "Fundamental Rights" in A. von Bogdandy and J. Bast (eds.), *Principles of European Constitutional Law* (Hart Publishing, 2006), p. 501

Kulick, A., "The Integration of International Investment Law" in N. Lavranos *et al.* (eds.), *Hague Yearbook of International Law*, 23 (2010), 159

and C. Wendler, "A Corrupt Way to Handle Corruption? Thoughts on the Recent ICSID Case Law on Corruption," *Legal Issues of Economic Integration*, 37 (2010), 61

Kuttner, S.G., *Harmony from Dissonance. An Interpretation of Medieval Canon Law* (Latrobe, 1960)

Lambsdorff, J. Graf, "What Nurtures Corrupt Deals? On the Role of Confidence and Transaction Costs" in D. Della Porta and S. Rose-Ackerman (eds.), *Corrupt Exchanges: Empirical Themes in the Politics and Political Economy of Corruption* (Nomos Verlagsgesellschaft, 2002), p. 20

Lasok, K. P. E., *Law & Institutions of the European Union*, 7th edn. (Butterworths, 2001)

Lauwaars, R. H., "Institutional Structure" in P. J. G. Kapeteyn, A. M. McDonnell, K. J. M. Mortelmans and C. W. A. Timmermans, *The Law of the European Union and the European Communities*, 4th (rev.) edn. (Kluwer Law International, 2008)

Leben, C., "The Changing Structure of International Law Revisited by Way of Introduction," *Eur. J. Int'l L.*, 8 (1997), 399

"L'état de necessité dans le droit international de l'investissment," *Gazette du palais – cahier de l'arbitrage*, (2005), 32

Hans Kelsen and the Advancement of International Law, EJIL, 9 (1998), 287

Leff, N., "Economic Development Through Bureaucratic Corruption," *American Behavioral Scientist*, 8 (1964), 8

Lerche, P., "Grundrechtlicher Schutzbereich, Grundrechtsprägung und Grundrechtseingriff" in J. Isensee and P. Kirchhof (eds.), *Handbuch des Staatsrechts*, vol. V, 2nd edn. (C. F. Müller Juristischer Verlag, 2000), p. 739

"Grundrechtsschranken" in J. Isensee and P. Kirchhof (eds.), *Handbuch des Staatsrechts*, vol. V, 2nd edn. (C. F. Müller Juristischer Verlag, 2000), p. 775

Übermaß und Verfassungsrecht. Zur Bindung des Gesetzgebers an die Grundsätze der Verhältnismäßigkeit und der Erforderlichkeit (Carl Heymanns Verlag, 1961)

Liberti, L., "The Relevance of Non-Investment Treaty Obligations in Assessing Compensation" in P.-M. Dupuy, F. Francioni and E.-U. Petersmann (eds.), *Human Rights in International Investment Law and Arbitration* (Oxford University Press, 2009), p. 557

Lowe, V., "Precluding Wrongfulness or Responsibility: A Plea for Excuses," *Eur. J. Int'l L.*, 10 (1999), 405

Lowenfeld, A., *International Economic Law*, 2nd edn. (Oxford University Press, 2008)

"Investment Agreements and International Law – The Regulation of Foreign Direct Investment," *Col. J. Transnt'l L.*, 42 (2003–04), 123

Macdonald, R. St. J., F. Matscher and H. Petzold (eds.), *The European System for the Protection of Human Rights* (Martinus Nijhoff Publishers, 1993)

Malanczuk, P., *Akehurst's Modern Introduction to International Law* (Routledge, 1997)

Marboe, I., *Calculation of Compensation and Damages in International Investment Law* (Oxford University Press, 2009)

Mas, M. E., "Right to Compensation under Article 50" in R. St. J. Macdonald, F. Matscher and H. Petzold (eds.), *The European System for the Protection of Human Rights* (Kluwer Academic Publishers, 1993), p. 775

Mathijsen, P. S. R. F., *A Guide to European Union Law*, 9th edn. (Sweet & Maxwell, 2007)

Matsushita, M., T. J. Schoenbaum and P. C. Mavroidis, *The World Trade Organization – Law, Practice, and Policy* (Oxford University Press, 2003)

Mayeda, G., "International Investment Agreements between Developed and Developing Countries: Dancing with the Devil? Case Comment on the Vivendi, Sempra and Enron Awards," *JSDLP*, 4 (2008), 189

McCaffrey, S., "The Human Right to Water" in E. Brown Weiss, L. Boisson de Chazournes and N. Bernasconi-Osterwalder (eds.), *Fresh Water and International Economic Law* (Oxford University Press, 2005), p. 93

McDougal, M. S. and M. Reisman (eds.), *International Law Essays: A Supplement to International Law in Contemporary Perspective* (Foundation Press, 1981)

et al., "The World Constitutive Process of Authoritative Decision" in M. S. McDougal and M. Reisman (eds.), *International Law Essays: A Supplement to International Law in Contemporary Perspective* (Foundation Press, 1981), p. 191

McNair, Lord, *The Law of Treaties* (Clarendon Press, 1986)

Menard, C. and M. Shirley (eds.). *Handbook of New Institutional Economics* (Edward Elgar, 2005)

Merten, D. and H.-J. Papier (eds.), *Handbuch der Grundrechte*, vol. I (C. F. Müller Verlag, 2004)

Miller, R. A. and R. M. Bratspies (eds.), *Progress in International Law* (NV, 2008) von Moltke, K., *The Vorsorgeprinzip in West German Environmental Policy*, in Twelfth Report, Royal Commission on Environmental Pollution (UK, HMSO, Cm. 310, 1988), 57

Morgenthau, H. J., *Politics Among Nations: The Struggle for Power and Peace* (McGraw-Hill, 1948 (repr. 1993))

Morgera, E., "The UN and Corporate Environmental Responsibility: Between International Regulation and Partnerships," *Eur. Com. & Int'l Env. L. Rev.*, 15 (2006), 93

Mosler, H., "The International Society as a Legal Community," *Recueil des Cours*, 140 (1974), 1

Muchlinski, P., "Caveat Investor? The Relevance of the Conduct of the Investor under the Fair and Equitable Treatment Standard," *Int'l & Comp. L. Q.*, 55 (2006), 527

Multinational Enterprises and the Law, 2nd edn. (Oxford University Press, 2007)

"Trends in International Investment Agreements – Balancing Investor Rights and the Right to Regulate: The Issue of National Security" in K. P. Sauvant (ed.), *Yearbook on International Investment Law & Policy 2008–2009* (Oxford University Press, 2009), p. 35

F. Ortino and C. Schreuer, *The Oxford Handbook of International Investment Law* (Oxford University Press, 2008)

Müller, J. P. and L. Wildhaber, *Praxis des Völkerrechts*, 3rd edn. (Stämpfli Verlag AG Bern, 2001)

Nelson, J. M., C. Tilly and L. Walker (eds.), *Transforming Post-Communist Political Economies* (National Academy Press, 1997)

Nettesheim, M., "UN Sanctions Against Individuals – a Challenge to the Architecture of European Union Governance," *C.M.L. Rev.*, 44 (2007), 567

"Von der Verhandlungsdiplomatie zur internationalen Verfassungsordnung – Zur Entwicklung der Ordnungsformen des internationalen Wirtschaftsrechts" in C. D. Claassen *et al.* (eds.), *"In einem vereinten Europa dem Frieden der Welt zu dienen ... ": Liber amicorum Thomas Oppermann* (Duncker & Humblot, 2001), p. 381

Newcombe, A. and L. Paradell, *Law and Practice of Investment Tribunals – Standards of Treatment* (Kluwer Law International, 2009)

Nguyen Quoc Dinh, P. Daillier and A. Pellet, *Droit International Public*, 6th edn. (Librairie Générale de Droit et de Jurisprudence, 1999)

Nolte, G., "General Principles of German and European Administrative Law – A Comparison in Historical Perspective," *Mod. L. Rev.*, 57 (1994), 191

North, D. C., "Understanding Economic Change" in J. M. Nelson, C. Tilly and L. Walker (eds.), *Transforming Post-Communist Political Economies* (National Academy Press, 1997), p. 13

Understanding the Process of Institutional Change (Princeton University Press, 2005)

Northmann, M., "Non-State Actors in International Law" in B. Arts, M. Northmann and B. Reinalda (eds.), *Non-State Actors in International Relations* (Ashgate, 2001), p. 59

Norton, P. M., "A Law of the Future or a Law of the Past? Modern Tribunals and the International Law of Expropriation," *Am. J. Int'l L.*, 85 (1991), 474

Nowrot, K., "Die UN- Norms on the Responsibilities of Transnational Corporations and Other Business Enterprises with Regard to Human Rights – Gelungener Beitrag zur transnationalen Rechtsverwirklichung oder das Ende des Global Compact?," *Beiträge zum Transnationalen Wirtschaftsrecht*, 21 (2003), 1

Olásolo, H., *The Criminal Responsibility of Senior Political and Military Leaders as Principals to International Crimes* (Hart Publishing, 2009)

Oppermann, T., *Europarecht*, 2nd edn. (C. H. Beck Verlag, 1999)

Paparinskis, M., "Investment Arbitration and the Law of Countermeasures," *Brit. Yb. Int'l L.*, 79 (2008), 264

Papier, H.-J., "Das Bundesverfassungsgericht als 'Hüter der Grundrechte'" in M. Brenner, P. M. Huber and M. Möstl (eds.), *Der Staat des Grundgesetzes – Kontinuität und Wandel, Festschrift für Peter Badura zum siebzigsten Geburtstag* (Mohr Siebeck, 2004), p. 411

Paulsson, J., *Denial of Justice in International Law* (Cambridge University Press, 2005)

Pearson, C. S., "Testing the System: GATT+PPP=?," *Cornell In'l L. J.*, 27 (1994), 553

Pechota, V., "The Limits of International Responsibility in the Protection of Foreign Investments" in M. Ragazzi (ed.), *International Responsibility Today – Essays in Memory of Oscar Schachter* (Martinus Nijhoff Publishers, 2005), p. 171

Pescatore, P., *Le Droit de l'Intégration* (A. W. Sijthoff, 1972)

Petersmann, E.-U., "Constitutional Theories of International Economic Adjudication and Investor-State Arbitration" in P.-M. Dupuy, F. Francioni and E.-U. Petersmann (eds.), *Human Rights in International Investment Law and Arbitration* (Oxford University Press, 2009), p. 137

"Introduction and Summary: 'Administration of Justice' in International Law and Adjudication?" in P.-M. Dupuy, F. Francioni and E.-U. Petersmann (eds.), *Human Rights in International Investment Law and Arbitration* (Oxford University Press, 2009), p. 3

Peterson, L. E., "More Details Emerge of Miner's Case Against South Africa," *investmenttreatynews*, November 30, 2007, available at www.investmenttreatynews.org/cms/news/archive/2009/03/23/

and K. R. Gray, "International Human Rights in Bilateral Investment Treaties and in Investment Treaty Arbitration," IISD Research Paper, April 2003, available at www.iisd.org

Petrochilos, G., *Procedural Law in International Arbitration* (Oxford University Press, 2004)

Porta, D. Della and S. Rose-Ackerman, "Corrupt Exchanges: An Introduction" in D. Della Porta and S. Rose-Ackerman (eds.), *Corrupt Exchanges: Empirical Themes in the Politics and Political Economy of Corruption* (Nomos Verlagsgesellschaft, 2002), p. 1

and S. Rose-Ackerman (eds.), *Corrupt Exchanges: Empirical Themes in the Politics and Political Economy of Corruption* (Nomos Verlagsgesellschaft, 2002)

Poudret, J.-F. and S. Besson, *Comparative Law of International Arbitration*, 2nd edn. (Sweet & Maxwell, 2007)
Puvimanasinghe, S. F., *Foreign Investment, Human Rights and the Environment* (Martinus Nijhoff Publishers, 2007)
Raeschke-Kessler, H. and D. Gottwald, "Corruption" in P. Muchlinski, F. Ortino and C. Schreuer (eds.), *The Oxford Handbook of International Investment Law* (Oxford University Press, 2008), p. 584
Ragazzi, M., *The Concept of International Obligations Erga Omnes* (Oxford University Press, 1997)
(ed.), *International Responsibility Today – Essays in Memory of Oscar Schachter* (Martinus Nijhoff Publishers, 2005)
Ramasastry, A., "Corporate Complicity: From Nuremberg to Rangoon – An Examination of Forced Labor Cases and their Impact on the Liability of Multinational Corporations," *Berkeley J. Int'l L.*, 20 (2002), 91
Rasmussen, H., *On Law and Policy in the European Court of Justice* (Martinus Nijhoff Publishers, 1986)
Ratner, S. R., "Corporations and Human Rights: A Theory of Legal Responsibility," *Yale L.J.*, 111 (2001–02), 443
Reiner, C. and C. Schreuer, "Human Rights and International Investment Arbitration" in P.-M. Dupuy, F. Francioni and E.-U. Petersmann (eds.), *Human Rights in International Investment Law and Arbitration* (Oxford University Press, 2009), p. 82
Reinisch, A., "Necessity in International Investment Arbitration – An Unnecessary Split of Opinions in Recent ICSID Cases? – Comments on CMS v. Argentina and LG&E v. Argentina," *J. World Invtm't & Trade*, 8 (2007), 191
Reisman, W. M., "The Regime for Lacunae in the ICSID Choice of Law Provision and the Question of its Threshold," *ICSID Review – FILJ*, 15 (2000), 362
"The View from the New Haven School of International Law," *Am. Soc'y Int'l L. Proc.*, 86 (1992), 118
and R. D. Sloane, "Indirect Expropriation and its Valuation in the BIT Generation," *Brit. Yb. Int'l L.*, 74 (2004), 115
Ripinsky, S. and K. Williams, *Damages in International Investment Law* (British Institute of International and Comparative Law, 2008)
Rivers, J., "Proportionality and Variable Intensity of Review," *Cambridge L.J.*, 65 (2006), 174
Rogers, C. A. and R. P. Alford (eds.), *The Future of Investment Arbitration* (Oxford University Press, 2009)
Rose-Ackerman, S., "Governance and Corruption" in B. Lornberg (ed.), *Global Crises, Global Solutions* (Cambridge University Press, 2004), p. 301
Ross, W. D., *The Right and the Good*, ed. P. Stratton-Lake (Oxford University Press, 2002)
Ruggie, J. G., "Current Developments – Business and Human Rights: The Evolving International Agenda," *Am. J. Int'l L.*, 101 (2007), 819

Ryssdal, R., "The Conscience We Need" in R. St. J. Macdonald, F. Matscher and H. Petzold (eds.), *The European System for the Protection of Human Rights* (Kluwer Academic Publishers, 1993), p. xxv

Sachs, A. L., "The Challenges of Post-Apartheid South Africa," *Green Bag*, 7 (2003), 63

Salbu, S. R., "Transnational Bribery: The Big Questions," *Nw. J. Int'l L. & Bus.*, 21 (2001), 435

Salman, S. M. A. and S. McIneray-Lankford, *The Human Right to Water* (The World Bank, 2004)

Samra, H., "Five Years Later – the CMS Award Placed in the Context of the Argentine Financial Crisis and the ICSID Arbitration Boom," *U. Mia. InterAm. L. Rev.*, 38 (2007), 667

Sanders, P. (ed.), *International Arbitration: Liber Amicorum Martin Domke* (Martinus Nijhoff Publishers, 1967)

Sands, P., *Principles of International Environmental Law*, 2nd edn. (Cambridge University Press, 2003)

R. Mackenzie and Y. Shany, *Manual on International Courts and Tribunals* (Butterworths, 1999)

Sauvant, K. P. (ed.), *Yearbook on International Investment Law & Policy 2008–2009* (Oxford University Press, 2009)

Scanlon, J., A. Cassar and N. Nemon (eds.), *Water as a Human Right?* (International Union for Conservation of Nature and Natural Resources, 2004)

Scelle, G., *Pacte des Nations et sa Liaison avec le Traité de Paix* (Sirey, 1919)

Scheinin, M., "Economic and Social Rights as Legal Rights" in A. Eide, C. Krause and A. Rosas (eds.), *Economic, Social and Cultural Rights – A Textbook* (Martinus Nijhoff Publishers, 1995), p. 41

Scherer, M., "Circumstantial Evidence in Corruption before International Tribunals," *International Arbitration Law Review*, 5 (2002), 29

Schill, S. W. (ed.), *International Investment Law and Comparative Public Law* (Oxford University Press, 2010)

"International Investment Law and Comparative Public Law – An Introduction" in S. W. Schill (ed.), *International Investment Law and Comparative Public Law* (Oxford University Press, 2010), p. 3

"International Investment Law and the Host State's Power to Handle Economic Crises – Comment on the ICSID Decision in LG&E v. Argentina," *J. Int'l Arb.*, 24 (2007), 265

The Multilateralization of International Investment Law (Cambridge University Press, 2009)

"Umbrella Clauses as Public Law Concepts in Comparative Perspective" in S. W. Schill (ed.), *International Investment Law and Comparative Public Law* (Oxford University Press, 2010), p. 317

Schilling, T., "The Autonomy of the Community Legal Order: An Analysis of Possible Foundations," *Harv. Int'l L.J.*, 37 (1996), 389

Schlosser, P., *Das Recht der internationalen privaten Schiedsgerichtsbarkeit*, 2nd edn. (Mohr Siebeck, 1989)

Schneiderman, D., *Constitutionalizing Economic Globalization – Investment Rules and Democracy's Promise* (Cambridge University Press, 2008)

Schokkenbroek, J., "Chapter 4 – The Supervisory Function of the Secretary General of the Council of Europe" in P. van Dijk, F. van Hoof, A. van Rijn and L. Zwaak (eds.), *Theory and Practice of the European Convention on Human Rights*, 4th edn. (Intersentia, 2006), p. 323

Schreuer, C., "Fair and Equitable Treatment in Arbitral Practice," *J. World Inv. & Trade*, 6 (2005), 357

The ICSID Convention – A Commentary (Cambridge University Press, 2001)

"Non-Pecuniary Remedies in ICSID Arbitration," *Arbitration International*, 20 (2004), 325

"Unjustified Enrichment in International Law," *Am. J. Comp. L.*, 22 (1974), 281

L. Malintoppi, A. Reinisch and A. Sinclair, *The ICSID Convention – A Commentary*, 2nd edn. (Cambridge University Press, 2009)

Schwab, F., *Der Europäische Gerichtshof und der Verhältnismäßigkeitsgrundsatz: Untersuchung der Prüfungsdichte* (Peter Lang, 2002)

Schwarze, J. (ed.), *Globalisierung und Entstaatlichung des Rechts – Ergebnisse der 31. Tagung der Gesellschaft für Rechtsvergleichung vom 20. Bis 22. September 2007 in Halle, vol. I: Beiträge zum Öffentlichen Recht, Europarecht, Arbeits- und Sozialrecht und Strafrecht* (Mohr Siebeck, 2008)

Schwebel, S. M., "The Influence of Bilateral Investment Treaties on Customary International Law," *Am. J. Int'l L.*, 98 (2004), 27

Justice in International Law (Cambridge University Press, 1994)

Seerden, R., "Comparative Remarks" in R. Seerden, *Administrative Law of the European Union, its Member States and the United States – A Comparative Analysis* (Intersentia, 2007), p. 401

Shaw, M. N., *International Law*, 6th edn. (Cambridge University Press, 2008)

Shihata, I. F. I. and A. R. Parra, "Applicable Substantive Law in Disputes between States and Private Foreign Parties: The Case of Arbitration under the ICSID Convention," *ICSID Review – FILJ*, 9 (1994), 183

Simma, B., "From Bilateralism to Community Interest in International Law," *Recueil des Cours*, 250 (1994), 217

and T. Kill, "Harmonizing Investment Protection and International Human Rights: First Steps Towards a Methodology" in C. Binder *et al.* (eds.), *International Investment Law for the 21st Century – Essays in Honour of Christoph Schreuer* (Oxford University Press, 2009), p. 687

Smit, H. and V. Pechota, *International Commercial Arbitration and the Courts*, 4th edn. (Juris Publishing, 2004)

Smith, C., "An American's View of the Federal Constitutional Court: Karlsruhe's Justices," *German L.J.*, 2 (2001), Issue 9, available at www.germanlawjournal.com/index.php?pageID=11_artID=17

Sornarajah, M., *The International Law on Foreign Investment*, 3rd edn. (Cambridge University Press, 2010)

Spiegel, H. W., "Origin and Development of Denial of Justice," *Am. J. Int'l L.*, 32 (1938), 63

Steiner, J., L. Woods and C. Twigg-Flesner, *EU Law*, 9th edn. (Oxford University Press, 2006)
Stone Sweet, A., "Investor-State Arbitration: Proportionality's New Frontier," *Law and Legal Ethics of Human Rights* (2009), available at: http://works.bepress.com/alec_stone_sweet/31
and J. Mathews, "Proportionality Balancing and Global Constitutionalism," *Colum. J. Transntl. L.*, 47 (2008–09), 72
Streinz, R., *Europarecht*, 5th edn. (C. F. Müller Verlagsgesellschaft, 2001)
Subedi, S., "Multinational Corporations and Human Rights" in A. Arts and P. Mihyo (eds.), *Responding to the Human Rights Deficit* (Kluwer Law International, 2003), p. 171
Szodruch, A., "Necessity and beyond – the legal aftermath of the Argentine financial crisis before the German Federal Constitutional Court," *Ger. Yb. Int'l L.*, 50 (2007), 523
Thielbörger, P., "The Human Right to Water Versus Investor Rights: Double-Dilemma or Pseudo-Conflict?" in P.-M. Dupuy, F. Francioni and E.-U. Petersmann (eds.), *Human Rights in International Investment Law and Arbitration* (Oxford University Press, 2009), p. 487
Thym, D. "'United in Diversity' – The Integration of Enhanced Cooperation into the European Constitutional Order," *German L. J.*, 6 (2005), 1731
Tienhaara, K., *The Expropriation of Environmental Governance – Protecting Foreign Investors at the Expense of Public Policy* (Cambridge University Press, 2009)
Tomuschat, C., "The European Court of Human Rights and Investment Protection" in C. Binder *et al.* (eds.), *International Investment Law for the 21st Century – Essays in Honour of Christoph Schreuer* (Oxford University Press, 2009), p. 636
Human Rights – Between Idealism and Realism (Oxford University Press, 2003)
"International Law: Ensuring the Survival of Mankind on the Eve of a New Century," *Recueil des Cours*, 281 (1999), 1
"Möglichkeiten und Grenzen der Globalisierung" in J. Schwarze (ed.), *Globalisierung und Entstaatlichung des Rechts – Ergebnisse der 31. Tagung der Gesellschaft für Rechtsvergleichung vom 20. bis 22. September 2007 in Halle*, vol. I: *Beiträge zum Öffentlichen Recht, Europarecht, Arbeits- und Sozialrecht und Strafrecht* (Mohr Siebeck, 2008), p. 21
"Obligations Arising from States without or against their Will," *Recueil des Cours*, 241 (1993), 195
Trebilcock, M. and R. Howse, *The Regulation of International Trade*, 3rd edn. (Routledge, 2005)
Trouwborst, A., *Evolution and Status of the Precautionary Principle in International Law* (Kluwer Law International, 2002)
Vandevelde, K., *United States Investment Treaties – Policy and Practice* (Kluwer, 1992)
Várady, T., J. J. Barceló III and A. T. von Mehren, *International Commercial Arbitration – A Transnational Perspective*, 3rd edn. (Thomson/West, 2006)
de Vattel, E., *Le droit des gens ou principes de la loi naturelle appliqués à la conduite et aux affaires des nations et des souverains* (1758)

Verdross, A., *Die Verfassung der Völkerrechtsgemeinschaft* (J. Springer, 1926)
Vessey, J., "The Principle of Prevention in International Law," *Austrian Review of International & European Law*, 3 (1998), 181
Virally, M., "Réflexions sur le 'jus cogens'," *Annuaire Français de Droit International*, 12 (1966), 5
Vis-Dunbar, D., "Norway Shelves its Draft Model Bilateral Investment Treaty," *investmenttreatynews*, June 8, 2009, available at www.investmenttreatynews.org/cms/news/archive/2009/06/08/
"South African Court Judgment Bolsters Expropriation Charge over Black Economic Empowerment Legislation in the Mining Sector," *investmenttreatynews*, March 23, 2009, available at www.investmenttreatynews.org/cms/news/archive/2009/03/23/
Vitanyi, B., "Les Positions Doctrinales Concernant le Sens de la Notion de 'Principes Généneraux de Droit Reconnus par les Nations Civilisé'," *Revue Générale de Droit International Public*, 86 (1982), 48
Waibel, M., "Two Worlds of Necessity in ICSID Arbitration: CMS and LG&E," *Leiden J. Int'l L.*, 20 (2007), 637
Waldock, H., "General Course on Public International Law," *Recueil des Cours*, 106 (1962), 1
Waldron, J. (ed.), *Theories of Rights* (6th impr.) (Oxford University Press, 1995)
Walker, N., "Sovereignty and Differentiated Integration in the European Union" in Z. Bankowski and A. Scott (eds.), *The European Union and its Order* (Blackwell, 2000), p. 31
Waltz, K., *Theory of International Politics* (McGraw-Hill, 1979)
Weil, P., "The State, the Foreign Investor and International Law: The No Longer Stormy Relationship of a Ménage à Trois," *ICSID Review – FILJ*, 15 (2000), 401
Weiler, J. H. H., "Does Europe Need a Constitution? – Demos, Telos and the German Maastricht Decision," *Eur. L. J.*, 1 (1995), 219
"The Transformation of Europe," *Yale L.J.*, 100 (1990–91), 2403
and U. Haltern, "The Autonomy of the Community Legal Order – Through the Looking Glass," *Harv. Int'l L.J.*, 37 (1996), 411
Weiler, T., "Prohibition against Discrimination in NAFTA Chapter 11" in T. Weiler (ed.), *NAFTA Investment Law and Arbitration* (Transnational Publishers, 2004), p. 27
Weiss, T. G. and S. Daws (eds.), *The Oxford Handbook on the United Nations* (Oxford University Press, 2007)
Weissbrodt, D., "Stefan A. Riesenfeld Symposium 2008, March 14, 2008, Berkeley, California – Keynote Address: International Standard-Setting on the Human Rights Responsibilities of Businesses," *Berkeley J. Int'l L.*, 26 (2008), 373
and M. Kruger, "Current Developments – Norms on the Responsibilities of Transnational Corporations and Other Business Enterprises with Regard to Human Rights," *Am. J. Int'l L.*, 97 (2003), 901
and M. Kruger, "Human Rights Responsibilities of Businesses as Non-State Actors" in P. Alston (ed.), *Non-State Actors and Human Rights* (Oxford University Press, 2005), p. 315

Wellens, K., "General Observations" in T. Komori and K. Wellens (eds.), *Public Interest Rules of International Law – Towards Effective Implementation* (Ashgate, 2009), p. 15

Wendt, A., *Social Theory of International Politics* (Cambridge University Press, 1999)

Werle, G., *Principles of International Criminal Law*, 2nd edn. (T. M. C. Asser Press, 2009)

de Wet, E., "The Prohibition of Torture as an International Norm of Jus Cogens and its Implications for National and Customary Law," *Eur. J. Int'l L.*, 15 (2004), 97

Wildhaber, L., "A Constitutional Future for the European Court of Human Rights," *Hum. Rts. L. J.*, 23 (2002), 161

Willoweit, D., *Deutsche Verfassungsgeschichte – Vom Frankenreich bis zur Wiedervereinigung Deutschlands*, 6th edn. (C. H. Beck, 2009)

Wilske, S. and M. Raible, "The Arbitrator as Guardian of International Public Policy?," in C. A. Rogers and R. P. Alford (eds.), *The Future of Investment Arbitration* (Oxford University Press, 2009), p. 249

Winkler, F., "Fatal in Theory and Strict in Fact: An Empirical Analysis of Strict Scrutiny in the Federal Courts," *Van. L. Rev.*, 59 (2006), 793

Winroth, A., *The Making of Gratian's Decretum* (Cambridge University Press, 2000)

Wyatt, D., "New Legal Order, or Old?," *Eur. L. Rev.*, 7 (1982), 147

Yasseen, M. K., "L'interprétation des traités d'après la Convention de Vienne sur les Droit des Traités," *Recueil des Cours*, 151 (1976), 1

Zimmermann, A., C. Tomuschat and K. Oellers-Frahm (eds.), *The Statute of the International Court of Justice – A Commentary* (Oxford University Press, 2006)

Zippelius, R. and T. Würtenberger, *Deutsches Staatsrecht*, 32nd edn. (C. H. Beck, 2008)

Zwaak, L., "Chapter 1 – General Survey of the European Convention" in P. van Dijk, F. van Hoof, A. van Rijn and L. Zwaak (eds.), *Theory and Practice of the European Convention on Human Rights*, 4th edn. (Intersentia, 2006), p. 1

"Chapter 3 – Supervisory Task of the Committee of Ministers" in P. van Dijk, F. van Hoof, A. van Rijn and L. Zwaak (eds.), *Theory and Practice of the European Convention on Human Rights*, 4th edn. (Intersentia, 2006), p. 291

Zweigert, K. and H. Kötz, *Introduction to Comparative Law*, 2nd edn. (Oxford University Press, 1993)

Index

Books in the series

Cyberwarfare and the Laws of War Heather Harrison Dinniss
The Right to Reparation in International Law for Victims of Armed Conflict: The Role of the UN in Advocating for State Responsibility Christine Evans
Global Public Interest in International Investment Law Andreas Kulick
State Immunity in International Law Xiaodong Yang
Reparations and Victim Support in the International Criminal Court Conor McCarthy
Reducing Genocide to Law: Definition, Meaning, and the Ultimate Crime Payam Akhavan
Decolonizing International Law: Development, Economic Growth and the Politics of Universality Sundhya Pahuja
Complicity and the Law of State Responsibility Helmut Philipp Aust
State Control over Private Military and Security Companies in Armed Conflict Hannah Tonkin
'Fair and Equitable Treatment' in International Investment Law Roland Kläger
The UN and Human Rights: Who Guards the Guardians? Guglielmo Verdirame
Sovereign Defaults before International Courts and Tribunals Michael Waibel
Making the Law of the Sea: A Study in the Development of International Law James Harrison
Science and the Precautionary Principle in International Courts and Tribunals: Expert Evidence, Burden of Proof and Finality Caroline E. Foster
Legal Aspects of Transition from Illegal Territorial Regimes in International Law Yaël Ronen
Access to Asylum: International Refugee Law and the Globalisation of Migration Control Thomas Gammeltoft-Hansen
Trading Fish, Saving Fish: The Interaction between Regimes in International Law Margaret Young
The Individual in the International Legal System: State-Centrism, History and Change in International Law Kate Parlett
The Participation of States in International Organisations: The Role of Human Rights and Democracy Alison Duxbury
'Armed Attack' and Article 51 of the UN Charter: Evolutions in Customary Law and Practice Tom Ruys
Science and Risk Regulation in International Law: The Role of Science, Uncertainty and Values Jacqueline Peel
Theatre of the Rule of Law: The Theory, History and Practice of Transnational Legal Intervention Stephen Humphreys
The Public International Law Theory of Hans Kelsen: Believing in Universal Law Jochen von Bernstorff
Vicarious Liability in Tort: A Comparative Perspective Paula Giliker
Legal Personality in International Law Roland Portmann
Legitimacy and Legality in International Law: An Interactional Account Jutta Brunnée and Stephen J. Toope

The Concept of Non-International Armed Conflict in International Humanitarian Law Anthony Cullen
The Challenge of Child Labour in International Law Franziska Humbert
Shipping Interdiction and the Law of the Sea Douglas Guilfoyle
International Courts and Environmental Protection Tim Stephens
Legal Principles in WTO Disputes Andrew D. Mitchell
War Crimes in Internal Armed Conflicts Eve La Haye
Humanitarian Occupation Gregory H. Fox
The International Law of Environmental Impact Assessment: Process, Substance and Integration Neil Craik
The Law and Practice of International Territorial Administration: Versailles, Iraq and Beyond Carsten Stahn
Cultural Products and the World Trade Organization Tania Voon
United Nations Sanctions and the Rule of Law Jeremy Farrall
National Law in WTO Law: Effectiveness and Good Governance in the World Trading System Sharif Bhuiyan
The Threat of Force in International Law Nikolas Stürchler
Indigenous Rights and United Nations Standards Alexandra Xanthaki
International Refugee Law and Socio-Economic Rights Michelle Foster
The Protection of Cultural Property in Armed Conflict Roger O'Keefe
Interpretation and Revision of International Boundary Decisions Kaiyan Homi Kaikobad
Multinationals and Corporate Social Responsibility: Limitations and Opportunities in International Law Jennifer A. Zerk
Judiciaries within Europe: A Comparative Review John Bell
Law in Times of Crisis: Emergency Powers in Theory and Practice Oren Gross and Fionnuala Ní Aoláin
Vessel-Source Marine Pollution: The Law and Politics of International Regulation Alan Tan
Enforcing Obligations Erga Omnes in International Law Christian J. Tams
Non-Governmental Organisations in International Law Anna-Karin Lindblom
Democracy, Minorities and International Law Steven Wheatley
Prosecuting International Crimes: Selectivity and the International Law Regime Robert Cryer
Compensation for Personal Injury in English, German and Italian Law: A Comparative Outline Basil Markesinis, Michael Coester, Guido Alpa, Augustus Ullstein
Dispute Settlement in the UN Convention on the Law of the Sea Natalie Klein
The International Protection of Internally Displaced Persons Catherine Phuong
Imperialism, Sovereignty and the Making of International Law Antony Anghie
Necessity, Proportionality and the Use of Force by States Judith Gardam
International Legal Argument in the Permanent Court of International Justice: The Rise of the International Judiciary Ole Spiermann
Great Powers and Outlaw States: Unequal Sovereigns in the International Legal Order Gerry Simpson
Local Remedies in International Law C. F. Amerasinghe
Reading Humanitarian Intervention: Human Rights and the Use of Force in International Law Anne Orford

Conflict of Norms in Public International Law: How WTO Law Relates to Other Rules of Law Joost Pauwelyn
Transboundary Damage in International Law Hanqin Xue
European Criminal Procedures Edited by Mireille Delmas-Marty and John Spencer
The Accountability of Armed Opposition Groups in International Law Liesbeth Zegveld
Sharing Transboundary Resources: International Law and Optimal Resource Use Eyal Benvenisti
International Human Rights and Humanitarian Law René Provost
Remedies Against International Organisations Karel Wellens
Diversity and Self-Determination in International Law Karen Knop
The Law of Internal Armed Conflict Lindsay Moir
International Commercial Arbitration and African States: Practice, Participation and Institutional Development Amazu A. Asouzu
The Enforceability of Promises in European Contract Law James Gordley
International Law in Antiquity David J. Bederman
Money Laundering: A New International Law Enforcement Model Guy Stessens
Good Faith in European Contract Law Reinhard Zimmermann and Simon Whittaker
On Civil Procedure J. A. Jolowicz
Trusts: A Comparative Study Maurizio Lupoi
The Right to Property in Commonwealth Constitutions Tom Allen
International Organizations Before National Courts August Reinisch
The Changing International Law of High Seas Fisheries Francisco Orrego Vicuña
Trade and the Environment: A Comparative Study of EC and US Law Damien Geradin
Unjust Enrichment: A Study of Private Law and Public Values Hanoch Dagan
Religious Liberty and International Law in Europe Malcolm D. Evans
Ethics and Authority in International Law Alfred P. Rubin
Sovereignty Over Natural Resources: Balancing Rights and Duties Nico Schrijver
The Polar Regions and the Development of International Law Donald R. Rothwell
Fragmentation and the International Relations of Micro-States: Self-determination and Statehood Jorri Duursma
Principles of the Institutional Law of International Organizations C. F. Amerasinghe